CHICAGO'S GREATEST YEAR, 1893

CHICAGO'S GREATEST YEAR, 1893

The White City and the Birth of a Modern Metropolis

Joseph Gustaitis

Southern Illinois University Press
Carbondale and Edwardsville

16 15 14 13   4 3 2 1

Library of Congress Cataloging-in-Publication Data
Gustaitis, Joseph Alan, date
Chicago's greatest year, 1893 : the White City and the
birth of a modern metropolis / Joseph Gustaitis.
    pages cm
Includes bibliographical references and index.
    ISBN 978-0-8093-3248-9 (paperback : alkaline paper)
    ISBN 0-8093-3248-5 (paperback : alkaline paper)
    ISBN 978-0-8093-3249-6 (ebook) (print)
    ISBN 0-8093-3249-3 (ebook) (print)
1. Chicago (Ill.)—History—1875– 2. Chicago (Ill.)—
Social life and customs—19th century. 3. Chicago
(Ill.)—Intellectual life—19th century. 4. City and town
life—Illinois—Chicago—History—19th century.
5. Social change—Illinois—Chicago—History—19th
century. 6. Civic improvement—Illinois—Chicago—
History—19th century. 7. Urbanization—Illinois—
Chicago—History—19th century. 8. Architecture—
Illinois—Chicago—History—19th century. 9. Chicago
(Ill.)—Biography. I. Title.
F548.5.G95 2013
977.3'1103—dc23   2012037898

The author gratefully acknowledges *American History*
magazine for permission to reprint material on William
Wrigley Jr. (October 1998, copyright Weider History
Group); and Richard W. Sears (July/August 1993,
copyright Weider History Group).

To Catherine, my partner in exploring all things Chicago,
with love and gratitude

Contents

List of Illustrations   ix

Introduction   1
1. The White City and the Gray City   13
2. Three Museums and a Library   31
3. Sears, Roebuck and Company   57
4. Frances Willard's Bicycle   76
5. Open-Heart Surgery   95
6. A Church for Father Tolton   113
7. The Illinois Institute of Technology   133
8. The Birth of Urban Literature   151
9. The West Side Grounds   181
10. The Chicago Hot Dog   203
11. Wrigley's Gum   221
12. The Chicago School of Architecture   237
13. Reforming Chicago   265
14. Epidemics and Clean Water   285
    Epilogue: Chicago's Next Great Year   301

Notes   309
Index   337

Illustrations

Randolph Street in 1890 2

State Street in 1893 10

Neoclassical architecture of the White City 14

Architect and planner Daniel Burnham and colleagues 16

Grover Cleveland, who turned on the lights of the
    White City 18

Opening Day of the Columbian Exposition 19

Ferris wheel, the world's first 23

Grand parade on Dedication Day for the Columbian
    Exposition 24

Smoking tugboats on the Chicago River 27

Burnham in a contemporary caricature 29

Art Institute of Chicago 35

Old Art Institute of 1887 37

Field Museum 43

The Ruined Cities of the Yucatan 44

Anthropological Building at the Columbian Exposition 45

Marshall Field 47

Charles Atwood's Fine Arts Building 53

Richard W. Sears 59

Montgomery Ward's headquarters 64

Sears Administration Building and Merchandise
    Building 70

Julius Rosenwald 71

Both of Chicago's Sears Towers 73

"Safety bicycle" 77

Frances Willard's bicycle, Gladys 78

Temperance leader and reformer Frances Willard 81

British satirical view of U.S. temperance forces 83

Woman's Temple in downtown Chicago 86

Willard's home, Rest Cottage 94

Dr. Daniel Hale Williams at about the time of his historic surgery 98

"Darkies' Day" at the Columbian Exposition 99

Clerk and customer at a black-owned store 100

"Only Negro store of its kind in the U.S." 101

First Provident Hospital 104

Second Provident Hospital 106

St. Mary of the Angels Catholic Church 114

Father Augustus Tolton 115

Tolton in the 1890s 118

Tolton's first parish, St. Joseph's, in Quincy, Illinois 120

Reverend Patrick Augustine Feehan 122

St. Katharine Drexel 124

St. Monica's Church 125

Tolton immortalized on a mural at St. Elizabeth's Church 131

Main Building of the Armour Institute of Technology 133

Philip Danforth Armour 135

Machinery Hall at the Illinois Institute of Technology 137

Electricity Building at the Columbian Exposition 138

Union Stock Yards 142

Cartoon representation of Chicago's meatpackers 144

Crown Hall at the Illinois Institute of Technology 149

Interior of Crown Hall 150

Chicago writer Henry Blake Fuller 152

William Dean Howells 156

Finley Peter Dunne   164

Frantic activities of a Chicago newspaper in the 1890s   171

George Ade's character Artie   172

Ade's character Pink Marsh   173

George Ade   175

World Series match between the Cubs and the
    White Sox   182

Chicago White Stockings   191

Spalding's Official Baseball Guide, 1890   192

Adrian "Cap" Anson   194

West Side Grounds in 1909   198

Plaque marking site of old West Side Grounds   202

Hot dog vendor at Coney Island in 1904   205

"Wiener" vendors at Columbian Exposition   208

Old Vienna on the Midway Plaisance   211

Samuel Ladany, father of the "Chicago Hot Dog"   212

Horse-drawn wagon, original delivery method for Vienna
    Beef   213

Vienna Beef smokehouse in 1913   215

William Wrigley Jr.   223

Wrigley as owner of the Chicago Cubs   228

Wrigley Building of 1921   232

Cartoon view of Chicago's architectural boom in the
    1890s   239

Tacoma Building (1889), by Holabird and Roche   245

Monadnock Building   247

Charles Bowler Atwood   250

Atwood's Marshall Field Annex   252

Reliance Building, by Atwood   255

Chicago Stock Exchange of 1893   258

Medallion on the Stock Exchange's entry arch   259

Frank Lloyd Wright's studio and home   261

One of Wright's so-called bootleg houses   263
William T. Stead's "Map of Sin"   267
Chicago-based evangelist Dwight Lyman Moody   268
British journalist and reformer William T. Stead   274
Frontispiece of Stead's *If Christ Came to Chicago!*   278
Social worker and reformer Jane Addams   292
Foul crust on Chicago's notorious "Bubbly Creek"   296
How Chicago got its water in the 1850s   297
Sanitary and Ship Canal   299

CHICAGO'S GREATEST YEAR, 1893

Introduction

The year is 1893. Chicago's elite intends the Columbian Exposition to make their young metropolis world famous. It does. That majestic fair becomes the most magnetic event in the city's history and draws visitors from home and abroad. Whether they view Chicago as glorious or startling, the crowds of fairgoers find the city unforgettable and recognize it as a force to be taken seriously.

Held in Jackson Park from May 1 to October 30, the fair offered a dazzling display of vast neoclassical buildings laid out on a pattern by Daniel Burnham and designed by the likes of Richard Morris Hunt, Henry Ives Cobb, and the trio of Charles McKim, William Mead, and Stanford White. The one major nonclassical structure, the Transportation Building, was the work of Dankmar Adler and Louis Sullivan. The Midway Plaisance showcased cultures from around the globe; its focal point was the world's first Ferris wheel. Nearly twenty-seven million people attended the fair—a figure that is even more astounding when one realizes that the population of the United States was barely sixty-three million.

Yet, ironically, the "White City" of 1893 has cast such a long shadow that it has obscured many other events that also occurred within that single year—all of which played central roles in Chicago's growth. When was Chicago's most important skyscraper completed? In what year did Chicago writers launch the urban literature movement? When did Sears, Roebuck and Company get started? When did the Art Institute of Chicago open? When did architect Frank Lloyd Wright open his office? When did William Wrigley invent Juicy Fruit? When did the "Chicago hot dog" begin? When did the Cubs unveil the ballpark in which they last won the World Series? When did the Illinois Institute of Technology get started? These all happened in 1893. Even if Chicago had not built the White City and hosted the fair, 1893 would still have been its banner year.

By 1893, Chicago had completed its transition from a provincial city to a world metropolis. It had now acquired all, or nearly all, of the components that make up a great modern city—museums, a rapid-transit system, a symphony orchestra, powerful business enterprises of national and international scope, universities, hospitals, a championship sports team, a progressive upper class keen on civic improvement, a willingness to do what was needed to provide clean water and air, a group of authors and journalists able to express city life, and, perhaps most famous of all, a school of architects that was doing more than just erecting impressive buildings but was revolutionizing world architecture. And, with the Columbian Exposition, Chicago had a showcase that proclaimed all these achievements not just to the nation, but to the world.

When this photograph of bustling Randolph Street was taken in 1890, Chicago was well on its way to becoming a world metropolis. (ICHi-59567, Chicago History Museum; photographer, J. W. Taylor)

It is to be remembered, however, that as the year 1893 approached its end, many in the city and the nation were probably beginning to think that things were not quite so shiny after all. Beginning in January, the economy began to weaken, and by December both the weather and financial prospects were bleak. The country was mired in the "Panic of 1893," which, before the 1930s, was also known as the "Great Depression." The unemployment rate, which had been around a healthy 3 percent in 1892, was now hovering near 11 percent, although it was probably nearer 25 percent among industrial workers. Bankruptcies were epidemic, railroads were failing, and the worst effects of the downturn were being felt in manufacturing cities like Chicago. Chicago, like the nation, would ride it out, but the financial predicament did loom in the background of most of the events described here. It considerably slowed the progress of Chicago's celebrated architecture, for one, and it inspired the civic reformer William Stead, the subject of chapter 13, "Reforming Chicago," to write one of the most detailed and chilling accounts of nineteenth-century urban destitution. The year began in bright light—the radiance of the White City—but it ended in shadow.

Concentrating on a single year in the history of Chicago makes it possible to concentrate on specific stories that are usually not covered in depth in histories of the city that employ a wider scope. To take one example, consider the story of Daniel Hale Williams, a black physician who in Chicago in 1893 performed one of history's first open-heart surgical operations. He rates a sentence in Donald L. Miller's history of nineteenth-century Chicago, *City of the Century*, and a paragraph (in the entry on "Provident Hospital") in the *Encyclopedia of Chicago*, but because the scope of this book is more limited, it can devote an entire chapter to this pioneer. Beyond that, his achievement allows us to consider why Chicago has become one of the premier medical centers in the United States and why the medical industry is one of the city's major employers. Another example might be the story of William Wrigley; as prominent as the name remains in Chicago, the man himself has rarely been discussed in detail in histories of the city. Father Augustus Tolton has even been put forth for canonization by the Roman Catholic Church, but, again, standard histories of Chicago don't have the space to tell his story. Cities are not buildings; cities are people. And, ultimately, this is a book about people and about how Chicago was a place where people could innovate and succeed.

One of the strategies of this book is to connect events that happened in 1893 with the Chicago of today—to demonstrate, in a way, that these occurrences, which might seem distant, still resonate. For example, another characteristic of today's Chicago that often escapes notice is that it has quietly acquired one of the largest student populations in the United States. A 2009 study by DePaul University found the Loop to be "the biggest college town" in Illinois. Among the city's thirty-seven colleges and universities are some of the nation's best educational institutions, including the Illinois Institute of Technology (IIT), which began life as the Armour Institute in 1893. An examination of how that forceful meatpacking titan, Philip Armour, established the school will allow us to survey Chicago's development as a major capital of higher education while also enabling us to take a quick look at the all-important meatpacking business.

. . . the story of Frances Willard helps us understand why Chicago was the bicycle capital, as well as the temperance capital, of the United States.

The method of this book is to move from the specific to the general. Each chapter analyzes a particular person or event not only because that person or event is worthy of note, but also because this approach makes it possible to study larger phenomena and to formulate generalizations. For example, the story of Frances Willard helps us understand why Chicago was the bicycle capital, as well as the temperance capital, of the United States. The account of Father Tolton, the first black Roman Catholic priest in the United States, enables us to examine the importance of Catholicism in Chicago's development. Recounting the smallpox epidemic of 1893 leads to an investigation of how the city took steps to clean up its water supply once and for all by constructing the Sanitary and Ship Canal. Similarly, the "tugboat war" that occurred in the summer of 1893 enables us to take a wider look at how the city dealt with its serious air pollution problem. The chapter on the Cubs' new ballpark, which opened in 1893, examines the rise of professional sports in the United States, a development that many historians have cited as central to the development of new modes of American leisure. One doesn't need to be reminded that Chicago is a great museum center; it is, however, startling to recognize that all three of Chicago's most distinguished museums trace their origins to 1893—the Field Museum was incorporated in September and the Art Institute and the Museum of Science and Industry are both housed in buildings that were first used for the Columbian Exposition. That the writers George Ade and Finley Peter Dunne both made newspaper debuts in 1893 and Henry Blake Fuller's groundbreaking Chicago novel, *The Cliff-Dwellers*, was also published in that year is quite a coincidence, but taking note of it also opens the door to considering Chicago's place as a literary center. The stories of Wrigley's gum and Cracker Jack, although interesting in themselves, are even more significant in the context of Chicago's earning the reputation as the "unofficial candy capital of the world." And to take one final example: some might regard a chapter on the Chicago hot dog as an exercise in triviality, but guidebooks to the city invariably cite the hot dog as one of Chicago's "don't miss" aspects. (When Fodor's guide says "Chicago's got it all," it lists "piled-high hot dogs" right up there with museums, lake views, and parks.) It has become a culinary emblem of the city, as indispensable to its identity as the Water Tower. In other words, although this book is about 1893, much of what it describes took place after that year because those 1893 events resonated in the city for decades (most are still being felt).

In 1893, as well as today, more than a few Chicagoans seemed to take a perverse pride in the city's raffish and unruly side as a sign of energy and exuberance. Stephen Longstreet recorded that a visitor at the turn of the century stated that "Chicago is the wickedest city in the world" and added, "As this remark was often printed in the local press, it would appear that many citizens were proud of the title."[1] The reporter and playwright Ben Hecht remarked, "The good-citizen majority looked on the wrongdoers as a sort of vaudeville, more entertaining than harmful. They watched these vaudevillians bilk the town, batten on its vices, and their virtuous citizen hearts applauded furtively."[2] A few historians have enjoyed doing the same thing. Engaging and edifying volumes such as Stephen Longstreet's *Chicago, 1860–1919*; Emmet Dedmon's *Fabulous Chicago*; Curt Johnson's *Wicked City*; Norman Mark's *Mayors, Madams, and Madmen*; Richard Lindberg's *Chicago Ragtime* and *Chicago by Gaslight*; and Karen Abbott's *Sin in the Second City* contain many tales of the city's animated characters, hustlers, boodlers, madams, and gamblers. They are key components of the city's history and won't be ignored here—hence the chapter on William Stead's exposure of the city's low life—but they tend to overshadow those individuals who strove for civic betterment, those persevering people discussed in Helen Lefkowitz Horowitz's *Culture and the City: Cultural Philanthropy in Chicago from the 1880s to 1917.* In 1893, Chicago's iniquitous Levee district did indeed sport wall-to-wall brothels and gambling joints, but just a short stroll away one could hear the recently founded Chicago Symphony Orchestra playing Wagner and Tchaikovsky. Henry Blake Fuller, a stern critic of Chicago's grasping capitalism, wrote in 1897:

> The date of the Fair was the period at once of the city's greatest glory and of her deepest abasement. But at the very moment when the somewhat naif and officious strictures of foreign visitors seemed to present Chicago as the Cloaca Maxima of modern civilization, the best people of the town found themselves, for the first time, associated in a worthy effort under the unifying and vivifying impetus of a noble ideal. . . . The sense of shame and of peril aroused by the comments of outside censors helped to lead at once to a practical associated effort for betterment, and scarcely had the Columbian Exposition drawn to a close when many of the names that had figured so long and familiarly in its directorate began to appear with equal prominence in the councils of the Civic Federation.[3]

Many of the chapters in this book are intended to serve as reminders that in 1893, Chicagoans were creating many of the public institutions that today make the city celebrated.

Analysts of urban development once took it for granted that civilizations in general, and cities in particular, went through a course of development that paralleled the human condition—they had their infant struggles, their vigorous youth, their powerful maturity, and their inevitable senescence and decline. In the 1830s, The Course of Empire, a series of outsized canvases by the American artist Thomas Cole, depicted this process: *The Savage State, The Pastoral or Arcadian State, The Consummation of Empire,*

Destruction, and, finally, *Desolation*. It is a useful metaphor, although not one that can be pressed too hard (cities can decline and rise again). Cole, of course, was thinking of Rome, but if he had lived to see the World's Columbian Exposition, he surely would have seen an empire on its way to consummation.

In the United States, writers commonly use the term "adolescent" to describe cities at a certain stage of development. As Anselm Strauss, an insightful observer of urban life, has pointed out, this metaphor entails the inherent difficulty of determining when a city has moved from one stage to another: "When a city changes, how much must it do so before a claim can legitimately be made, or safely supported, that a new stage has been reached in the city's development? When does a city stop being young and become adolescent? How long can a city exist without being regarded as old, or even as middle-aged and settled down?"[4] With Chicago, it is persuasive to view the city in 1893 as young, and so it was seen. One visitor in 1891–92 said, "It seems to me to have ever been, as it is now, a city of young men."[5] The social worker Jane Addams, who founded Hull House in 1889, called the Chicago of her day "a city in the first flush of youth, impatient of correction and convinced that all would be well with its future."[6] In 1892, an anonymous bard penned a lyric entitled "Chicago's Soliloquy on Her Childhood," which ran in part:

> Like the flash of a meteor, my childhood has vanished.
> It came and it went like a summer night's dream,
> And swiftly as thought has maturity banished
> The dalliance of childhood that did intervene . . .
>
> The chirp of the quail in my ear is still ringing,
> So brief has it been since her callow brood came,
> But briefer the changes that progress is bringing
> To clothe me with manhood, and honor my name.
>
> To clothe me in manhood's becoming attire
> Of urban devices in towers and domes,
> And sky piercing buildings, that higher and higher
> Rise up and o'ershadow our beautiful homes.[7]

Chicago's adolescence, however, seems to have lasted a long time. A writer in 1930 spoke of its "stage of adolescence—an adolescence beautiful but dumb."[8] And as late as 1947, a reporter in the *Saturday Evening Post* was still referring to Chicago as adolescent.[9] Perhaps it's most accurate to say that in 1893 Chicago was young, but that like a lot of young people it was trying to look and act older. One of the major goals of the Columbian Exposition was to prove to the world that this one-time rough frontier town was now a mature metropolis, with all the cultural and financial attributes required. And visitors were in fact astonished to discover how far Chicago had come in such a short time. In 1893, the French diplomat François Edmond Bruwaert wrote, "Those who come here will wonder how, in less than fifty years, that is, in less than a man's lifetime, it has been possible to transform a swamp, producing only a sort of wild onion, into a powerful and flourishing city."[10]

Although there probably is a point in the development of any great city at which it bursts into greatness, it's unlikely that for most cities that moment could be concentrated into a single year. A major reason it can be done for Chicago is that its expansion was so rapid—Chicago was probably the fastest growing big city in world history. When it was incorporated as a city in 1837, it had a population of about four thousand; by 1860, the population was over 110,000. Between 1880 and 1890, the city's population doubled—from half a million to over a million. In the ensuing decade, it nearly doubled again, arriving at a population of 1.7 million by 1900. Chicago was also expanding in area. Just four years before the Columbian Exposition, the city annexed the towns of Jefferson and Lake, the city of Lake View, and the village of Hyde Park (in 1893 it added a few smaller plots). In 1880, the area of Chicago was 35.2 square miles; in 1890, it was 178.1. When a city grows like that, changes come quickly, events follow one after the other with an irresistible momentum, and it's possible—even likely—that one specific year will stand out as the focal point of its swift success. Today, Chicago is classified as a "global city."[11] Such a thing as a "global city" might be possible only in an age of rapid travel and instant communication, but tracing the history of Chicago's ascendance to the top rank of urban metropolises would lead one back to the 1890s. As an observer noted at the time, between the Great Fire and the Columbian Exposition, "Chicago has passed from the position of a mere receiving point for the produce of a limited area to that of a metropolitan city."[12] It is noteworthy that, if we enlarge the time frame a little, how many other events take place in the first few years of the 1890s. The Chicago Symphony Orchestra was established in 1891. In the following year, the present University of Chicago was founded; the first "El" train began operation; Burnham and Root's Masonic Temple, briefly the tallest building in the world, was opened; and, an ominous sign for the future of cities everywhere, an automobile appeared on a Chicago street for the first time.[13] The great Pullman strike, one of the most important episodes in U.S. history, occurred in 1894.

Lewis Mumford, the well-known analyst and critic of cities, said that it is in the nature of expanding cities to want the biggest of everything—the biggest university, the biggest department store, the biggest hospital, and so on.[14] The year after the Columbian Exposition, the architecture critic Montgomery Schuyler wrote, "In this country mere bigness counts for more than anywhere else, and in Chicago . . . it counts for more, perhaps, than it counts for elsewhere in this country. To say of anything that it is the 'greatest' thing of its kind in the world is a very favorite form of advertisement in Chicago. One cannot escape hearing it and seeing it there a dozen times a day, nor from noting the concomitant assumption that the biggest is the best."[15] This is where Chicago was in 1893; the city's ambitions were illimitable. It had come to a point of development at which its citizens were saying, in effect, we possess a great mercantile and industrial city—it is time we also owned the civic institutions a true metropolis should have. An essay in the Chicago magazine *Dial* in 1892 entitled "Chicago's Higher Evolution" said that "Chicago has put all her energy of this half century of her adolescence into the development of a material body which is magnificent in its functional structure and health. . . . But already the signs are clear that the season of mere physical life is over."[16]

State Street in 1893. Even before the elevated trains were built, the streetcars gave the name "Loop" to Chicago's downtown.
(Wikimedia Commons)

Ironically, Chicago arrived at its year of greatness at a time when a lot of people thought cities in general were hopeless. Many a critic saw Chicago in particular, and industrial cities in general, as so disorderly that they might be unsustainable. For example, the reformer Henry George, in his *Progress and Poverty* (1879), viewed urbanization with alarm, arguing, "Where the conditions to which material progress everywhere tends are most fully realized—that is to say, where population is densest, wealth greatest, and the machinery of production and exchange most highly developed—we find the deepest poverty, the sharpest struggle for existence, and the most of enforced idleness."[17] In a vision worthy of Thomas Cole, he feared that the city was breeding new "Huns" and "Vandals" who would raze civilization. In *Wealth against Commonwealth* (1894), William Demarest Lloyd argued that "liberty produces wealth, and wealth destroys liberty," citing cities as one of the "obesities of an age gluttonous beyond its powers of digestion."[18] In 1891, the minister Josiah Strong put it bluntly: "The city has become a serious menace to our civilization."[19] From the opposite side of the political spectrum, the socialist Eugene V. Debs wrote an essay in 1902 entitled "What's the Matter with Chicago?" He stated, "Chicago is the product of modern capitalism, and, like all other great commercial centers, is unfit for human habitation." The best thing for it, he argued, would be "depopulation" and the release of its miserable population to "spread out over the country and live close to the grass." Finally, after visiting Chicago, the city planner Ebenezer Howard rushed home to England and began designing what he called "garden cities"—progenitors of the modern suburb—using Chicago as an example of what human habitation should *not* be.[20]

Many utopian visions of humane cities created in the late nineteenth and early twentieth centuries were inspired by the problems found in cities like Chicago. Daniel Burnham himself turned to the question of city planning with his 1909 *Plan of Chicago*, a visionary proposal that, although not completed, was responsible for many of the amenities that make Chicago so appealing today. In addition, as Jane Addams astutely noted, the decade that followed the Columbian Exposition was an era of "propaganda" and radicalism, what we now see as the beginning of the Progressive movement that addressed so many festering urban social problems (*McClure's Magazine*, the leading journal of the muckrakers, was founded in 1893).

Nearly all visitors who commented on the city's shortcomings were equally impressed by its energy, and they commonly used contrasting terms to describe Chicago—"splendor and squalor" was William Archer's phrase, and Price Collier more colorfully called it "a city of pork and Plato." Writing in 1888, Charles Dudley Warner recognized that, for all its social ills, Chicago was "in fact a metropolis, by-and-by to rival in population and wealth any city in the world."[21] What happened was that Chicago in 1893 proved that livable cities were *not* impossible. The White City of the Columbian Exposition was meant to be an object of reassurance—proof that with careful planning cities could be enlightened, secure, and habitable. As the fair closed, the *Chicago Tribune* described it as "a little ideal world, a realization of Utopia," adding that "this splendid fantasy of the artist and architect seemed to foreshadow some faraway time when all the earth should be as pure, as beautiful, and as joyous as the White City itself."[22]

Yet at least two visitors to the fair recognized that as inspiring as the fair was, Chicago itself was even more so. Julian Ralph commented, "Those who go to study the world's progress will not find in the Columbian Exposition, among all its marvels, any other result of human force so wonderful, extravagant, or peculiar as Chicago itself."[23] And François Bruwaert said that it would not be "the Exposition itself that will most surprise the foreigner who is enterprising enough to come as far as Chicago. The most beautiful exhibition will be Chicago itself, its citizens, its business, its institutions, its progress."[24] The *New York Times* realized the same thing, stating in an article on Christmas Eve 1893 that "outsiders only know half the truth about this city. . . . What gave it the courage to produce the Columbian Exposition at the cost of a third of a billion dollars was the conviction that it had already done greater things."[25] Chicago in 1893 *was* a city of pestilence, pollution, and poverty, but, as the following pages will show, it was also a city of museums and merchants, skyscrapers and schools, candy and clerics, writers and reformers, entrepreneurs and engineers, bicycles and ballparks.

1

The White City and the Gray City

The Scottish writer James Fullarton Muirhead, author of the 1899 Baedeker's guidebook to the United States, summed up Chicago as a "city of contrasts." He knew that many outsiders called Chicago "Porkopolis" in reference to its slaughterhouses, but he warned, "Chicago ought never to be mentioned as Porkopolis without a simultaneous reference to the fact that it was also the creator of the White City, with its Court of Honour, perhaps the most flawless and fairy-like creation, on a large scale, of man's invention."[1]

It was a rare visitor to Chicago in 1893 who did not come away from the Columbian Exposition without a sense of wonder. And many marveled at the city's variations and disparities. The White City represented what a city, any great city, might, and should, be—an idealization, to be sure, but a vision worth imitating. Another thing that most visitors remarked upon was that Chicago was enveloped in a vast cloud of smoke, the result of burning tons of bituminous coal. That was the other city—the Gray City.[2]

The White City

The great Columbian Exposition was the crowning event of 1893. Even more, it was one of the most celebrated experiences in U.S. history and arguably the finest world's fair ever staged.

At first it seemed as if the exposition to commemorate the four hundredth anniversary of Christopher Columbus's first

The neoclassical architecture of the White City was meant to evoke the grandeur of ancient Greece and Rome. (Library of Congress)

voyage to the New World would not be held in Chicago at all. Other cities with more prestige were vying for that honor. When the idea of a great fair was first proposed, most people assumed that it would be held in Washington, D.C., the nation's capital. However, other cities realized what a boost such an extravaganza would be to their economy and status, and soon New York and St. Louis were in the running. Chicago entered the competition in the summer of 1889. St. Louis and Washington gradually dropped out, and a heated rivalry between New York and Chicago emerged.

For years a story has been passed down that it was during this competition for the fair that Charles Dana, editor of the *New York Sun*, called Chicago the "Windy City," thus giving it its nickname (Dana, it has been said, was referring to the hot air being emitted by the city's politicians and not to the gales blowing off the lake). However, historians have been unable to find an actual citation in which Dana used the term, although after Chicago won the fair, the *Sun* did run an article that said, "All of the talking, blowing, and boasting for years has been on the part of the Windy City."[3] But even if the use of the term in that article came from Dana himself, scholars have determined that the term "Windy City" had been in use long before 1893. As far back as 1858, the *Chicago Tribune*, in an article about young Chicagoans' failed efforts to be accepted as volunteers in a federal military expedition to Utah, wrote, "An hundred militia officers, from corporal to commander, condemned to air their vanity and feathers only for the delectation of the boys and servant girls in this windy city."[4] That usage doesn't amount to a city nickname, but the employment of "Windy City" in that manner can be traced to 1876, when it was being used in Cincinnati newspapers. Interestingly, in the latter decades of the nineteenth-century "Windy City" was used to refer both to Chicagoans' bragging *and* to its winds. (Compared to other U.S. cities, meteorologists report, Chicago is not especially windy.)

In any case, the U.S. House of Representatives voted on February 24, 1890, to give the fair to Chicago. "Great is Chicago," crowed the *Chicago Tribune*; "it gets the World's Fair."[5] The common feeling was that Chicago had finally arrived as a city, a view shared around the nation, which is why the significance of 1893 as a pivotal year in Chicago's history is both psychological and practical. Millions of people would come to appreciate that here, indeed, was a great metropolis, a rival not only of New York, but also of Paris and London.

But the fair would be a coming-out not only for Chicago, but also for the nation. The industrial and technical exhibits, the confidence of the architecture, and the grand scale of the enterprise all signaled a new, vigorous world power, bristling with innovation and self-assurance. In addition, the evocations of ancient Rome raised by the exposition's neoclassical architecture appealed to expansionist Americans who viewed their country as being on the verge of becoming itself an imperial power destined to fulfill its "manifest destiny."

A group called the Chicago Exposition Company oversaw the project. Comprised of prominent business and civic leaders, it was headed by Harlow N. Higinbotham, an executive with Marshall Field's. The directors moved quickly and by the summer had hired Frederick Law Olmsted as landscape designer and the firm of Burnham and Root as chief architects. The sixty-eight-year-old Olmsted, famous as the designer of Central Park in Manhattan, was no stranger to Chicago, having planned the acclaimed suburb of Riverside in the 1870s. Daniel Burnham and John Wellborn Root had already put up some of Chicago's finest buildings, including the Rookery (1885).

Within a year of congressional approval, it was decided that the fair should be located in Jackson Park on the South Side, which was well served by public transportation and where land had

Architect and planner Daniel Burnham and colleagues at the site of the Columbian Exposition. Ernest R. Graham is at the far left, Burnham is third from the left, Charles B. Atwood is at the far right, and the others are unidentified.
(ICHi-02208, Chicago History Museum)

already been set aside for public use. Burnham considered giving a single architect the job of designing all the major structures but realized that a team would be more expedient, and for the most part he invited distinguished architects from the East trained in the neoclassical Beaux-Arts tradition. Among them were Richard M. Hunt; George B. Post; Peabody and Stearns of Boston; and the New York firm of McKim, Mead, and White. Architects from Kansas City were assigned the Electricity Building, and Chicagoans were given the Fisheries, Horticulture, and Transportation Buildings. The Transportation Building, the work of Louis Sullivan, was, with its Golden Doorway (a series of receding arches with gold leaf ornament), one of the few to go against the overall neoclassical look of the White City, which looked like a fantasy of imperial Rome as seen through a nineteenth-century utopian lens. Another building to buck the neoclassical trend was the Fisheries Building, the work of Chicagoan Henry Ives Cobb, which had blue glazed tiles on the roof and employed polygonal, conically roofed towers in a Romanesque revival style.

Because the term "White City" has ever since been a synonym for the fair, it's interesting to note that Burnham at first considered that the buildings could be of different tones. Evidence exists that speed was a major reason for selecting white as a uniform hue—the paint was easily sprayed on by compressed-air squirt guns, which were used here for the first time on an important undertaking.[6] Most of the buildings were not intended to be permanent. They largely consisted of iron or wood skeletons clad with a wrapping of "staff," a material made of plaster, cement, and jute fibers. Although the term White City is often used to describe the entire fair, it more properly applies to the Court of Honor, which was the prospect that imprinted itself most vividly on visitors' memories. Many other styles, such as French Gothic and Romanesque Revival, could be found in state pavilions and other structures, not to mention the ethnic styles used in many of the buildings representing foreign countries.

The great fair sprang into life on May 1, 1893, when President Grover Cleveland pressed the button that illuminated the entire scene in a network of electric lights. The effect was staggering.

The British journalist William T. Stead commented, "Never before have I realised the effect which could be produced by architecture. The Court of Honour, with its palaces surrounding the great fountain, the slender columns of the peristyle . . . and the golden dome of the Administration Building, formed a picture the like of which the world has not seen before."[7]

What was it like to be there? First, the fair was immense. The Paris Exposition of 1889 covered 160 acres. The Columbian Exposition, however, covered 633 acres, a size guaranteed to fatigue the most stalwart legs, which was one reason for the popularity of "rolling chairs," which were pushed by college students for forty cents an hour (there was also an elevated train, as well as boat transportation on the lagoons, and many people rented folding camp stools to carry about with them). A popular guide suggested that just to "comfortably" see the delights of the Midway Plaisance alone, "one week should be given to the excursion," and one estimate calculated that to see the entire fair would take a visitor three weeks and 150 miles of walking.[8] To cope with this immensity, visitors often stayed in Chicago for a couple of weeks and visited just one or two buildings in a day.

Another thing that must have astonished visitors was the crowding. During the six months it was open, more than 27.5 million people

President Grover Cleveland himself pressed the switch that turned on the dazzling electric lights of the White City. (Library of Congress)

visited the exposition (21.5 million admissions were paid), and it's been calculated that about 25 percent of the population of the United States saw the fair. Opening day drew nearly 130,000, and the largest one-day attendance was on October 9, "Chicago Day," when 716,881 visitors came through the gates. Another thing that brought much comment was how bright the fair was in the daytime—staring at all those glaring white buildings hurt the eyes. A modern visitor would also have been struck by the heat. Fairgoers in 1893 would not have dreamed of walking around in T-shirts, shorts, and sandals; it was jackets and hats for the men, long skirts and buttoned collars for the women. Visitors regularly got sick or fainted from the heat.

At Opening Day of the Columbian Exposition, the world got its first look at the "White City." (Library of Congress)

Finally, there was the scene after sunset. If there was one aspect of modernity that stood out, it was electricity. Although electric-powered devices of all sorts were featured in the displays, it was the incandescent bulb that elicited the greatest awe. Many rural Americans at the fair had never seen a single light bulb; now they were dazzled by thousands. The buildings of the Court of Honor, as one visitor expressed it, were "etched in fire against the blackness of the night."[9] It can fairly be said that the year 1893 marked the decisive transition from the age of steam to the age of electricity, and visitors to the fair were well aware of it.

Unlike Disneyland, this was not a fair primarily of recreation and amusement; it had a strong didactic, even encyclopedic, educational mission. Above all (an aspect easily overlooked today) it was a celebration of Christopher Columbus. Americans in the 1890s were in the habit of rating the courageous explorer as one of the greatest figures in history. One of the many booklets published about the fair was one called "Classification of the World's Columbian Exposition." This 104-page volume simply listed, without comment, all the categories covered by the exhibits in the various buildings, and the list goes on and on, ranging from (just to give a sample) "wheat and its culture," "cheese and its manufacture," "cigars, cigarettes," "blast furnaces," "aluminum alloys," and "steam, air, and gas engines" to "lithography," "wire-working machinery," "rolling-mills and forges," "artists' colors and artists' materials," "jewelry and ornaments," "cotton fabrics," "toys and fancy articles," "electroliers and electric lamps," "refrigerators," "sculpture," "paintings in oil," "the nursery and its accessories," "elementary instruction," "books and literature," "bridge engineering," "government and law," "religious organizations and systems," and "the North American Indian." The final item is "Class 968: The Latin-American Bureau," and, yes, the list does begin with "Class 1." Obviously, this was an exposition in the true sense of the term—not an amusement park, but an encyclopedic display of contemporary life and enterprise.

In order to house all these displays, the architects put up buildings on a colossal scale. Covering more than eleven acres of space, the Manufactures and Liberal Arts building was promoted as the largest building in the world. Boosters pointed out that its 540,000 square feet could encompass Madison Square Garden, Winchester Cathedral, the U.S. Capitol, and the Great Pyramid. And it was just one of several similar huge structures surrounding the Court of Honor—buildings devoted to electricity, mines, machinery, and agriculture. Dominating the west end of the basin was Richard Morris Hunt's Administration Building, whose towering dome, higher than the national capitol's, served as the focal point. Finally, at the north end of the fairgrounds, surrounded by a variety of state pavilions, stood the Palace of Fine Arts, which many thought the most beautiful of all the structures. Because it was built to contain art treasures, it was constructed with greater durability, and today it houses the Museum of Science and Industry.

Fortunately, Higinbotham and Burnham realized that although all this technology and high culture was fine, fairgoers would need diversions. Burnham enlisted the talents of twenty-three-year-old Sol Bloom, an Illinois-born entrepreneur and showman who had made a name for himself in San Francisco, where he had been a theater manager and a fight promoter. Bloom was the genius behind what was known as the Midway Plaisance, a mile-long strip of amusements extending west of the fair (it is now a wide linear park flanked by University of Chicago buildings). At first the midway was meant to be a kind of living display of world culture, a sort of anthropological expo, and was placed under the supervision of the Harvard anthropologist Frederick Ward Putnam. This was too professorial for Bloom, who transformed the idea into a colorful Street of All Nations, which was more like a carnival than a classroom (although anthropology was taken seriously at the fair—see chapter 2). An indication of his showmanship was the immensely popular Street in Cairo, in which Bloom introduced the "hootchy-cootchy" version of the belly dance. Other attractions included the Dahomey Village, the German Village, the Javanese Settlement, the Brazilian Music Hall, the Hungarian National Orpheum, the Turkish Village, and a display of Samoan Islanders "so recently rescued from cannibalism."

Most likely the single most impressive attraction of the entire exposition was the Ferris wheel, Burnham's answer to the Eiffel Tower. As a display of technological skill, the Eiffel Tower was until then unrivalled, and Burnham challenged American engineers to come up with something to outdo it. Many proposals came in, some impractical, some uninspired, some bizarre. One engineer, for example, devised what might be the first conception of bungee jumping, but in this case a car carrying passengers would be pushed off the top of a tower. Connected by a long rubber cable, the car would snap back before reaching the ground. On August 15, 1890, the *Chicago Tribune* published a piece entitled "The Columbian Exposition Cranks," in which it poked fun at some of the outlandish schemes, and it listed dozens. Just to take a sampling, this is from the section on tower proposals:

> a tower to run about on rollers and towers to be mounted on wheels, self-propelling, and adapted to the work of carrying the visitors in and out of various buildings; hanging towers; a tower half a mile high, surmounted by a globe and statue of Columbus; a tower seventeen stories high, the roof forming an airy promenade; a tower of the plan of the tower of Babel, forty stories high; another Babel tower with numerous landings, a different language to be spoken on each; and, finally, a gigantic tower in the shape of a ladder, up whose immense rungs the crowd will climb.

Fortunately, an engineer from Pittsburgh named George Washington Ferris Jr. conceived something different *and* practical. Much has been written about the dimensions of the fair's 264-foot-tall Ferris wheel, but probably the most salient fact is that each of the cars weighed twenty-six thousand pounds and was the size of a city bus. The wheel went into operation on June 16, and during its months of operation (it ran until November 6) it carried some 1.5 million passengers, each of whom paid fifty cents for the twenty-minute ride. It has been estimated that the Ferris wheel earned over $750,000. After the fair it was moved

The most spectacular structure at the Columbian Exposition was the mighty Ferris wheel, the world's first, which was meant to outdo the Eiffel Tower. (Library of Congress)

to a site on North Clark Street, where it operated until 1903. Many local residents considered it a nuisance, but even so, it did not draw the crowds its owners had hoped. It was taken to St. Louis for the Louisiana Purchase Exposition of 1904, and, after serving its role there, it was demolished on May 11, 1906, by a huge controlled explosion of dynamite. If it had somehow been preserved, it would be one of Chicago's most appealing tourist attractions, if not a symbol of the city itself.

Crowds lined Adams Street on October 21, 1892, for the grand parade on Dedication Day for the Columbian Exposition. (ICHi-64435, Chicago History Museum; photographer, J. W. Taylor)

The Gray City

One event that occurred in 1893 might seem to be a minor one in that remarkable year, but its symbolic value was large. This was the "tugboat war."

Visitors to the White City, while wondering at its beauty, could not fail to notice one major characteristic of Chicago. The air was dark. Or, as Rudyard Kipling put it, "Its air is dirt."[10] Another visitor spoke of the "enveloping pall of smoke and puffing steam jets that rise above the buildings," and the French novelist Paul Bourget said, "Far as the eye can reach Chicago stretches away, its flat roofs and its smoke—innumerable columns of whitey-gray smoke."[11]

These foreign observers weren't telling Chicagoans anything they didn't already know. How could they ignore the carpet of smoke that covered their city when, for example, on November 30, 1892, Chicagoans woke up in the morning and saw that the sky was still as dark as midnight? It got a little lighter later in the day, but, as the *Chicago Tribune* put it, "Over all the city lay the heavy pall of black, sooty smoke and dimly through it gleamed the gas lamps like stars on a foggy night."[12]

The problem was that Chicago burned tons and tons of bituminous, or soft, coal ("the coal of the West"), a major source of air pollution and considerably cheaper than anthracite coal, which burned more cleanly. By 1893, Chicago was burning some eight million tons of bituminous coal every year, making it the largest soft-coal-burning city in the United States. In the downtown business district alone, there were over two thousand boilers and twelve hundred chimneys.[13] In 1888, the *Chicago Tribune*, which took the lead on this issue, interviewed several architects and recorded their complaints. Not only did soot quickly blacken new buildings and make them look decades old, but also it corroded the stone and metal. Furthermore, the soot crept into the architects' offices through the windows and darkened the drawings on the tables.[14] In the same week the newspaper sent a reporter to Wabash Avenue, which contained establishments involved in the millinery and drapery trade. One after another, proprietors grumbled about how the smoke and soot disfigured their wares and how they were compelled, at great cost, to wrap their goods in special paper or store them in specially constructed drawers.[15]

In 1891, five prominent Chicagoans formed the Society for the Prevention of Smoke in Chicago. Their self-appointed task was to promote a two-pronged solution: punishment and prevention. First, they would seek vigorous legal prosecution of polluters, and, second, they would urge the use of smoke-abatement devices and help owners of boilers to adopt such equipment. Several companies were installing a new type of coal-burning furnace called the down-draft furnace and were finding that smoke emissions could be reduced by as much as 90 percent.

Other enterprises were turning to the use of hard coal, natural gas, or oil (the White City was powered by oil, all the better to keep it white).[16]

Within a year, the society's membership had expanded to two dozen or more, and it was able to report some successes. One of the greatest was its victory over the operators of the power plant owned by the Chicago Edison Company. This huge facility, with ten boilers, had been a major source of soot, but Chicago Edison had finally agreed to equip all the boilers with down-draft furnaces, which eventually brought a great improvement in air quality. The society had also been able to persuade local railroads to adopt smoke abatement devices, and it reported a 75 percent reduction in locomotive smoke. The society had its own attorneys and, working with the city's lawyers, had brought over three hundred suits against violators of the smoke ordinances. The violators fell into three categories: stationary plants, locomotives, and tugboats, which brings us back to the "tugboat war."[17]

As the history of the environmental movement has shown, efforts to compel industry to practice environmentally sound practices are inevitably met with resistance that is usually based on the claim that such efforts, because they involve great expense, threaten the economic health of businesses, and, by extension, the economic health of the country as a whole. In addition, business leaders commonly challenge or disregard medical studies suggesting a link between pollution and illness. The antismoke crusade was an early example of this. In Chicago, resistance to the antismoke movement began to organize early in 1893. On February 25, a group of businessmen met at the Sherman House to make plans to combat the efforts of the Society for the Prevention of Smoke. They charged that the society threatened "the manufacturing and business interests of Chicago" and that its endeavors to block the use of bituminous coal threatened the jobs of some thirty thousand Illinois coal miners. Industry and business, they complained, needed "protection" against "a sentimental, namby-pamby, ignorant discrimination against the vital interests of our city and State," and they implied that somehow the society was in cahoots with the producers of anthracite coal.[18]

The tugboat owners were some of the antismoke society's most hostile opponents. In August 1892, the society had announced that they were now becoming more aggressive. The directors noted that they had written the tugboat owners a cordial letter reminding them of the practical advice they had given on how the boats could curtail smoke emissions but that they had been met with indifference and enmity. "The tugboat owners," they charged, "have not shown the slightest intention of adopting measures looking toward the abatement of the smoke nuisance." Consequently, the society was going to station observers along both branches of the Chicago River and bring suit against polluting tugboats. In addition, the society had secured the services of a young, aggressive

The smoking tugboats on the Chicago River were a main target of reformers who wanted to clean up Chicago's dirty air. (Library of Congress)

lawyer named Rudolph Matz of the firm of Matz and Fisher. "Matz & Fisher," warned the society, "had charge of the suits against delinquent World's Fair subscribers, and are thoroughly familiar with the pushing of this class of suits."[19]

On July 25, 1893, the *Chicago Tribune* announced in a headline, "War Begun on Smoking Tugboats." The article said that the antismoke society had secured the backing of Mayor Carter Harrison and that the city government had brought lawsuits against the main tugboat companies. The society also charged that the tugboat owners, by stalling and impeding the legal process, hoped to exhaust the society's financial resources. The tugboat industry fought back by forming a group called the Citizens' Protective Association, the kind of benign title often used by antireform groups. They made the now-familiar argument that a cabal of elites was working to prevent honest workingmen from carrying on their trades—worse, they were doing it for profit because, the tugboat owners pointed out, nearly all the directors of the antismoke society were also directors of the Columbian Exposition. The juries sided with the tugboat owners, and in August the cases were dismissed. The *Chicago Herald* concluded, "If the voice of the people is the voice of God it is evident that the Almighty is exercising a special providence over smoke makers."[20]

The term "Gray City" may be used in reference not only to smoke but also to all the urban ills that the city confronted.

It might be going too far to say that its defeat in the tugboat war caused the Society for the Prevention of Smoke to run out of steam, so to speak, but it did expire soon after, largely because it ran out of funds. The society was also losing in the court of public opinion because the crippling depression that began in 1893 made it difficult to propose measures that would increase the cost of doing business. But the crusade for cleaner air did not die. It would be revived in 1908 by a group of determined women, led by the redoubtable Annie Sergel, who organized a new antismoke campaign. Their foe was the Illinois Central Railroad, which ran smoke-belching locomotives through their South Side lakefront neighborhoods. Sergel found an ally in

Mayor Frank Busse, and eventually all of Chicago's steam railroads had to adopt electrification within the city.[21]

The smoke-covered city was the Gray City that stood in contrast to the White City.[22] The term "Gray City" may be used in reference not only to smoke but also to all the urban ills that the city confronted. No one was more aware than Chicagoans themselves that the city had major problems. Smoke was one of them, and others— impure water, slum housing, epidemic disease, political corruption, rampant vice, and open gambling—will be discussed in later chapters of this book.

Although the White City, designed in large part by eastern architects, made little direct reference to Chicago itself, visitors did not remain insulated from the Gray City. Many were seeing Chicago for the first time. Some, like Kipling, were repulsed; others were dazzled by its energy, by its architecture, and by the speed with which it had re-created itself in the twenty-two years since it had burned to the ground.

Sixteen years after the Columbian Exposition, Daniel Burnham published his *Plan of Chicago*, an inspired view of what the city might become. The plan, which envisioned a system of lakefront improvements, wide boulevards, and spacious parks, was clearly influenced by the White City. Burnham's plan was realized only in part, but what it did accomplish brought significant improvements to the city, especially in creating its system of lakefront parks.

Daniel Burnham, the architect in charge of building the Columbian Exposition, as seen in a contemporary caricature. (P&S-1954.236, Chicago History Museum; artist, Theodore L. Wust)

The White City and the Gray City, then, were inescapably linked. Although one was fantasy and the other was reality, those citizens of Chicago who were dedicated to civic improvement would always have a reminder of what collective effort could accomplish. The historian Carl Smith has pointed out that although the fair might have looked like a dreamscape, its developers were assiduous in employing modern technology (electricity, especially, and, as noted, the use of oil for fuel), and the builders "devoted as much attention to plumbing and garbage removal as they did to monumental display."[23] The White City was a dream, but it taught lessons in how a city could better be operated. In the following chapter we shall see how the Columbian Exposition bequeathed to Chicago three of its most celebrated institutions.

2

Three Museums and a Library

Any city that wants to be taken seriously in the twenty-first century has to have at least one notable museum, either an institution from the Gilded Age or an edifice designed in high modern style by an architect with a name—or better yet, both. It's where locals go on a Sunday, it's something that tourists come to see, and it proclaims that the city is of consequence. This, however, is not a modern idea: similar sentiments animated a great wave of museum building in the second half of the nineteenth century—and most definitely in Chicago, where civic-minded citizens were anxious to shed their city's image as a frontier boomtown and demonstrate that it could support the arts and culture as much as New York or Boston or the great European capitals.

The founding of New York's Metropolitan Museum of Art in 1870 put Chicagoans on notice that if they were going to challenge New York for urban supremacy, they had better have a large art museum of their own. And more than an art museum would be needed. Chicagoans knew that there were other types of museums—New York's American Museum of Natural History had opened in 1869, and nearby Milwaukee had opened the encyclopedic Milwaukee Public Museum in 1882—so Chicagoans would have to own examples of these. Americans in the post–Civil War era were so enamored of museums that they envisioned a great variety, perhaps even more than today. For example, George

Brown Goode, the assistant secretary of the Smithsonian, argued the value of six kinds of museums—art, history, anthropology, natural history, technology, and commerce.[1] This kind of list was enough to challenge any city's ambitions to cultural importance. Fortunately, in Chicago the arrival of the World's Columbian Exposition in 1893 boosted these efforts. All three of Chicago's most celebrated museums—the Art Institute, the Field Museum of Natural History, and the Museum of Science and Industry—can trace their origins to 1893.

Culture and Its Benefactors

Chicago's civic leaders were vigorous supporters of the arts, and without them the city would not likely have its museums. They had been involved in charitable and cultural activities from the city's early days. In the decades before the Civil War, it was taken for granted that those—male and female—who enjoyed wealth and success were obliged to take the lead in civic betterment. Often urged on by their churches, women became involved in institutions such as orphanages, hospitals, shelters for unmarried mothers and the homeless, and establishments that taught domestic skills to the poor. Men were expected to aspire to the ideal of the "Christian Gentleman." As one historian has expressed it, "In assessing each other's achievements, wealthy Chicagoans continually stressed their gentlemanly qualities rather than their material accomplishments. Erudition, bibliophilia, charity, cultural patronage, and refined but modest life styles were the qualities most frequently singled out for commendation."[2]

Things changed after the Civil War as a new class of self-made millionaires appeared in Chicago. The earlier generation had gone out in search of the needy and had entered their homes, but the recent super-rich, especially society's *grandes dames*, preferred to conduct their beneficent activities from a distance. The wives of the millionaires were more concerned about their ranking in society, and to demonstrate their preeminence they fostered the development of highly visible cultural institutions, such as art galleries and opera houses. In addition, it became *de rigueur* to make the Grand Tour of Europe, and many of these women, such as Bertha Palmer and Lydia Hibbard, returned determined that Chicago should possess the same great museums and musical institutions as the European capitals. It was left to their husbands, however, to actually do the basic work of organizing and founding the institutions. These men were great joiners of clubs, sometimes belonging to half a dozen or more, and it was there that they usually met to discuss plans for civic improvement.

Today, the purpose of art is commonly viewed as something provocative: art, it is said, challenges people's perceptions and value systems and forces them to think in different ways. Therefore, art that is shocking, alienating, or deliberately upsetting is assumed to be beneficial. The mainstream mid-nineteenth-century view was otherwise: art was an expression of the ideal. It was a secular, ethical religion because it inspired and uplifted. Beauty could make people morally better and motivate noble deeds, and it was the task of the elite to bring beauty to the masses. The English poet and essayist Matthew Arnold, author of *Culture and Anarchy* (1869), sounded this theme often: art could ennoble the soul and thus help bring society closer to perfection. Arnold's writings had a wide readership in the United States, and in 1884, the great man himself even came to Chicago, where he gave a speech at the Central Music Hall before some four hundred people, including many of the city's upper crust. He warned that America faced the dangers of "hardness" and "materialism" and expressed hope that an "all-transforming remnant" of society (the privileged) would secure the triumph of "whatsoever things are elevating."[3]

Another reason that Chicago's plutocrats were drawn to the foundation and administration of cultural institutions was that they realized that they were being pushed out of city politics. The city's changing demographics had led to the rise of politicians who were either from specific immigrant ethnic groups or who were able to present themselves as their champion.[4] The executive board of a privately endowed and administered museum was beyond the reach of city hall—it was a place where the upper class could still exercise uncontested authority without having to consort with "coarse" ethnic politicians.

A third motive for promoting cultural uplift, and one not often mentioned, was fear. Labor unrest, as exemplified in such events as the Haymarket affair of 1886, in which a bomb went off at a labor rally and killed eight policemen and several civilians, stirred feelings of near panic among Chicago's elite, who were already dismayed at the influx of immigrants, some of whom were bringing anarchistic and communistic ideas with them. Creating institutions that would civilize the masses, then, was a form of self-protection.

The Art Institute of Chicago

The stately building facing Michigan Avenue that today houses the Art Institute of Chicago opened on May 12, 1893.[5] Although the structure was intended to be an art museum from its inception, for its first six months of existence the directors of the Columbian Exposition used it to host what was called the World's Congress Auxiliary. The idea behind this enterprise was to invite "representatives of all interests, classes, and peoples" to come and present papers on issues of the day. To give an example, on just one day (June 22, 1893) the following lectures were given: "Essential Elements of a Monetary System"; "Governmental Regulation of Transportation and Its Practical Effects"; and "Boards of Trade: Their History, Utility, Effect on Prices, Results to Producers, Results to Consumers."[6] It was at the congress that the historian Frederick Jackson Turner delivered in 1893 his famous paper "The Significance of the Frontier in American History," which argued that the development of the leading traits of the American character was tied to the moving frontier, which had now disappeared. The most popular segment of the congress was the World Parliament of Religions, in which representatives of Roman Catholics, Protestants, Jews, Buddhists, Hindus, Muslims, and others met to discuss their common interests in an atmosphere of toleration. The assembly had at least one profound effect on American culture: the star of the parliament was a turbaned Indian monk named Vivekananda, who introduced Americans to a spiritual discipline known as "yoga." That small spark, kindled in Chicago in 1893, ignited what is today an annual $6 billion industry in the United States.

When the World's Congress Auxiliary shut down in October, the Art Institute was free to become a public gallery of artistic masterpieces. The writer George Ade, then a reporter for the *Chicago Record*, was there in 1893 to record the new museum, and he decided that it was "in Chicago but not of it," largely because it was so peaceful:

> Any place as quiet as the Art Institute is a relief. The walls are dark-hued and restful, and there can be no more deadly silence than that made by a roomful of heroic casts and bronzes. The people who move along, usually two and two,

In contrast to today, the Art Institute of Chicago was a lonely presence in Grant Park when it opened in 1893. (Library of Congress)

fingering their catalogues and reading the unpoetic sticker labels, converse in whispers or a mumble. An occasional bell or whistle on the Illinois Central tracks interrupts for a moment, but the rattle of wheels on Michigan Avenue seems a long distance away. The Art Institute is beginning to realize all hopes.

Ade went on to report how a museum guard told him, "They have some of the greatest pictures up there you ever put your eyes on. I heard a man say here the other day it was one of the best collections in the world. I'd like to have what just one of them cost. I wouldn't kick."[7]

Although the present museum opened in 1893, the history of the Art Institute itself can be traced to 1866, when a group of artists established the Chicago Academy of Design in a rented space on Clark Street. Within four years, the academy had moved into its own home on Adams Street, but that building burned in the Great Fire of 1871, and the academy struggled through lean years before reorganizing as the Chicago Academy of Fine Arts in 1879. The first president was George Armour, who served one year; he was followed by L. Z. Leiter, who stayed on for two years. The presidency then went to banker Charles L. Hutchinson, who would lead the Art Institute from 1882 until his death in 1924. In 1882, the name was changed to the Art Institute of Chicago, and the society purchased a lot at the corner of Michigan and Van Buren. John Wellborn Root of the firm Burnham and Root designed for this space a modest Elizabethan-style building that opened in January 1883. The trustees then acquired the adjacent property and hired Burnham and Root to design a second building, a four-story Romanesque Revival brownstone that measured eighty by a hundred feet and which opened to great acclaim in November 1887.[8]

Charles Hutchinson serves as a good example of the kind of civic-minded Chicagoan who got involved in institution building in the late nineteenth century. His father, Benjamin F. Hutchinson, was one of those buccaneer types who had come to Chicago from the East. "Old Hutch," who made a fortune in banking, grain trading, and meatpacking, had no patience for his

The old Art Institute of 1887, designed by Daniel Burnham and John Wellborn Root, had an exhibition area consisting of just a dozen small galleries. (ICHi-64434, Chicago History Museum; photographer, J. W. Taylor)

son Charles's love of art and wouldn't let him attend college, but Old Hutch did give Charles (as well as each of his other children) a million dollars to get started in business. Old Hutch eventually became mentally unstable and had to be institutionalized; Charles turned his father's bequest into an even larger fortune and was free to collect art. In the 1880s, accompanied by his friend Martin Ryerson, Charles traveled extensively in Europe, both to study museum organization and to collect masterpieces. Hutchinson eventually became the acknowledged dean of cultural life in Chicago. A colleague tried to count the number of organizations with which Hutchinson had been involved and came up with more than seventy, adding: "Of half a dozen he was president. Of twenty or more he was treasurer. He was a director or trustee of more than forty."[9]

Hutchinson's conception of what the Art Institute should be was highly democratic and sometimes strikingly modern. "Art is not destined for a small or privileged group," he said. "It is of the people, and for the people." He went so far as the express his wish to make his museum a "three-ring circus," one that offered lectures, music, an art school, and free admission on Sunday.[10] All this was a major reason that he needed an even larger building. The 1887 Burnham and Root building had good attendance, but half of its twenty-four rooms were rented to societies, private firms, artists, and other tenants, leaving the exhibition area with a dozen small galleries.[11]

Hutchinson set his eyes across the street—to what is now known as Grant Park—and in March 1891, he negotiated a deal with the city council for the right to build there. Part of the cost of the new edifice would come from the sale of the current Art Institute building; some would come from the World's Columbian Exposition, which would use the building for its congresses; and some would come from private funding; the city was to donate the land. Legal ownership of the new building was given to the city, which would allow the Art Institute to remain there indefinitely. Actually, the land was not vacant but was occupied by the Interstate Industrial Exposition Building of 1872, Chicago's first convention center. This flamboyant building had in 1883 hosted a major railroad fair. It had also served as an armory, as a hall for national political conventions, and as the first home of the Chicago Symphony Orchestra.

Although the city agreed to raze the Exposition Building to make way for the Art Institute, there was disagreement on whether anything at all should be built on the site. In 1836, when plans were drawn for a canal linking the Chicago and Des Plaines Rivers, the commissioners decided not to sell the land between Michigan Avenue and Lake Michigan but to forever keep it as "Public Ground—A Common to Remain Forever Open, Clear, and Free of any Buildings, or other Obstruction Whatever." Most Chicagoans seemed to believe that this stricture could be ignored, but others did not, the most prominent being the mail-order magnate Aaron Montgomery Ward, who waged a twenty-year campaign to keep the lakefront free of buildings. He did not, however, oppose the Art Institute, partly because he understood that the building would remain modest in size (which it certainly didn't, leading him to regret his decision). Other Michigan Avenue property owners were not as accommodating as he was, and one of them, Warren F. Leland, secured an injunction against construction. Although he withdrew his opposition, at the end of May 1892, opposition was renewed by an intractable woman named Sarah E. Daggett, who argued that the erection of the Art Institute would diminish the value of her nearby property. At this point the museum's directors had already spent $30,000 to lay the building's foundation, and if Mrs. Daggett were able to delay further construction long enough, the directors might lose the $200,000 they were due to receive from the World's Fair fund. A proposal was made to buy Mrs. Daggett's Michigan Avenue property, but her asking price was much greater than anyone would meet. In June 1892, however, a panel of judges ruled against Mrs. Daggett, and work resumed. It's interesting to remember, however, that, strictly speaking, the Art Institute probably should stand elsewhere.

In June 1890, the trustees appointed a building committee that selected two architectural firms to draw designs in an "academic classical style." Root drew up at least three separate versions of a Romanesque Revival building before he died in January 1891. Charles B. Atwood, his successor, took over the project and submitted his design nine months later. His competition was the Boston firm of Shepley, Rutan and Coolidge, which was awarded the commission in October 1891. It has been speculated that they were given the assignment partly because the directors believed that they had been slighted by not being invited to contribute a building to the Columbian Exposition, but it also appears that they were the architects most eager to comply with the directors' desire to keep the cost of the building as low as possible.[12]

The objects on display ranged from Egyptian antiquities to photographs by the French photographer Adolphe Braun . . .

When the World's Congress Auxiliary wrapped up its business, a demolition company came in to remove the two large temporary wooden assembly halls in the rear of the building in which the delegates had met. Then a "large force of painters, calciminers, and janitors" got to work "making the Art Institute presentable."[13] The building opened as an art museum on December 8 with a grand evening reception. It was announced that the museum would "be open to the public, free of charge, from 9 A.M. until sunset every Saturday and Wednesday hereafter and also Sunday afternoon from 1 to 5 the museum will be open to everyone, without money and without price."[14]

The objects on display ranged from Egyptian antiquities to photographs by the French photographer Adolphe Braun, which had been given by Mrs. D. K. Pearsons. The contents of some of the galleries indicate the museum's dependence on gifts from wealthy patrons, and at the time, such donations were not considered standard practice. As one contemporary observer put it, "While in other cities many priceless treasures of art are kept aloof from the many and for the enjoyment of the few fortunate to possess enough wealth to own them, in Chicago there has been that public spirit which has donated them to a public institution for the benefit of all."[15] Besides Mrs. Pearsons's photographs, there were the "Elbridge G. Hall Collection of Sculpture," the

"Ryerson-Hutchinson Collection of Metal Work," the "Higin-botham Collection of Naples Bronzes," "Oil Paintings, lent by A. A. Munger," and the "Henry Field Memorial Collection." The Munger Collection was said to have cost its lender a quarter of a million dollars, and the Field Collection, consisting mostly of works from the nineteenth-century French Barbizon school, was an exceptionally valuable addition. It included *Song of the Lark* (1884) by Jules Breton, which was all the rage at the Columbian Exposition; a newspaper contest in 1934 determined that it was the most popular painting in the United States. In 1900, the banker and museum trustee Samuel M. Nickerson donated a collection of Japanese, Chinese, and East Indian works, along with a group of contemporary paintings. One of the Art Institute's greatest coups involved the acquisition in Florence of thirteen seventeenth-century Dutch masterpieces known as the Demidoff Collection.

Although one of the Demidoff paintings, Rembrandt's *Young Woman at an Open Half-Door* (1645), remains one of the glories of the Art Institute, today the most popular works in the museum are the impressionist paintings. When the museum opened, the queen of Chicago society was Bertha Honoré Palmer, wife of the millionaire hotel owner Potter Palmer. Potter Palmer built a huge Gold Coast mansion aptly called "the castle," and his wife filled it with treasures (she was especially fond of jade). The couple traveled to Paris in 1889, and their agent, Sara Tyson Hallowell, introduced them to the American impressionist painter Mary Cassatt, who in turn led them to Claude Monet and several Parisian art dealers. Bertha Palmer had developed advanced artistic tastes at a time when many considered impressionism to be barbaric and incomprehensible. She came to be especially fond of Monet's work—she bought twenty-two of his paintings in 1892 alone and eventually owned thirty-two. She also enjoyed Degas, Pissarro, Sisley, and, of course, Cassatt, and her favorite painting was said to be Renoir's *Dans le Cirque*.[16] Although Hutchinson pleaded with her to lend some of these treasures to his museum, she could not bear to see them leave her home. However, after her death in 1918, many of her finest paintings made their way to the Art Institute in 1922, according to the terms of her will.

Over the years, the Art Institute has expanded well beyond its original 1893 home, both in size and scope. The Fullerton Auditorium was added in 1898 and the Ryerson Library three years later. In the 1920s, the museum built over the railroad tracks on the east and added the McKinlock Court and the Goodman Theater. In 1925, the Art Institute was given the Helen Birch Bartlett Memorial Collection, which included Georges Seurat's *Sunday Afternoon on La Grande Jatte*. A few years later, the collection of Martin A. Ryerson was added; the largest bequest ever given to the Art Institute, it brought a wealth of treasures, including American and European paintings, prints, and decorative arts as well as Asian art. Later additions to the building included the Ferguson Building (1958), the Morton Wing (1962), and the Daniel F. and Ada L. Rice Building (1988). In the spring of 2009, the new Modern Wing was opened. With this 264,000-square-foot addition, designed by Renzo Piano, the Art Institute now contained more than a million square feet of space and was the second largest art museum in the country. It had come a long way from John W. Root's four-story brownstone.

The Field Museum

Today, culture supports what has been called a "hierarchy" of museums in which the most prestigious are the museums of art.[17] There are several reasons for this—first, the objects within an art museum are of immense value; second, the objects are, for the most part, aesthetically pleasing and are enjoyed visually; and third, even in the twenty-first century, many art lovers still adhere to a nineteenth-century romantic view of the artist as a specially inspired, often misunderstood, being who rises above the common herd, and museumgoers draw comfort from stories of underappreciated geniuses who become vindicated by sophisticated viewers such as themselves. But this museum hierarchy did not exist in 1893, when museums of natural history were considered every bit as important—perhaps even more so, than art museums. In 1893, the founding of Chicago's Field Museum was of equal importance to that of the Art Institute.

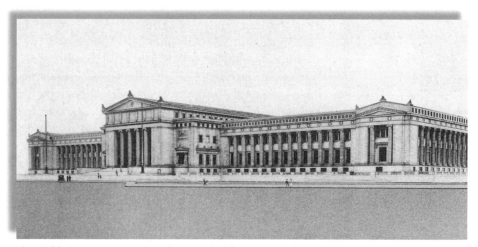

The Field Museum was originally intended for Grant Park, but the objections of business-man Aaron Montgomery Ward forced its founders to find an alternate site. (ICHi-62466, Chicago History Museum)

The nineteenth-century fervor for natural history had a theological component—the idea was that a study of the natural world would reveal its organization and demonstrate God's design of creation. Scientists scoured the world for specimens of that creation; cataloged, classified, and arranged them; and then put them on display. As the naturalist Louis Agassiz put it, the "great object of our museums should be to exhibit the whole animal kingdom as a manifestation of the Supreme Intellect."[18] Museums were not showcases of curiosities—P. T. Barnum could do that—but places of research and education. It was expected that it was in museums that scientific discoveries would be made; it was only in the twentieth century that the locus of original research shifted to the universities. Agassiz also argued that museums needed to scrutinize what contemporaries called "the natural history of civilization." Thus museums became crucial in the development of anthropology, and the Field Museum was at the forefront of this trend.

The primary force behind both the anthropology exhibits at the Columbian Exposition and the establishment of the Field Museum was Frederick Ward Putnam, professor of archaeology and ethnology at Harvard. In February 1891, he was appointed the chief of the Department of Ethnology of the great fair. He recruited a team of assistants numbering some hundred—university students, government officials, military officers, anthropologists, even missionaries—to travel widely, excavating, researching, cataloging, and borrowing objects to be displayed in the Anthropological Building. There fairgoers could see, just to take a few examples, specimens from the newly discovered Hopewell culture in Ohio; teepees and bark houses from the American West; amulets, shrines, and devotional sculptures exemplifying various world religions; items used by the inhabitants of Greenland and collected for the exposition by the explorer Robert E. Peary; a miniature cemetery illustrating burial customs in ancient Peru; and ten thousand square feet of castings made in the "ruined cities of the Yucatan."[19] (The exhibits came in for some criticism for concentrating so heavily on the Western Hemisphere.) The activities of Putnam's researchers, the organization of the exhibits, and the exposure to anthropology given to thousands of fairgoers combined to make the Columbian Exposition the springboard for the scientific study of anthropology in the United States.

It had cost some $100,000 to assemble the material in the Anthropological Building, and Chicago now possessed one of the richest ethnographical collections in the world. As early as November 28, 1891, Putnam had been one of the speakers at a meeting of the Commercial Club at which was proposed some sort of institution to

The Ruined Cities of the Yucatan was one of the most impressive displays at the Anthropological Building at the Columbian Exposition. The structures were castings of Mayan buildings. (Goodyear Archival Collection, Brooklyn Museum)

perpetuate the achievements of the Columbian Exposition. One of the participants pointed out that there were already enough wealthy men interested in the idea to make its success nearly certain.[20] A week later, the directors of the fair released a long statement by Putnam explaining why the proposed establishment was needed and how it would be organized. Chicago's natural history museum, he advised, should not only display objects but also accommodate meetings and lectures, house a library, and support research and the publication of papers, and he proposed that it have five departments—geology, mineralogy, botany, zoology, and anthropology. Museums of natural history, he pointed out, already existed "in nearly all the prominent cities," making such an institution "imperative for the culture and fame of Chicago." Otherwise, he warned, the objects collected for the fair would "be sent elsewhere."[21] The museum was incorporated as the Columbian Exposition was nearing its end. The *Chicago Tribune* predicted that the new establishment would become "one of the greatest features to welcome the great-great-grandchildren of those who now throng the grounds at Jackson Park" when Chicago held another Centennial Exhibition in 1993.[22]

The name of the institution was planned to be the Columbian Museum of Chicago in commemoration of the fair. It did not, obviously, retain that title. Despite Putnam's advocacy, he was not the one with the resources and connections to make the museum a reality. Leading that effort was Edward E. Ayer, a businessman and collector of

The contents of the Anthropological Building at the Columbian Exposition later formed the nucleus of the collection of the Field Museum. (Goodyear Archival Collection, Brooklyn Museum)

American Indian artifacts who was the chairman of the temporary finance committee (he later became the museum's first president and one of its greatest benefactors). The Great Depression of 1893 was in full swing, fund raising was slow, and Ayer was going to have to find someone with really deep pockets. He turned to a Chicagoan who had some of the deepest pockets in the country—the department store mogul Marshall Field. Ayer knew Field well enough to go on fishing trips with him, and more than once he sounded him out on donating a million dollars, which Ayer considered the minimum needed. Field inevitably replied, "I don't know anything about a museum and I don't care to know anything about a museum. I'm not going to give you a million dollars."[23]

As the end of the fair approached, Ayer was persuaded to try Field just one more time. He went to see him in his office in the morning, and Field, a busy man, asked how much time he needed.

"If I can't talk you out of a million dollars in fifteen minutes," Ayer answered, "I'm no good, nor you either."

"Fire ahead," responded Field.

Ayer went on to argue, "You can sell dry goods until Hell freezes over; you can sell it on the ice until it melts; and in twenty-five years you will be absolutely forgotten. You have an opportunity here that has been vouchsafed to very few people on earth."

Field listened for, not fifteen, but forty-five minutes and then said, "You get out of here."

Ayer, relieved that Field had not actually said no, asked for one thing—that Field come with him to the Columbian Exposition to see "what is there that can be used in a natural history museum." They went out the next morning, and upon leaving the fair in the afternoon, Ayer asked if he could see Field the next day. Field said yes, and when Ayer arrived in his office, he was handed the check.

The museum was incorporated in the State of Illinois on September 16, 1893. Field continued to support it, and other members of the Field family also became backers.

Other wealthy Chicagoans quickly followed with their donations, but Field's gift was the biggest philanthropic story of the year, and at a meeting of the museum incorporators on November 25, 1893, Ayer proposed that it be called the "Marshall Field Columbian Museum." The name change did not become official until May 21, 1894, when the museum trustees approved it (minus Field's first name). The new institution opened on the following June 2. It was to be free to the public on Saturdays, Sundays, and all public holidays, and free to schoolchildren at all times. Its director, Frederick Skiff, had organized it into four departments: botany, zoology, geology, and anthropology. The museum was housed in the former Palace of Fine Arts of the world's fair, the only building left standing from the exposition. Designed by Charles B. Atwood, it was in 1893 universally admired as one of the great buildings of its time. The American sculptor Augustus Saint-Gaudens, for example, considered it the finest piece of architecture since the Parthenon.

The Field Museum's ambitions were great, and so was its success. In 1896, the curator of zoology, Daniel Giraud Elliot, went on the first expedition to Africa ever sponsored by a U.S. museum. He wrote back to Skiff, "We will make the Field Columbian Museum lick all creation as a scientific museum and a Mecca for naturalists to visit."[24] By 1899, more than a quarter of a million people were visiting every year, the collection was

It took some doing, but eventually the department store magnate Marshall Field was persuaded to lend his money—and his name—to Chicago's new natural history museum. (*The Biographical Dictionary and Portrait Gallery of Representative Men of Chicago and the World's Columbian Exposition* [Chicago and New York: American Biographical Publishing Company, 1892]).

growing at a rapid rate, and it became obvious that it would soon outgrow its home.

The search for a new location intensified with the death of Marshall Field in 1906 because he left in his will $8 million for a new Field Museum. Just like their counterparts at the Art Institute had done, the trustees quickly cast their eyes on Grant Park, which had been renamed in 1901 after the former president. Their wishes were seconded by Daniel Burnham, who said in a speech to the Merchants Club, "The principal feature of the Grant Park should be the Field Columbian Museum. Picture to yourselves a stately white museum, resting on the Grand Terrace called the Lake Front. . . . No structure in the world has ever had a nobler setting than this would be."[25] If Burnham and the museum trustees had had their way, today visitors would face a vast building across the street from the Auditorium Building at Congress Parkway and Michigan Avenue.

Montgomery Ward, however, was still insisting on a building-free lakefront. In 1907, his lawyer warned than an injunction would follow the first sign of building on the disputed site, whereupon Harlow Higinbotham, president of the trustees, fumed, "The people of Chicago have expressed themselves as overwhelmingly in favor of this project. . . . Who is Mr. Montgomery Ward that he should dictate what the people are to have and what they are to go without? He might as well try to dictate what Chicago is to eat."[26] By November 1908, Ward appeared ready to compromise. In a lengthy statement, he said that he would drop his opposition to the Grant Park location if the South Park commissioners and the museum trustees could guarantee that no other buildings would ever be erected there. The Crerar Library and several administration buildings were already being planned for the park (Ward himself counted twenty proposed projects), and the trustees refused Ward's offer. The money in Field's will was contingent upon the finding of a new site within six years of his death, which gave the trustees only until 1912 to settle the matter. The prospect of losing the money, and the new museum building, turned the newspapers and Chicago's elite against Ward, calling him "stubborn" and "undemocratic." The *Tribune* labeled him "a human icicle, shunning and shunned in all but the relations of business."[27] Chicago's leaders might have been against Ward, but the law was not, and he prevailed in the Illinois Supreme Court in a decision handed down on October 26, 1909.

In 1914, an alternate site was found on landfill just below Grant Park east of the Illinois Central tracks and south of Twelfth Street. Construction on the new $5 million museum began in July 1915. The design, by Graham, Burnham and Company, was hailed as "a modern masterpiece in classical architecture," and the *Chicago Tribune* said, "When completed, it will be the largest marble building in the world."[28] The low-lying site required extensive amounts of landfill and over nine thousand deep pilings had to be driven into the ground to reach the level of rock. During World War I, the federal government contracted to use the building for three years as a hospital. The war ended before this became necessary, but Skiff complained that the episode had a "confusing and disturbing effect upon the affairs of the museum."[29] In the spring of 1920, the work began of transferring 560 carloads of exhibits from the old building to the new. The process took a year, and the new Field Museum opened on May 3, 1921.

The Museum of Science and Industry

The origin of the Museum of Science and Industry can be traced to 1893 in two ways. The first is in the building itself, which opened in that year as the Palace of Fine Arts at the Columbian Exposition. The second is less obvious—it was in 1893 that the firm of Sears, Roebuck and Company was incorporated, and it might be argued that had there been no Sears, there would be no Museum of Science and Industry. The building that houses it would be there, but most likely as a school, not as a place where a visitor can descend into a coal mine, walk through a submarine, and manipulate the dynamics of a tornado. The reason it is what it is today is because it was a Sears executive, Julius Rosenwald, who was the driving force behind its establishment. The story of Rosenwald's rise to the presidency of the Sears mail-order firm is recounted in the following chapter. This chapter explores how Rosenwald was instrumental in getting the museum started.

After the new Field Museum opened, its glorious former home sat empty and at the mercy of the Chicago weather—"semi-ruined" was how one observer described it[30]—and the South Park commissioners, who administered the building, voted three-to-two to demolish it, whereupon a coalition of individuals and citizens' groups rallied to conserve the structure. William Nelson Pelouze, the president of Chicago's Association of Arts and Industries, called it simply "the most beautiful building of classic architecture in existence."[31] In 1922, the Chicago chapter of the American Institute of Architects published a booklet entitled "A Challenge to Civic Pride," in which architects extolled the building's beauty and its importance in world architecture. They also put forth a modern idea—recycling an old building can have economic benefits. "Do you know," the booklet pointed out, "that it can be restored in permanent form for $2,000,000 and made ready for use, but would cost $12,000,000 if built new?"[32] The cause of preservation got a powerful lift when the Finnish architect Eliel Saarinen, who had finished second in the competition to design the Tribune Tower, visited the building and proclaimed it "perfect architecturally," adding "this is the age in which America should be inspired to preserve its monumental public buildings."[33]

In May 1921, the *Chicago Tribune* listed several organizations that had come out in favor of preserving the Palace of Fine Arts, including the Union League, the Illinois chapter of the American Institute of Architects, the Illinois Society of Architects, the Chicago chapter of the American Association of Engineers, the City Club, the Municipal Art League, and the Chicago Federation of Women's Clubs.[34] Early in 1922, six thousand clubwomen proposed raising $7,500 to restore the pavilion at the northeast tip of the building in order to demonstrate that restoration could be done smoothly and that the effect would be so "strikingly beautiful" that public opinion would rally to the structure's cause.[35] By the end of the summer, the money had been collected, and the designated section of the building was refurbished.[36] In February 1923, a meeting of the Chicago Woman's Club was given over to reminiscences of the glories of the Columbian Exposition, and among those attending were several women who had played major roles in organizing that fair. It was reported that there were "many tear filled eyes" when the Chicago sculptor Lorado Taft recalled the "beauty that is lost forever." And, in referring to that sole survivor, the Fine Arts Building, he exclaimed, "They are today asking for bids, for offers to tear it down and take it away forever. We must not permit it. We must rise in protest."[37] In April 1923, the South Park commissioners appropriated $500,000 for preliminary restoration work and ordered the placing of a $5 million bond issue on the November ballot so that the voters themselves could decide the future of the structure. The referendum passed, forty-nine thousand votes to thirteen thousand, and the building was saved.

And yet, saved for what? There was no shortage of proposals. When the Union League voted to save the building in May 1921, the group envisioned it vaguely as "a great art memorial for the encouraging of the fine arts." Early the following year, the *Chicago Tribune* listed some of the suggestions: "For the building of a great model of the entire Columbian Exposition in replica, to be illuminated; for a branch museum of sculptural casts for the Art Institute; for a collection of large current architectural and sculptural exhibits that might otherwise be destroyed for lack of storage space; for space for loan exhibits of Chicago artists; for a school in industrial art; for a great center for the liberal arts; for park field house purposes, such as gymnasium, swimming pools, assembly halls, public library branch, etc."[38] Most observers leaned toward making the building into some kind of technical school with perhaps a theater and a museum. Everything seems to have been thought of except what it actually became. No one could have known it, but the building's fate had already been determined as long ago as 1911 in, of all places, Bavaria.

That was the year in which Julius Rosenwald took his family to Germany. One stop on the tour was Munich, the location of the Deutsches Museum, an institution that show-cased technology and science (it's still thriving). Rosenwald's eight-year-old son, William, loved the place and requested several visits. This, Rosenwald decided, was the kind of museum Chicago needed.[39]

Chicagoans might not be especially excitable, but it's fair to say that they were flabbergasted when, on August 17, 1926, the *Tribune* screamed in a banner headline "CITY TO GET GREAT MUSEUM" and explained that Rosenwald was donating an astounding $3 million for the foundation of an "industrial museum, bringing under one roof realistic, moving miniatures of the great mechanical achievements of the ages."

Rosenwald said, "I would like every young growing mind in Chicago to be able to see working models, visualizing developments in machines and processes which have been built by the greatest industrial nation in the world." Similarly, Edward Kelly, the president of the South Park Commission, said, "A boy visiting a show is inspired by what he sees. He starts making things at home instead of stealing autos and running wild."[40] These quotations illustrate a key difference between the Museum of Science and Industry and the institutions built during the great age of museum building in the nineteenth century. In a sense, all museums are educational, but the Museum of Science and Industry, unlike its Victorian predecessors, was planned with children in mind. Although actual "children's museums" are now common, Rosenwald's museum was an innovation in its specific aim of reaching out to young people. If we think of museums today as a place to take the kids on the weekend, Julius Rosenwald had a lot to do with it.

All those people who made the Museum of Science and Industry happen were at the forefront of another trend that is common today but was nearly unheard of at the time—historic preservation. In that era, it was common practice to tear down notable buildings that had been praised only thirty or forty years before. A list of buildings erected during the golden age of Chicago architecture and torn down in the 1910s and 1920s would include the Insurance Exchange, the Second Rand McNally

Building, the Borden Block, the Chicago Opera House, the Chamber of Commerce Building, the Virginia Hotel, the Tacoma Building, and the Woman's Temple. Burnham and Root's Montauk Building, which opened in 1882, lasted only twenty years. The idea that one might want to save an old building for its aesthetic or historical value is recent—in fact, Chicago lost many of its greatest structures in the 1960s. It was not until 1949 that President Harry Truman signed the legislation creating the National Trust for Historic Preservation, which made Chicago's civic leaders in the 1920s way ahead of their time. The Museum of Science and Industry is seldom, if ever, viewed in this light, but it was one of the first triumphs of historic preservation and should be considered one of the movement's most distinctive landmarks.

Visitors to the Columbian Exposition admire Charles Atwood's Fine Arts Building, now the Museum of Science and Industry. (Library of Congress)

The museum opened on June 19, 1933, just in time for Chicago's second world's fair, the Century of Progress International Exposition. Since then the museum has gone on to add many memorable features—Christmas around the World (1942), Colleen Moore's Fairy Castle (1949), the U-505 submarine (1954), the Baby Chick Hatchery (1956), the Apollo 8 capsule (1971), a Boeing 727 (1994), The Great Train Story (2002), ToyMaker 3000 (2003), and Science Storms (2010). The Henry Crown Space Center opened in 1986. Rosenwald would surely be proud—and so would Charles B. Atwood, whose masterpiece could well have been carted away to a landfill.

The Chicago Public Library

November 30, 1893, was Thanksgiving Day. The weather in Chicago was cold and crisp, which was considered a good thing because the mud was frozen and not a hindrance to travel. The University of Chicago hosted a football game against Michigan, Northwestern played Wabash, and the Scotch Football Association squared off against the Gaelic Association, which must have been a colorful scene. The newsboys were given a Thanksgiving dinner at the Fifth Avenue Bakery Lunchroom, and the prisoners in Cook County jail were treated to turkey and to cigars. Helena Modjeska starred in *Mary Stuart* at Hooley's, and over at McVicker's, theatergoers could see *Blue Jeans*, which was described as an "Indiana melodrama." That entertainment caused a sensation—and launched one of popular entertainment's most durable clichés—because the intended victim was tied to a belt moving toward a large spinning buzz saw. And over at the northwest corner of Michigan Avenue and Washington Street, a group of about eight hundred men and half a dozen women witnessed the laying of the cornerstone of the new public library. To Chicagoans it was just another indication that their city was becoming an eminent cultural center. Housed in a neoclassical/Renaissance hybrid structure designed by Shepley, Rutan and Coolidge, the architects of the Art Institute, the library opened on October 9, 1897. Today, it is the home of the Chicago Cultural Center, which contains a tourist office and serves as a venue for free music, dance, and theater events, as well as lectures, films, and art exhibits.

As the historian Daniel Bluestone has expressed it, "The Chicago Public Library was one building that the 1871 fire created rather than destroyed."[41] That conflagration caused a huge upwelling of sympathy both domestically and internationally, and in Great Britain, A. H. Burgess came up with the idea of an "English Book Donation" to replace the library books that he assumed Chicago had lost. The author and parliamentarian Thomas Hughes enthusiastically backed the idea, and at his urging more than eight thousand volumes were collected, some donated by Britain's most prominent citizens, including Tennyson, Browning, Darwin, and even Queen Victoria herself. All this philanthropy was somewhat embarrassing for Chicagoans because they actually hadn't lost any books in the fire—there had been no public library to burn down. Obviously, that was a situation that had to be corrected, and the state legislature passed the Illinois Library Act of 1872, which authorized municipalities to found tax-supported libraries. Chicago got its public library rather quickly—on the first day of 1873—although it was located in a circular water tank that had survived the fire.

The library moved into several venues over the next couple of decades (for eleven years it was located on the fourth floor of city hall). A building fund for a lasting library building was established in 1881. The backers, many of them clergymen, sounded a refrain often heard in Chicago at the time—the city's cultural achievement did not equal its material prosperity. Even so, the project proceeded erratically, and it took more than a decade before the architects could be hired and the cornerstone put in place.

Not everyone welcomed the new building's neoclassical style. The former head of the library, William Frederick Poole, sounded a modern note: "The same secular common sense and the same adaptation of means to ends which have built the modern grain elevator and reaper are needed for the reform of library construction." However, for almost everyone else, classicism meant class. As *Harper's Weekly* expressed it, "We have so long been accustomed to think of Chicago architecture as a rather crude embodiment of brute force, asserting itself by Brobdingnagian height and ponderousness, that it is a delightful relief to find that Messrs. Shepley, Rutan and Coolidge . . . have adopted the classical style."[42]

The Chicago Public Library's main branch is now the Harold Washington Library Center on West Congress Parkway, one of the largest public library buildings in the world. Yet Chicago also boasts some distinguished specialized libraries. The Library of International Relations (1932) became part of the Illinois Institute of Technology's downtown campus in 1983. The Ryerson Library is part of the Art Institute. The Chicago History Museum has a research center rich in resources on the city's past. The John Crerar Library (1897), now affiliated with the University of Chicago, is one of the world's great science libraries. And, finally, the Newberry Library, which specializes in history and the humanities, has a spectacular collection of books, manuscripts, and maps. Located on the north side of Washington Square, it is housed in a handsome edifice designed by Henry Ives Cobb. The library, which is free and open to the public, opened in 1893.

3

Sears, Roebuck and Company

A huge city like Chicago affects many more people than the ones who live in or near it. For example, Chicago's aggressive and efficient meat packers transformed the High Plains prairies into cattle country, induced farmers to turn millions of acres over to the raising of corn for feeding animals, and put independent cattle raisers in the East out of business. Another profound effect came from Chicago's insatiable need for lumber, which denuded the Great Lakes region of its white pine forests. A third was how Chicago's mail-order houses linked the city and the country in new ways and transformed rural life.

Historically, one of the biggest divides between the country person and the city dweller was their ability to buy goods of almost any kind. In the colonial era, many of the manufactured goods purchased by farmers were sold by peddlers, whose wares were few and of variable quality. Many of these itinerant vendors settled down in towns and opened small general goods stores, where prices were high, choices were few, and satisfaction was definitely not guaranteed. It was different in the cities, where department stores emerged in the mid-nineteenth century. Marshall Field, Chicago's most famous department store owner, came to the city in 1850; he first went into partnership with Potter Palmer and Levi Leiter and opened his own firm in 1881. Other important Chicago department stores of the period were Schlesinger and Mayer, the Fair, Carson Pirie Scott, and

Mandel Brothers. They gave urbanites an extensive choice of goods, but unless a farmer (and his family) came to the city, these stores did not do the same for country people. That was the job of the great mail-order houses, another unique feature of Chicago.

Sears and His Catalog

Sears, Roebuck and Company was incorporated on September 16, 1893.[1] Its founder, Richard Warren Sears, had been in the retailing business, in one form or another, for some seven years. When Sears, Roebuck and Company. was incorporated, Sears was not quite thirty years old, having been born in Stewartville, Minnesota, on December 7, 1863.[2] His father died when Richard was fourteen, and the lad went to work for the Minneapolis and St. Louis Railroad as a telegrapher. Soon he became the manager of the railroad station two miles from Redwood Falls, Minnesota, and it was there he began dabbling in sales. The railroad gave him, as station agent, special rates on such commodities as coal and wood, and he began selling to locals at attractive prices.

As the story goes, in 1886, a jeweler in town received a shipment of watches from Chicago but found the merchandise unsatisfactory. The shipper offered the watches to Sears at $12 each, and he began retailing them for $14 to other station agents, who were then free to sell them for whatever they could get. This is the narrative given in *Send No Money* by Louis E. Asher and Edith Heal, the first book-length narrative about Sears, Roebuck and Company, and it has been repeated in dozens of publications. Because Asher became general manager of Sears, Roebuck in 1906 and corresponded with and was a friend of friend of Richard Sears, this story presumably came from Sears himself. However, in an interview with a reporter from the *Chicago Tribune* in 1907, Sears told a somewhat different tale. The reporter, Hollis W. Field, related that Sears himself received a $9 watch C.O.D. along with "a suggestion from the shipping house that the young telegraph operator could make a nice profit selling them to agents and railroad men throughout the northwest." Sears knew that railroaders, who relied on good timepieces, normally purchased watches for $20, so he contacted the shipping company and agreed to take a batch of slightly better watches at $9.40 each. Then by means of Western Union, Sears wrote "forty letters to forty men in forty different towns" offering the watches at $11.90. He soon had made himself a profit of $200.[3]

Whatever the exact details, within six months Sears had made $5,000, moved to Min-neapolis, and opened the R. W. Sears Watch Company. He quickly decided that Minneapolis was too small and too remote, and a year later he was in Chicago. As part of his business, Sears was called upon to repair watches, and he needed to find someone to handle that side of operations. His want ad was answered by a young Hoosier named Alvah Curtis Roebuck, and they teamed up in 1887.

And then Sears suddenly decided to get out of the business. In March 1889, he sold his firm and decided to try banking and investment, only to re-alize that this was not the field in which his talents lay. Un-fortunately, when he sold the company he had agreed not to do business under the Sears name for three years. So he moved back to Minneapolis and opened the Warren Com-pany (his middle name), but Sears, who seemed to find it hard to settle down, sold this business too—to Alvah Roe-buck. Just a week later, Sears changed his mind yet again and persuaded Roebuck to take him back as a partner, although the company now operated under the name A. C. Roebuck.

Few people had a greater impact on Chicago than Richard W. Sears, a brilliant businessman and copywriter who revolutionized U.S. retailing. (ICHi-51971, Chicago History Museum; photographer, Wallinger)

By this point, the two young merchants were expanding beyond watches and jewelry and were selling silverware, pistols, and various other items.

Finally, by 1893, the time limit on the use of the Sears name expired and Sears, Roebuck and Company was officially in business. At this time, however, the firm was still headquartered in Minneapolis, a city that Sears still did not regard highly, so it was back to Chicago, where an office was established on West Van Buren Street in December 1893. At the end of 1894, Sears, Roebuck and Company signed a five-year lease on a five-story building on West Adams Street for $5,000 a year, and within a month the entire operation had been moved to Chicago.

The first catalog to bear the Sears, Roebuck name came out late in 1893 (it was dated 1894). On the cover the company calls itself the "Largest Watch House in the World," but the inside pages show that Sears was selling much more than watches. Diamonds, jewelry, and silverware were major

"We guarantee that any article purchased from us will satisfy you perfectly . . . [and] that it represents full value for the price you pay.

sellers, but the company also offered, among other things, harnesses, saddles, buggies, baby carriages, furniture, men's suits, ladies' shoes, bicycles, and firearms. Sears also prominently featured a mandolin for $6.95, which makes one wonder why, with all the instruments available, Sears was pushing this one. The mandolin is just one indication of how the Sears catalog can give insight into the culture of the era—the mandolin was *the* fashionable instrument of the 1890s, and the decade saw the beginning of a craze for mandolin orchestras that lasted almost until World War I (some still exist).

The Sears catalog came to be known as the "Nation's Wish Book." With the plethora of choices available today, we might have difficulty appreciating the huge cultural impact the Sears catalog had from, say, 1893 to 1940. "The Big Catalog," Sears pointed out, "is your right arm to reach out and touch the whole world. Workmen, designers, and inventors of all nations may be summoned to your service. In this Book you have a modern convenience to be classed with electric power, the telephone and the telegraph." The Sears catalog epitomized home and America: when secretary of state Newton D. Baker visited France during World War I, he was surprised to learn that the book most requested by hospitalized Yanks was the Sears catalog, which supplied them with images of home.

During an era when fair pricing and customer satisfaction were scarce, Sears's policy stated, "We guarantee that any article purchased from us will satisfy you perfectly . . . [and] that it represents full value for the price you pay. . . . If for any reason whatever you are dissatisfied with any article . . . we expect you to return it to us at our expense." Today, the prices in an old Sears catalog are striking. Who wouldn't love to pay $10.95 for a bicycle or $9.95 for a solid gold ring with "8 fine rose diamonds and 4 almandines"? As startling as the prices is the abundance. Every conceivable need could be met within the catalog's pages, whose immense index ran from abdominal bands to Zylonite rugs, with Bibles, chain hoods, dynamite, ear muffs, flannel shirts, gold toothpicks, horseshoes, Indian clubs, jams, kites, lace, mole traps, nursing bottles, oyster forks, paints, quick-silver, road wagons, salt fish, tombstones, union suits, valves, wire ropes, xylophones, and yarns in between. About the only thing missing were houses themselves, and Sears remedied this omission in 1908—and for three decades thereafter—by selling through the catalog pre-cut materials for complete houses. Many Sears houses still exist.

In a sense, an old Sears catalog is about as close as one can come to a time machine. So clearly does it illuminate the evolution of American culture that a book could be written on just that subject, and one has been—a thick volume from 1940 by David L. Cohn entitled *The Good Old Days: A History of American Morals and Manners as seen through the Sears, Roebuck Catalogs 1905 to the Present*. The book contains a flowery introduction by novelist Sinclair Lewis, who commented, "By your eyebrow pencils, your encyclopedias, and your alarm clocks shall ye be known."

Montgomery Ward

Sears, Roebuck and Company would eventually go on to become the largest retail operation in the world, but it was not the first major mail-order business. That was Montgomery Ward, also headquartered in Chicago.

Aaron Montgomery Ward was born in Chatham, New Jersey, on February 17, 1844, and his family settled in Michigan when he was nine. As a youngster, he realized he was not suited for heavy labor so he took jobs clerking in stores of different types. At age twenty-one he headed to bustling Chicago, where he found a job at the Field, Palmer and Leiter department store. He performed well but was restless and became a traveling salesman. It was probably while touring through the small towns of the Midwest that he conceived his great idea—to undercut the high prices of general stores by selling direct to the farmer by mail at near wholesale prices.

Montgomery Ward astutely observed two phenomena that made his scheme workable. First, farmers might have been isolated and uneducated, but the rural economy was expanding. From 1860 to 1900, the farm acreage in the United States nearly doubled, and the value of agricultural products tripled, while the value of farm property had gone from $8 billion to $20 billion.[4] At the same time, rural isolation was disappearing: railroads were pushing their way west, linking all regions of the country (and centering on Chicago). These railroads transported goods from the farms to the cities for distribution, but in return they also carried manufactured items to the farmers. Second, as the farmers grew more prosperous, they became more dissatisfied. In the farmers' view they were the ones who created the wealth of a nation; speculators, mortgage lenders, equipment manufacturers, railroad magnates, eastern merchants, and operators of grain elevators were parasites. Farmers began to organize, and an association called the Patrons of Husbandry, better known as the Grange, was founded in 1867 to represent their interests. Within just a few years, membership grew to more than a million and a half. Grange meeting halls were used for meetings, dances, and other social functions, and Grange farmers formed cooperatives to buy machinery in bulk and thus at lower prices. Also, Grange stores were set up in many towns to compete with local retailers who, it was believed, were oppressing farmers with their unfair prices. What the Grangers really detested was the "middleman"—the scoundrel who schemed to buy farm products for as little as possible while retailing to farmers for prices that amounted to extortion.[5] Consequently, when merchants like Ward and Sears told farmers that they would dispense with at least one middleman—the retailer—they were eager to listen . . . and to buy.

Ward's retailing vehicle was the catalog. Ward decided that he would try to sell just about anything a farmer and his family could want. In addition, the catalog would expose rural citizens to products that they didn't even know they wanted. Ward quit his traveling salesman trade, returned to Chicago, found work in a retail company, and saved every penny he could spare while investigating the firms that could serve as suppliers for his enterprise. He had finally accumulated enough funds to begin in 1871—a bad time to launch a business because the Great Chicago Fire consumed his stocks. But Ward rallied quickly, found investors, and was back in action in late 1872.

Ward targeted Grange members as his first customers, and his first offering—one page long—went to them. He advertised as "The Original Wholesale Grange Supply House," and the title of one of his first price lists read: "Grangers supplied by the Cheapest Cash House in America. . . . You can readily see at a glance the difference between our Prices and what you have to pay your Retailer for the same quality of goods."[6]

The first bound catalog (thirty-two pages) appeared in 1874, and a year later Ward issued his famous pledge of customer satisfaction: "We guarantee all our goods. If any of them are not satisfactory after due inspection, we will take them back, pay all expenses, and refund the money paid for them."[7] By 1893, Montgomery Ward and Company had a seven-story headquarters on Michigan Avenue. The catalog, now known as the "Big Book," was well over five hundred pages long. In that year over three hundred thousand people toured the building and the immense

Montgomery Ward's headquarters building on Chicago Avenue was a major tourist attraction in the early twentieth century. Ward, Sears's predecessor, is today best remembered as the savior of Grant Park. (Library of Congress)

warehouse. Most were visitors to the Columbian Exposition, and Ward provided for their comfort a Customer's Parlor. By the end of the nineteenth century, Ward's catalog had twelve hundred pages and offered some seventy thousand items. If one of the prime goals of American enterprise is to persuade customers to buy things they don't need, Montgomery Ward and Sears, with their enticing catalogs, were two of the most convincing initiators of this policy.

For Montgomery Ward and Sears, one of the most important events of 1893 had nothing to do with Chicago or their catalogs. It was the approval by Congress of what was called rural free delivery, although the actual implementation of the process did not take place until 1896. Rural free delivery was the policy of providing free mail delivery to rural homes. Before this, a farmer had to pick up the family's mail at the post office, which was often located in the general store. As a contemporary article put it, "many a farmer must travel 10 to 15 miles for his mail. . . . No other errand may require him to visit the post-office village more than once a fortnight or a month except to get his letters, and often he allows them to accumulate, perhaps to his loss, simply because he cannot spare the time to go after them."[8] Parcel post took a bit longer to get started, but by 1913, the U.S. government was delivering packages to farm homes across the country. Newspapers, books, and goods of all sorts were now easily available to nearly anyone anywhere, and as long as the buyer had the money, there was no reason the interior of a farmer's home could not look like one on the West Side of Chicago. The era of the "country bumpkin" was over.

Although Sears would overtake Montgomery Ward as a retailer and the Montgomery Ward company would declare bankruptcy in 1997 and close every single one of its stores four years later, Aaron Montgomery Ward himself had an enduring, even crucial, effect on Chicago. This contribution can be traced back to yet another key event of Chicago history that occurred in 1893. As we have seen in the previous chapter, Ward fought hard to keep the Field Museum off the lakefront, but this effort was just part of a larger campaign. On January 23, 1893, Ward summoned a group of Michigan Avenue property owners to his office to discuss the creation of a park stretching two blocks along the east side of Michigan Avenue from Randolph Street to Madison Street. Chicagoans today would recognize this area as Millennium Park, but in Ward's time the city had plans to maintain all sort of things on it, from exposition halls to race tracks to garbage dumps. When Ward looked out upon this expanse from his office window, he saw a firehouse, freight cars, an armory, piles of trash and ashes, shacks, and stables. However, the participants in the meeting envisioned a differ-ent vista and stated, "The cupidity or corruption of city fathers and others who were periodically to use these blocks, originally dedicated to the public for private purposes, should be at once and forever thwarted." The best way to do this would be to create a new public space, which would gradually be extended several more blocks to the south. Ward noted that "this is the age of commercial activity, but there should be something in life besides this ceaseless grasping for the dollar."[9] The attendees agreed to fund the $10,000 that would be initially required to prepare the grounds.

Although Chicago's Grant Park is the envy of cities around the world, practically no one wanted it. Not the mayor. Not the city council. And certainly not the businessmen. One alderman groused that the downtown lakefront is "no place for a park." But the enemies of Ward's vision had a problem: as discussed in the previous chapter, back in 1836, when three eminent Chicagoans drew up plans for a canal linking the Chicago and Des Plaines Rivers (and thus Lake Michigan and the Mississippi), they de-cided not to sell the patch of land between Michigan Avenue and the lake. Instead, this part of the map bore the legend "Public Ground—A Common to Remain Forever Open, Clear, and Free of any Buildings, or other Obstruction Whatever."

When there's money to be made, however—and developing the lakefront promised a lot of it—what are a few words on an old map? As Chicago got bigger, so did the appetites of the patricians and the hustlers. The mayor envisioned a power plant, a city hall, stables for garbage cart horses, and, very important, an armory to house soldiers brought in to subjugate striking workers. The power elite visualized museums and monuments, but not a park. Three years before calling his meeting, Ward had sued the city to tear down the structures that were accumulating on the lakefront and to clean up the area. Thus began a fight that cost Ward twenty years, $50,000, and not one, but four, Illinois Supreme Court cases. In 1908, he said,

> It has been my purpose to preserve the Lake Front park for the people in accordance with the plain intent of the government which gave to the city the land for an open park, free from all buildings, and I am still of the opinion that in so doing I have done the city and the people a real service. Had I not done what I have it seems fair to say the open park we now have would long ago have been covered by buildings that would not add to the beauty or usefulness of the surroundings and the park would be destroyed.[10]

He prevailed, finally, in 1909, but by the time of that final Illinois Supreme Court decision, he was pretty fed up. "Perhaps I may yet see the public appreciate my efforts," he grumbled. "But I doubt it."[11] Montgomery Ward's preservation of the land is an example of philanthropy at its finest—a gift that required not only money, but also time and perseverance.

The Sears Empire

Sears Roebuck caught up to Ward surprisingly quickly. It was in 1900 that Sears first surpassed his older rival; sales at Sears in that year were over $10 million—$2 million more than Ward's.[12] Probably the leading reason for Sears's rise to the top was Richard Sears's salesmanship. His natural gifts as a copywriter are demonstrated on every page of his catalogs. To take an example from the first Sears Roebuck catalog, it lists a "genuine nickel stem wind watch" for 98 cents, and the copy reads "War to the Knife! We are Waging War Against Combinations, Associations, Trusts and High Prices. Let Competitors Meet Our Prices Or else forever hold Their Tongues." And in especially bold large type: "We Defy Them!" Older Sears catalogs contain a lot of prose, nearly all of it is persuasive, and most of it was written by Richard Sears.

Sears was also a believer in advertising and made his managers edgy by the amount of money he was willing to pour into it. Although Sears placed ads in some of the finest magazines of the period, he spent the bulk of his advertising budget on publications that targeted the rural market. These monthly or semimonthly periodicals were known as "mail-order magazines" because their pages were filled with advertisements from mail-order firms; their subscription prices were low, and they reached great numbers of readers who did not read daily newspapers or more expensive magazines. Some of the mail-order magazines had as many as a million and a half subscribers.[13] In 1901, a Chicago publication called the *Mail Order Journal* reported that "Sears, Roebuck and Company of Chicago are at present the largest mail order advertisers. . . . The January issue of *Comfort* contained 70 different ads of Sears, Roebuck and Company. More than 75% of the ads were therefore from Sears, Roebuck and Company. . . . In other mail order publications, Sears, Roebuck and Company are using even larger space."[14]

Yet Sears was not a good manager. In the middle 1890s, the company's liabilities commonly dwarfed its net worth. In July 1894, for example, the firm's liabilities were over $78,000, which was more than three times the $25,000 cap that had been fixed in the charter of incorporation, and the company's assets were worth less than $55,000.[15] Sears and Roebuck were both putting in sixteen-hour days, seven days a week, and the threat of bankruptcy was constant. The stress eventually caught up to Roebuck, and in August 1895, he announced that he was quitting the business. Sears bought him out for $25,000. Roebuck then went out on his own. He owned a company that manufactured movie projectors and typewriters (both sold by Sears) and in the mid-1920s got into a failed Florida real estate venture. When he returned to Chicago, he came back to the Sears fold and became something of a corporation figurehead, attending store openings and greeting customers. He died in 1948 at the age of eighty-four.

Sears needed a new partner to put the company on a sound financial footing, and, curiously, he had found one even before Roebuck left. An entrepreneur named Aaron Nusbaum, who had made $150,000 selling ice cream and soda pop at the Columbian Exposition, decided to get into the business of selling pneumatic tube systems for department stores and other buildings. Sears declined to buy, but Nusbaum was impressed enough with the Sears Roebuck company to invest $75,000 to purchase a half interest. He also brought his brother-in-law, Julius Rosenwald, into the deal. As it turned out, Sears was already acquainted with Rosenwald, who was a manufacturer of men's suits: Sears had shown up at Rosenwald's office one day and placed an order for fifty suits. Rosenwald was skeptical that Sears could sell that many only to be informed that they had already been sold.

Here was a man with whom Rosenwald could do business. Sears was reincorporated on August 23, 1895, with Sears as president, Rosenwald as vice president, and Nusbaum as treasurer. The triumvirate did not last long. Nusbaum apparently was an abrasive personality. On a day early in 1901, Sears strode into Rosenwald's office and, so the story goes, said, "Someone's got to go. Either you and Nusbaum buy me out, or you and I buy him out." Rosenwald chose the latter option, and henceforth Sears, Roebuck and Company became a two-man operation. It was an ideal match—Sears the salesman and Rosenwald the businessman.

As the firm rapidly expanded in the 1890s, it haphazardly acquired a disparate collection of Chicago properties to house its operations. Rosenwald saw the need to construct a centralized headquarters, which would have to be colossal. It just so happened that as a young man Rosenwald had formed a friendship with one Henry Goldman, who had gone on to become one-half of the New York investment firm Goldman Sachs. Goldman helped Sears and Rosenwald raise some $40 million by selling stock, and in 1905, a throng of construction workers descended upon Chicago's North Lawndale neighborhood.

The downtown Sears Tower (now the Willis Tower) is actually the city's second Sears Tower. The first was opened in

The Sears Administration Building and Merchandise Building in 1908. The massive complex on the West Side centralized the company's operations. (Library of Congress)

1906; it's the fourteen-story spire that was attached to what was known as the Sears Merchandise Building, a behemoth of 125,000 square feet that stretched a quarter of a mile along Arthington Street (then known as Harvard Street). The complex included four other large structures—the Printing Building, the Advertising Building, the Administration Building, and the Power House. To these were added in 1920 the Wallpaper Factory and the Grocery Building, and in 1925, Rosenwald opened on the site the company's first retail store. The entire complex functioned under what was known as the "schedule system," devised by plant superintendent Otto Doering. The 1906 Sears catalog described the plant's operations: "Miles of railroad tracks run through, in and around this building for

the receiving, moving and forwarding of merchandise; elevators, mechanical conveyors, endless chains, moving sidewalks,
gravity chutes, apparatus and conveyors, pneumatic tubes and
every known mechanical appliance for reducing labor, for the
working out of economy and dispatch is to be utilized here in
our great Works."[16]

Most of these buildings have been demolished, but the original Sears Tower still stands alone without
the Merchandise Building, and a visitor
positioned in the right spot can see
both Sears Towers, the older one in
the forefront and the newer one in
the distance. What remains of the
complex is today known as the
Sears Plant Historic District.

In 1906, the company was
thriving with sales of over $50
million. The following year,
however, saw the arrival of a
recession, and Sears's fortunes
declined. A salesman to the
end, Richard Sears judged that
the best way to meet the crisis
was to increase advertising even
more. Rosenwald disagreed, and
when two of the firm's key managers sided with him, Sears resigned as
president of his own company. Health
was another factor in Sears's stepping down;
his wife had been ill and recently had had her leg
amputated. Sears himself, although only forty-four, was not in
the best condition either; for years he had put been putting in
very long work days. In a letter, Sears mentioned his need for
relaxation, his wish to care for his mother, and his wanting "a
little time for my family."[17] Sears remained on the board of directors, first as chairman and then as a member, but he did not
go to meetings. He died on September 28, 1914.

Julius
Rosenwald,
seen here on a
visit to the White
House in 1929,
took over the Sears
company after the
founder's retire-
ment and rescued
it from bankruptcy.
(Library of Congress)

Sears, Roebuck and Company enjoyed years of steady growth under Rosenwald's leadership, although when farm prices tumbled after World War I, the company again teetered on the brink of bankruptcy. Rosenwald pledged some $21 million of his personal fortune, in cash, stock, and other assets, and by 1922, the company was back in the black. Rosenwald resigned as president in 1924, although he stayed on as chairman of the board until he died in 1932.

Rosenwald's later years were filled by energetic philanthropic activity (it has been reported that he gave away some $63 million during his lifetime).[18] Rosenwald grew especially interested in the education of black children and established more than five thousand "Rosenwald schools" throughout the South for the education of African Americans.[19] As we saw in the previous chapter, Rosenwald was the primary force behind the founding of the Museum of Science and Industry. By the 1920s, Sears Roebuck was in the midst of a transition from a mail-order company to an operator of retail stores. As mentioned, the first Sears retail store, which opened for business on February 2, 1925, was located at the Sears complex on the West Side. Seven more retail stores opened later in that year, and in 1925, retail sales counted for 4.5 percent of Sears's total sales. A year later, the figure was 8.5 percent. By 1928, there were twenty-seven Sears stores, and a year later, 324. By 1932, Sears's retail outlets eclipsed the catalog in sales.[20] In the late 1980s, the Sears catalog was giving way to an increasingly suburban population's preference for shopping at giant discount shopping centers. By 1989, the catalog was unprofitable; in 1992, it suffered a $175 million loss; and in 1993, it was discontinued, ending a major chapter in U.S. history.

The Sears Tower

In 1973, Sears was the country's largest retailer, employed 365,000 people, operated 837 retail stores, and had annual estimated sales of $11 billion. In the following year, the company opened the world's tallest building. The Willis Tower at 233 South Wacker Drive is an excellent example of how a corporation can benefit a city far beyond its contribution to the economy.

The two most recognizable towers on the Chicago skyline—the 110-story Willis Tower and the hundred-story John Hancock Center—were the work of the same architect: Bruce Graham of Skidmore, Owings and Merrill, who died at age eighty-four in March 2010. At the time of Graham's death, Joseph Rosa, chairman of the Department of Architecture and Design at the Art Institute of Chicago, commented, "With those two skyscrapers he singlehandedly put Chicago back on the map. Without them, Chicago architecture would have been frozen in time. They expressed the optimism in Chicago and pointed toward what the future could be."[21] Graham insisted that in his design for the Sears Tower he was thinking about a lot more than the corporation that commissioned it. "Unlike most tall buildings in New York," he commented, "it is a tower of the people, not the palace of a bank."[22] The Hancock Center is famous for its distinctive tapering shape and exterior X-shaped cross-bracing. However, in designing the Sears Tower, Graham, along with his innovative structural engineer, Fazlur R. Khan, produced an equally singular design—a "bundled tube" of nine seventy-five-by-seventy-five-foot column-free squares that rise to different heights until just two are left at the top.

By standing in just the right place, a viewer can see both of Chicago's Sears Towers, built sixty-eight years apart. (Photograph by the author)

In general, architectural critics prefer the Hancock Tower over the Willis Tower, which has been the subject of some cutting remarks, such as the view of the author of the "Sears Tower" entry in the second edition of the *AIA Guide to Chicago*, who wrote, "While Graham and Kahn were like a well-oiled, twin-cam engine firing on all cylinders when they designed the elegant John Hancock Center, the architectural manifold was slightly backfiring when they were running the Sears 500."[23]

The major reason the Sears Tower has a different profile from the Hancock Center, however, has to do with the wishes of Gordon M. Metcalf, who was chairman and chief executive of Sears from 1967 to 1973; as Bruce Graham put it, "Gordon said that he didn't want any of those damn diagonal things like the Hancock building."[24] Nevertheless, when it opened, the Sears Tower drew considerable praise. *New York Times* architecture critic Ada Louise Huxtable hailed its "almost nonchalant understatement" and called the Sears Tower a "richly rewarding experience":

> Mr. Graham has an architectural philosophy which holds that there is no point in overreaching (except in height), overcomplicating, striving for dubious originality, or going gratuitously beyond what amounts to an unbeatable basic solution. He thinks that good is good enough. There is no straining for effect. This is a principle that should be pasted in a lot of so-called "creative" hats. And if that makes for the paradox of an unpretentious tall building, so be it. God is still in the details, and SOM has a direct line to heaven.[25]

Paul Gapp, writing in the *Chicago Tribune*, said, "What we have here is a building whose exterior profiles are a bold, vital, and exciting departure from orthodox mediocrity; in sum, a finely engineered piece of sculpture."[26] Few subsequent Chicago buildings have equaled or surpassed the Sears Tower.

In 1994, Sears sold the building to Boston-based AEW Capital Management, and ownership of the tower has changed hands a couple of times since then (although Sears's naming rights did not expire until 2003). By 1995, the Sears Tower contained no Sears offices, and the company had moved to a campus in Hoffman Estates. In 2009, the British Insurance firm Willis Group Holdings Limited, as part of a cost-saving move to consolidate its Chicago-area offices, agreed to lease some 140,000 square feet of space on three floors of the building. As part of the deal, the structure was renamed the Willis Tower. The building remains a major tourist attraction, a symbol of Chicago, and a reminder of a corporation that changed the United States. Had Richard Sears never been born, it would not exist.

4

Frances Willard's Bicycle

When you're a fifty-three-year-old woman in 1893, you're ready for the rocking chair. Or so many people thought at the time. But Frances E. Willard of Evanston, Illinois, decided she was going to perch on a different kind of seat—the saddle of a bicycle.

Willard's health was not good. Although she had been a vigorous woman, by the spring of 1893, she had begun to note in her journal that red spots were appearing on her tongue and throat—a condition that soon made it difficult for her to eat. She tired easily and sometimes had to cancel speaking engagements. Eventually she developed skin lesions on her legs and ankles and grew so fatigued that she had to be carried down stairs. Willard's mother had died less than a year before, and now Willard began speculating that she might soon join her in paradise. "My thoughts are greatly on the future life," she wrote.[1]

But resignation soon turned into defiance. By the time the autumn breezes began to blow, Willard, after securing her doctor's blessing, had acquired one of those trendy new machines called a "safety bicycle."[2] This apparatus, which had been invented around 1885, had tangentially spoked wheels of approximately the same size, a sprocket and chain system that drove the bike from the rear wheel, and inflatable rubber tires. Unlike the precarious "high wheeler" bike, with its enormous front wheel, this machine could be easily mastered by both sexes and all ages.

Frances Willard was, at the time of her bike lessons, a guest of Isabel (Lady Henry) Somerset at that eminent lady's suburban home in Reigate, England.[3] As Willard recounted in *A Wheel within a Wheel*, her 1895 book on her bicycle learning experience, "At fifty-three I was at more disadvantage than most people, for not only had I the impedimenta that result from the unnatural style of dress, but I also suffered from the sedentary habits of a lifetime."[4] She began her training by climbing upon the bicycle's saddle while "three young Englishmen" firmly held the machine in place. Once she was aboard, two "well-disposed young women" grasped both sides of the handlebar while Willard tried to maintain her balance. Finally, one of the women walked along, clutching the bike, as Willard began to roll. Her command to her instructor was "Let go, but stand by." Though unsteady, Willard managed to pedal, turn, and get off the bicycle. Getting on unaided was a skill that eluded her for a long while.

Nineteenth-century feminists considered the "safety bicycle," which helped launch a revolution in women's dress, one of the greatest forces for women's liberation. (Library of Congress)

Willard had named her two-wheeler "Gladys," thinking of it as a kind of steed that, like any other horse, could be mastered only as the rider determined its peculiar characteristics. "Gradually," she reported, "I learned the location of every screw and spring, spoke and tire, and every beam and bearing that went to make up Gladys. This was not the lesson of a day, but of many days and weeks."[5] In her characteristically reflective way, she derived life lessons from the adventure. "Indeed," she

Frances Willard's beloved bicycle, Gladys, which she learned to ride at the age of fifty-three. (Photograph by the author)

wrote, "I found a whole philosophy of life in the wooing and winning of my bicycle." For one, the process reinforced her belief in the importance of "time and patience." Often, she mused, people "will not take the pains, they have not enough specific gravity, to balance themselves in their new environment."[6] She realized that any time we manage to surmount an obstacle, we attain the strength to surmount another: "The totality of native forces and acquired discipline and expert knowledge stands us in good stead for each crisis that we have to meet. . . . There is a momentum, a cumulative power on which we can count in every new circumstance."[7]

Perhaps the keenest insight she derived was the one that concerned how people are taught and how they learn. "Let go, but stand by" she came to appreciate as "the golden rule for parent and pastor, teacher and friend," and as she contemplated how difficult it can be for a teacher to know a student's mind and ability, she considered that this was a problem for all of human interaction. "The opacity of the mind," she said, "its inability to project itself into the realm of another's personality, goes a long way to explain the friction of life. . . . We are so shut away from one another." "Mutual non-comprehension," she concluded, "is "the greatest disadvantage under which we labor."[8]

Willard dealt with her inability to climb aboard the bike without help by performing the act fifty times a day until she had done it no fewer than five hundred times. After her one fall, she simply decided that she would suffer no more accidents—and she didn't. And she reassured her younger readers that although an old lady might take a tumble, for any young woman to fall off a bike is "inexcusable": "the lightsome elasticity of every muscle, the quickness of the eye, the agility of motion, ought to preserve her from such a catastrophe." January 20, 1894, was the day of triumph. She got on by herself and rode off unassisted. "From that hour the spell was broken," she wrote, "Gladys was no more a mystery."[9]

Willard calculated that because she practiced only fifteen minutes a day, her total training time was some thirteen hundred minutes, which comes out to about twenty-two hours, or "less than a single day as the almanac reckons time." She concluded with this advice for other women: "Go thou and do likewise." A great many women did because *A Wheel within a Wheel* became a best seller.

The Greatest American Woman

Although the name of Frances E. Willard remains something of an inspiration to feminists, her fame is hardly what it was in 1898, when a publication called her simply "the greatest American woman."[10] Her celebrity was not due to her bicycling; she was the president of the Woman's Christian Temperance Union (WCTU), an organization dedicated to the "total prohibition" of alcoholic beverages.[11]

Frances Willard was born on September 28, 1839, in Churchville, New York, a small town about fourteen miles from Rochester. She was barely two when her parents settled in Oberlin, Ohio, where they took advantage of the educational opportunities afforded by recently founded Oberlin College. Mr. Willard intended to study for the ministry, but when he developed symptoms of tuberculosis he pulled up stakes again, this time proceeding on to Wisconsin, to a farm near Janesville, where Frances grew up.

A daguerreotype taken of Frances at around age nine shows a rather pretty, fine-featured girl, with a serious expression. Actually, she was a lively lass, stoutly resisting womanly chores like cooking and sewing and instead joining her brother, Oliver, in climbing trees, walking on stilts, and shooting homemade cross-guns (her mother called her "Frank," which was the nickname she used for the rest of her life). "I knew all the carpenter's tools and handled them," Willard wrote. "But a needle and a dishcloth I could not abide."[12] Many times Willard remarked how she detested at age sixteen having to put up her loose hair and to forgo her boyish childhood trousers in favor of the constricting garb of a mid-nineteenth-century woman, "the long skirts that impeded every footstep," as she put it.[13] As she explained in her autobiography, "No girl ever went through a harder experience than I, when my free, out-of-door life had to cease, and the long skirts and clubbed-up hair spiked with hair-pins had to be endured. . . . Mine was a nature hard to tame."[14] On the other hand, upon arriving at age eighteen she felt a great sense of liberation from her father's rule, writing a poem entitled "I Am Eighteen" in which she exclaimed, "The clock has struck!/ O! heaven and earth I'm free."[15]

Willard's learning was haphazard until 1857, when she entered the Milwaukee Female College, which was considered one of the best women's schools in the Midwest. Unfortunately, her father withdrew her after one term because he preferred a school of a different religious denomination. He then found a solidly Methodist school in Evanston, Illinois—the North Western Female College. Frances studied an impressive range of courses there, but she chafed at the rules and graduated in 1859 with relief (she was labeled the "most reckless" girl in the school).[16]

Willard went into teaching, beginning as head of a one-room schoolhouse, and, although she was successful, she hated it and was set on greater achievements. She then taught in a school in Kankakee, Illinois, but thought the town disgracefully irreligious.

In 1862, she found a place in a public school in Evanston, and then she briefly returned to the North Western Female College as a science instructor. She also taught at schools in Pittsburgh and in Lima, New York, before returning to Evanston, where she preferred to remain. In the meantime, she became friends with a young woman named Kate Jackson, whose wealthy father agreed to bankroll a two-year grand tour of Europe for the pair, who traveled mostly alone, visiting such places as Russia, Egypt, Turkey, and the Holy Land, as well as western Europe.

In 1869, the trustees of fourteen-year-old Northwestern University voted to admit women to university classes. It was thought, however, that more women would attend if the women's college was established as a separate entity within the university. In February 1871, Willard was named president of the new Ladies College. Two years later the Ladies College merged into Northwestern, where it became known as the Woman's College. Willard became dean and professor of aesthetics. She probably would have remained a university instructor indefinitely, but soon Northwestern acquired a new president, Charles Henry Fowler. It certainly didn't help that Fowler had once proposed to Willard and had been rejected, but the pair almost immediately found themselves at odds. In June 1874, Willard resigned, stating, "The world is wide and full of elbow room; this atmosphere is stifling—I must leave it."[17]

As it turned out, a new career—and international fame—was awaiting her.

In her day, temperance leader and reformer Frances Willard was called "the greatest American woman." (Library of Congress)

Do Everything

Nowadays the WCTU likely evokes images of grim hatchet-wielding Carrie Nations zealously attacking cozy neighborhood taverns. Although the charismatic Willard, with her light blue eyes, fair hair, and a figure often described as "elegant," was not unattractive to men (although she thought she was), her wearing of rimless pince-nez glasses and her severely pulled-back hair gave her the appearance of the stereotypical spinster schoolmarm.[18] In addition, it is often thought that the WCTU's disapproval of alcohol arose in part from an anti-immigrant bias, where Anglo-Saxon jingoists viewed with horror the beer gardens of the Germans, the pubs of the Irish, and the homemade wine of the Italians. Critics also judge the WCTU by its having given the United States the failed experiment of Prohibition, with the resulting burden of organized crime.

Yet the WCTU, which Willard served as president from 1874 until her death in 1898, was in many ways one of the most progressive forces of its day and the crucible in which the modern women's movement was forged. As the historian Ruth Bordin has pointed out, the WCTU "became one of the most powerful instruments of women's consciousness-raising of all time. Through the Union women learned of their legal and social disabilities, gained confidence in their strengths and talents, and became certain of their political power as a group and as individuals."[19] Frances Willard put it this way: "Woman, like man, should be freely permitted to do whatever she can do well. . . . Women are slowly and surely coming to their own. Their own is to work side by side with men everywhere."[20]

Although men participated in the temperance movement, it was largely run by women—the WCTU was by far the largest woman's organization of its time. Including its auxiliaries, the WCTU by 1893 had over two hundred thousand members, compared to the thirteen thousand members of, to take one example, the National American Woman Suffrage Association.[21] It's difficult to measure the extent of alcoholism in the mid-nineteenth century, but part of the reason so many women were zealous about abolishing alcohol was because women were dependent

In 1906, the British humor magazine *Puck* took a satirical view of U.S. temperance forces.
(Library of Congress)

on men, both legally and economically. It's been pointed out that most women's novels of the nineteenth century end with a wedding; but temperance novels, of which there were many, usually *begin* with a wedding.[22] After the nuptials, the new bride's torment commences as her spouse succumbs to the curse of demon rum, rendering her subject to penury and violence. Even today, it's difficult for women to escape abusive partners; in the Victorian era it was nearly impossible. And children always remained the legal property of the father, whether he drank whiskey or soda water.[23]

The WCTU held its first national convention in November 1874. Willard was named corresponding secretary, and five years later she was elected president. Willard's motto summed up the scope of her interests and ambitions: "Do Everything."[24] She traveled throughout the nation (often staying in rough accommodations), speaking at rallies, organizing local chapters, and writing speeches, letters, and tracts. Although the primary purpose of the WCTU was to achieve the national prohibition of alcoholic beverages through a constitutional amendment, Willard gradually pushed the organization toward adopting a wider set of progressive reforms, including the kindergarten movement, children's aid societies, free school lunches, federal aid to education, prison reform, labor unions, the five-and-a half-day week and eight-hour day for workers, dress reform, and women's suffrage. Willard herself moved further left than most of her organization's members and adopted what she called "Christian Socialism," a system under which the government owned the factories, railroads, and the public utilities and even regulated the theaters so that only "uplifting" plays would be presented. Willard's progressivism made her instrumental in a fundamental shift in the ideology of the anti-saloon forces. Previously, excessive drinking was considered a sin, and poverty was viewed as the result of alcoholism. Willard reversed that analysis so that alcoholism became seen as an illness—not the cause of poverty but the result of it.

By 1893, Chicago had become the center of the WCTU's reform efforts. According to Bordin, in 1889, the WCTU in Chicago "was sponsoring two day nurseries, two Sunday schools, an industrial school, a mission that sheltered four thousand homeless or destitute women in a twelve-month period, a free medical dispensary that treated over sixteen hundred patients a year, a lodging house for men that had to date provided temporary housing for over fifty thousand men, and a low-cost restaurant."[25] Among the most common indications of the WCTU's presence were the water fountains the union installed throughout the city—the organization offering a salubrious alternative to beer for the thirsty summer laborer.[26] For those who favored a tastier drink, in 1893, the WCTU established street fountains that dispensed "wild cherry phosphate" for a penny. The *Chicago Tribune* called them a "Chicago institution," with about thirty of the dispensers distributed throughout the business district: "Although the project is not entirely a profitless one to the temperance people, the main purpose is to place within easy access of everybody a cheap and agreeable beverage and to reduce the number of saloon frequenters."[27]

One of the most notable events in Chicago in 1893 was the opening by the WCTU of its massive office building known as the Woman's Temple (or simply "the Temple"), located on the corner of LaSalle and Monroe Streets. Designed in a mixed Romanesque–French Gothic style by John Wellborn Root of the architectural firm of Burnham and Root, the building looked something like a gargantuan French chateau; its steeply pitched roof with multiple dormers, its huge arched entrances, and its heavy rusticated base indicated a building of importance, and Root's design was considered a triumph.[28] (The story goes that at the ceremonial laying of the cornerstone, Root suggested to his colleagues that they could all use a drink.) The somewhat frilly nature of its ornamentation, unusual for Root, has sometimes been described as "feminine," but if that was Root's intention it probably would not have suited the taste of Willard, who spent her life combating feminine stereotypes. As the architectural historian Carl W. Condit put it, "The so-called femininity of the design may well have embodied the very thing that she and her cohorts fought against and ultimately triumphed over."[29] The ground floor contained a space called Willard Hall, which held seven hundred people and was where midday prayer meetings were held.

The economic depression that began in 1893 brought difficulties. The Temple was constructed with borrowed money and was intended to support itself through office rentals, but the rentals were inadequate, and shortly after Willard's death in 1898, the WCTU would repudiate its debt and relinquish control of the building. The WCTU convention of 1899 voted to move the organization's headquarters to Willard's modest cottage in Evanston.[30] The building was demolished in 1926;

Opened in 1893, the Woman's Temple in downtown Chicago was an inescapable sign of the power and prestige of the Woman's Christian Temperance Union. (Chicago Public Library)

the editor of the *Inland Architect* mourned the destruction of what he called such a fine example of the "romantic period in American architecture."[31]

Freedom on Wheels

Today, the link between temperance and bicycling might not be obvious, but to Frances Willard they meant the same thing: the emancipation of women. As the temperance movement would empower women in a manner that would lead to the vote, the bicycle would bring liberation in dress and in movement. The best known quotation to that effect comes from Susan B. Anthony, who said in 1896 that she believed that bicycling had "done more to emancipate women than anything in the world."[32]

American women first began participating in outdoors sports soon after the Civil War—they first took up the genteel activities of croquet and skating and then moved on to tennis.[33] These sports were difficult to play when clad in whalebones, corsets, hoops, and bustles and cried out for a streamlined mode of dress. Such a style had been proposed as early as 1851 by Amelia Bloomer, who advocated a "freedom dress" consisting of full trousers clutched at the ankles beneath a dress that came just below the knees (Bloomer unveiled her creation in her temperance publication, *The Lily*, which she published from 1840 until 1853).[34] A few hardcore feminists wore these so-called "bloomers," but the outfit was decades in catching on.

Once the safety bicycle appeared, women took to it with passion, and both mobility and dress reform followed. Aboard their two-wheelers, women could meet one another and venture, unescorted, along the boulevards and into the parks. Charlotte Holt of the Chicago Society for the Protection of Women and Children commented, "Of course, wheels have made greater freedom possible among our young women. It is nothing uncommon for a girl to be away all day with her wheel, but what of it? One reason I like the wheel so thoroughly is that it has done away with the chaperone who was beginning to be foisted on us."[35] Women could also use the bicycle to commute to work and save themselves the indignity of being jostled in a streetcar.[36]

The bicycle craze helped bring about a new era in women's clothes. As the *New York Times* explained in 1895, "If it is true that without wheelwomen there would be no dress reform, it is no less true that without dress reform there would be no wheelwomen." Women, the article said, are "looking forward to the time when women shall have escaped from the bonds of fashion and demand a walking dress as comfortable as the wheeling gown."[37] In 1893, a reformist publication called the *Arena* reported on a symposium on women's dress reform that had been held at the Columbian Exposition.[38] The article contained a photograph of "Mrs. Marie Reidsdelle in Her Bicycle Costume" and described the outfit as "a divided skirt of two breadths of black cashmere . . . with tan leather gaiters meeting the divisions half way from the knee to the ankle."[39] This was not a bloomer outfit, but it was similar, and the divided skirt proved a worthy alternative for women cyclists. Another garment that was tried was called a "rainy day skirt." Originally intended to keep hems dry in inclement weather but then used for bicycling, these could be surprisingly short. In 1899, the *New York Times* reported that a few women were wearing skirts "eight inches from the ground."[40] At an 1897 meeting of the Health Culture Club in Brooklyn, New York, attended by some forty women concerned with dress reform, one anxious member reported that "I went out one fine day with my rainy-day skirt on, and a lot of horrible men laughed at me and ridiculed me so that I had to fly back in a hurry."[41] In 1895, the *Chicago Tribune* sent a reporter to interview Mrs. Perry A. Hull of the board of education, to ask whether teachers should be permitted to wear bloomers—a topic of interest because, the paper said, "Chicago is distinctively a bloomer city and many women teachers are devotees of the wheel." Mrs. Hull was ambiguous; she questioned "the good judgment of a woman who wears bloomers" but did not consider them to be "immoral," which meant that unless the board decided to revisit the issue, Chicago teachers could wear what they chose.[42]

The November 1895 issue of the *Delineator*, a publication created by E. Butterick and Company, the sewing pattern firm, contained illustrated pages of "Bicycle Garments." It took some time for cautious women to abandon skirts for trousers, but in 1895, the *Delineator* was able to report that "those who adopt reforms readily have welcomed the new bloomers or trousers as a most radical innovation, and so rapidly has this fashion grown in favor that the so-called 'rational dress' is now worn without provoking comment."[43] In the spring of 1895, the *Chicago Tribune* announced that anyone who thought that bloomers were a fad was mistaken. A reporter visited the parks and boulevards of the South Side and recounted that "there were hundreds of bicycles out and among them more than the usual proportion of women, young and old, and where there was one woman attired in skirts there were a dozen who wore bloomers of one sort or another. . . . It was plain that . . . the undivided skirt has practically been discarded by women who ride the wheel."[44] Frances Willard was not a bloomer wearer herself but described her bicycling costume as "a skirt and blouse of tweed, with belt, rolling collar, and loose cravat, the skirt three inches from the ground; a round straw hat, and walking-shoes with gaiters," adding: "It was a simple, modest suit, to which no person of common sense could take exception."[45]

Nevertheless, it would be many decades yet before women would wear trousers as street clothes. The next stage in dress reform came from the women's colleges, where the need for suitable garb for gymnasium activities and field sports resulted in the further development of bloomers, the acceptance of knickers, and ultimately trousers for women, à la Katharine Hepburn. But by the time the Great Kate was flaunting her patrician sports-wear, women were taking their fashion cues from Hollywood stars—not from temperance reformers.

Chicago, the Bicycle Capital

As Chicago in 1893 was the epicenter of the American temperance movement, so was it also the nucleus of the American bicycle mania. In the mid-1890s, so many bicycle firms went into operation in Chicago that soon there was a glut of bicycles on the market, and prices dropped, which only increased ridership further.[46] Some bicycles went for as much as $120, which was not exactly cheap, but you could buy a less expensive model for as little as $20, and there were always second-hand bikes to be had.[47] In addition, one could purchase a bicycle on time by providing a down payment and then a dollar a week.[48] In 1882, there were about twenty thousand bicycles in the United States; in 1900, there were ten million.[49]

Chicago's diverse industrial base was just one reason that it became the nation's bicycling capital. Other reasons were the ideally flat terrain, the extensive park system, the success of bicyclists in forming organizations that pressured state and local government to enact bicycle-friendly legislation (such as smooth pavement and a ban on dumping grass clippings in the street), the popularity of bicycling racing as a spectator sport (the first six-day bicycle race in the United States took place in Chicago in 1879), and the approval of the elite and of the medical profession, who generally viewed bicycling as a wholesome alternative to wicked pleasures for the middling classes.

The oldest and largest bicycling club in the country was the Chicago Cycling Club . . .

The oldest and largest bicycling club in the country was the Chicago Cycling Club, founded in 1879, and the subsequent proliferation of cycling clubs gives some indication of the sport's popularity. The historian Perry R. Duis, citing the *Chicago Tribune*, reports that by 1895, Chicago had thirty-three cycling clubs with ten thousand members.[50] Another historian, Richard Lindberg, agrees that there were ten thousand members but counts forty-eight cycling clubs.[51] However, according to George D. Bushnell, "By 1895, there were five hundred clubs of varying size, each with its own colors and a distinctive uniform for endurance rides and competitive events."[52] The Chicago Cycling Club, as the most venerable of the cycling associations, had the poshest club headquarters. The organization moved into a new Michigan Avenue facility in April 1895. The building's first floor was spacious enough to contain a ballroom, and the club had reading rooms, showers, a dining hall, billiard parlors, and a "rubbing down" room. The women's auxiliary had its own well-appointed quarters on the second floor.[53]

Just one year after Frances Willard first climbed aboard Gladys, the Chicago baseball and sporting goods magnate Albert G. Spalding bought out the Lamb Bicycle Company and began producing his own line. The *Sporting News* hailed the Spalding machine as "coming to the front as a favorite with all lovers of cycling" and commented that many other bicycles were now "has beens."[54] Spalding made sure that his displays at big-city cycling shows were the most impressive ones there, he contracted with professional bicycle racers to promote his gear, and in 1895, he became president of the National Board of Trade of Cycling Manufacturers. When the bicycle craze waned at the end of the century, Spalding got out of the business, but in 1895, Ignaz Schwinn opened his factory on the corner of Lake and Peoria streets, and Schwinn bicycles are still being sold. Soon after Schwinn's opening, there were thirty bicycle manufacturers on Lake Street alone,[55] and Chicago was the "bicycle-building capital of America." In 1895, one newspaper counted forty bicycle manufacturers in Chicago producing some 144,000 bikes; the following year another paper reported eighty-eight bicycle makers and said that two-thirds of all of the bicycles in the United States were being made within 150 miles of the city.[56]

Chicago's Columbian Exposition, being the showcase of America, was not about to ignore the bicycle. August 10, 1893, was wheelman's day, as 699 members of the League of American Wheelmen paraded through the White City. Because each of the bicycles carried two Chinese lanterns, the procession, as the *Chicago Tribune* described it, looked like "a dancing river of fire rushing along at breakneck speed." Several cyclists brought highly elaborate rigs, some festooned with as many as fifty gleaming lanterns. One rider towed a wagon that held a model of the fair's Ferris Wheel, with each car containing a lantern that "produced a pretty effect as it revolved when the car was in motion." A wheelman named Mark Kennicott "started out under a pagoda with sixty lanterns on it, but lost about half of them." A pair of brothers from Evanston pedaled a tandem bike with "two immense wheels covered with white cloth, on which in bronze were the winged signs and the initial letters of the league," and another cyclist came dressed as Uncle Sam. Although this was the so-called wheelmen's club, "a hundred or more of the women of the various clubs rode beside escorts at the head of the procession." All the while, bands played and judges carefully scrutinized the vehicles so as to award prizes later.[57]

Bicycle riding brought some tensions—drivers of delivery wagons glowered when bicycles got in their way, and pedestrians were occasionally struck by bikes. Taxpayers resented the cost of the silky pavements that cyclists demanded, and people in poor neighborhoods especially opposed asphalt because they feared bikers tearing down their smooth, crowded streets and knocking into pedestrians (bicycles, not automobiles, were the force that initiated the asphaltization of America).[58] The police had a word for bikers who rode recklessly fast—"scorchers." A patrol officer on foot couldn't catch a speeding cyclist, but enterprising constables discovered that a well-aimed billy club would become entangled in the spokes of the wheel.

By and large, however, the elite and the reformers welcomed the machine as a salutary alternative to iniquitous pastimes. In addition to acting as a vital force in the emancipation of women, the bicycle, Willard insisted, was "perhaps our strongest ally in winning young men away from public-houses,"[59] and in 1896, the *Chicago Tribune* reported that bicycling's allure had turned many away from bars, pool halls, and cigar shops.[60] (It was a common refrain among temperance advocates that the bicycle discouraged drunkenness because an inebriated rider could not maintain his balance. A sardonic article in the *Chicago Tribune*, however, said that this simply was not true and that "a man with a wabbly [*sic*] head if he has ever learned to ride can ride.")[61]

Cyclists were fortunate to have a powerful advocate in Mayor Carter Harrison II. His wife's twin brothers manufactured the popular Hibbard bicycle, and he saw the machine as a way to attract the youth vote. Campaign posters went up depicting Harrison in cycling garb; their slogan was "NOT THE CHAMPION CYCLIST BUT THE CYCLISTS' CHAMPION!" He was said to have completed no fewer than eighteen "centuries" (hundred-mile rides). The wheelmen were not unaware of their political power. Chicago's Viking Bicycle Club released a statement that said, "This club and associates controlled 1,500 political votes and would support those candidates favorable to wheelmen and wheeling."[62]

In the manner of all crazes, bicycling soon lost its attraction. When, in the days of high wheelers, it was expensive and difficult, it had a great cachet for young gentlemen, but they found little glamor in it when bicycles were ridden by shopgirls. They quickly turned to an even more exciting machine—the automobile. In the late twentieth century, however, a strange thing happened. It turned out that the bicycle in Chicago was not dead after all. Under the administration of Mayor Richard J. Daley in the 1970s, Chicago began developing an extensive network of bicycle lanes and paths. Daley opened a thirty-four-mile bicycle route in May 1971, and in August of the following year, rush-hour bike lanes were instituted on Clark and Dearborn Streets.[63] His son, Mayor Richard M. Daley, a keen cyclist himself, furthered the process by establishing the Mayor's Bicycle Advisory Council in 1991, and in the following year, the Bike 2000 Plan, which led to the creation of a hundred miles of on-street bike lanes and fifty miles of off-street trails, the placement of bike racks on buses, and the installation of ten thousand bike racks across the city, more than in any other in the United States. In January 2006, the city unveiled an even grander Bike 2015 Plan. Its goals included a five-hundred-mile bikeway network with a bikeway within a half mile of every Chicago resident and bike parking inside and outside transit stations. Shortly after taking office, Rahm Emanuel, Daley's successor as mayor and arguably an even greater bicycle enthusiast, announced plans for a new system of a hundred miles of "protected bike lanes" (lanes placed between parked cars and the curb) and stated his ambition to make Chicago the "bike-friendliest city in the country."

Gladys Discovered

Frances E. Willard is gone, but Gladys is still with us. She can be found at the Frances Willard House on Chicago Avenue in Evanston. The house, which is the possession of the WCTU, has been lovingly preserved, although its renovation is slow and expensive and has not been completed. Gladys is in a display room on the second floor in a rather rundown condition, although she is, after all, 120 years old. She's an Imperial Rover built in Coventry, England, by the firm of Starley and Sutton (the Rover Safety Bicycle was extremely popular and was exported around the world).

Between her many travels, Frances Willard recuperated at her home, Rest Cottage, in Evanston, Illinois. (Photograph by the author)

Many other mementos of Frances Willard are in the attractive Gothic Revival house, which was Willard's home from 1866 until her death and which she called "Rest Cottage" because it was where she returned to recuperate after her travels. Prominently displayed is the old Willard family Bible, in which Frances, at age seventeen, signed a temperance pledge. Family portraits peer down from the walls, one of Willard's graceful black gowns hangs behind glass, and a collection of wooden gavels, which Willard employed to conduct meetings, lies in a case. The study, with its many bookcases and well-stocked desk, has a much-lived-in aspect. There one can see a small metal sign on which are painted the words "THIS IS MY BUSY DAY." Willard would hang it on the doorknob as a polite way of saying "stay out." Frances Willard was a hard-working woman.

5

Open-Heart Surgery

After the Fourth of July in 1893, the weather in Chicago turned oppressive. The temperature reached ninety-four at five in the afternoon on July 8, the hottest day yet of that year. A policeman riding a streetcar was hit by sunstroke and fell from the conveyance at the corner of Halsted and Indiana. The *Chicago Tribune* noted that because of the heat, "nearly everything in the social world was at a standstill, and almost no entertainments, whether large or small, were given."[1]

The heat was still gripping the city the next day, when a black deliveryman named James Cornish, having ended his day's work, went into a South Side saloon. Somehow a fight broke out, and an assailant plunged a knife into Cornish's chest. In the 1890s, this kind of wound was almost always fatal, but Cornish had the great fortune to have been stabbed just down the street from a facility known as Provident Hospital, headed by a thirty-seven-year-old surgeon named Daniel Hale Williams. Cornish was taken to the hospital, and Dr. Williams examined the injury.

At first the wound did not look too bad—about an inch long. But then the patient's pain and bleeding increased, and it appeared he was going into shock. Williams then began to suspect that a major blood vessel had been damaged, if not the heart itself. This was another thing entirely. Williams had two choices: administer a painkiller, put Cornish to bed, and hope for the best, or operate. To take the first course would have been the recommended medical practice of the day. To take the second would have been a step into the unknown. As far as Williams knew, no one had ever before attempted to operate on the human heart.

However, when Williams had graduated from medical school ten years before, the practice of surgery was in the midst of a revolution. The British surgeon Joseph Lister had pioneered the modern use of antiseptics to kill the microorganisms that caused the infections that accompanied unsterile operations. Lister's system relied on the use of carbolic acid, or phenol, which was liberally sprayed into the air, into wounds, and onto surgical instruments, and the incidence of infection declined dramatically. Lister's breakthrough had been made possible by the research of Louis Pasteur, who had demonstrated that living microorganisms caused infection and other effects. Germ theory and antisepsis took some time to catch on, especially in the United States, and even in the 1890s, when Listerian technology was the general practice in Europe, the American medical profession was divided into conservative skeptics and progressives. Fortunately for Cornish, Dr. Williams was in the second camp.

We can tell that Williams recognized that he was undertaking something significant because he asked five other doctors to observe the operation. Williams had no x-ray, no antibiotics, no blood transfusion, no trained anesthesiologist to administer the painkillers—and no air conditioning; the heat in the operating room was intense. But he did sterilize thoroughly. Then, as Williams later explained, the "wound was lengthened to the right, second incision was made from the centre of the first, carried over the middle of the cartilage and fifth rib about six inches in length. Sternum, cartilage, and about one inch of the fifth rib were exposed. Cartilage of the fifth rib was separated at its junction with the sternum."[2] Once he had enlarged the wound, Williams discovered a damaged artery. He probed further and saw that the pericardium, the membrane sac that surrounds the heart, had sustained a wound 1 ¼ inches long, although the heart itself was barely scratched. Working quickly, he washed the wound with a salt solution, clamped it with forceps, and sewed it up with catgut. He then closed the incision, placed a dressing over it, and prayed that Cornish would live.

Cornish endured a high fever and a weak, rapid pulse for two days and then gradually returned to normal. About three weeks after the surgery, Williams drained excess fluid from his patient's lungs and then, on August 30, Cornish was discharged. On July 22, however, the *Chicago Inter Ocean* had published a sensational article entitled "Sewed Up His Heart," in which a reporter described Williams's operation. Such a splashy notice in the newspaper would surely have made Williams famous in Chicago, but he was a celebrity already. Three years before, the *Chicago Tribune* had run a lengthy article discussing several of Chicago's prominent citizens, and the profile of Dr. Williams was one of the longest. The article was entitled "Chicago Colored People."[3] James Cornish was a black man, and so was his surgeon.

From Barber to Doctor

At the time of Williams's operation, an acquaintance described him this way: "He has a very small strain of colored blood about him, but to all appearance is a white man. I was well acquainted with him for two years before I knew that he was 'colored' so little does it show in his appearance."[4] Unlike many other black leaders, Daniel Hale Williams did not come from a background of slavery. His family had long been solidly middle class, and his forebears had so intermingled with Europeans—German, Welsh, Irish, and Scots—that many of them freely passed between races, intermarrying and sometimes relinquishing their African heritage and becoming, for all intents and purposes, white. Williams's grandfather, for example, had married a white woman. But Williams himself, although he could have passed for white, never considered it.

Daniel Hale Williams was born in Hollidaysburg, Pennsylvania, on January 18, 1856. His mother, the former Sarah Price, came from a prosperous family in Annapolis. Daniel's father did well in Hollidaysburg but died when his son was eleven. Daniel's mother proved to be an erratic parent and apprenticed Daniel to a shoemaker in Baltimore while she herself moved to

Dr. Daniel
Hale Williams at
about the time of
his historic open-
heart surgery.
(ICHi-31926, Chicago
History Museum; creator,
Graphic News)

Rockford, Illinois. Daniel followed her, on his own, but she abandoned him yet again, and by age seventeen Daniel was running his own barbershop in Edgerton, Wisconsin. He then moved with his sister to nearby Janesville, where he worked part-time in the shop of a black barber named Harry Anderson and attended, first Jefferson High School, and then an institution called the Classical Academy. After graduation, Williams at first considered following in the footsteps of his brother Price, who had become a successful lawyer in the East, but he then made the acquaintance of Janesville's leading doctor, Henry Palmer, and decided that medicine was his future.

In that period, it was common for aspiring physicians to get their training by spending a few years as an apprentice to an experienced doctor before moving on to medical school, and this is what Williams did, studying Palmer's medical texts and following him on his rounds. In the fall of 1880, Williams entered Chicago Medical College. The training was rigorous, and Williams, always strapped for money and supported largely by Harry Anderson, worked hard, graduating in March 1883.

Williams did not return to Janesville but chose instead to open a small office in a building at 3034 South Michigan Avenue. The chance of greater opportunity probably influenced his decision; there were just three other black physicians in the city, and they did not practice in his neighborhood. He also secured a position as attending physician at the nearby Protestant Orphan Asylum. Although the job was unpaid, it provided valuable experience in the care of children.

His practice grew quickly. Patients admired his flawless grooming and good looks, his professionalism, and his confidence, and he became known widely as "Dr. Dan." Surgery came naturally to

Williams, and his dexterous fingers, combined with his up-to-date knowledge of antisepsis and sterilization, made him a standout. He prospered and invested in several pieces of property. An indication of his stature was his appointment to the Illinois State Board of Health in 1889, a remarkable honor for a black physician.

Chicago's Black Citizens

Chicago's black population was still small at the time of the Columbian Exposition. The black community had begun to form in the 1840s as freedmen and fugitive slaves settled in the young city, but by 1860, the black population was only around a thousand. After the Civil War and emancipation, migration from the South caused Chicago's black population to grow from sixty-five hundred in 1880 to fourteen thousand in 1890, and to forty-four thousand in 1910, at which time a ghetto was beginning to form.

Some eight out of ten black people living in Chicago in 1900 came from outside Illinois, mostly the upper South, especially

A depiction of "Darkies' Day" at the Columbian Exposition illustrates the rampant racial stereotyping of the era. (Library of Congress)

Kentucky and Missouri. Some of them lived in the "Black Belt," a strip running along State Street from Twenty-Second Street to Thirty-Ninth Street, a historic neighborhood now known as Bronzeville. Other sizeable black neighborhoods were to be found on Lake Street west of Ashland Avenue, on the Near West Side near Hull House, on the Near North Side, and down around Hyde Park and other far south neighborhoods, which attracted the more prosperous black inhabitants. Still, in the 1890s there was no ghetto per se; only two wards in the entire city had a black population of more than 10 percent, and in 1898, only one-fourth of Chicago's black population lived in precincts that were more than half black. As the historian Allan H. Spear has explained, "As late as 1910, Negroes were less highly segregated from native whites than were Italian immigrants. . . . The Negro neighborhoods were by no means exclusively black."[5] However,

A clerk and his customer at a black-owned store at 2933 State Street on Chicago's South Side. A small black entrepreneurial class emerged in Chicago in the 1890s.
(Library of Congress)

their housing choices were narrow. As Sophonisba Breckenridge of Hull House described it, "With the Negro the housing dilemma was found to be an acute problem, not only among the poor, as in the case of the Polish, Jewish, or Italian immigrants, but also among the well-to-do."[6] In an ugly episode in 1909, white residents in Hyde Park organized to prevent the black population from expanding into white areas—and these were affluent blacks. In one incident, all the windows in a black-owned home were broken, and the family quickly moved out. Some white citizens began agitating for a city law mandating residential segregation.[7] As the economist Edward Glaeser has explained, "Northern racists didn't bother to enact laws when there were only a handful of urban blacks, but as their numbers increased, so did discriminatory legislation, and Northern cities increasingly found ways to isolate their growing African-American populations."[8]

This store at 2933 South State Street was called "the only Negro store of its kind in the U.S." The area in which it was located later became known as Bronzeville.
(Library of Congress)

At the time of the Columbian Exposition, Chicago's blacks worked mostly as domestic servants and laborers. Although blacks made up just 1.3 percent of Chicago's population, they comprised 43.3 percent of the city's female servants and 37.7 percent of the male servants.[9] Nevertheless, a small elite of black business people and professionals like Dr. Dan was emerging. The black population was described in this way: "A small, compact, but rapidly growing community divided into three broad social groups. The 'respectables'—churchgoing, poor or moderately prosperous, and often unrestrained in their worship—were looked down upon somewhat by the 'refined' people, who, because of their education and breeding, could not sanction the less decorous behavior of their racial brothers. Both of these groups were censorious of the 'riffraff,' the 'sinners'—unchurched and undisciplined."[10]

In 1885, the state legislature passed a bill banning racial discrimination in municipal services and public accommodations, including "inns, restaurants, eating houses, barber shops, theaters, and public conveyances on land and water."[11] The legislation was widely ignored, and many white businesses were not covered under the law; enterprises such as cemeteries and insurance companies openly discriminated against blacks. Even the jails and prisons were segregated.[12] For the most part, so were hospitals. Black patients, even if they were upper class, were typically sent to the charity wards.

But the black population of Chicago, small as it still was, was beginning to take progressive steps. Another important event of 1893 was the coming to Chicago of Ida B. Wells. Two years later, this well-known antilynching crusader married F. L. Barnett, the editor of the *Conservator*, one of Chicago's early black-owned newspapers. She went on to become one of the founders of the National Association of Colored People (NAACP) and the first black woman to be admitted to the bar in Illinois. Dr. Dan was, of course, acquainted with Ida B. Wells. The most dramatic of their meetings came in the company of the celebrated writer (and former slave) Frederick Douglass. That had to do with Dr. Dan's hospital.

Provident Hospital

What happened at Bethel A.M.E. Church on Dearborn at Thir-
tieth Street on December 12, 1893, was by no means the most
spectacular event that took place in Chicago in that momentous
year—except for the six young black women who were attending
their graduation ceremony. They made up the second graduating
class of the nursing school of Provident Hospital, the institution
that had been founded by Dr. Daniel Hale Williams.

In 1890, the Reverend Louis Reynolds had asked Williams
to stop by and discuss the case of his sister Emma. She wanted
to become a nurse, but all of Chicago's nursing schools had
rejected her because of her color. Williams speedily assembled
many of his friends and acquaintances, formed committees, and
began raising funds. Several wealthy benefactors donated to the
founding of Provident Hospital, but Williams and others also
solicited contributions from across the black community, and
contributions came in from donors rich and poor. Keeping track
of the funding was Williams's friend James Madden, the first
black bookkeeper to work for a white Chicago accounting firm.
Donations also came in the form of equipment and supplies.
Also crucial to the enterprise was the work of black volunteers.[13]

The meat packer Philip Armour gave the money for the
down payment on a three-story brick building on the corner
of Dearborn and Twenty-Ninth Streets. The facility, which
opened in 1891, hardly looked like a hospital—more like, as the
Chicago Tribune described it, "the home of a moderately well-
to-do man"—and, indeed, it contained but twelve beds.[14] But its
importance was huge. It was the first black hospital in the city,
and it was owned and operated by African Americans. But it
took in white patients, leading the *Tribune* in 1891 to call it "the
opening attack on race discrimination." As the article explained,
"The other hospitals may pretend to receive all the sick and the
maimed that come to them, but dark patients and white nurses
have never been found who will establish themselves on terms
of mutual good-will. Knowing this, Dr. Daniel H. Williams
. . . conceived the idea of starting a hospital for his race several
years ago. It was originally intended exclusively for the colored,

The first Provident Hospital, which had only twelve beds, was described as looking like "the home of a moderately well-to-do man." (Chicago Public Library)

but out of the idea has grown the Provident Hospital, which has taken down the barriers and will admit every one who has a claim to the attention of a physician."[15] The reporter seemed amused that the first announced patient of the new facility was an Irishman.

Two months after Provident Hospital opened, it was caring for nine patients (only one white one, a woman suffering from alcoholism), and it had already brought its first baby into the world. The furniture was "light and new and bright," laboratories and an operating room were going strong on the third floor, and several nurses were in training. The first four nurses graduated in October 1892, by which time the hospital had expanded to eighteen beds. In his first annual report, Williams stated that of 189 patients treated, 141 had recovered entirely, twenty-three had "improved," three had not improved, and twelve had died. Most patients had been black, but Provident had also treated twelve Irish patients, six Germans and Swedes, and twelve "others."[16]

One of the most singular fund-raising events held by Provident Hospital was a pageant entitled "Thirty Years of Freedom" staged at the Auditorium Theater in May 1896 before an audience of three thousand.[17] The purpose of the review was to illustrate the advancement of black people since emancipation. It began with depictions of slavery days and then moved on to tableaux showing black troops fighting in the Civil War. The Emancipation Proclamation was read, and then the third act, entitled "Education," began. An actor performed a scene from *Oedipus Rex*, and Joseph H. Douglass, Frederick Douglass's grandson, played several pieces on the violin. The concluding act began with the singing of contemporary "jubilee songs," and the performers then acted out a picnic, which provided the occasion for dances and games and a crowd-pleasing drill by black soldiers. The grand evening concluded with a performance of *Penelope*, a comic opera.[18]

The performance was almost certainly staged in order to raise funds for a new Provident Hospital because the cornerstone of that edifice was laid some three weeks later. The opening reception of the new facility, located at Dearborn and Thirty-Sixth, was held on November 17, 1896. In the audience was Malvina Armour, the wife of the meatpacking magnate; she had donated the funds for the obstetrical ward. Provident Hospital now had beds for sixty-five patients and employed sixteen physicians and twelve nurses. A reporter on the scene was especially impressed by the operating room, surely the work of Dr. Dan: "The walls and apparatus are constructed entirely of marble, iron, and enamel, no wood whatever being used. Every possible means is employed to prevent germ infection. An adjacent bath-room is provided for the attending physicians. To prevent contact of the hands with the faucets for running water foot pedals are used for turning on the supply."[19]

Only five years after the first Provident Hospital, a second, much finer one was established at Dearborn and Thirty-Fifth Streets. (Chicago Public Library)

Serving mostly poor patients and relying predominantly on patients' fees for income, Provident, as the years went by, was almost always in financial difficulties. In order to weather the depression of the 1930s, it formed an affiliation with the University of Chicago and moved to the university's neighborhood, Hyde Park. In the late 1970s, the federal government provided grants and loans toward the construction of the present building on East Fifty-First Street, which opened in 1982. However, Provident fell on especially hard times; it declared bankruptcy in July 1987 and closed two months later. But it was not quite dead. The Cook County Board of Commissioners, seeking to increase access to health care for the residents of Chicago's South Side, acquired it in 1991 and reopened it in August 1993. It now goes by the name of Provident Hospital of Cook County and is no longer considered a black-run establishment.

Dr. Dan's Later Years

In 1893, Dr. Williams served on the Sanitary Board of the Columbian Exposition, but he did not remain in Chicago much longer. When Grover Cleveland began his second term as president earlier that year, he named as his secretary of state Walter Q. Gresham of Chicago, a backer of Provident Hospital. Gresham persuaded Williams to take the job of chief surgeon at Freedman's Hospital in Washington, D.C. Williams brought energy and innovation to his new position, reorganizing the hospital and establishing new departments and an internship program. In addition, in 1895, Williams helped establish an association for black physicians, the National Medical Association. It was at this time that Williams shaved off his beard, leaving a full, but dapper, mustache.

Ultimately, however, Williams's tenure at Freedman's Hospital was unhappy. Congressional committees interfered with the running of the institution, and Williams grew weary of the political intrigue. He resigned in the spring of 1898 and returned to Chicago and Provident Hospital. He surprised his acquaintances at home by bringing back a bride, the former Alice Johnson, who was considered a great beauty among Washington's black middle class. In 1900, Williams began a relationship with Meharry Medical College in Nashville, Tennessee, the first medical school in the South for African Americans. He traveled there every year for a week or ten days to act, without pay, as visiting clinical professor of surgery. He also was appointed to the attending staff of Cook County Hospital, and in 1913, he became the first black physician to be inducted into the American College of Surgeons. However, while Williams was away at Freedman's Hospital, an ambitious young black physician named George Cleveland Hall had joined the board of trustees of Provident Hospital, and Hall became a bitter rival of Williams. A superior politician, Hall outmaneuvered Williams who, for all his skill, could sometimes come across as aloof, proud, and, for some blacks, it seemed, too "white." Hall successfully campaigned to deny Williams the presidency of the National Medical Association. As the original members of Provident's board of trustees either retired or died, Williams's influence waned. When Williams was given the extraordinary honor (for a black doctor) of being appointed an attending surgeon at St. Luke's Hospital, Hall pushed through the board a resolution that all Provident physicians, including Williams, should be required to bring all their patients to Provident. Williams, who had patients in several other hospitals and was the only black doctor in Chicago with a large number of white patients, could not agree to this, and in 1912, he resigned.

Dr. Dan continued as a highly successful surgeon at St. Luke's for years. He died at his summer home in Idlewild, Michigan, on August 4, 1931. An editorial in the *Journal of the National Medical Association* stated, "Let us be reminded that the race had enjoyed barely twenty years of freedom when this remarkable genius joined the ranks of the trail blazers of the more favored race. Throughout a professional life of nearly fifty years he remained in the vanguard. . . . He was a medical missionary, a veritable Moses to the Negro profession." In 1975, the house on East Forty-Second Street to which Williams and his wife had moved in 1905 was designated a National Historic Landmark.

Although many reference books and Web sites report that Williams was the first surgeon in history to perform open-heart surgery, that isn't quite accurate. In the first place, on September 6, 1891, Dr. H. C. Dalton of St. Louis sewed up the lacerated pericardium of a stabbing victim in an operation quite similar to that later done by Williams. Dalton, however did not report the surgery in a medical journal until 1894, so Williams would not likely have known about it.[20] Second, both doctors operated on the pericardium, not the heart itself, and experts question whether either of the operations therefore qualifies as true open-heart surgery. In fact, two histories of heart surgery—*Pioneers of Cardiac Surgery* by William S. Stoney and *To Mend the Heart* by Lael Wertenbaker—do not even mention Dalton and Williams. Both give precedence to Ludwig Rehn of Frankfurt, Germany, who sutured a stab wound of the left ventricle in 1896.

All of this, however, does not detract from Williams's achievement. Most likely not knowing of Dalton's operation, Williams had no precedent to guide him. Also, the distinction between the pericardium and the heart might be too fine. The pericardium sutured by Dr. Dan was throbbing, just like the patient's heart, at 130 beats per minute, and it is no easy task to put stitches into such an organ. Furthermore, Williams did observe that the heart itself had been nicked by the knife—it probably would not have been that difficult for him to stitch up that wound also, if he had thought it necessary. Finally, the received medical opinion of the day was that surgery on the heart was, by and large, impossible. Williams was probing into an undiscovered realm, and he needs no claim of primacy to ensure his reputation.

Chicago: Medical Center

The story of Daniel Hale Williams also enables a study of one of Chicago's most important, if not always recognized, characteristics. For it was in Williams's time that Chicago was turning into a medical center of first national, and then of international importance. Today, there are few meat packers in Chicago, but there are a huge amount of health-care workers. One-fifth of all the doctors in the United States have received all or part of their training in Chicago.[21]

Visitors to the city probably do not venture very far west of Ashland Avenue, but if they did they would discover the first and largest urban medical district in the United States. This 560-acre special-use zoning district, created in 1941, contains an impressive number of facilities, such as the University of Illinois Medical Center, the John H. Stroger Jr. Hospital (formerly Cook County Hospital), Rush University Medical Center, and the Jesse Brown VA Medical Center, as well as the Chicago Technology Park, which houses firms that conduct research in pharmaceuticals, medical devices and testing, genomics, and nanotechnology. The College of Medicine at the University of Illinois Medical Center is the largest medical school in the United States. The first years of the twenty-first century were ones of impressive growth in Chicago's medical facilities. Rush University Medical Center launched a major expansion plan on the West Side, Northwestern University inaugurated a new women's hospital, the Lurie Children's Hospital (formerly Children's Memorial) opened nearby, and the University of Chicago completed the ten-story Center for Care and Discovery.

Chicago's medical history begins with William Smith, the first surgeon at Fort Dearborn. The first resident physician in Chicago was Alexander Wolcott, a graduate of Yale who came to Chicago in 1818 as "Indian Agent to the Lakes" for the federal government.[22] Medicine in Chicago's frontier days was a rough-and-ready enterprise, and it would take some years for the city to evolve into a world medical capital. One of the key early events in that transformation was the arrival in Chicago in 1877 of the Danish surgeon and pathologist Christian Fenger (1840–1902). He joined the staff of Cook County Hospital, gave lectures and demonstrations, presented research papers, and introduced Chicago's medical community to the latest advances in Europe. Later, he became a consulting surgeon at Provident. In the 1880s, many Chicago physicians began traveling to Europe, absorbing the new knowledge and acquiring the latest equipment. Thomas Bonner, the author of *Medicine in Chicago, 1850–1950*, cites two Chicago physicians as nationally important in this period.[23] William T. Belfield of Rush Medical College lectured on the relationship of bacteria to disease, and Henry Gradle of Chicago Medical College delivered a series of papers entitled "Bacteria and the Germ Theory of Disease," which was published in book form in 1883.[24]

. . . no other midwestern city came even close to Chicago in the number of physicians being turned out annually by its medical schools.

Provident Hospital was just one of many hospitals founded in the Chicago in the nineteenth century. Chicago's very first hospitals, however, were founded to provide care for the poor, to house the insane and the incapacitated, or to isolate victims of epidemic disease, which was the purpose of the city's first official hospital, which dates to 1843. The original Cook County Hospital opened in 1866, and the first medical school in Chicago was Rush Medical College, established by Daniel Brainard in

1843. A second medical school came to Chicago in 1859, when Nathan S. Davis, who had been lecturing at Rush, founded the Lind University Medical School. The establishment later changed its name to Chicago Medical College, which was Dr. Dan's alma mater, and then became Northwestern University Medical College. Davis helped found the American Medical Association (AMA) and became its president in 1864. The AMA still maintains its headquarters in Chicago.

In 1847, physicians from Rush set up the city's first general hospital. This facility was too small and went out of business, whereupon the doctors from Rush founded a new general hospital and invited a Roman Catholic order of nuns, the Sisters of Mercy, to provide nursing care. In 1851, ownership was transferred to the sisters, and the facility, renamed Mercy Hospital, enabled the Archdiocese of Chicago to provide medical care to the growing population of Roman Catholics. It is the oldest continuously operating hospital in the city. Other religious groups founded their own hospitals. In 1865, the administrators of Grace Episcopal Church founded St. Luke's, and the Lutheran minister William Passavant founded Passavant Hospital. A year later, Chicago's Jews founded the establishment that eventually became Michael Reese Hospital. In 1888, the Methodists founded Wesley Memorial Hospital, and in 1891, the same year that Provident opened, Baptists established the Chicago Baptist Hospital.

Other Chicago hospitals concentrated on specialized fields. Examples include the Illinois Charitable Eye and Ear Infirmary (1858) and Children's Memorial (1882). A singular nineteenth-century establishment was the Hahnemann Hospital (1870), which specialized in homeopathic medicine. The original hospital burned in the Chicago Fire; it was replaced, and then the cornerstone of a newer, larger facility was laid in 1893.

By this time, writes Thomas Bonner, Chicago "could boast four regular medical schools, two post-graduate institutions, a dozen medical societies, numerous hospitals and clinics, ten medical journals, and more than twelve hundred regular practitioners of medicine."[25] In addition, no other midwestern city came even close to Chicago in the number of physicians being turned out annually by its medical schools. And not all of these students were men. Sarah Hackett Stevenson, the first woman to belong to the AMA, was a Chicagoan, and in 1865, Mary Harris Thompson, the first woman surgeon in the United States, founded the Chicago Hospital for Women and Children, the first hospital staffed by female physicians. Six years later, Thompson helped found a medical school for women named the Woman's Hospital Medical College of Chicago.

If the West Side of Chicago is today home to one of the world's greatest concentrations of medical facilities, that, in a sense, was already true in 1893. On July 21, the *Chicago Tribune* presented its readers with an article describing a new medical facility, the Post Graduate Medical School, on West Harrison Street. This fine five-story structure was to serve as a school, a dispensary, and a hospital all in one. However, the article noted that this building did not stand alone: "The medical quarter of Chicago, which with the County Hospital, Rush Medical College, and the Presbyterian Hospital as a focal center, fills so large a space on the West Side and practically monopolizes the territory between Congress and Polk streets, from Wood street west to Lincoln, is receiving important and valuable accessions in the way of new structures devoted to hospitals, schools, and medical and surgical purposes."[26]

As the saying goes, the more things change, the more they stay the same.

6

A Church for Father Tolton

From Italy they came. From Ireland, Poland, and Slovakia. From Bohemia, Lithuania, Croatia, Slovenia, Austria, French Canada, Bavaria, and the Rhineland. They were Roman Catholics, and they were dramatically altering Chicago, changing it from a city founded mostly by Protestant fortune seekers from New England and upstate New York to a city in which the bells of grand Catholic churches, heard throughout the neighborhoods, now counted the hours of the day.[1]

In 1893, three-fourths of the immigrants coming to Chicago were Catholic, and that year saw some significant developments for the Catholic population. For one, the "Edwards Law" was repealed. This 1889 legislation stipulated that instruction in all schools, public and parochial, had to be in English, and immigrant parents feared that the law meant that the Protestant-dominated state government would now dictate policy to parochial schools. German Lutherans joined with Catholics in fighting the law, and their victory was a great achievement. Then, in September 1893, a group of women launched the Chicago Catholic Women's League, which was dedicated to charitable activities. And in 1893, the fourth black Catholic congress was held in Chicago. As the historian Charles Shanabruch has expressed it, by 1893, "Chicago Catholicism was no longer insecure. Through strength of numbers, wise leadership, and increasing success in the marketplace and in the political arena, it had become

St. Mary of the Angels, built to serve Chicago's Polish community, is a striking example of the grand Catholic churches erected by immigrants. (Photograph by the author)

self-assured."[2] No wonder: in 1880, Chicago had thirty-eight Catholic parishes; in 1890, it had eighty-one. In that year, the Catholic Church counted 262,047 souls in its Chicago flock, which far outnumbered the Protestant count.[3]

Catholic churches and parishes were opening at a furious pace in Chicago in the early 1890s, creating a legacy of extraordinary buildings not regularly noted by historians. Although excellent churches were built before the fire of 1871 (Old St. Patrick's and Holy Family are the two finest surviving examples), the great surge of Catholic church building occurred from the 1890s through the 1920s. The Germans favored the Gothic style, as seen in such edifices as St. Alphonsus and St. Paul's. Polish churches, however, normally followed baroque and Renaissance designs—such as St. Mary of the Angels—and the Lithuanians followed suit (Holy Cross Church). The Irish opted for a mix of styles, as in the Romanesque Revival of St. Pius V (1893) but generally were partial to high Victorian Gothic, the style of Holy Name Cathedral itself, which was rebuilt shortly after the fire and then renovated—in 1893.

One of the less impressive churches to open in 1893 was St. Monica's on Thirty-Sixth and Dearborn. It was unfinished. Although backers had raised enough funds to begin construction, the money ran out before it could be completed. Nevertheless, the opening of St. Monica's doors was a landmark in the history of American Catholicism. Leading its congregation was a thirty-nine-year-old pastor named Augustus Tolton, the first black Catholic priest in the history of the United States.[4]

Actually, calling him the first black priest in the United States requires some qualification. Three black Catholic priests preceded him—brothers named James Augustine Healy, Patrick Francis Healy, and Alexander Sherwood Healy, who were the sons of an Irishman named Michael Morris Healy and his light-skinned slave mistress, Mary Eliza, with whom he appears to have lived with as a spouse. The boys were sent north to be educated at Holy Cross, and eventually all three were ordained—James in Paris in 1854, Alexander in Rome four years later, and Patrick in Belgium in 1864. James even rose to the position of bishop, and Patrick became rector of Georgetown University. Although some people recognized their African ancestry, the brothers took little interest in the condition of black people and seem to have been content to pass for white. For this reason, Cyprian Davis, the author of *History of Black Catholics in the United States*, calls Tolton "the first black American priest whom all knew and recognized as black."

Father Augustus Tolton. The berretta with the red tassel indicates his standing as a Vatican scholar. (Brenner Library, Quincy University)

From Slavery to the Seminary

Augustus Tolton was born a slave in Ralls County, Missouri, in 1854.[5] His father, Peter Paul Tolton, belonged to a Roman Catholic family named Hagar, or Hager. Augustus's mother, Martha Jane Chisley, had been a slave on the Manning plantation in Mead County, Kentucky, but when Susan Manning married Stephen Eliott of Ralls County she brought along Martha Jane, who had also been baptized a Catholic. In 1851, Peter Paul Tolton and Martha Jane Chisley were wed in St. Peter's Church in Brush Creek, Missouri. The couple had three children, of whom Augustus was the second.

There were many black Catholics, slave and free, in the portions of the New World settled by colonists from Catholic France and Spain, but there were also quite a few in the British colonies. Many of them lived in Maryland, which had been founded in 1634 as a sanctuary for oppressed Catholics. The percentage of slaves in the antebellum South who were Catholic was not large. It has been estimated that of some four million slaves, about 150,000 were Catholic.[6] Still, 150,000 is not an insignificant number, and, as their descendants multiplied, many moved to the cities of the North.

The extent to which black Catholics, slave or free, were fully instructed in the faith varied, and racist attitudes were widespread among the Catholic population and clergy. Some of this tendency was attributable to the Catholics' dislike of the abolitionists, whom they viewed as fanatics, but part was due to the conventions of the age, in which few white Americans could view black people as equals. On the other hand, there were those in the Catholic hierarchy who were troubled about the inadequate pastoral care given to black Catholics. One was William Henry Elder, the bishop in Natchez just prior to the Civil War. Writing in a Catholic newsletter, he described his diocese in this way: "These poor negroes form in some respects my chief anxiety. I believe they are generally well cared for, so far as health and the necessaries of life are concerned. But for learning and practising religion, they have at present very little opportunity indeed. . . . Catholic masters of course are taught that it is their duty to furnish their slaves with opportunities for being well instructed, and for practising their religion. And here is my anxiety, that I cannot enable those masters to do their duty because there are not Priests enough."[7] The Hagars and the Eliotts of Missouri were of those Catholic slaveholders able to provide religious instruction. Augustus's baptismal register reads: "A colored child born April 1, 1854. Son of Peter Tolton and Martha Chisley. Property of Stephen Eliott. Mrs. Stephen Eliott sponsor; May 29, 1854. Father John O'Sullivan."

The Civil War changed everything. On August 30, 1861, Union commander John C. Frémont put Missouri under martial law, which effectively freed the slaves of pro-Confederates. Thousands of slaves promptly fled, Peter Paul Tolton among them. Not much else is known about him, although he did reach St. Louis. He eventually became a solider in the Union army and died in a hospital in St. Louis. Martha Chisley Tolton also took to the road. At Hannibal, the family was suspected of being runaways, but Union soldiers smuggled her and the children across the Mississippi during the night, and from there they proceeded to Quincy, Illinois, which, as a border town, was receiving numerous fugitive slaves. In February 1864, Newton Flagg, the quartermaster at Quincy, wrote secretary of war Edwin Stanton that he was distributing rations to the "most needy and destitute" among them. There were about four hundred fugitive slaves, or "contrabands," as they were known at the time, nearly all women and children, the Tolton family surely among them, although Augustus's older brother had died the year before. Flagg said that they lived in "miserable hovels and stables" and that he had hired someone to look after them and find them homes.[8]

Martha Tolton found work in a tobacco processing facility, where Augustus joined her at age seven. The family attended St. Boniface Church, sitting along with other black Catholics in a separate section. Quincy was heavily German, and the pastor, Herman Schaeffermeyer, conducted services in that language, which Augustus came to speak fluently. Father Schaeffermeyer also admitted Augustus to the church's school, not realizing that many German parents would object, forcing Augustus to withdraw. Augustus then attended an all-black school. The family transferred to the parish of St. Peter's, where the Irish pastor, Peter McGirr, saw that Augustus was admitted permanently to the parochial school and had him trained as an altar boy. It was to Father McGirr that Augustus Tolton first made known his ambition to become a priest. McGirr conferred with Schaeffer-meyer, who backed Augustus's appeal.

An ambition to become a teacher or a lawyer would have been difficult enough for someone in Augustus Tolton's circumstances, but Catholics viewed the priest as the mediator between God and mankind, and in nineteenth-century America, it was nearly impossible for many Catholics to view a black man in that part. In fact, after the Civil War, the number of black Catholics dropped as many left the church in repulsion against segregated pews and lack of opportunity to participate fully in church life. As one black Catholic priest later put it, "Negroes have followed their masters into the Catholic Church, but have fallen away in great numbers because they have not been given an active part in the organic life of the church."[9]

Father Augustus Tolton in the 1890s. In 2010, the archbishop of Chicago announced the introduction of Tolton's cause for sainthood.
(Brenner Library, Quincy University)

No seminary in the United States would accept Tolton, and he began his training with a private tutor, Father Theodore Wegmann, who taught him Latin, Greek, English, German, history, and geography. In 1878, Tolton was admitted to St. Francis College as a special student. It was there that Father Michael Richardt solved the quandary of finding a seminary. He wrote to the minister general of the Franciscan Order in Rome. A handful of black priests from Africa had already been studying in the Eternal City, training to be missionaries to their homelands, so Tolton's color would be no obstacle. Tolton entered the Urban College in Rome in March 1880.

Tolton performed well and was described as "truly a man to be trusted on account of his industry and obedience."[10] He was ordained on April 24, 1886. At first he was meant to become a missionary in Africa, but as Tolton himself explained in a speech in 1889, he was told that he was instead to be sent to the United States: "When on the eve of going to St. John Lateran to be ordained, the word came expressing doubt whether I would be sent here. It was said that I would be the only priest of my race in America and would not be likely to succeed. All at once Cardinal Simoni said, 'America has been called the most enlightened nation; we will see if it deserves that honor. If America has never seen a black priest, it has to see one now.'"[11]

Tolton's initial foray into the United States was euphoric. On July 12, 1886, the *New York Times* published a brief report stating, "The Reverend Augustus Tolton, the first Catholic colored priest ordained for the United States, took part in the services at the Church of St. Benedict the Moor yesterday morning." It neglected to mention that the church was overflowing with black Catholics from New York City and beyond who viewed the occasion as historic. Some of the elation can be glimpsed in an article published in the *St. Joseph Advocate* in January 1887. It enthused, "And so we have in our midst to-day a colored priest, a native American, once a slave and the son of slaves . . . said to be incapable of education." The author was especially delighted that Tolton was "no hybrid, but the genuine article; a typical Africo-American, the very one of all others we long to see chosen; not your ideal octoroon if possible, quadroon at most, Caucasian in chiseling, Semitic in coloring, a pinch-nose, straight-haired 'look-at-me,' as if picked out for a compromise because of his proboscis and not of his brains." He was "the *vivid and striking* likeness of a solid man, true as steel, without a shadow of pretension, well up in his sacred duties, able to converse and preach in more than one language, humble as a child, boasting of his African blood, and all aglow with devotion and love for his race." The article went on to say, "As he passes through the streets of

Quincy, white gentlemen raise their hats, and priests at tables take back seats to give him the place of honor."[12]

On the Sunday following his appearance in New York, Father Tolton said his first Mass in Quincy. Reports say that

Father Augustus Tolton's first parish, St. Joseph's in Quincy, Illinois. The young pastor was so popular that many white Catholics attended his services, angering other priests in the town. (Brenner Library, Quincy University)

the crowd was the largest ever to fill the church, and many of the blacks were Protestant but proud of the local boy who had made good. In a letter to Rome, Tolton said, "In America everyone received me kindly, especially the Negroes but also the white people: Germans, Irish, and all the others. I celebrated Mass on July 18, in the Church of Saint Boniface with more than 1,000 whites and 500 colored people present. After the Mass all shouted, 'Hail to the Propaganda College; long live the college in Rome.'"[13] Tolton was assigned his own parish, St. Joseph, a black church. Although he found it difficult to make converts among the black population, it seems, oddly, that his major trouble was a very result of his popularity. The church, ostensibly black, attracted a significant number of white Catholics— Tolton reported that as many as two hundred white Catholics were attending regularly. A white woman named Mrs. Joseph Ducker became organist and choir leader and trained "a choir of Negro and white girls and practiced the necessary liturgical singing" while the St. Joseph's Altar Society had eighty women members, both white and black. Tolton himself was praised for his education, his oratory, his rich voice, and his fine singing. Some white priests grew resentful, or, as Tolton put it in a letter to the archbishop of Baltimore, his success provoked "a little jealous feelings among other neighboring brother priests." He said that "the priests here rejoiced at my arrival, now they wish I were away because too many white people come down to my church from other parishes." The white people of Quincy, Tolton noted, were "really good-hearted, charitable, and non-prejudicial, no feeling of bitterness at all against a man on account of complexion."[14]

In 1887, a new pastor, Father Michael Weiss, was appointed to St. Boniface. He was aghast that so many of his parishioners were attending St. Joseph's. Tolton viewed Weiss as a racist who actually presented a physical threat to him, and he complained that Weiss had asked the bishop to relocate Tolton. An additional problem was that the black Protestant churches redoubled their efforts to keep black worshipers away from St. Joseph's, and Tolton despaired of attracting enough black parishioners to keep the church viable. In 1887, he reported to Rome, "During the year that I have been pastor the number of Negro Catholics has not increased. It seems they do not care much for religion . . . I had only six converts this year." He added, "The Negroes in Chicago, Illinois, complain that I am here in Quincy and that they do not have a Negro priest. They have asked Archbishop Feehan of Chicago to appeal to Rome for my transfer to Chicago."

And that was how it worked out.

Going to Chicago

The Archbishop Feehan to whom Tolton referred in his letter was the Right Reverend Patrick Augustine Feehan, who had been archbishop of Chicago since 1880. He was born in Ireland in 1829 and came to America in 1850. He was tall, blue-eyed, and handsome and, according to one reporter, looked "every inch a prince of the church."[15] Today, he is most remembered as the founder of Chicago's parochial school system.

The Right Reverend Patrick Augustine Feehan, who became the Roman Catholic archbishop of Chicago in 1880, was instrumental in bringing Father Augustus Tolton to the city. (ICHi-10251, Chicago History Museum; Century Printing and Engraving Company, Chicago)

Chicago's Catholics were fragmented by nationality and language. In 1880, there were thirty-eight Catholic parishes in Chicago and sixteen of them were considered "national"—that is, given over to a single non-English-speaking ethnic group. There were nine German, three Polish, three Bohemian, and one French. By 1902, the year of Feehan's death, there were fifty-two "national" parishes—nineteen German, fifteen Polish, five Bohemian, three French, three Lithuanian, three Italian, one Croatian, one Slovenian, one Slovak, and one Dutch. This rise in the proportion of national parishes was not church policy; Feehan was responding to the demand of immigrants who preferred churches where they could hear and preserve their languages.

Actually, there were fifty-three "national" parishes—if you counted one that was not immigrant and not non-English-speaking. This was the one "Negro" parish—St. Monica's. It had its origin in a small organization called St. Augustine's Society, which had been founded in 1881 at the request of black Catholics who were permitted to hold services in the basement of St. Mary's, a white church. They wanted their own parish "where they might retain and build up their faith which was beginning to be greatly hampered by the growing prejudice in the white church."[16] In 1882, St. Augustine's Society became St. Augustine's Church, although it still did not have a separate facility. It was this church that made the request to have Father Tolton transferred from Quincy, and, accordingly, it was to St. Mary's that he was sent just before Christmas 1889.

Building the Church

When Father Tolton arrived in Chicago, nineteen black converts from Quincy came with him (his mother and sister would join him later). His initial meeting with Archbishop Feehan went well; Tolton was given charge of all the black Catholics in the city and was told that a donation had already been made toward the construction of a church. Shortly after the meeting, Tolton, in a letter, said of Feehan, "He is an elegant bishop. I love him." There were not a lot of black Catholics in Chicago, but there were enough to make Father Tolton badly needed. In 1894, the *Chicago Tribune* reported that "there are in this city about 140 families of colored people who profess the Catholic faith" and went on to say that amounted to some eight hundred people in all.[17]

Tolton's first Mass was said in the basement of St. Mary's. In early 1890, he wrote, "Here I am hard at work. . . . We have secured a site on which to build a church as soon as we have the means to begin. . . . I had to refuse going to some places to give addresses as I had too much to do going around getting the names of my people and organizing a parish. These poor people have been left in a bag with both ends open if I may say it that way."[18] One of the first persons he wrote to for help in funding the new church was Katharine Drexel, who came from a wealthy Philadelphia family and who became a nun in 1891 (she was canonized in 2000). Tolton wrote to her that he had "altogether 500 souls but they have become like unto the dead limbs on a tree and without moisture because no one had taken care of them: just Sunday night last I was called to the death bed of a colored woman who had been 9 years away from her duties because she was hurled out of a white church and even cursed at by the Irish members."[19] Drexel responded with an initial donation of $100; eventually she would contribute at least $30,000.[20] A black parishioner and trustee, Lincoln C. Valle, acted as Tolton's representative in the matter of fundraising and received many donations from Chicago's white population.

In 1891, Archbishop Feehan gave Tolton permission to take his congregation to a storefront church next door to Tolton's rooming house on South Indiana Avenue, but this was a temporary

St. Katharine Drexel, seen here with school children in Beaumont, Texas, was a great help to Father Tolton. (From the Archives of the Sisters of the Blessed Sacrament)

arrangement. In January 1893, Father Tolton told a reporter, "I have worked in the Catholic cause since 1889 and now celebrate mass for 2,000 parishioners. Mrs. Patrick O'Neil heads the subscription list with $10,000. The fund has assumed considerable proportions, and we will be able to begin work in March."[21]

The architect of the new church at the corner of Dearborn and Thirty-Sixth Streets was Julius Wegman of the Chicago architectural firm of Julius Wegman and Son; G. W. Brown, a black contractor, was in charge of construction.[22] It was a gritty neighborhood, almost entirely black. As the *Tribune* stated, the Gothic structure, built of "pressed brick with trimmings of Bedford stone" was going to have large twin towers, each a hundred feet high, a front with "two large windows of cathedral glass," "fancy ornaments," and a tile roof. These aspirations could not be met because the fund-raising came up short. It's likely that the onset of the depression that began in 1893 was partly responsible for a drop-off in donations. Many of Father Tolton's parishioners were already needy, and the economic crisis surely caused more to come into financial difficulty. Funds intended for construction were diverted to help them with food, housing, clothes, and medicine.

In late 1893, the building was as finished as it would ever get; a temporary roof was put on, and services began. It was an odd-looking building—half a church, with one sturdy tower abruptly terminating in a squat flat roof. Although Tolton began using it in 1893, the formal dedication took place on January 14, 1894. Father Hodnett of St. Malachy's Church delivered a sermon in which he "congratulated the members upon the distinction of being pioneers among their people in the creditable work of erecting a church for worship according to the faith of the Catholics."[23] The church was named St. Monica's after the mother of St. Augustine of Hippo. That the two saints were native to the African continent gave them special resonance with black Catholics—it was Catholic tradition that some of its early saints were black. As a prominent black Catholic expressed it in 1892, "There were holy women like St. Monica, St. Felicita, and St. Perpetua. There were holy men like St. Augustine, St. Basil, St. Cyprian, St. Moses, St. Benedict the Moor, St. Cyril, all of whom, as the Church affirms, were of pure Ethiopian blood."[24]

A small house at 448 Thirty-Sixth Street was found for the new pastor, and he was now able to bring his mother and sister from Quincy. A priest who visited in 1896 wrote that "they lived in a poorly furnished but very clean house. The meals were simple affairs. Father Tolton, his mother, and I sat at a table having an oil cloth cover. A kerosene lamp stood in the middle. One the wall directly behind Father Tolton's place hung a large black rosary, most

St. Monica's Church in Chicago was left in an unfinished state after fundraising fell short, but nevertheless it opened in 1893. (Brenner Library, Quincy University)

likely one he had brought from Rome."[25] Tolton's recreation was to play the accordion; he was known for his beautiful singing voice, which he put to good effect at Mass. Once St. Monica's opened, a contemporary priest wrote, Tolton's congregation "grew by leaps and bounds."[26] Eventually, some six hundred black Chicago Catholics registered at St. Monica's. However, they were scattered about the city and many lived far from the church. When some of them discovered that they would not be barred from attending Mass closer to home, they left St. Monica's, which suffered a loss of parishioners, although some members of nearby white parishes found it convenient to continue to attend St. Monica's. One of Tolton's parishioners later wrote, "The intermingling of races in the churches did begin to stir up feelings of segregation and prejudice. This hurt Father Tolton keenly because after six years in Rome he had not completely realized the difference between white and black."[27]

Father Tolton became a celebrity and a symbolic leader of all the black Catholics in the nation. Even before he came to Chicago, a prominent black Catholic newspaperman hailed him as "the most conspicuous man in America."[28] Tolton had been the star attraction at the first Catholic Afro-American Congress, which was held in Washington, D.C., in January 1889. Tolton's parish duties prevented him from accepting all of the invitations he received. At one time, he wrote, he had "27 letters . . . asking me to come and lecture, come and give my assistance." And he said, "I wish at this moment that there were 27 Father Toltons or colored priests at any rate who could supply the demands." Tolton also came to feel that he was under an uncomfortable scrutiny. As he wrote to Katherine Drexel, "They watch us, just the same as the Pharisees did our Lord."[29] And being in the spotlight did not translate into receiving assistance. One observer commented, "Poor Father—it seems strange that after all the gush about the 'dear Negro,' he is left to struggle alone in poverty and humility, grappling with the giant task of founding a church and congregation in Chicago."[30] The remark about his "poverty and humility" is telling because if Father Tolton had a flaw it was a lack of assertiveness. When Archbishop John Ireland, a leader of the liberal wing of the Catholic Church in the United States, began looking for a young black man to enter a seminary, he pointedly said, "I want no Toltons." Ireland seems to have felt that Tolton was not aggressive enough, which might have been the case because all indications are that saintly Father Tolton was uncommonly sensitive.

In 1895, Father Tolton's health declined and he took a leave of absence. His duties were taken over by Father Riordan of the nearby Irish church of St. Elizabeth. Riordan recognized the struggles of the new church and wrote a letter entitled "An

Appeal on Behalf of the Black Catholics." As he put it, "As the colored Catholics are few in number, it was not expected that they would be able to meet the large expense necessary for the building of their church. . . . The church, though only partially built, is burdened with a very large debt, and I find myself greatly embarrassed in trying to meet even the current expenses. During a whole year I have practiced the most rigid economy, and am now obliged, though reluctantly, to appeal to the public for assistance."[31]

July 9, 1897, was an unusual weather day in Chicago. Although the temperature did not reach ninety, the night did not bring the usual cooling. It was eighty-six at noon and eighty-six at midnight. As the *Chicago Tribune* explained in reporting the death of fifteen people, it was "torture day and night": "The slaughter of the sun's rays was due mostly to the continuous heat. . . . The suffering at night was intense, especially in the tenement districts. . . . For another day and another night 1,600,000 people have been broiling on the gridiron of a large city."[32] The newspaper also reported that two priests had died from the heat. One was Father Otto Groenbaum of St. Nicholas German Catholic Church; the other was the "Rev. August Tolton," who had died at Mercy Hospital at 8:30 P.M. The story went on to say, "He was prostrated at Thirty-sixth street and Ellis avenue, only a short distance from his home. . . . He was about to make several calls in his parish just before noon. He was seen to reel and then fall heavily to the sidewalk. Several men rushed to his assistance and removed him to a cool spot, where everything possible was done to relieve him until the arrival of the Stanton avenue police patrol, which removed him to Mercy Hospital."[33] Father Tolton was forty-three years old, which might seem young, except that in the nineteenth century, most Catholic priests died before their fiftieth birthdays, a state of affairs attributed to their almost daily visits to sick parishioners in an age without antibiotics.

On March 17, 2010, Francis Cardinal George, the archbishop of Chicago, announced that Father Tolton's cause for sainthood was being introduced.

His body was returned to Quincy for burial in St. Peter's Cemetery, where today a memorial plaque marks his resting place. On March 17, 2010, Francis Cardinal George, the archbishop of Chicago, announced that Father Tolton's cause for sainthood was being introduced. Catholics were encouraged to pray for and to Father Tolton and to report any spiritual or physical favors granted through prayer in his name.

The Struggle for a Black Priesthood

It would be satisfying to report that Augustus Tolton was the Jackie Robinson of the Catholic priesthood, that he opened the door for dozens, and then hundreds, who quickly followed him. That was not the case. The cause of the black Catholic priesthood would be a long, difficult effort.

A second black priest had actually been ordained even before St. Monica's was dedicated. Charles Randolph Uncles, the first black priest ordained in the United States, had been ordained in 1891. He had been sponsored by a priest named John R. Slattery (1851–1926), one of the most intriguing and tragic figures in the history of U.S. Catholicism.

The cause of a native black priesthood in the United States was the mission of an organization called St. Joseph's Society of the Sacred Heart. They had originated in Britain, where they were known as the Mill Hill Fathers, and had sent missionaries to the United States in 1871 to work with freed slaves. In 1893, the Americans cut ties with their British counterparts to become an independent entity, and Slattery became the superior general of the new group, the Josephites.

When Slattery met Uncles, he was impressed by his "vivid intelligence" and saw that he was admitted to St. Hyacinth's College in Quebec, where Slattery personally paid for his education. Slattery purchased a former hotel and turned it into St. Joseph's Seminary, which, Slattery said, "would receive the black as well as the white man." Uncles received holy orders in Baltimore cathedral on December 19, 1891. The relationship between Slattery and Uncles did not turn out well. Slattery wanted Uncles to tour the United States, but Uncles protested that he would not be "trotted out before the public gaze" to become a "show priest."[34] Eventually a position was found for Uncles as a teacher at Epiphany College. He spent most of his career there, and died in 1933.

It would be eleven years before Slattery succeeded in elevating another black man to the priesthood—John Henry Dorsey, who was ordained in Baltimore in 1902. Unlike Uncles, he was delighted to conduct missions. He was sent to Alabama, but the atmosphere was not welcoming. He was transferred to Pine Bluff, Arkansas, but there he felt isolated from the white priests, who were wary of "social equality" for blacks. Attendance at Dorsey's masses was small, and he returned to Alabama, to St. Joseph's College for Negro Catechists. In 1913, he became a missionary to black Protestants on the Gulf Coast. His health weakened, and he was transferred to St. Monica's in Baltimore, a poor black parish. He died in 1926.

A third Josephite black priest, John Joseph Plantevigne, was ordained in 1907. He conducted several successful missions in the South until Archbishop James H. Blenk of New Orleans denied him permission to speak there, leaving Plantevigne despondent and insulted. Plantevigne offered to take over Tolton's parish in Chicago, but Archbishop James Quigley preferred a local (white) man. A plan to send Plantevigne to St. Augustine, Florida, was rejected by the bishop there who said he "could never think of placing a colored priest."[35] He ended up at a parish in Baltimore and died in 1913 at age forty-two. Tuberculosis was the official cause, but many attributed his passing to "a broken heart."

By this time, Slattery was long gone from the Josephites. As the Jim Crow laws hardened and prospects for American blacks worsened, nativists began to crowd out Catholic moderates, and as the twentieth century approached, Slattery said that there was "fresh opposition to negro priests."[36] By 1902, he had had enough. At the first Mass performed by Father Dorsey, he delivered an angry sermon denouncing the Church on the race issue. "The fact is clear that many Catholics are prejudiced against the Negro," he said.[37] The sermon set off a furor; one priest called it "the most incendiary pronouncement which I can recall coming from a Catholic priest." In 1904, Slattery retired as superior general. Two years later, he said, "There is no hope of reforming the Catholic Church." He left the priesthood and the Church, got married, became a lawyer in California, and died in 1926.

By the early 1920s, the Josephites had nearly ended the policy of cultivating black priests, with a few light-skinned exceptions. Three black priests were ordained in the 1920s and about a dozen in the 1930s, but many of these were active outside the United States. With the arrival of the civil rights movement, the Catholic Church finally made progress, but the black Catholic community continued to be underserved. The numbers of black Catholics began to increase sharply in the late 1940s, but by 1990, there was but one black priest for every five thousand black Catholics while among the larger Catholic population there was one priest for every eight hundred Catholics.[38] As one historian has explained, "the failure of the American Catholic Church to develop an African-American clergy until the mid twentieth century was a crucial factor in the slow growth of Catholicism among black Americans."[39]

The End of St. Monica's

With the help of Mother Katharine Drexel, who sent five members of her Sisters of the Blessed Sacrament, St. Monica added a school in 1912. The church was then under the care of Reverend John S. Morris, a white pastor. In 1922, it was reported that over twelve hundred people had attended Easter Mass at St. Monica.

Yet the church had only two years left. Nearby St. Elizabeth, founded as an Irish parish in 1881, had become black, and the diocese decided that the two churches should be made one. The merger took place in 1924, and St. Elizabeth became the "mother" black Catholic church.

In January 1930, St. Elizabeth Church burned down, and the parish assembly hall was remodeled to serve as the church. The church that stands on the site today was dedicated in 1989. Although the modern church looks nothing like the original St. Monica's, in other respects not much has changed. It continues

The saintly Father Tolton is immortalized on an outdoor ceramic mural at St. Elizabeth's Church in Chicago. (Photograph by the author)

to serve a disadvantaged community—96 percent of the families who have children in St. Elizabeth School have incomes below the poverty level. The exterior of the edifice boasts a large ceramic mural created by Ildiko Repasi, a Hungarian-born artist. It was installed in 1995 to narrate the history of St. Monica's and St. Elizabeth's. On the Michigan Avenue side can be found a depiction of Father Tolton. Looking rather hieratic in his Byzantine pose and with his blank eyes, his arms spread and his palms open in benediction and prayer, he also appears wise, saintly, and perhaps a bit sad. In that regard, a good likeness.

7

The Illinois Institute of Technology

When the light is right, its russet bricks gleam as you make your way along the Dan Ryan Expressway near Thirty-Third Street. It's a commanding Romanesque Revival hulk, with pyramidal roofs, prominent gables, round-arched windows, and heavily rusticated walls. The creation of architects Normand Patton and Reynolds Fisher, this proud structure was the Main Building of the Armour Institute of Technology, which opened in 1893.

To understand how it happened to be built, one has to go back to a Sunday early in 1890 at the Plymouth Congregational

The Main Building of the Armour Institute of Technology, designed by the firm of Patton and Fisher, opened in 1893. (Photograph by the author)

Church on Indiana Avenue. The preacher giving the sermon was Frank W. Gunsaulus, one of those forgotten personages who was once a towering figure in Chicago.[1] An acquaintance once said, "He had a kingly presence, and came to his ceaseless tasks confessedly dominant in build, demeanor, gesture, and voice."[2] In addition to being a minister and educator, he was also a founding board member of the Field Museum and a trustee and board member of the Art Institute. To the latter establishment he donated collections of Wedgwood and oriental pottery, and he persuaded other prominent Chicagoans to make similar bequests. At the University of Chicago, he was considered the "the patron saint" of the library system.[3] Gunsaulus was described as "a preacher, a lecturer, an author, a novelist, a historian, a lover of art, a connoisseur of china and Persian pottery, collector of tapestries and of valuable manuscripts, versed in book lore, and conversant with not a few of the notable epochs of ecclesiasticalism."[4] Finally, in an era that valued oratory as both an art form and an entertainment, Gunsaulus was a star.

Gunsaulus's philosophy envisioned the "union of things intellectual and material," by which he meant that modern technology could best benefit humanity if guided by a spiritual ethos. He was aware that other cities boasted technical schools with this goal and concluded that Chicago could also use a progressive establishment of that type. So on that Sunday he delivered what has since become known as the "Million Dollar Sermon." Listening to the oration, the title of which was "If I Had a Million Dollars," was Philip Danforth Armour, the meatpacking tycoon. Gunsaulus described what he would like to see done with a million—the building of a school in which students from all walks of life could acquire the skills needed in a new age of technology and therefore better both themselves and all of humanity.

The story of what happened next has two versions. In the first, Armour invited Gunsaulus to lunch to discuss the idea. In the second, he burst into the parson's study right after the service and said, "Young man, do you believe what you just preached?"

"I do, or I would not have preached it."

"I will give you a million dollars if you will give me five years of your life."

The agreement was that Armour would fund the dream school and Gunsaulus would run it.[5]

Armour, who had a fortune estimated at $25 million and was the richest man in Chicago, once said, "I don't want any more money. . . . I have more than I want. I do not love money. What I love is getting rid of it."[6] Like many of his contemporaries, he believed that one of the best ways to alleviate the social problems created by poverty and slums was to help the young, or at least the ones with aspirations. In addition, allowing poor students to mingle with the well-off would benefit both classes: one would profit from the example set by the better sort and the other would be shorn of their snobbery. Armour once said, "I like to turn bristles, blood, bones, and the insides of pigs and bullocks into revenue now, for I can turn the revenue into these boys and girls, and they will go on forever."[7]

Philip Danforth Armour was in 1893 the richest man in Chicago. (ICHi-62463, Chicago History Museum)

Joseph Francis Armour, the millionaire's brother, had been an active member of Plymouth Congregational Church long before Gunsaulus arrived and had helped found a mission on State Street near Thirty-Fifth that was run by the church's Sunday school department. When Joseph died in 1881, he left the mission $100,000 in his will. Philip Armour determined to see that the money was well spent, and on December 5, 1886, the new Armour Mission, the largest of its kind in the country, opened in a fine new building designed by Burnham and Root. *Rand, McNally & Co.'s Handy Guide to Chicago*, published in 1893, described it as follows:

The basement is occupied by a kindergarten, creche, work-rooms for boys and girls, and a free dispensary, open daily to the poor. On the first floor are two large classrooms, flanking the main hall and stairway. These rooms are each about twenty-five feet square, and there is on the same floor a large assembly hall, about eighty feet square, and forty-five feet high, fitted with gallery and stage.... Opening into this hall, on the line of the gallery, and situated above the class-rooms just mentioned, is a large room, about 30 × 80 feet, intended to be used as a lyceum.... The object is industrial, moral, mental, and religious training for the poor of the neighborhood, the religious instruction being "non-sectarian."[8]

Gunsaulus was a frequent visitor to the mission, and he observed that the rooms containing the secular classes were overcrowded—another factor that convinced him of the need for a new school. In 1886, Armour also opened the Armour Flats (now demolished), also designed by Patton and Fisher. This was a group of twenty-nine three-story and four-story buildings containing 194 apartments for middle-class renters. The plan was that the rents would provide an income for the mission.

So it made sense that when Philip Armour decided to found a school he would place it near the mission. In 1892, Gunsaulus and his brother-in-law traveled to Germany, where they visited the new technical school at Charlottenburg. What Gunsaulus saw there altered his plans for the new school. At first he had envisioned it as a place where students would learn to become mechanics and technicians; but Charlottenburg was an engineering school, and Gunsaulus decided that the Armour Institute should be one too. Gunsaulus reasoned that for a country to develop into an industrial power it needed professional engineers.[9]

To ensure that the students were prepared, Armour took care to establish a preparatory school, the Armour Scientific Academy, which enrolled a class of four hundred boys and girls a month before the opening of the institute itself. "The religion of Armour Institute will be sixteen ounces to the pound, but undenominational," Armour said, "and it makes no difference to me whether its converts are baptized in a soup bowl, a pond, or the Chicago River."[10]

The cornerstone was laid in 1891, and the building was finished late in the following year.[11] In 1901, a companion building, Machinery Hall, was added across the street.[12] When in 2004 the Commission on Chicago Landmarks approved landmark status for both buildings, it described them as "fine examples of the Romanesque Revival architectural style, sharing a common visual aesthetic of deep red brick and sandstone walls, red terra cotta and molded-brick trim, and picturesque round-arched windows and entrances. Although once a common style for late 19th-century institutional buildings, the Main Building and Machinery Hall survive as rare, large-scale Chicago examples of the style as used for college buildings."[13]

Machinery Hall at the Illinois Institute of Technology, completed in 1901 and also designed by Patton and Fisher, is a companion to the Main Building. (Photograph by the author)

At the opening of the school, Gunsaulus duly gave a ring-ing oration, but Armour himself sat at the rear of the dais. The students clamored for a speech from the meat packer–philanthropist, but he smiled and declined. Armour did not consider himself a public speaker; he was content that he had finally witnessed the birth of the right kind of school—one that would, as Gunsaulus put it in his speech, "show how to make life worth living," rather than "how to make a living."[14] The school began with nine departments—scientific academy, electrical engineering, mechanical engineering, mining and metallurgical engineering, kindergarten, library science, com-merce, art, and domestic arts, which, with an enrollment of a hundred women, was the largest department. The domestic arts department, reported one newspaper, was "divided into educational and technical courses. The former is for those who merely wish to learn household work, and the latter is intended for persons who wish to become proficient as teachers or as professional milliners or dressmakers."[15] The faculty numbered twenty-six full-time teachers and seven special lecturers. W. M. Stine, the chairman of the electrical engineering department,

The Electricity Building at the Columbian Exposition. Philip Armour considered electricity the dominant technology of the age, and the Armour Institute purchased many of the exhibits. (Library of Congress)

was also on the jury that judged the electrical exhibits at the Columbian Exposition, and he took advantage of his position. The *Chicago Inter Ocean* reported that in the Electricity Building at the fair, "Armour Institute purchase tags are tied on almost everything worth having."[16]

Soon after the school opened, Arthur Warren, a writer for *McClure's Magazine*, paid a visit.[17] "A large and handsome building of red brick, trimmed with brownish stone, and open on all sides to the light and air, is the home of the Institute," he wrote. "It is a hive of pleasant lecture-rooms and spacious laboratories." He explained that the school was not free, but "the terms of tuition are so low that any one who is determined to get an education can easily defray the cost of it." He went on to say, "If he or she have no money for this purpose, then the term charges can be worked out, or an undertaking can be given that after graduating from the Institute and finding employment, the charges will be paid in the course of time. For there is this healthy fundamental idea about the work—it is devoid of all appearance of charity."

Armour and Gunsaulus themselves guided the visitor. Warren wrote that "While he was showing us the Institute that morning, a class of bright-faced youths came unexpectedly tumbling out from one of the lecture- rooms, and as we paused to watch the merry groups, a sort of quiet smile played over Mr. Armour's face; his eyes twinkled with pleasure, and then he turned to me and said: 'This is worth living for.'" Warren saw the electrical experiments and the girls' classes and especially noted the immigrant students. "We want to make some fine Americans out of rough material," Armour told him. On the top floor of the building, the visitor had a look at the cooking school, which was surprisingly important to Armour, who said, "This is a vital spot. We do not sufficiently appreciate in this country the national importance of cooks. There are plenty of people who can paint well and sing well, but there are few who can cook well." Finally, Armour said, "The institute has been open ten days, and I am already ten years younger."

The Rise of Philip D. Armour

Perhaps one reason that Armour was so keen on the value of an education was that he was disappointed in his own. Armour was born in Stockbridge, New York, on May 16, 1832. After going to a nearby primary school, at age fourteen he entered the Cazenovia Academy, where he showed little interest in learning. On one occasion, he took a girl, a fellow student, out buggy riding; the faculty deemed the hour too late for such an outing and voted to expel Armour, who thereupon went to work for a neighboring farmer, his formal education ended. Many years later, when Armour was one of the most powerful men in the United States, an elderly gentleman appeared in his LaSalle Street office. The reason he was there, he explained, was that "I was the only member of the faculty to vote against your expulsion." Armour replied curtly: "It took you a damn long time to tell me that."

In January 1848, gold was discovered in California, and four years later, Armour headed west. He worked first as a miner and then as a contractor selling water and digging water ditches. In four years, he accumulated $6,000 and then headed back east. He went home briefly (he discovered that his buggy companion had gotten married) and then moved to Milwaukee, where his brother Herman had already set up a business. Philip Armour opened a soap factory, but after it burned down, he moved to St. Paul. He made a little money there, returned to Milwaukee, and partnered in a grocery and grain business with a friend. In 1862, Armour visited Cincinnati and saw how the meat packers were thriving by filling orders for the Union army. While there, he found a bride, Malvina Belle Ogden. Back in Milwaukee, Armour formed another enterprise, this time in partnership with John Plankinton, an experienced butcher. This alliance was the beginning of the Armour empire. Armour followed the course of the Civil War closely and after the battle of Gettysburg became convinced that a Union victory was inevitable, which meant a drop in the price of pork. He contracted to sell pork for $40 a barrel, and when the price did indeed fall, he was able to fulfill that contract with pork that cost him $18 a barrel. He made about a million dollars, and he had established himself as a man to be reckoned with.

Philip Armour was not the only one in his family with commercial talents. He had four brothers who went into related businesses—Simeon, Andrew, Herman (also known as H.O.), and Joseph (a brother named Charles was killed in the Civil War). Simeon and Andrew settled in Kansas City, where they owned a packing company and a bank. In 1865, Herman went into business in New York, where he handled Philip's eastern financial contacts. But before going east, Herman had opened a packing business in Chicago, and upon Herman's departure, Joseph took it over. When Joseph's health weakened, Philip came to Chicago in 1875 to step in, although he still maintained operations in Milwaukee.

The Chicago firm was already large, but Philip turned it into the largest packing company in the world. By the end of the 1890s, Armour was employing some fifteen thousand workers and had a payroll between $6 million and $10 million a year. On the side of his refrigerated railroad cars was the slogan "We Feed the World."

Hog Butcher for the World

In 1893, the stockyards and the surrounding district of "Packingtown" were Chicago's number one tourist attraction. Visitor after visitor came away astonished by its efficiency, its scope, and its ghastliness. The French actress Sarah Bernhardt summed up her visit as "horrendous but fascinating,"[18] and others were driven to deep musings on death. As the novelist Upton Sinclair expressed it, "One could not stand and watch very long without becoming philosophical, without beginning to deal in symbols and similes, and to hear the hog-squeal of the universe."[19] In 1893, one-fifth of Chicago's population was in one way or another connected to the meatpacking industry.[20] From the time of the "big three" of the industry—Armour, Gustavus Swift, and Nelson Morris—until the stockyards closed in 1971, the meatpacking business practically defined Chicago in the eyes of outsiders.[21]

Chicago became the nation's meatpacking capital because it was also the railroad capital. Railroads linked the cattle raisers of the West and Midwest to the markets of the East (and Europe). The animals were ferried by rail to Chicago, where they

The great Union Stock Yards were Chicago's biggest tourist attraction in the 1890s.
(Library of Congress)

were slaughtered and processed, and trains hauled the packaged meat out. To consolidate operations, entrepreneurs opened the Union Stock Yard on Christmas Day 1865. This huge facility received all the animal shipments for the packers, who opened their plants nearby. By 1893, the Union Stock Yard was receiving some twelve million hogs and cattle every year; over the course of its existence, it is reckoned that more than one billion animals passed through the facility. In 1870, the packers were proud that the value of their products was about $19 million; twenty years later the value had increased tenfold, to some $194 million.[22] A "Stockyards settlement" quickly grew up near the plants in order to house thousands of workers, who lived in neighborhoods such as Back of the Yards, Town of Lake, New City, and Englewood.[23]

Armour famously described himself as "just a butcher trying to go to Heaven." He said, "I can stand a lot for my hide is thick. . . . That is the result of my early habits. I was raised like a farmer and I still have a pitcher of water in the center of the table as we used to at home."[24] But more than just a smart, hard-working businessman, he was a technological innovator. One of his most astute accomplishments was the utilization of the whole hog, as it were. Whereas earlier packers discarded what they considered worthless byproducts, Armour found uses for, as he put it, "all but the squeal." As Armour himself explained it:

> So recently as twenty-five years ago, in Chicago, the blood was allowed to run into the river, and men were paid five dollars a load to cart the heads, feet, tankage, and other waste material upon the prairie and there bury it in pits and trenches. Instead of being a source of profit, the offal, in this respect, was a distinct source of expense. . . . The large packing establishments of to-day manipulate their own horns, hoofs, bones, sinews, hide-trimmings, etc., in their own glue works. The sweet fat of the cattle forms the basis of butterines [margarines], made in their own butterine factories; the sheep pelts are scoured, and the wool removed in their own wool-houses, cleansed, and sold direct to the large Eastern cloth-mills. The intestines are cleansed and salted and used for sausage casing in their own sausage factories. The blood and all animal refuse are treated in their own fertilizer factories . . . and in one or two packing houses there has been established a laboratory where the inner lining of the hog's stomach is made into pepsin.[25]

The French novelist Paul Bourget, who visited Chicago in 1894, reported a contemporary witticism to the effect that "a pig that went to the abattoir at Chicago came out fifteen minutes later in the form of ham, sausages, large and small, hair oil, and binding for a Bible."[26] Other items that emerged from Armour's factories were buttons, hairbrushes, and pharmaceuticals. By 1893, his plants covered thirty acres. Armour was also in the forefront in the development of tin cans for the vacuum packing

As John T. McCutcheon's cartoon shows, Chicago's meatpackers in the 1890s had most efficient ways of turning pigs into products. (*The French Emissary Studies Our Industrial Methods*. Originally printed in the *Chicago Record-Herald*. The complete series of "French Emissary" cartoons was published in *Cartoons by McCutcheon* [Chicago: A. C. McClurg, 1903].)

of meat products and of refrigerated railroad cars, which had been pioneered by Gustavus F. Swift. By 1900, Armour owned some eleven hundred refrigerated cars.[27]

Before the advent of refrigeration, butchers in the East bought animals from nearby cattle raisers and slaughtered them themselves, providing their customers with the freshest meat. The Chicago packers were able to sell pre-cut refrigerated "dressed" beef at lower prices, and a whole eastern industry of local packers, wholesalers, and butchers disappeared almost overnight.[28] And Chicago's packers were not content with conquering the

East; they soon would be shipping their products to Europe and beyond. The Chicago meat packers not only transformed their city, they also profoundly changed the nation. The prairies in the High Plains of the West were turned into cattle country, and millions of buffalo were slaughtered to make room for the steers. The great cattle drives, beloved of cowboy movies, were instituted to bring the cattle to the railroad and then to Chicago, and acres and acres of farmland were given over the raising of corn for feeding both cattle and hogs.

Historians of technology credit Henry Ford as the one who perfected the assembly line, but Ford's innovation was previewed decades before by what might be called Armour's "disassembly line." Armour didn't invent the process, but he refined it into what might be called a science. It was the kind of rationalization of production that preceded much of twentieth-century mechanization.[29] In the disassembly line, the hog, after it was killed, was moved along a course in which each worker had a specific task to fulfill, over and over again, until the animal was completely processed. On an assembly line, an automobile is put together. On a disassembly line, a hog is taken apart.

Chicago: College Town

In 1893, *Rand, McNally & Co.'s Handy Guide to Chicago* surveyed the educational scene in Chicago and reported: "It is greatly to the credit of Chicago, the distinguishing characteristic of which has been said to be the pursuit of wealth with an energy and a singleness of purpose almost unexampled, to have made the splendid provision it has for the education of the young. Two hundred and fifty-three public, primary, grammar, and high schools; fifteen colleges of law, medicine, and theology; half-a-dozen academies of art and science, and two universities are not the marks of a community wholly given up to the acquisition of wealth."[30] The guide had much to say about the brand-new University of Chicago, which in 1893 was just concluding its first year. Had the University of Chicago opened three months later than it did, it would have had its own chapter in this book, with its admittedly artificial parameters. But although it officially opened on October 1, 1892, mention must be made of this university, still Chicago's most prestigious.

The 1892 University of Chicago had been preceded by an earlier University of Chicago, which had been founded in 1857 but went bankrupt in 1886, although not before the trustees appealed to the great oil magnate John D. Rockefeller for help. The institution was Baptist, so was John D., and he agreed to fund a new one in a different location. Rockefeller eventually would contribute $35 million. The school's president was William Rainey Harper, one of the most distinguished scholars in the nation, and the faculty was similarly illustrious. Harper wanted the school to be the equal of any in the Ivy League or even the greatest of British universities—at first architect Henry Ives Cobb meant to use the same Romanesque Revival style employed by Patton and Fisher, but he was persuaded to use instead the Gothic Revival style: limestone buildings arranged around quadrangles, which would be more evocative of Oxford and Cambridge.

Chicago has quietly become one of the great university cities in the world, an enormous "college town."

When the second University of Chicago opened in 1892, Northwestern University in Evanston was already forty-two years old. Lake Forest College, just north of Evanston, had been founded in 1857; Wheaton College had opened in 1860; and Plainfield College (now North Central College in Naperville) had come along a year later. The School of the Art Institute of Chicago dates as far back as 1882. The Roman Catholics were also creating their own institutions of higher learning—Saint Xavier (1846), Barat (1858), St. Ignatius (1879, later renamed Loyola), and St. Vincent's (1898), now DePaul, which is the nation's largest Catholic university. The twentieth century saw the establishment of many more colleges and universities in Chicago—the University of Illinois at Chicago, Roosevelt University, Chicago State, Robert Morris, Northeastern Illinois University, and Harold Washington College (originally Loop College). The Columbia School of Oratory (1890) became Columbia College in 1944 and today has more than twelve thousand students.

Chicago has quietly become one of the great university cities in the world, an enormous "college town." In 2005, researchers at DePaul released a study of higher education in Chicago's Loop and South Loop.[31] They began by saying, "The first thing to say about higher education in Chicago's Loop/South Loop is that there is more of it than almost anyone expected to find at the outset of this study." They counted twenty-one institutions in the area (this number is flexible as schools constantly move in and move out), with a total of 52,230 students. The researchers calculated that the total direct and indirect effect on economic output in the Chicago area was nearly \$1.3 billion. This study was updated in 2009; at that time, twenty-five institutions of higher learning were counted, with an enrollment of 65,524, an increase of 25 percent.[32] The researchers wrote that sixteen reporting institutions had spent over \$857 million on goods and services in the five-year period since the 2005 study, compared to the previous figure of just over \$345 million, an increase of 148 percent. They also reported that twelve institutions were using over eight million square feet of space, or more than two Willis Towers.[33] And all this activity is just in the Loop/South Loop. The University of Illinois at Chicago (UIC), which is not far away, has more than twenty-five thousand students. The list of Chicago's colleges, universities, and technical training schools is huge. As city planner Richard Galehouse has pointed out, "In many ways, *intellectual* might now competes with industrial might as the engine of growth for American cities. In Burnham's era, power was held by great Chicago dynasties such as Wrigley, Armour, Field, and McCormick and their associated enterprises. Now we look to fields such as biotechnology, computer science, and other disciplines that are, almost by definition, tied to colleges and universities."[34] Because of efforts by education visionaries like Armour and Gunsaulus, Chicago has been able to place itself in a position of intellectual and academic strength.

The Merger

With its seven hundred students, the Armour Institute was off to a fine start. In July 1894, the *Chicago Evening Post* reviewed the school's first year and reported: "Mr. Armour and Dr. Gunsaulus feel greatly encouraged to say that the expenditure of nearly $100,000 this year, outside of equipment which cost about $300,000, has been entirely justified by the results"[35] A department of civil engineering was added in 1899, and chemical engineering was added two years later. The course in metallurgical and mining engineering was dropped, and the library science department was closed. This latter action meant a reduction in the number of women students, a development that reportedly greatly displeased the men. Things got even worse for the men when courses in shorthand and typing were discontinued, the kindergarten department was closed, and, finally, in June 1901, the domestic arts department shut its doors. The school now enrolled few women at all.

When Philip Armour died in 1901, one of his sons, J. Ogden Armour, quickly quelled fears that the family might lose interest in the school by announcing a donation of $1 million. About a hundred happy students, buoyed by the realization that this meant the continuance of low tuition, celebrated the news by running outside in their nightshirts, clambering aboard a southbound El (without paying), and alarming the passengers with their unrestrained cheers. The next morning, fifty-nine rioters were hauled before a judge, but the railroad's lawyer had the charges dropped. A newspaper explained, "Youth must have its fling and boys will be boys. There is nothing the matter with the Armour Institute boys. Please forgive them."[36]

Three years after the opening of the Armour Institute, a similar school opened on Chicago's West Side—the Lewis Institute, which had been funded by a bequest made by Allen C. Lewis, a Chicago entrepreneur. His will stated that the institute should offer "courses of a kind and character not generally taught in public schools . . . studies that would be directly useful to students in obtaining a position or occupation for life."[37] The Lewis Institute has been called the first junior college in the United States.[38] By the time of the depression of the 1930s, both the Armour Institute and the Lewis Institute were in debt. The boards of trustees approved a merger, and the two schools united in July 1940 with the new name of Illinois Institute of Technology (IIT).

Mies Remakes the Campus

A great number of students and admirers of architecture visit the campus of IIT today, but it's doubtful that many are coming to see the work of Patton and Fisher. This tour is for those who wish to see the work of the man who is considered in most quarters to be the titan of modern architecture in the twentieth century—Ludwig Mies van der Rohe (1886–1969), the champion of the minimalist "glass box," who will be forever linked with the city of Chicago. It was in Chicago that Mies built some of his most celebrated structures, and many consider the finest of Mies's Chicago buildings to be Crown Hall at IIT.[39]

Born in Aachen, Germany, in 1886, Mies van der Rohe had been the director of the famous Bauhaus from 1930 to 1933.[40] As the atmosphere in Nazi Germany grew increasingly hostile to modern art, Mies was drawn to America. On a trip through Chicago he met the architect John Holabird, who was seeking someone to head the School of Architecture at the Armour Institute. Holabird told the president of the institute that he didn't know Mies personally, but he knew his work. As he put

Crown Hall at the Illinois Institute of Technology is considered one of Mies van der Rohe's greatest buildings.
(Photograph by the author)

it, "He is so much better than any of the people you could get to head a school of architecture, why not take a chance?"[41] An agreement was made, and Mies moved permanently to Chicago in 1938. Soon after Mies took the job at Armour, the president, Henry Heald, decided that Mies should design an entire new campus covering eight city blocks. Today, IIT boasts twenty buildings designed by Mies, and in 2005, the entire campus was placed on the National Register of Historic Places.

Philip Armour would undoubtedly be delighted to see today's students working on projects in the Illinois Institute of Technology's Crown Hall.
(Photograph by the author)

It's difficult to say what Philip Armour would have thought of today's campus. On the one hand, he was an advocate of technology and efficiency, and if Mies's buildings are about anything, they're about that. Yet it's doubtful whether he would have appreciated or understood Mies's "less is more" minimalism. That the name Armour is no longer on the school might displease him, although he was not the kind of person given to self-promotion. However, one thing cannot be doubted. If he could walk into Crown Hall and gaze at those hard-working young students, both men and women, hunched over their drafting tables, thinking, learning, and testing new ideas, he would be as happy as he was when the Armour Institute was ten days old and he felt ten years younger.

8

The Birth of Urban Literature

The February 1893 issue of the *New England Magazine* carried an article entitled "Literary Chicago." Written by William Morton Payne, it stated that the city was emerging from its rough-and-tumble origins and was launching "the positive growth of the literary spirit." However, of the three dozen or so writers the author listed as examples of Chicago's literary accomplishments, all are now either unknown or the subject of specialists, except perhaps three—Henry Blake Fuller, Eugene Field, and Harriet Monroe. The author admitted that the achievements he described were meager, but he expected that the future would be bright: "Chicago is still mewing her mighty youth, and what she has done as yet towards the production of literature is but the merest foretaste of what the future may reasonably be expected to bring."

Payne couldn't have known it, but the future was coming fast. Before 1893 was over, three Chicago writers would signal a new direction in American letters—a literature of the city, one that employed urban themes; examined the social, cultural, and economic life of the metropolis; and employed the jargon of the streets. A mere ten years after Payne's article, the novelist and critic William Dean Howells wrote in the *North American Review* that no group of American writers compared with the "admirable artists" in Chicago. In praising what he called the "Chicago School of Fiction," Howells stated that the city's writers were "ahead of New York in a direction where none, possibly, would be more surprised than Chicago to find them in the van."[1] And by 1917, H. L. Mencken was hailing the city as the literary capital of the United States, the home of the nation's most original authors. "I give you Chicago," he said. "It is not London-and-Harvard. It is not Paris-and-buttermilk. It is American in every chitling and sparerib, and it is alive from snout to tail."[2]

Henry Blake Fuller

The first Chicago writer cited by Mencken was Henry Blake Fuller (1857–1929), whom he called "the first American novelist to get away from the moony old spinsters of New England and depict the actual human beings of America." The statement is an indication of how high was once the reputation of Fuller, who is no longer widely known. The publication of Fuller's *The Cliff-Dwellers* in 1893 brought something new— an actual urban novel, literally from basement to cornice, and a book of many protagonists, of which the most commanding was not a person but a building, a skyscraper that presided over the affairs of the scuttling, grasping, insecure cliff-dwellers who toiled inside its towering walls.[3]

Henry Fuller was, as Henry Regnery has expressed it, "not the first Chicago writer, but the first Chicago writer to win national recognition as a literary figure."[4] The accuracy of this evaluation explains why Fuller usually comes first, or nearly so, in surveys of the history of Chicago literature. Yet the city had produced a number of published authors before Fuller.[5] Early publications include Horatio

The Chicago writer Henry Blake Fuller, whose groundbreaking novel *The Cliff-Dwellers* was published in 1893, was one of literature's first "urban realists."
(ICHi-10342, Chicago History Museum)

Cooke's *Gleanings of Thought* (1843), the first book of poetry published in the city, and William Asbury Kenyon's *Miscellaneous Poems, to which are added writings in prose on various subjects* (1845). This volume contained such poems as "A Prairie Song" and "A Winter Morning on the Prairie." A literary weekly entitled the *Gem of the Prairie* appeared in Chicago in 1844; it was the first of many literary periodicals in Chicago's history, a trend that culminated with the *Dial* of 1880, which became the leading literary magazine in the United States, and, later, the *Chap-Book* (1894–98).

Wau-bun, the "Early Day" in the North-West (1856) by Juliette Augusta Magill Kinzie, daughter-in-law of Chicago pioneer John Kinzie, is sometimes described as the first Chicago novel, but three works of fiction preceded it. *The Banditti of the Prairies* and *The War Scout of Eighteen Hundred Twelve* both appeared in 1850; the author of *Banditti* is uncertain; it was either Edward Bonney or Henry A. Clark. Clark was, however, the undisputed author of *The War Scout*. Also appearing in 1850 was John Richardson's *Hardscrabble; or, The Fall of Chicago; A Tale of Indian Warfare*. Richardson's subsequent novel, *Wau-Nan-Gee; or, The Massacre at Chicago: A Romance of the American Revolution* (1852), earned the author praise in some quarters as the heir of James Fenimore Cooper.[6]

Chicago authors published numerous other novels before 1893.[7] Another historical saga was *Prairie Fire: A Tale of Early Illinois* (1854) by William H. Bushnell. In 1866, J. E. Chamberlain published the novel *Cotton Stealing*, an exposé of the cotton trade.[8] The year 1887 brought four noteworthy frontier romances—Joseph Kirkland's *Zury, the Meanest Man in Spring County*; John McGovern's *Burritt Durand*; William Bross's *Tom Quick, Legend of the Delaware*; and *Theophilus Trent: Old Times in the Oak Openings* by Benjamin Franklin Taylor. Although such novels pleased older readers, they had little relevance for young people who had come to Chicago to escape rustic drudgery. It was readers of this type that the newer writers cultivated as they sought to fashion stories set in the challenging new world of the city.

In his survey of Chicago literature, Hugh Dalziel Duncan wrote that "between 1872 and 1890, a dozen novels, including three novels of the Fire" attempted to forge a new kind of literature reflecting life in the new urban metropolis.[9] One such book was *Barriers Burned Away* (1872), a novel of the fire by the widely popular E. P. Roe (it was said that he sold more books than Mark Twain). Roe's book was one of the first to sound a theme that would become increasingly familiar: the story of a young person who arrives in the city from the country and must learn to avoid its traps. Kenny J. Williams has argued that with the appearance of Roe's opus, "there was a 'Chicago novel' which was destined to continue to the present day."[10]

Hobart C. Chatfield-Taylor's *With Edge Tools* (1891) was what might be called a genteel novel of manners, but it took a cynical look at the city's social structure. As one of the main female characters expresses it, in Chicago "one has the choice . . . between parvenu vulgarity and Puritanic narrow-mindedness. . . . I actually believe one would find the pork-packers more distracting." Although much of *With Edge Tools* is set in Chicago and offers some insightful comments on it, it is not a "Chicago novel" in the sense that it gives a vivid and varied picture of life in the city. Its plot centers on a bounder named Duncan Grahame who preys on married women. His designs on a Chicagoan named Marion Sanderson are foiled, however, when she comes to realize that her husband is smarter, more capable, and more honorable than her tempting suitor. Opie Read's *The Colossus*, published, like Fuller's *The Cliff-Dwellers*, in 1893, took a major step toward urban realism by describing the affairs of businessmen.

Several woman writers were active in Chicago before 1893. Some wrote what might be called "family dynasty" novels, although Mary Healy Bigot's *Lakeville* (1873) took a candid look at Chicago and the status of women in the 1870s. *Shadowed by Three* (1879) by Emma Murdock Deventer and *For Her Daily Bread* (1887) by Lillian Sommers sounded the theme of the "new woman"—the resolute heroine who comes to the city and learns to deal with it on its own terms. For example, Norma Southstone in *For Her Daily Bread* boldly enters, and succeeds in, the male-dominated world of Chicago business. Kathryn

Donelson's *Rodger Latimer's Mistake* (1891), which follows the fortunes of a young man who comes to Chicago fresh out of Harvard, contrasts the vacant life of those who pursue money with the idealism of the social worker. *A Wilful Heiress* (1892) by Emma Scarr Booth has been called a good account "of the stringent legal, social, and moral code by which women were bound in the latter half of the nineteenth century."[11]

Despite all this activity, the output of fiction in Chicago before the 1890s remained small in comparison to eastern cities. That would change dramatically. According to Duncan, one study of Chicago literature counted forty-eight authors of books written in the city from 1890 to 1900. These writers created 175 books, ninety-seven of which were published in Chicago.[12]

Leading the charge was Henry Blake Fuller. If today Fuller is mostly a footnote in the history of American literature, he should not be. He was a trailblazer for what might be called the school of American realism. Stephen Crane's gritty *Maggie: A Girl of the Streets*, often hailed as a pioneering work of American realism (or naturalism) appeared in 1893—the same year as Fuller's *The Cliff-Dwellers*. The father of American realism, William Dean Howells, preceded nearly everyone, but it was Howells himself who compared Fuller to Émile Zola and hailed *The Cliff-Dwellers* and *With the Procession* as masterpieces of realism. In Howells's opinion, no writer in the East compared with Fuller "in scale and quality of work."[13] When we think of American realism, we think of Frank Norris, Theodore Dreiser, Upton Sinclair, Hamlin Garland, and so on, but Fuller preceded all of them.[14]

Fuller went beyond Howells in turning a scathing eye on the urban environment itself. The main protagonist of *The Cliff-Dwellers* is not a person, but a building, the Clifton—the malevolent skyscraper that encased its inhabitants like a cage. In that regard, Fuller is at the forefront of urban literature. As Carl S. Smith put it, "Fuller's most original achievement was that he shaped a whole novel around this landscape which he found so appalling. . . . Fuller skillfully uses the Clifton as the objectification of the field of social movement and aspiration in Chicago."[15]

William Dean Howells, the father of American realism, compared Henry Blake Fuller to Émile Zola and hailed Fuller's *The Cliff-Dwellers* as a masterpiece. (Library of Congress)

Unlike so many who made their fame and fortune in Chicago in the nineteenth century, Fuller was actually born there—on January 9, 1857. Fuller's grandfather, who was born in Northampton, Massachusetts, settled in Chicago in 1849. He became successful in various ventures, especially railroading and real estate, and also served as a judge. His son, George Wood Fuller, became a bank vice president. Henry Fuller was a shy, quiet lad; complicating matters was his development of a speech impediment. Although he was an excellent student, he did not pursue his education past high school. He was an aesthete and hungered for the Grand Tour of Europe. He set off from Chicago on August 17, 1879, financing the journey with money he had earned working in his father's bank. The trip gave Fuller an educational and artistic awakening, and he managed to stay away for almost a year, visiting Britain, France, Italy, Switzerland, Germany, Belgium, and the Netherlands. He revered Rome most of all, and for the rest of his life, Italy and Chicago would be the twin poles of his sensibility (he returned to Europe in 1883 for a second tour).

Although he was already an avid reader of Henry James and William Dean Howells, his first novel was not a study of American manners but a suave Italian romance entitled *The Chevalier of Pensieri-Vani*. The book is about an American midwesterner named George Occident who journeys to Italy and encounters a stereotypical group of Europeans: in addition to the Chevalier of the title, there's the British duke of Avon and Severn; a German nobleman from Schwahlbach-Schrekenstein; a French aristocrat; and a German historian who specializes in Roman history. Despite the appeal of all these sophisticated personalities, Occident concludes (as Fuller did) that his future lies in the United States. Fuller might have been describing himself when he wrote, "He delighted in the pictorial aspects of the Southern civilizations, but he was by no means blind to the merits of his own, and he felt that the more he defended the social scheme of which he was a part, the more he would be obliged to defend himself for having detached himself from it."[16]

The Chevalier of Pensieri-Vani was published in 1890 and was hailed by two of Boston's elite literati—Charles Eliot Norton of Harvard and James Russell Lowell, who were surprised and delighted that such a charming book could emerge from such a rough environment as Chicago. Chicagoans were in turn pleased that one of their own could so impress the Eastern establishment; in July 1891, the *Chicago Tribune* proudly noted that the book was a triumph in New York and that an editor there had hailed the "discovery of a new genius."[17] Fuller followed *The Chevalier* with a similar romance called *The Chatelaine of La Trinité*, which was completed in August 1891. This book, set mostly in Switzerland, was, he said, "meant to do for the Alps . . . what its predecessor had done for Italy itself."[18] Like *The Chevalier*, the book deals with a young American—a woman named Aurelia West—who interacts rather brashly with a group of distinguished Europeans. Fuller's second novel was not as enthusiastically received as his first, and he abandoned plans to write a third romance, this one set in Spain. One does get the impression that, though these novels were brief, he had pretty much exhausted that vein of amused observation of charming European aesthetes. He became an entirely different writer.

Fuller, like so many, admired the neoclassical architecture of the 1893 Columbian Exposition with its European overtones, but the exposition also prompted him to contrast it with the other Chicago, the city of skyscrapers, corruption, immigrants, and the unrelenting pursuit of wealth. The result was *The Cliff-Dwellers*, which Fuller called his "magnum opus" and "my first essay in 'realism'" and which prompted Hamlin Garland to say that Fuller "had beaten the realists at their own game."[19] Fuller set to work in the middle of January 1893 and finished the novel in just six weeks; it was serialized in *Harper's* in the summer and appeared in book form in the late fall.

The cliff-dwellers are those who work in an eighteen-story skyscraper called the Clifton. The plot of the book is complicated—Kenneth Scambray has counted no fewer than "thirteen married couples of various ages that play significant roles in the novel" (nearly all put the institution of marriage in a bad light).[20] The core of the plot concerns one George Ogden, who comes to Chicago from New England and finds himself torn between two prospective brides—Abbie Brainard, who is bright and compatible but who comes from a family of dubious character, and Jessie Bradley, a superficial woman who aspires to social status and makes profligate purchases to help secure it. Ogden marries Jessie and learns bitterly how ambitious women can help secure the ruin of their husbands. Describing Cecilia Ingles, the wife of the developer of the Clifton, Fuller writes, "It is for such a woman that one man builds a Clifton and that a hundred others are martyred in it." Another main character is Ogden's employer, the cold-hearted Erastus Brainard. Brainard's conflict with his artistic son, Marcus, parallels Fuller's own tensions with his businessman father (Marcus, however, kills his father with a paper cutter). Another revealing character is Cornelia McNabb, an example of one of those spunky, ambitious midwestern girls who were arriving in Chicago every day in 1893. Beginning as a waitress, she eventually becomes a stenographer and then snares the ultimate prize—she marries Brainard's son Burton and goes to live in a faux chateau on Lake Shore Drive.

Howells's review of *The Cliff-Dwellers* in *Harper's Bazaar* compared Fuller to Zola and Henry James, called the novel "a work of very great power," and hailed the "rich poetry of the imagination."[21] In a letter to Fuller, Howells exhorted him to write more novels of Chicago, "whether you like it or not," which is what Fuller did. *With the Procession*, an arguably stronger work than *The Cliff-Dwellers*, appeared in 1895.[22] The "procession" referred to in the title is the grand pageant of society, and Fuller satirizes the need to keep up "with the procession" as one of the most distasteful facets of Chicago's social order. The novel follows the fortunes of the Marshall family. David, the businessman patriarch, is one of the "old settlers" who resent the aggressive, money-seeking, conspicuous consumers of the generation that came to great wealth after the Great Fire. His son Truesdale is an aesthete recently returned from the Grand Tour who paints in the modern style. Although Fuller portrays him as idle and self-important, they share many qualities, not least their jaded view of Chicago. Truesdale's assessment of the city is "so little taste, so little training, so little education, so total an absence of any collective sense of the fit and the proper!" One of David Marshall's daughters, the pretty Rosamund, manages to fulfill her social ambitions by ensnaring a lower-level English aristocrat. The other, Jane, falls under the spell of one of Chicago's wealthiest women, Mrs. Granger Bates. As she tells Jane,

"Keep up with the procession is my motto, and head it if you can. I *do* head it, and I feel that I'm where I belong." Spurred to ambition, Jane persuades her father to build a newer, more opulent mansion, forcing him to leave the old homestead that he loved.

For the most part, reviewers greeted *With the Procession* with the same keenness with which they had praised *The Cliff-Dwellers.* Some were pleased to note that a more rounded portrayal of the characters softened somewhat the harshness of the earlier novel. In his review, Howells said that Fuller "was himself born to the manner of the people he depicts, and the wonder in this case is that he is able to regard them sufficiently aloof to get them and their belongings into such true perspective." The critic James Huneker wrote, "The conflict of the old and new social order could not have been better done by Mr. Howells," adding, "in Fuller we have at last met the American novelist."[23]

James Huneker wrote ". . . in Fuller we have at last met the American novelist."

"The American novelist"—that's how illustrious Fuller's reputation was. However, his was a promise unfulfilled. After finishing *With the Procession*, Fuller would not complete another Chicago novel for twenty-two years. He was not entirely idle; he followed *With the Procession* with a volume of one-act plays entitled *The Puppet-Booth*, and he wrote a few short stories and many reviews and editorials. In 1899, he wrote *The New Flag*, a denunciation of the Spanish-American War and American imperialism, but few people knew about it or read it. A year later, he published another narrative set in Europe, *The Last Refuge: A Sicilian Romance*; it sold hardly at all. By the time Fuller finished his third Chicago novel, a slender volume entitled *On the Stairs*, in 1917, American letters had long passed him by. In 1927, Samuel Putnam, a writer for the *Chicagoan* magazine, penned a profile of the elderly Fuller in which he described his "merry" and "satiric" eyes, hailed his groundbreaking fiction, and noted that he looked a bit like Santa Claus. "He was the stylist in the wilderness," Putnam wrote. "His literary approach was the salad-fork. It was he who first told

Chicago to pull down her skirts; she was a big girl now. And do you think Chicago appreciated him? To this day, she doesn't even know there was a Santa Claus."[24]

Surprisingly, Fuller experienced an extraordinary burst of creativity at the very end of his life. In 1929, at age seventy-two, he completed not one, but two, novels—*Gardens of This World* (a travel romance) and *Not on the Screen* (a satire of the movie business)—and even began a third. It was a remarkable case of a flame burning brightest just before going out; Fuller died on July 19, 1929. As his biographer John Pilkington has said, "Fuller made his really significant contribution to American literature in the 1890s; the last thirty years of his life were, in the main, an anticlimax."[25]

Yet there is one intriguing footnote to Fuller's career. In 2000, he was inducted into the Chicago Gay and Lesbian Hall of Fame, and today his name has been kept alive by specialists in the cross-disciplinary academic specialty of gay and lesbian studies. Critics speculate that Fuller's feelings of not fitting in to Chicago society, his distrustful opinion of marriage, and his craving for privacy were due to his homosexuality. It is hardly surprising that he did not broadcast his sexual preference, but he did take the daring step of openly treating homosexuality in at least some of his fiction. One of the plays in *The Puppet-Booth*, "At Saint Judas's," describes how a young man forsakes his male lover to marry a woman, with tragic, melodramatic results. A broader treatment of the theme appeared in Fuller's novel *Bertram Cope's Year* (1919), which contains a subtle, veiled description of what might be called the "gay marriage" of Cope and Arthur Lemoyne. Fuller couldn't find a publisher and published the book at his own expense. Although the novel contains a comical scene in which Arthur performs in a theatrical presentation dressed as a woman and carries his characterization a bit too far, the few people who did read *Bertram Cope's Year* probably would have missed its sexual messages, homosexuality not then figuring prominently in cultural consciousness. The book went nowhere, but when it was reissued in 1998, it met with praise. Joel Connaroe, writing in the *New York Times*, described it as an "engaging and quite undeservedly neglected comedy of bad manners,"[26] and at the end of the year, the same newspaper placed Fuller's novel on its list of "Notable Books of 1998." It might be ironic that Fuller, who stood at the forefront of literary realism and might well be considered the father of the Chicago novel, should today be remembered mostly for an example of gay fiction, but such are the changing tastes of readers and historians of literature.

Finley Peter Dunne

Jacques Barzun, one of America's best-known cultural historians of the twentieth century, said of Chicago writer Finley Peter Dunne that his "political understanding and gift of satirical phrasing put him on a level with all the other American and English writers who made the 1890s an age of sagacity and wit." And he added, "It is a disgrace to American scholarship that he is not studied, and thus republished and enjoyed on a par with Mark Twain and Ambrose Bierce," and labeled the neglect of Dunne "a reproach to the American mind, that is to say the academics and the critics."[27]

It was on October 7, 1893, that Dunne introduced the readers of the *Chicago Evening Post* to one Martin Dooley, "a bachelor, saloon-keeper, and a Roscommon Irishman." The very first words out of the saloon-keeper's mouth burst like firecrackers, announcing a major new voice in American literature: "Hellow, Jawny. How's thricks? I don't mind, Jawny, if I do. 'Tis duller here than a raypublican primary in the fourth wa-ard, th' night. Sure, ye're like a ray iv sunlight, ye are that. There's been no company in these pa-arts since Dominick Riley's big gossoon was took up be the polis." Mr. Dooley would go on to become one of the most beloved fictional characters in early-twentieth-century America, and Dunne would become the most famous journalist of his day.

Mr. Dooley's saloon is located on Archer Avenue (or "Archey Road," as Mr. Dooley expresses it) in the Irish blue-collar neighborhood of Bridgeport, and it is from behind the bar that he expresses his wide range of opinion on just about any and all topics. If Dunne is no longer well known, many of Mr. Dooley's aphorisms are still widely quoted, especially by political analysts. What follows is just a sampling:

- Politics ain't beanbag.
- Thrust ivrybody—but cut th' ca-ards.
- A fanatic is a man that does what he thinks th' Lord wud do if He knew th' facts iv th' case.
- No matther whether th' constitution follows th' flag or not, th' supreme court follows th' illiction returns.
- I think a lie with a purpose is wan iv th' worst kind an' th' mos' profitable.
- Th' dimmycratic party ain't on speakin' terms with itself.
- I care not who makes th' laws iv a nation if I can get out an injunction.
- Life'd not be worth livin' if we didn't keep our inimies.
- An appeal is when ye ask wan court to show its contempt for another court.
- Vice goes a long way tow'rd makin' life bearable. A little vice now an' thin is relished by th' best iv men.
- Whiniver I see an aldherman an' a banker walkin' down th' sthreet together, I know th' Recordin' Angel will have to ordher another bottle iv ink.
- Th' newspaper does ivrything f'r us. It runs th' polis force an' th' banks, commands th' milishy, controls th' ligisla-chure, baptizes th' young, marries th' foolish, comforts th' afflicted, afflicts th' comfortable, buries th' dead an' roasts thim afterward. (The source of the adage "comfort the afflicted, afflict the comfortable.")

As the quotations illustrate, Mr. Dooley's wisdom is immortal, but his Irish brogue can be an obstacle, and, in fact, some lists of Mr. Dooley quotations are "translated" into contemporary English. Dunne's own son, Philip, conceded as much: "The Irish brogue in which he wrote, a blessing in days when people had time to read, enhancing as it did his wit and wisdom, has become a curse in these times when reading has been replaced by staring at the boob tube."[28]

Finley Peter Dunne won literary immortality with his creation in 1893 of Mr. Dooley, "a bachelor, saloon-keeper, and a Roscommon Irishman." (ICHi-10168, Chicago History Museum)

Like Henry Blake Fuller, Finley Peter Dunne was a native Chicagoan, born in the city on July 10, 1867. He was christened Peter Dunne but decided to add his mother's maiden name after she died while he was still in high school. His parents, Peter Dunne and Ellen Finley, had both been born in Ireland and had come to the United States as children. Dunne grew up in the Irish heart of Chicago (the parish of Old St. Patrick's). Once, when someone asked him if he was a Roman Catholic, Dunne replied that he was not—he was a Chicago Catholic. After graduating last in a high school class of fifty, he was hired by the *Telegram* at age sixteen as a newspaper office boy. He was soon assigned to cover the police beat, largely, it seems, because he would work for next to nothing and because he knew the streets of Chicago so well. Dunne worked for five newspapers before landing at the *Sunday Post*. Along the way he managed to revolutionize sportswriting during his stint covering the Chicago White Stockings. Previously, sports reporters tended to merely list the actions on the field, but Dunne employed the players' slang and described the game with gusto (he is credited with inventing the term "southpaw" to describe a left-handed pitcher).

Dunne's rise from cub reporter to national celebrity serves as a reminder of the importance of the newspaper as an incubator of writers in the nineteenth century. Besides Mencken and Dunne, American writers who started out in newspaper work include

Stephen Crane, Lincoln Steffens, Jack London, Edna Ferber, Frank Norris, Carl Sandburg, Jacob Riis, Theodore Dreiser, Eugene Field, Ring Lardner, Ernest Hemingway, Ben Hecht, and George Ade.

Eugene Field, who wrote a humorous column called Sharps and Flats for the *Chicago Daily News*, was a beacon and inspiration for Chicago's younger columnists (Carl Sandburg once commented, "May Field's sin in pioneering modern columnists be forgiven").[29] Chicago's writer/reporters organized informal clubs, and Field was a member of the Press Club, which had been founded in 1880. It was succeeded in 1889 by the Whitechapel Club, whose regulars included Dunne, Ade, Opie Read, Alfred Henry Lewis, Frederick Upham (Grizzly) Adams, Hobart C. Chatfield-Taylor, and one of America's greatest cartoonists, John T. McCutcheon. The members named their association after the site of some of Jack the Ripper's crimes and decorated their meeting room with murder weapons, hangman's ropes, skulls, and a bar shaped like a coffin. Their most notorious escapade was the cremation in the Indiana Dunes of the body of an alcoholic poet named Morris Allen Collins atop a twenty-foot-high funeral pyre. This was an early example of a publicity stunt—the cost was paid for by the editor of the *Chicago Herald*, who splashed the story over the front page of his paper's Sunday edition.

Dunne began using the Irish brogue in reporting the doings of certain Chicago aldermen and then began writing a column about a Colonel Malachi McNeery, who made wry observations on the Columbian Exposition. McNeery was modeled on a real-life Chicago saloon-keeper named James McGarry, who wearied of the unwanted publicity (customers started teasing him and calling him McNeery) and asked Dunne's publisher to find his columnist someone else to imitate.[30] Dunne was directed to working-class Bridgeport, where he found the perfect Irish neighborhood for his humor. Over the next five years, he would contribute no fewer than 215 Dooley essays, all written in the Irish brogue, to the pages of the *Evening Post*; over the course of his long writing career, Dunne would write more than seven hundred Dooley pieces.

Dialect humor has a long tradition in the United States. From today's perspective it is easy to view it as condescending, if not racist, but it was a way for a nation of strangers to come to terms with its ethnic and regional differences. Twenty years before Mr. Dooley made his debut, Charles H. Harris of Chicago launched *Carl Pretzel's Magazine Pook*, a successful publication written in a mock German American dialect.[31] Carl Pretzel and Mr. Dooley came along when large numbers of European immigrants were crowding into Chicago and many Americans of older stock feared that these newcomers would never assimilate. Mr. Dooley served as a representative of all these immigrants, from whatever country, and reassured Chicagoans that they were not threatening. Mr. Dooley was a patriot, solidly middle-class, and a hard worker. He demonstrated to Americans mistrustful of Catholicism that although he was a son of the Church, this by no means involved surrendering his intellectual independence or giving his primary allegiance to a "foreign" institution. Although Mr. Dooley was critical of crooked Chicago aldermen, he realized that they provided social services and, especially, jobs for the uneducated, and he was also skeptical of "rayformers," who, in his eyes, were often upper-class do-gooders who wanted to restrain the personal liberties of the working class. Businessmen he regarded as materialistic plutocrats heedless of the public good. One good example of Mr. Dooley's enduring relevance is his ridicule of the oft-recurring illusion that, as one writer described it, "Business ethics are superior to political ethics, hence businessmen make superior public officials."[32] One of the most quoted and popular of Dunne's Mr. Dooley pieces was entitled "What Does He Care?" in which the Bridgeport philosopher lambasted the railroad car tycoon George Pullman, who, during the Pullman strike of 1894, cut his workers' wages without reducing their rents:

> Mr. Dooley swabbed the bar in a melancholy manner and turned again with the remark: "But wat's it all to Pullman? Whin Gawd quarried his heart a happy man was made. He cares no more f'r thim little matthers iv life an' death thin I do f'r O'Connor's tab. 'Th' women an' childhern is

dyin' iv hunger,' they says. 'Will ye not put out ye'er hand to help thim?' they says. 'Ah, what th' 'ell,' says George. 'What th' 'ell,' he says. 'James,' he says, 'a bottle iv champagne an' a piece iv crambree pie. What th' 'ell, what th' 'ell, what th' 'ell."

After completing the column, Dunne went down to the composing room to check the proofs before publication. As he came in, the typesetters began to drum their sticks on their cases and then burst into applause. Dunne always treasured the moment as one of the greatest in his life.

Mr. Dooley was certainly original, but he was not without predecessors. Dunne's character came from a long line of similar types in American humor—democratic philosophers who, though uneducated, had through experience gained a native shrewdness and informed view of life and society. One of the first classic types was the "Yankee," a canny northeasterner skeptical of intellectuals and "book-larnin." His democratic preference for "horse sense" can be traced at least to Benjamin Franklin, whose Poor Richard remarked, "Tim was so learned that he could name a horse in nine languages. So ignorant, that he bought a cow to ride on."[33] Probably the first fictional character to embody the rustic Yankee was Major Jack Downing, a creation of Seba Smith, who first appeared in print in 1830. He was followed by Sam Slick, the creation of Thomas Chandler Haliburton, and Hosea Biglow, invented by James Russell Lowell. Another well-known American type was the shrewd frontiersman; some of the most popular were Nimrod Wildfire (invented by James Kirke Paulding), Simon Suggs (Johnson Jones Cooper), Major Jones (William Tappan Thompson), Mike Hooter (William C. Hall), and Sut Lovingood, the creation of George Washington Harris, whom some critics still regard as a rival of Mark Twain. One of the most popular frontier characters was a real person—Davy Crockett. Two great wisecracking philosophical characters that emerged in the Civil War era were Artemus Ward, the invention of Charles Farrar Browne, and Petroleum V. Nasby, the creation of David Ross Locke. Also in this period, some writers sought to capture the speech of African Americans, the most famous being Joel Chandler Harris, the creator of Uncle Remus. None of these characters used standard English, which was, to their audiences, proof of their democratic credentials, an indication of their authenticity, and, in a counterintuitive way, a sign of their cleverness. Obviously, Mr. Dooley fits into this legacy, but with one crucial difference—these characters were rustics. Mr. Dooley was an *urban* character, and Dunne was writing *urban* literature.

Mr. Dooley also differed from some other notable predecessors—the other comic Irishmen of the nineteenth century. One of the first in American literature was the character Teague O'Regan, who played Sancho Panza to the Don Quixote–like figure of Captain John Farrago in H. H. Brackenridge's *Modern Chivalry* (1792).[34] Buffoonish Irish servants are to be found in *The Irish Emigrant* (1817) by "An Hibernian" (probably Adam Douglass), and the quintessential stereotypical depiction of the drunken, dishonest Irishman can be found in Harriete Keyser's anti-Catholic novel *Thorns in Your Sides* (1884). Nor was Dunne the first journalist to employ the Irish brogue. Charles Fanning, a specialist in Irish American studies, has identified such characters as the Widow Magoogin in the *St. Louis Post-Dispatch*; the "Gowanusians," a Brooklyn Irish family invented by Maurice E. McLoughlin; and ten-year-old Mickey Finn, whose adventures were related by Ernest Jarrold. There were even brogue-speaking characters in Chicago newspapers before Mr. Dooley, such as "the Connemara cop" in the Chicago *Times-Herald*.[35] But many of these characters were dim-witted and mostly unattractive, if not treacherous. Mr. Dooley was nothing like these. He has all the shrewdness of the Yankee and the frontiersman, and despite his brogue, he is a genuine American. Dunne once said that for him the brogue served as a kind of journalistic self-defense. As he explained it, Dunne and his editor, Cornelius McAuliff, were at the time engaged in combat with certain dishonest aldermen. The newspaper's publisher, however, "wasn't so eager. He was nervous about libel suits and loans at banks that were interested in franchises for sale in the council. It occurred to me that while it might be dangerous to call an alderman a thief in English no one could sue if a comic Irishman denounced the statesman as a thief."[36]

Shortly before he died in 1895, Eugene Field suggested to Dunne that he should collect some of the best Dooley pieces and publish them in book form. Dunne resisted; his biographer, Elmer Ellis, suggested that Dunne didn't want to be known as a humorist but as a serious writer.[37] In January 1898, it even seemed that Dunne was ready to abandon the Dooley character. He wrote a farewell piece in which Mr. Dooley announced his intention to leave Chicago and go perhaps "to Boolgahria" and then turned out the lights of his saloon. But Dunne's fame was soon to go national. When the United States entered the Spanish-American War and invaded Cuba later in 1898, Dunne brought Mr. Dooley back. His series of Dooley articles on the conflict were wildly popular, the foremost being "On His Cousin George," in which Mr. Dooley claimed kinship with Admiral Dewey, who had defeated the Spanish fleet at Manila: "Dewey or Dooley, 'tis all th' same." This time, Dunne responded to pleas to collect some articles in book form, and the result was *Mr. Dooley in Peace and in War*, published in November 1898. It stayed on the best-seller list for a year and was followed over the next twelve years by six further Dooley collections. The first two of these volumes made Dunne nationally famous, and the income from his books was such that he no longer needed to have a newspaper job. Dunne at last saw the chance to become a full-time serious writer, and he decided that the best place to forge a literary career was New York. Thus this writer, so identified with Chicago and its characters, in 1900 packed up and moved to New York City to stay.

Two years later, he married Margaret Abbott, the first American woman to win an Olympic Gold Medal (in golf at the 1900 games in Paris). They had four children, one of whom was the screenwriter Philip Dunne. Mr. Dooley's popularity began to wane around the time of World War I, but by then, Dunne was writing many nondialect articles for various publications, especially *Collier's*, for which he contributed a series of editorials. In 1927, he unexpectedly inherited half a million dollars from his old friend Payne Whitney, the super-rich investor and philanthropist, and he was able live well without ever having to write another word.

Dunne continued to be a popular figure in New York, where he died of throat cancer on April 24, 1936. He was buried in Wood-lawn Cemetery in the Bronx. The following month, a memorial mass was celebrated at St. Bridget's Church on "Archey Road."

George Ade

In the years before World War I, George Ade was universally admired as a genius. A new play by Ade was a major event, he was the first American playwright to have three works running on Broadway at the same time, and his writing made him a millionaire. Mark Twain, William Dean Howells, and H. L. Mencken hailed his prose, and more than one critic speculated that if anybody were going to write the great American novel, it would be George Ade. Obviously, he didn't do that, but by taking the language of the streets and putting it on paper, he made a lasting contribution to the literary evolution of the United States.

Ade's rise to fame began on November 20, 1893, the day on which readers of the *Chicago Record* found a new column, Stories of the Streets and of the Towns. Ade's editor had simply told him to wander through the city and report on whatever caught his attention, to "go ahead and revel in the inconsequential."[38] The very first column, "A Young Man in Upper Life," demonstrated the young reporter's wit and dexterity. It tells of one "Mr. Ponsby" who works in an office on the sixteenth floor of a Chicago skyscraper. One day he notices that workmen are tearing holes in the roof of the small building next door. A few days later, that building is gone—a new one is taking its place. Day after day, he watches the framework go up. As the workers clamber over the steel cage, he is constantly distracted for fear that one of them will fall. Finally, the new skyscraper is finished, and "Mr. Ponsby, finding some relief in a bare wall, went back to his neglected work." It's a tale that's Chicago to the bone. It's fiction, but it mixes in the reality of a city that is constantly pushing upward.

"A Young Man in Upper Life" was followed by a succession of columns that delved into the life of the city with vitality and surprise. Stories of the Streets and of the Towns ran every day

The frantic activities of a Chicago newspaper in the 1890s as seen by cartoonist John T. McCutcheon. (The French Emissary Studies Our Industrial Methods. Originally printed in the Chicago Record-Herald)

for seven years (many were reprinted in book form, eight volumes in all). They were accompanied by witty illustrations from the hand of Ade's old college chum, John T. McCutcheon. Ade's stories, McCutcheon later remarked, "will be of great value to the future historian," which is true, for in them one can find unique details of Chicago life in the 1890s.[39] Subjects treated in the columns, some fiction, some reportage, include Chicago's French restaurants; an incident in the "Pansy Saloon;" the

"Junk-Shops of Canal Street;" the discussions around the breakfast table at a Dearborn Street boardinghouse; a farmer who trucks his vegetables into the city to sell in Haymarket Square; tiny stores, some just three feet wide, that squeeze themselves into the gaps between tall buildings; politicians buying the votes of tavern-goers; sidewalk merchants; a restaurant where you could get real Southern cooking, including "chidlins;" the life of a Chicago coachman; river tugboats; Chinese laundries; and an opera spoof called "Il Janitoro."

Ade discovered that recurring characters were a good way to keep readers coming back, and three of his characters eventually had books of their own—*Artie* (1896), *Pink Marsh* (1897), and *Doc Horne* (1899). Artie is a young man-about-town who works in an office. He sometimes gambles too much or comes to work with a hangover, he joins the bicycle craze, and he's fond of the ladies (he eventually settles down with a "peach" named Mamie). But what is unique about Artie is his language—this is the book to consult in order to learn how the hip and trendy were talking in the 1890s. Here's how Artie dresses down a pool shark who tries to con him into a game: "Drop it! Do n't try to con me with no such talk. I'm on to you bigger 'n a house. I know about you and the whole push o' ringers. Me and my friend here play a gentleman's game, understand? I might stand some show against you, only I do n't take my meals off of a pool table. I ain't no shark that hangs around these places all day lookin' for somethin'

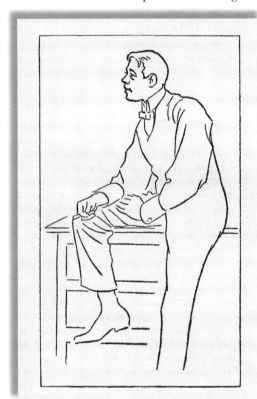

The colorful slang of George Ade's character Artie reveals how the fast young crowd talked in the 1890s. (Author's collection)

easy, and I'm just foolish enough to think that I'm too good to play pool with a skin like you."

Pink Marsh also explores unconventional English, but the book can be discomforting because the title character is a black man who works the shoeshine stand in a barbershop and Ade's attempts to render his language comes across as condescending: "I may be baihfoot an' need mo' undeh-cloze, but I sutny will have my chidlin's on Ch'is'mas, an' any man 'at thinks diff'ent wants to make a new guess, suah. If 'at ol' box up on 'e wall uses me good I'll be a wahm baby 'iss Ch'is'mas— yes, seh, I'll eat oystehs 'ith my true love." At the time, however, *Pink Marsh* delighted many celebrated readers. In a letter to William Dean Howells, Mark Twain wrote, "My admiration of the book has overflowed all limits, all frontiers. . . .

Mark Twain said of George Ade's character Pink Marsh that "he deserves to live forever." (Author's collection)

Pink, oh the shiftless, worthless, lovable, black darling! Howells, he deserves to live forever."[40] *Doc Horne* relates the exploits of an elderly gentleman who resides in a hotel with a group of colorful companions—the actor, the lush (that is how he is designated), the lightning dentist, the race-track man, and the freckled boy. The parallels to *The Pickwick Papers* are easy to spot; Doc, like Mr. Pickwick, socializes with a quaint collection of personalities and is badgered by the law: Mr. Pickwick is sued for breach of promise of marriage, and Doc Horne is unjustly accused of running a fake medicine company. Doc is given to telling braggadocio-laced stories about his supposed feats of derring-do. His monologues sound a lot like the yarns related in the movies by W. C. Fields, so much so that one wonders if the great comedian, who was born in 1880, imbibed the Horne stories as a young man.

After years of writing the Streets and Town columns, Ade was running out of variations. "One morning," he explained, "I sat at the desk and gazed at the empty soft paper, and realized the necessity of concocting something different. . . . Why not a fable for a change?"[41] But this was going to be a fable with a twist; it would use language that was "fly"—"modern, undignified, quite of the moment." It would be in slang.

The first of Ade's *Fables in Slang* appeared on September 17, 1898. He thought of it as a one-time thing, but at the time his publisher was nagging him to complete the "great American novel" people were waiting for—it was going to be entitled *The College Widow*. Ade, admitting to himself (if to no one else) that he was never going to write it, agreed to substitute an entire volume of slang fables (despite their title, the fables—and some argue that they're not even fables—do not use a lot of slang, not nearly as much as *Artie*). The titles of some them give an idea of their character: "The Fable of the Visitor Who Got a Lot for Three Dollars," "The Fable of the Kid Who Shifted His Ideal," "The Fable of a Statesman Who Couldn't Make Good." In Aesopian fashion, each fable ended with a moral, and Ade's idiosyncratic ones perhaps give an even better idea of the nature of the pieces: "If it is your Play to be a Hero, don't Renig;" "Get a good Make-Up and the Part plays itself;" "Don't begin to Forget until you have it in Government Bonds." *Fables in Slang* arrived in bookstores at the end of 1899 and was a sensation. Nearly seventy thousand copies were sold in 1900, and when Ade started writing the fables for national syndication, he was bringing in over $1,000 a week. He became so rich that he was able to leave the newspaper and become a full-time writer. Ade was no longer a Chicago author; he was an *American* author.

George Ade was not a city kid like Fuller and Dunne but was born in Kentland, Indiana (population six hundred), on February 9, 1866. As a child, Ade was an eager reader of magazines, newspapers, dime novels, and, especially, the works of Dickens and Mark Twain. An essay he wrote in high school entitled

The immensely popular George Ade was the first American playwright to have three works running on Broadway at the same time. (Library of Congress)

"A Basket of Potatoes" so impressed his teacher that she sent it to be published in the local paper. The superintendent of schools thereupon paid a visit to the Ade home and convinced John Ade that his gifted son should be sent to college—an unusual step for a Kentland lad. Fortunately, father John's concerns over how to pay for it were alleviated when George was awarded a scholarship to a new school not too far away—Purdue University, which is where he went in September 1883.

Ade thrived in the college town of West Lafayette, Indiana. Traveling groups of thespians found it a convenient stopping point on the way to Chicago, and the theater scene was unusually active for a municipality of fifteen thousand. Ade was a regular at the Grand Opera House, where he saw many of the era's biggest stars and enjoyed a succession of bubbly light operas (*The Mikado* made the biggest impression on him). He joined a literary society and a fraternity, learned to dance and smoke cigarettes, collected a sizeable library of second-hand books, went on picnics, and edited for a semester a literary periodical called the *Purdue*. He also made friends with McCutcheon and fell in love with a blonde coed named Lillian Howard. She married a Baptist minister, and Ade remained a bachelor for the rest of his days. When he became famous, he received plenty of offers from women, but he used to say, "I didn't marry because another man married my girl."

After college, Ade took a job on a newspaper in West Lafayette and then he found a better paying position as a patent-medicine salesman. McCutcheon, however, had gone to Chicago after graduation and was quickly hired by a newspaper. He wrote back to Ade, describing Chicago in alluring terms and saying that his rented room had a large double bed and was big enough for two. The patent-medicine company went bust, and Ade was soon on the train.

That was in June 1890. McCutcheon soon introduced his pal to the city editor of the *Morning News*, Charles H. Dennis, who agreed to give Ade a trial with a starting pay of $12 a week writing about the weather, an assignment coveted by no other reporter. Ade set about portraying the weather with a verve and color that no one had ever thought achievable. He asked hotel workers how the heat was affecting the guests; he queried wagon drivers about how their horses were faring; he found out how the weather bureau made its predictions and explained the process to his readers. Ade was demonstrating (and probably discovering for himself) that he was a born reporter—he was curious about everything and would ask questions of anybody and everybody. On one occasion a steamer exploded in the Chicago River, and because all the other reporters were off doing something else, the managing editor had no other choice but to send the weatherman. Ade's reporting on the story was so dramatic and precise that he soon left the weather beat. Before long, he was mentoring even less experienced reporters (one who never forgot Ade's kind advice and assistance was Theodore Dreiser).

After *Fables in Slang* made Ade rich enough to leave his newspaper job, he decided to try his hand at writing for the stage, first a couple of short pieces and then musical comedy. His first venture into musicals was *The Night of the Fourth*, which was a flop. His second, *The Sultan of Sulu*, with music by Alfred Wathall, was inspired by a trip to the Philippines and clearly influenced by *The Mikado*. It was first produced in Chicago, but the authors revised it, and it made its Broadway debut on December 29, 1902. It was a smash, ran for nearly the entire season, and took in some $10,000 a week at the box office. A second musical, *Peggy from Paris* (music by William Loraine), was not as much of a success but still made money.

Ade then resolved to write plays "for talking actors instead of singing dancers."[42] His first Broadway comedy, *The County Chairman*, a satire on local elections, was such a sensation with both the critics and the public that Ade might have believed he could never top it. But he did—with his next comedy, *The College Widow*, which opened in New York on September 20, 1904. Comedies about college life are such a Hollywood staple these days that it is hard to imagine that in 1904 the idea of a college comedy seemed unfeasible. As Ade once recalled, "I was either very courageous and far-sighted or else very foolhardy. I wanted to write a play dealing with college life and football. No play dealing with those two subjects had ever been produced on the American stage. Henry W. Savage, who had been producing my plays, and many other wise people connected with the theater were of the opinion that the general playgoing public was not keenly interested in under-graduates or college athletics."[43] After the second act, the cheering audience demanded that Ade get up and give a speech, and after the curtain went down on the third act, the patrons stood and applauded throughout the entire intermission. The play was one of the biggest triumphs in the history of the American theater. The *Morning World* called it "a real, old-fashioned, howling success," and the *Telegraph* wrote that Ade was "the great American master of comedy." And less than a month after it opened, Ade's musical *The Sho-Gun* made its Broadway debut. It was less than a triumph, but it did give Ade the satisfaction of having three shows running in New York at the same time.

Ade was hardly a Chicago writer anymore, but he was not exactly a New Yorker either. All along he had been sending his money back to Kentland (his father, still a bank clerk, deposited the checks himself), and his brother Bill had been investing in prime Indiana farmland, which steadily grew in value. Although he still maintained ties to Chicago (he often went to visit McCutcheon), Ade used some four hundred acres of his Indiana land to erect an estate called Hazelden, and there he lived the life of a country squire, playing golf on his own private nine-hole course and holding huge picnics for visiting celebrities and for local folk.

And then Ade started to lose his touch. His next three shows after *The Sho-Gun* were failures. His final play for Broadway, a musical entitled *The Old Town*, which opened on January 10, 1910, ran for 179 performances, and Ade thought so little of it he didn't bother to have it copyrighted. He stayed active in his remaining years, however, writing essays and short stories and quite a number of scripts for silent movies. He began spending the winters in Florida, and in 1931, he published *The Old-Time Saloon*, a lament for the demise of the local tavern in the age of Prohibition. He was a great benefactor of Purdue, and the football stadium there is called Ross-Ade Stadium after Ade and his fellow alumnus, David Ross. Ade died in Kentland on May 16, 1944.

In regards to culture, one of the most characteristic aspects of modernity is its high estimation of originality. Terms such as "unorthodox," "fringy," "revolutionary," "uncommon," "progressive," "avant-garde," "modish," "edgy," and "cutting edge" are high praise for works of art. Yet the works of Ade, as well as Fuller and Dunne, show that originality is not enough to secure immortality because in their day they were as "cutting edge" as anyone. Their originality was central to their success—they were doing something truly new and people responded. But nothing brings imitation like originality, and when hordes of other authors began crowding through the doors that these writers had opened (often improving on their achievements), their successes no longer looked so new—they looked, in fact, like achievements bound to a particular time and place. Nevertheless, in 1893, three Chicago writers opened a trail for other American authors to follow. Other authors did follow, and American literature was forever changed.

Chicago's Literary Fortunes

The list of writers who either got their start in the Chicago area or became firmly identified with the city is long and impressive: besides Fuller, Dunne, Ade, and the early writers mentioned in this chapter, one can cite Frank Norris, Theodore Dreiser, Hamlin Garland, Carl Sandburg, Upton Sinclair, Ring Lardner, Edna Ferber, Edgar Lee Masters, Ben Hecht, Sherwood Anderson, James T. Farrell, Richard Wright, Lorraine Hansberry, Nelson Algren, Gwendolyn Brooks, Saul Bellow, Studs Terkel, Mike Royko, Harry Mark Petrakis, Stuart Dybek, Sandra Cisneros, Sara Paretsky, and Scott Turow. Nevertheless, Chicago did not become, as Mencken thought, the literary capital of the United States. One reason is that many so-called Chicago writers did not stay in the city. Once they became famous, Dunne and Ade headed for New York, and others who made the same journey include Dreiser, Garland, Ferber, Hecht, Anderson, Masters, Lardner, Farrell, and Algren (who actually went to Paterson, New Jersey). Even Saul Bellow headed east, moving from Chicago to Brookline, Massachusetts, although very late in life. As Emmett Dedmon put it, "When H. L. Mencken bestowed the accolade of literary capital of the United States on Chicago, most of those who had been the legislators of the new rules of literature were gone."[44]

Certainly, money was a factor in this migration—New York was, and remains, the center of the publishing industry. Hamlin Garland once said that Henry Blake Fuller told him, "Why stay in this town if you can get out of it? No writer can earn a living here except on the newspapers."[45] Other factors were the desire to be part of a larger literary culture and to associate with authors from different backgrounds—as well as the time-honored challenge that to truly prove one's worth, one most prove it in New York City.

On the other hand, one could argue that New York did not turn out to be the literary capital of the United States either. Many of the most famous twentieth-century American writers, such as William Faulkner, Eugene O'Neill, Ernest Hemingway, John Steinbeck, John Updike, Flannery O'Connor, and Toni Morrison, were not especially associated with either New York or Chicago, which is understandable, given the geographic and cultural variety of a large country like the United States. Nor is the challenge of making it in New York what it used to be. As the writer and professor Joseph Epstein recently expressed it, "Young writers no longer feel this way about New York. For them New York is not a city that they feel they must conquer; they scarcely feel they have to visit it. . . . Where once New York was indisputably the center of literary culture in this country, it is now so chiefly in the institutional sense: the publishers, slick magazines, agents, and engines of publicity remain in New York. But, increasingly, writers are finding jobs in universities—and in universities all over the country."[46] Saul Bellow said pretty much the same thing—the universities have become the focal point of intellectual and cultural life in the United States (Bellow himself was a university professor for years).[47] Nowadays, aspiring novelists don't look for jobs on daily newspapers in rousing cities like Chicago, they look for M.F.A.'s in creative writing in bucolic burgs like Iowa City. Readers themselves will have to decide whether or not this is a good thing.

9

The West Side Grounds

What was the best baseball team of all time? The 1927 Yankees, with Ruth, Gehrig, Lazzeri, and Meusel? Or one of Cincinnati's Big Red Machines of the early 1970s, with Johnny Bench, Pete Rose, and Joe Morgan? What about the Dodgers when they had Duke Snider, Jackie Robinson, Roy Campanella, Gil Hodges, and Pee Wee Reese?

Well, as Casey Stengel used to say, "You could look it up." None of these teams holds the record for the best single season in baseball history. Or the best three consecutive seasons. Or the best *five*. The best three-year record in major league history is 322–136 (a winning percentage of .703). The best five-year record is 530–235 (.693). And the most wins ever achieved in one year was 116. Every one of these feats was accomplished by the same team. The best team of all time was the Chicago Cubs.

Consider the team that won 116 games in 1906. Manager Frank Chance's stalwarts led the league in runs (705), batting average (.262), hits (1,316), triples (71), slugging average (.339), fielding average (.969), strikeouts by pitchers (702), shutouts (30), and earned run average (an ungodly 1.75). Now that the season lasts 162 games, the number of victories notched by the '06 Cubs was bound to be equaled, as it was by the Seattle Mariners in 2001. But that team lost forty-six games, ten more than the Cubs. And it will be a long time before we witness a club that plays .800 ball *on the road*, as the 1906 Cubs did. That team inexplicably lost

During sold-out games, such as this World Series match between the Cubs and White Sox in 1906, spectators at the West Side Grounds were allowed to stand around the edge of the outfield. (Library of Congress)

the World Series, to, of all people, the Chicago White Sox, the "Hitless Wonders," but it was essentially the same group that won the World Series in 1907 and 1908.

The Stadium and the Team

The Cubs are practically synonymous with Wrigley Field, but those victories did not take place there because Wrigley Field opened in 1914. Those Cub teams played in a ballpark known as West Side Grounds, which opened on May 14, 1893. The West Side Grounds (also known as West Side Park II) stood on a plot bounded by Polk Street on the north, Taylor Street on the south, Wood Street on the east, and Lincoln Street (now called Wolcott) on the west.

As the ballpark was not Wrigley Field, the team was not the Cubs. The name of Chicago's entry in the National League has a complicated history, made more confusing by the fact that during its first years the team was called the White Stockings (although not the "White Sox").

The first organized professional baseball league, the National Association of Professional Base Ball Players, was founded in New York City on St. Patrick's Day, 1871. Chicago was one of eight cities represented. Late in 1875, baseball's leading pitcher,

Albert Spalding, and William Hulbert, a Chicago entrepreneur, began discussing a new league. Spalding, who was a straight arrow and a smart businessman, was dismayed by the gambling and liquor sales that blighted the professional game; he also envisioned a system in which each team would have two "interdependent divisions, the executive and the productive."[1] That is, the players would work, under contract, for the owners. The result was the establishment in 1876 of the National League of Professional Baseball Players, the league in which the Cubs play today.

One of the best young players on the Chicago White Stockings in 1876 was Adrian "Cap" Anson, who would go on to manage the team. He became so identified with the team that eventually it became known as Anson's White Colts, or just the Colts. After Anson was fired in 1898, the writers viewed the team as leaderless and called it the "Orphans" or the "Remnants." But club names were fluid and sportswriters enjoyed inventing varied cognomens; thus Chicago's team was occasionally known as the "Zephyrs," "Microbes," "Spuds," and "Cowboys." It didn't matter much because baseball teams were more commonly called after their cities, such as "the Chicagos beat the Detroits, 5–2." City names, not team names, appeared on uniforms.

After the American League made its debut in 1901, Chicago had two teams, and use of a team name now became necessary. The name "Cubs" appears to have come from an article in the *Chicago Daily News* on March 27, 1902, in which a sportswriter, speaking of the team's new manager, wrote, "Frank Selee will devote his strongest efforts on the teamwork of the new Cubs this year."[2] Because the word "cub" was then habitually used for young players (just as the term "colt" was), it might be that a typesetter mistakenly set the "C" in upper-case, but the name stuck, and by 1907, manager Chance was insisting upon its use.

Another way 1893 was a remarkable year is that one could argue it was the year modern baseball was born. Baseball in the 1870s was different in many ways from today's game. Sports historian Peter Levine described it as a time "when pitchers stood forty-five feet from home plate and tossed the ball underhanded and straight-armed to a bare-handed catcher located some thirty feet behind the batter; when batters were permitted to ask for the ball to be pitched high or low as many as nine times before a single umpire awarded them first base; when infielders rarely moved from their bases; and when balls caught on the fly by gloveless fielders were rarities."[3] Gradually, the rules were changed. In 1884, pitchers were able to use any arm motion they preferred, and the practice of calling for high or low pitches ended in 1887. Four balls became a base on balls in 1889, and catchers' mitts were introduced two years later. Finally, in that landmark year of 1893, the official distance from the pitching mound to home plate was increased from fifty feet to today's sixty feet, six inches. This has been called "arguably the most significant rule change in major league history" and was the final milestone in the shaping of modern baseball.[4] A fan of today seeing a game in 1893 would find nearly all aspects familiar.

Professional Baseball and the Public

Games involving hitting a ball with a stick have been around for a long time. Children in colonial America played games of this type. The earliest organized baseball in the United States was centered in the New York City area, although not exclusively. According to the reminiscences of an early player named Daniel "Doc" Adams, baseball was being contested in New York City as early as 1840, and historians have uncovered evidence that the game was being played there even in the early 1830s.[5] In 1845, a bank clerk named Alexander Cartwright organized a team called the New York Knickerbockers and set down standards and rules that are remarkably similar to those still in use (ninety-foot base paths, nine players on each team, three strikes you're out, three outs in an inning, and so on). Baseball began heading west in the 1850s, and during the Civil War soldiers helped spread the game's popularity. In his autobiography, Cap Anson likened the spread of baseball to an "epidemic fever" that began in the East and "gradually worked its way over the mountains and across the broad prairies until the sport had obtained a foothold in every little village and hamlet in the land."[6]

By 1856, a team called the Union Baseball Club was playing in Chicago, and Chicago also had a team called the Excelsiors. There were teams in other Illinois towns even before that.[7] The Lockport *Telegraph* of August 6, 1851, reported a baseball match between the Joliet Hunkidoris and the Lockport Sleepers.[8] In that era, Rockford was something like the capital of Illinois baseball (both Spalding and Anson got their starts there). In 1866, Rockford held a tournament for the "championship of the Northwest." The Chicago Excelsiors prevailed and returned to Chicago bearing a silver tea set.[9]

The sport changed greatly in the years immediately following the Civil War as professionalism began creeping in. The National Association of Base Ball Players (NABBP), made up of sixteen clubs in the East, had been founded in 1857 as a league of amateur teams, but as early as 1866, the NABBP was investigating a Philadelphia club for paying some of its players. By 1867, sportswriters were already writing of "professional teams," even though there weren't supposed to be any.[10] In Washington, D.C., it was an open secret that ballplayers were hired as "clerks" in various government departments and played baseball for "free."[11] Soon the best players began jumping from one club to another, and sportswriters excoriated these players as "revolvers."[12] By the end of 1868, the NABBP bowed to reality and allowed the establishment of professional teams. The first was the Cincinnati Red Stockings (1869).

Chicago and Cincinnati were rivals for the position of leading city of the Midwest. If Cincinnati was going to have a professional baseball team, then so would Chicago. The *Lakeside Monthly* asserted that Chicago "could not see her commercial rival on the Ohio bearing off the honors of the national game."[13] As sports historian Steven A. Riess put it, "A city was not seen as much of an urban area unless it had a professional nine, and furthermore, it should be in the best league possible."[14] Therefore, some of the most important men in Chicago—department store owner Charles Farwell, General Philip Sheridan, publisher Joseph Medill, and hotel owner Potter Palmer—assembled late in 1869 to create the Chicago Base Ball Association. As a Boston newspaper reported, they "raised $20,000 with which to employ a nine that should sweep the board."[15]

Sports: Good for America

In the latter half of the nineteenth century, team sports entered American culture, and ever since, historians, sociologists, and anthropologists have speculated about the significance of sports. One theory holds that on the frontier, a young man could prove his worth by his survival skills—building a cabin, shooting a deer. A society of offices and factories did not offer these challenges; instead, a young man could demonstrate his masculinity on the sports field. In 1906, William James wrote an essay entitled "The Moral Equivalent of War," in which he pondered the problem of how a nation could maintain its political unity and civic virtue without being challenged by an external threat. The phrase "moral equivalent of war" soon became associated with sports as observers recognized that team sports in particular were a simulacrum of combat and that participation fostered "manly virtues."[16] Central to this development was the publication in 1857 of British author Thomas Hughes's *Tom Brown's Schooldays*, a book that extolled the value of team sports as a character builder and which was very popular in the United States. In 1893, Theodore Roosevelt praised the nation-building virtues of "vigorous manly out-of-door sports"[17] Finally, today it is common to view sports in general as a way for testosterone-driven young men to sublimate their aggressive impulses, but H. Addington Bruce was viewing baseball in just that light as early as 1913. The game, he wrote, was "a harmless outlet for pent-up emotions, which unless thus gaining expression, might discharge themselves in a dangerous way. . . . Baseball, then, from the spectator's standpoint, is to be regarded as a means of catharsis, or perhaps better, as a safety-valve."[18]

Today, baseball is much less of a participatory sport than it was in the nineteenth century. In that era, many amateur leagues gave adults ample opportunity to play the game. The Inner-City Association of Chicago, for example, had 194 teams, each of which played at least once a week. There were leagues organized by profession and by religion; according to Riess there were four hundred teams in Chicago in 1906, and three years later, there were "over 550 registered amateur teams and twenty-six semiprofessional clubs."[19]

Baseball was also considered a bulwark of American ideology; it stood for the values of fair play, self-discipline, moral rectitude, and democracy. Americans dismayed by the huge numbers of immigrants coming to U.S. cities hoped that baseball would serve as a mechanism of assimilation. As the sportswriter Hugh Fullerton expressed it at the time, "Baseball, to my way of thinking, is the greatest single force working for Americanization."[20] Finally, baseball was seen as a link to an idealized rural past. Albert Spalding himself was paramount in establishing this myth. It was he who in 1907 urged the establishment of a commission to uncover the origins of baseball. On the flimsiest of evidence, the commission declared that the game had been invented by Abner Doubleday in Cooperstown, New York, in 1839, a determination that has since proved spurious. Baseball's origins do lie in New York State, just not on the banks of pastoral Otsego Lake but in the Murray Hill section of Manhattan.

Baseball and the City

Baseball was an urban sport. Riess has analyzed the backgrounds of the professionals who played in the Association of Professional Base Ball Players and determined that 83 percent of them came from cities, mostly in the Northeast.[21] One might wonder how it was that youngsters growing up in crowded cities found the space in which to play baseball, but "sandlot baseball" has long been an urban phenomenon and, especially in the nineteenth century, Chicago and other cities still had areas of vacant land large enough to accommodate a baseball game. As time went on, this changed. A report in the *St. Louis Post-Dispatch* from 1905 explains how it was once easy for boys to find places to play ball in Chicago but how open spaces were disappearing: "The passing of Chicago from recruiting fields was due wholly [*sic*] to the activity of the builders. Only a few years ago great spaces, even in the thickest settled parts of Chicago, lay vacant, and on

. . . baseball broke down barriers between ethnic groups . . .

these lots myriads of youngsters pitched, caught, and batted. As the city grew, these lots were covered one by one. Today, the boy who would play ball in Chicago has to travel long distances to find a diamond, and the ambitions of the Chicago juveniles seem to have shrunk in inverse ratio to the length of these journeys."[22]

Being, then, an urban sport, baseball influenced, and was influenced by, the conditions prevailing in great cities like Chicago. Historians of cities and of sports have ascertained a connection between the waves of immigrants coming to U.S. cities in the last half of the nineteenth century and the appeal of baseball. As baseball historian Roger I. Abrams expressed it, "Immigrants to America forged a new energetic society with a fascinating social history. Separated by class, race, and religion, they were united by an affiliation to an urban space—to a city. . . . Baseball was a cultural event that was involved in all their lives. It was a public activity that attracted a noteworthy, and perhaps unique, diversity of spectators. European immigrants came out to the ballpark to root for the men who represented the cities the immigrants had adopted as their own."[23] It is, how-ever, questionable how many arrivals from Europe—especially non–English–speakers—embraced the game. First-generation immigrants from eastern and southern Europe were not huge baseball fans, and it is difficult to imagine a Polish stockyard laborer opting for the ballpark instead of a comfortable tavern peopled by his countrymen. Besides, at its launch, the National League set a ticket price of fifty cents, which was about half the daily wage of a manual laborer (many club owners later added twenty-five-cent seats, taking care that the users of those seats would not mingle with the better-off patrons). The children of immigrants, however, were another matter, and second-gener-ation boys became baseball enthusiasts, playing in alleys and streets with broom handles and rubber balls and idolizing ball-players (all the better if they were of the same ethnicity). In addition, baseball broke down barriers between ethnic groups as well as between old-timers and newcomers; as Robert G. Spinney has said, baseball was "an activity in which anyone, regardless of ethnicity, could participate."[24]

Baseball also offered one more form of urban leisure and recreation in an era that was eager to produce them. Ballparks were "outdoor theaters," and the players in those theaters were much more real than distant political or cultural heroes—especially in the era before motion pictures. Although analysts of the day praised baseball for its healthful qualities, its powers of assimilation, and its capacity to redirect energy, they neglected the business aspect of the game and the role it played in forming a popular culture. Baseball was a form of mass entertainment; indeed, baseball and vaudeville could be described as the nation's two first (at the turn of the twentieth century, many professional ballplayers, including Cap Anson, earned extra money by appearing in vaudeville shows in the off-season).[25] The cultural significance of baseball likely has more to do with its power to draw crowds in search of entertainment (and enrich club owners) than with any of its putative health-giving powers or its evocation of a bucolic past.

Chicago Baseball

As Chicago was the capital of the nation's railroads and of bicycling, temperance, and meatpacking, one could argue that, in the 1880s at least, it was also the capital of baseball. Two Chicagoans—Albert Spalding and William Hulbert—had founded the National League, and after 1883, when the White Stockings' stadium was remodeled, the city boasted the finest and best-attended ballpark in the United States.

And the local team was terrific. The first team to win the National League championship was Spalding's Chicago White Stockings, who finished the season with a record of 52–14. In 1880, the pennant-winning club compiled a record of 67–17, for a winning percentage of .798 (even higher than that of the 1906 Cubs). The team then went on to dominate the decade, finishing first again in 1881, 1882, 1885, and 1886. The *Chicago Tribune* wrote about Chicago's "many baseball-maniacs," and another paper, describing baseball as "a tremendous source of revenue," reported that the Chicago team was "its richest corporation."[26] In an event that Henry Chadwick praised as "the greatest event in the history of athletic sports," this illustrious team made a bid for not just national, but international, fame when it made its worldwide tour from October 1888 to April 1889.[27] Embarking from San Francisco, Spalding took his lads to Hawaii, Australia, Ceylon (now Sri Lanka), Egypt, Italy, France, England, Ireland, and Scotland.

Albert Spalding is an almost unique figure in nineteenth-century sports in that his name is still familiar—the "Spalding" that is seen on NBA basketballs is indeed that of this son of Byron, Illinois. Born in 1850, he began playing ball with the Rockford Pioneers at age fifteen. At twenty-one he was a pitcher on the Boston Red Stockings, for whom he posted a record of 205–53 in five years. After teaming with Hulbert to create the National League, he joined the White Stockings, which caused a scandal (the day of the "revolvers" was supposed to be over). Yet in founding the National League, Spalding made sure that future players would not follow his example. He supported the establishment of the "reserve clause," that, until it was overturned in 1975, bound a player to a team with an iron-clad contract. In his first year with the White Stockings, Spalding acted as manager and star pitcher for the pennant-winning squad.

Spalding had no sooner arrived in Chicago when, along with his brother, he opened a sporting goods store. A clever marketer, he persuaded the National League to use none but Spalding baseballs. He supplied the baseballs at no cost; the money would be made from the millions of kids who wanted the same baseballs used by the pros. He also pioneered the use of baseball gloves. Old-timers viewed them as sissified, but when Spalding, the game's premier pitcher, began wearing them, they caught on—much to the profit of Spalding, who not only wore them, but also sold them. By the end of the nineteenth century, Spalding owned the largest sporting goods company in the United States, with a chain of fourteen stores. He was only twenty-eight when retired as a baseball player in 1878. He felt he was slipping, but it's likely that running his business had become his true calling, although he continued to function as a baseball executive. As Peter Levine has expressed it,

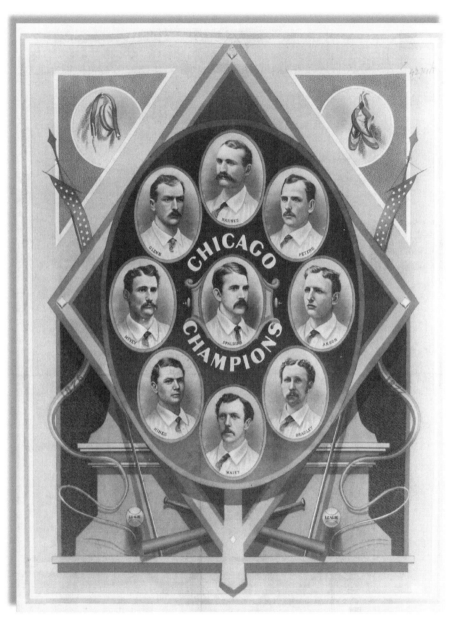

The Chicago White Stockings, winners of the first National League championship in 1876. The team later became known as the Cubs. (Library of Congress)

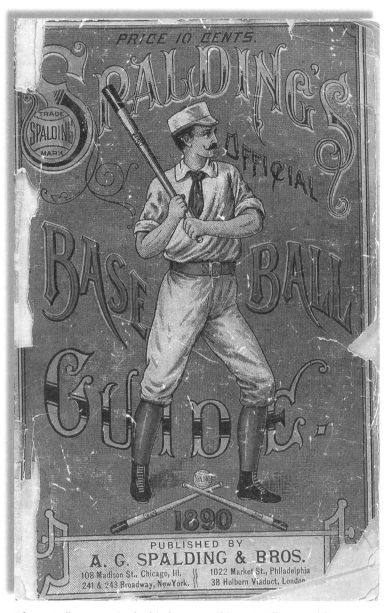

After a stellar career in the big leagues, Chicago's Albert Spalding became a baseball executive, sporting goods mogul, and publisher of sports-related material, such as this 1890 baseball guide. (Author's collection)

"Between 1876, when he helped form the National League, and 1901, when he became its president, Spalding figured in every major event in the early history of professional baseball."[28]

Spalding's mission was to make baseball a respectable, middle-class sport. The game's early days tended to be rowdy, and the players undisciplined. Its reputation was something like that of professional wrestling today—entertaining in its way, but hardly a sport for the educated and the respectable. That's why Spalding strove to prevent open gambling at the ballpark and did not sell liquor at games.[29] There is no better instance of his determination to keep the game clean than his handling of the idol of the 1880s, right fielder Mike ("King") Kelly. A splendid hitter, the flamboyant King was frequently spotted stumbling out of saloons at dawn. Fearing he was a bad influence on younger players, in February 1887, Spalding shocked baseball by selling Kelly's contract to Boston.

Chicago's second great baseball figure of the era was Cap Anson. Born in 1852, Anson was, like Spalding, a midwesterner. Due to his youth (not to his size—six feet, 227 pounds—nor his truculence), he was at first dubbed "Infant Anson" and "Baby Anson." He batted .356 in his first year with the White Stockings and went on to play twenty-two straight seasons for Chicago, becoming team manager in 1879. Anson was bossy, fiery, argumentative (he had epic bouts with umpires), and shrewd. When he died in 1922, the *New York Times* speculated that, despite the more recent achievements of Ty Cobb, Honus Wagner, and Babe Ruth, the case could be made that Anson was "the greatest player the game had produced."[30] He developed the practice of standing near third base and shouting instructions to runners—the first third-base coach. Anson is also credited with inventing the pitching rotation, with first using hand signals to instruct batters, and with coming up with the idea of platooning players. He also created one sinister innovation—racial bigotry in the big leagues. If another team fielded a black ballplayer, Anson would not let his men take the field. Black professional ballplayers did exist in the 1880s. One was Moses Fleetwood Walker, a catcher for the Toledo Blue Stockings in the American

ADRIAN C. ANSON.
ALLEN & GINTER'S
RICHMOND. Cigarettes. VIRGINIA

Adrian "Cap" Anson was a dominant force in Chicago baseball for over twenty years. (Library of Congress)

Association who is usually considered the first black major leaguer. The White Stockings were slated to play Toledo on July 20, 1884, but the Ohio club was warned that the Chicagos would not play if Walker was in the game. Three years later, a reporter described the incident as "the first time in baseball history that the color line had been drawn."[31] By 1897, partly at Anson's insistence, baseball had instituted an unwritten understanding that, although they were welcome to form segregated leagues of their own, there would be no more black players in the majors.

After the great years of the 1880s, the fortunes of the White Stockings declined, and they finished seventh in 1892 and ninth in 1893. The team remained in the second division throughout the decade, and new club president Jim Hart dumped Anson as player/manager before the beginning of the 1898 season. By then the newspapers were making jokes about Anson's age.

The Search for a Home

The lifespan of a ballpark in late-nineteenth-century Chicago was short. By the time the West Side Grounds opened in 1893, Chicago's baseball team had already played in six ballparks. One might say that with the West Side Grounds, the team finally found a home.

When Chicago businessmen first fielded their "Base Ball Club" in 1870, the White Stockings played in a facility known as Dexter Park, which had previously hosted amateur teams. Located on Halsted Street north of Forty-Seventh Street, it was a race track owned by the adjacent Union Stock Yards. For baseball games, a grandstand was built within the enclosure, and the top rows could be removed when the races were held.

Counting the baseball seats and the racing seats together, the facility had a capacity of thirty thousand, which, for the time, was enormous (although attendance never came even close to that). However, the owners decided that Dexter Park's location was too distant, given that public transportation consisted mostly of horse-drawn streetcars.[32]

In 1871, the team moved to the Union Base-Ball Grounds, also known as Lake Park or Lake Shore Park, which was on the southeast corner of Michigan and Randolph, exactly where Millennium Park is today. It had been open for only a few months when it was destroyed in the Great Chicago Fire. The White Stockings did not even field a team in 1872 and 1873, but in 1874, the team moved into another home—the Twenty-Third Street Grounds, which Cub historian Glenn Stout has dismissed as "ramshackle" and "a ballpark of sorts," although it had a reasonable capacity of seven thousand.[33] A better facility was then erected on the site of the old Union Base-Ball Grounds, and in 1878, the White Stockings moved back downtown. The park was now known as "Lakefront Park." Unfortunately, the site had been used as a dumping ground for debris from the Chicago Fire, and rocks, glass, bottles, and ashes had an annoying way of poking through the ground. This park was squeezed into a long, narrow lot, which resulted in the shortest fences in the history of major league baseball. The dimensions were: center field, 300 feet; left center, 280 feet; left field, 186 feet; right center, 252 feet, right field, 196 feet—so short that a rule was instituted that a ball hit over the fence would be not a home run but a ground rule double. However, in 1884, the team decided, for just that one season, to count the hits as homers. Home run totals shot up ridiculously; Cap Anson slugged twenty-one, and Ned Williamson hit twenty-seven, a record not surpassed until Babe Ruth broke it in 1919.

In 1882, attendance at Lakefront Park averaged almost twenty-nine hundred, the highest in the league, and in the following year, Spalding laid out $10,000 to remodel the facility. It now held ten thousand viewers (two thousand in standing room), making it the largest and finest ballpark in the nation. It even sported eighteen what might be called skyboxes that sported "cozily draped curtains . . . and luxurious arm chairs" for "the accommodation of reporters, club officials, and parties of ladies and gentlemen."[34] The ballpark's staff included seven ushers, six policemen, four ticket sellers, eight musicians, six vendors of refreshments, and three cushion renters. The First Cavalry Band played in a pagoda overlooking the main entrance.[35]

As comfortable as Lakefront Park was, it was never supposed to be there. The federal government owned the land and long before had allowed Chicago to utilize it with the stipulation that no permanent structure be erected there. Lakefront Park, however, gave every indication of being permanent, and in 1884, the government sold the land to the Illinois Central Railroad for $800,000, and the White Stockings had to move again. Their next home, called West Side Park (also known as West Side Park I) was bounded by Congress, Loomis, Harrison, and Throop Streets, which was reasonably close to downtown. It had larger stands than Lakefront Park, and as at Lakefront, the distances down the foul lines were short (216 feet); center field, however, was so deep that the far end was used as a parking ground for carriages.[36]

In 1890, most of the National League ballplayers (not Cap Anson, however) attempted to set up a rival league called the Players' National League of Professional Base Ball Clubs, or the Players' League for short. They were fed up not only with Spalding's reserve clause but also with the maximum salary of $2,000 he had fixed. Anson later recalled that the National League scheduled games on the same days as the Players' League, which threw "both clubs and public into confusion" so that the fans became "so disgusted as to stay away from the games altogether" and revenues plummeted.[37] Although the Players' League lasted just one season, Chicago's entry, the Chicago Pirates, had constructed a fine ballpark on the South Side at Wentworth and Thirty-Fifth. When the Pirates played there, it was called Brotherhood Park; after they folded, it became known as the Thirty-Fifth Street Grounds. Now that it was empty, Anson's team moved in, although the team didn't abandon West Side Park but split the schedule between the two venues. It was at this time that the team acquired the name "Colts." In his autobiography, Anson wrote that so many of the White Stockings' players had bolted to the new league that, except for third baseman Tom Burns and Anson himself, "the rest of the team was composed of a lot of half-broken 'colts.'"[38]

One problem with the lease on the Thirty-Fifth Street Grounds was that it prohibited Sunday games, which was probably one of the reasons that Spalding decided to construct yet another park. In addition, his real estate company owned the land on which it would be built, and he would be able to rent the stadium to the Colts for $6,000. Finally, a new elevated rail line was being planned that would enable fans to get to the new ballpark from downtown in seven minutes. This new facility was the West Side Grounds, which opened in 1893. During the ballpark's first year, it was used only for Sunday games. In 1894, nearly all home games were played there; in 1895, all home games were played there.

Fashioned from steel and wood and costing $30,000, the West Side Grounds sat some sixteen thousand spectators, although overflow patrons were permitted to stand at the perimeter of the outfield, which could bring total attendance to twenty-six thousand. Above the grandstand was a balcony containing fifty-eight boxes for plusher patrons. The roof had three green towers and a bandstand. Left center was a long 441 feet away, although right center was a more manageable 365. The depth of center field was altered over the years but was 475 feet when the park opened. In a preview of things to come at Wrigley Field, nearby homeowners erected rooftop bleachers. There is persuasive evidence that the much-debated origin of the term "out in left field" to mean "odd" or "out of it" lies in the location of Chicago's Neuropsychiatric Institute, which stood behind the park's left field.[39] Thus, someone "out in left field" was a mental patient, or someone who should be.

Although the West Side Grounds could accommodate twenty-six thousand, only rarely did that many people attend a game. In 1893, average attendance at a U.S. major league baseball game was about two thousand; Chicago teams appear to have averaged

The spacious outfield of the West Side Grounds can be seen in this view of a game between the Cubs and the White Sox in October 1909. (Library of Congress)

around thirty-three hundred spectators in the late nineteenth century. However, special days brought special crowds. On July 4, 1895, two games were played, and the crowd count for both matches was 34,942 (22,913 for the afternoon game). The record attendance for the West Side Grounds was 27,489 on a Sunday in 1899, which meant that over ten thousand people were standing at the periphery of the outfield.[40] According to the reference book *Total Baseball*, the Colts drew 382,300 fans in 1895, the first year in which every home game was played at the West Side Grounds, which makes the average attendance for the sixty-seven home games about 5,706. The team's best year was 1905, when the Cubs led the league with an attendance of 687,419, a huge number for the era. Games usually started at 3:00 P.M., which sounds odd but was actually a convenient time. The Chicago Board of Trade shut its doors at 1:30 P.M., and the Stock Exchange closed a half hour later, which meant that plenty of office workers were free to speed over to the ballpark for a game and still get home at a reasonable hour.

In 1893, the Colts opened their home season at the Thirty-Fifth Street Grounds. "Old Man" Anson had confidence in his team, telling reporters that he would be "knocking at the door when the league pennant is given out."[41] Opening day was May 13, and the Colts lost to the Cincinnati Reds, 10–8. The next day was a Sunday, so the game was played in the new West Side Grounds. The *Chicago Tribune* commented on the "fine new ball park," calling it "perhaps the best in the world," and opined that the splendid surroundings "ought to cheer any ball team on to new and nobler ways."[42] It was not to be. Again the Colts lost to the Reds, this time in epic fashion. After six innings, Chicago was leading 7–2, and then Cincinnati went on to score three in the seventh, four in the eighth, and four more in the ninth, for a final score of 13–12. Cincinnati's winning run was scored when a ground ball was hit toward Colts second baseman George Decker. Decker, the *Tribune* reported, "was spread out like a spider. The ball hit a lump of mud just before it reached him, changed its course so that it barked his shin, then rolled into right field." Scampering home on the play was one Charles Comiskey, who would eventually become the first owner of the White Sox. The Colts had a dismal season. Late in August, the *Chicago Tribune* was lamenting, "Never in the history of baseball has a Chicago team been so low in the race at this season of the year" and was pining for the White Stockings of a decade earlier.[43] The Colts finished the 1893 season in ninth place, twenty-nine games back of Boston.

The ballpark had been open barely a year when, during a Sunday game attended by about ten thousand fans on August 5, 1894, a spectator tossed a cigar butt into a pile of rubbish and touched off a fire in the grandstands. The narrow exits filled with smoke, and spectators panicked. Two years before, irate fans at the Thirty-Fifth Street Grounds had swarmed on to the field to berate the umpire, forcing Chicago to forfeit a game that they looked certain to win. So when the West Side Grounds were constructed, a barbed wire fence was put up to keep fans off the field. Another barbed wire fence had been erected to separate the twenty-five-cent seats from the fifty-cent ones. As the flames grew larger, as a newspaper report put it, "Women screamed in their fright and men got jammed against the sharp fence. The exits might as well have not been there."[44] About five thousand people were trapped between the spreading flames and the barbed wire. Some men managed to climb over it; others worked their way through. "Men came popping out through the wires," reported the *Chicago Tribune*, "their faces and hands torn and bloody, their clothes in rags, wild with fright. The crazed crowd behind pushed and pounded upon those near the barrier, driving them into the cruel barbs. Some of the men had sense enough to look after the few women in the bleachers—not over half a dozen."[45] Three Colt players bravely attacked the fence with baseball bats and the barrier gave way as the crowd spilled onto the field. No one was killed, but at least five hundred people were hurt, mostly with lacerations. Fortunately, County Hospital and Presbyterian Hospital were nearby and took in many of the injured. As the *Tribune* described it, "The whole medical staff of two big hospitals was kept busy the rest of the afternoon patching scratches and cuts." The burnt seats were fenced off and the park remained open the rest of the season, although the destroyed grandstands were not replaced until September 8.

One of the oddest episodes in the ballpark's history occurred in 1897, the year in which Chicagoans were mesmerized by the trial of meat packer Adolph Luetgert, who was accused of murdering his wife and melting her corpse in acid in a sausage vat. On September 29, 1897, two deputy sheriffs, apparently wishing to give the jurors a break, took the twelve men out to the empty West Side Grounds and got up an informal baseball game. There were seven players on a side, and after an hour of invigorating recreation, the team captained by a juror named Fowler was ahead, 10–3. (Luetgert was convicted and sentenced to life in prison, where he died in 1899.)

As has been noted, the West Side Grounds went on to become the scene of Chicago's greatest baseball glory. But a new age of larger fireproof ballparks was dawning. Philadelphia's Shibe Park (1909) seated twenty-three thousand; Sportsman's Park in St. Louis (1909) held 24,040; the Polo Grounds in New York (1911) held 31,316; and Braves' Field in Boston (1915) seated forty thousand.[46] It didn't take long for the West Side Grounds to start looking old and shabby. In 1912, a group of financiers founded a baseball league known as the Federal League to compete with the National and American Leagues. The Chicago entry was called the Whales, and the club played in a spacious new facility on the North Side called Weeghman Field after the team owner, Charles ("Lucky Charlie") Weeghman. The Whales actually won the Federal League pennant in 1915, but the league went broke after only two years of play. Weeghman, however, put together a team of investors and purchased a controlling interest in the Cubs for approximately half a million dollars. Despite warnings that fans would not troop all the way up to the North Side, he moved the Cubs to Weeghman Field. One member of Weeghman's team of investors was the chewing gum tycoon William Wrigley Jr., and when Weeghman fell into financial trouble in 1918, Wrigley became the team's major stockholder. By 1921, he was sole owner. The ballpark, which had been known as Cubs Park since 1919, officially became Wrigley Field in 1926.

The State of Illinois bought the West Side Grounds for $400,000 in 1917 and demolished it. In the 1920s, the land was used to erect two new medical college buildings and a hospital, and the site is now part of the 560-acre Illinois Medical District. The ballpark did not vanish without a few tears. In his "Wake of the News" column in the *Chicago Tribune*, Ring Lardner published a parody of Thomas Gray's "Elegy in a Country Churchyard" entitled "Elegy Written in a West Side Ball Yard." Here are two sample stanzas:

> Now fades the glimmering landscape on the sight,
> Save for the chatter of the laboring folk
> Returning to their hovels for the night,
>   All's still at Taylor, Lincoln, Wood, and Polk.

> Beneath this aged roof, this grandstand's shade,
> Where peanut shucks lie in a mold'ring heap,
> Where show the stains of pop and lemonade,
>   The Cub bugs used to cheer and groan and weep.

And then the West Side Grounds were pretty much forgotten—until 2006, when a Chicago policeman and student of baseball history named Mike Reischl formed a group called the Way Out in Left Field Society to raise funds to have a marker

A plaque outside the Neuropsychiatric Institute of the University of Illinois at Chicago today marks the site of the old West Side Grounds. (Photograph by the author)

placed at the site. He and a colleague named Brian Bernardoni secured the necessary landmark approval from the Illinois State Historical Society and cooperation from the Illinois Medical District. Reischl determined that the ideal place for the plaque was outside the University of Illinois–Chicago's Neuropsychiatric Institute at 912 South Wood Street, where the centerfield flag pole of the West Side Grounds once stood. The unveiling of the monument took place on September 6, 2008, about a month before the centennial of the Cubs' World Series victory of 1908. The very next day, the Cubs lost a road game to none other than the Cincinnati Reds, who, even more remarkably, scored three runs in the bottom of the ninth—a near duplication of the first game ever played at the West Side Grounds. Given that eerie similarity, Cub fans could be forgiven for feeling that the team's fortunes were somehow entwined with the supernatural.

10

The Chicago Hot Dog

The words "icon" and "iconic" are easily thrown about, but if anything deserves such language it's the hot dog. Although it has long been a symbol of American life, General Motors probably cinched the deal in 1975 when it devised the jingle, "Baseball, Hot Dogs, Apple Pie and Chevrolet, They Go Together in the Good 'Ole USA." And nowhere is a hot dog more "iconic" than in Chicago.

It's easy to find out when the first Chevrolet appeared (1911), apple pies appear to go back to the Middle Ages, and baseball, as discussed in the previous chapter, was invented in and around Manhattan. And the hot dog? Like most of America's favorite fast foods (pizza, "French" fries, tacos, and hamburgers), it comes from abroad. A sign of that is the two names by which it is known: "frankfurter" and "wiener," indicating origins in two German-speaking cities—Frankfurt am Main and Vienna (Wien).[1]

The hot dog is a type of sausage, and the art of sausage making is ancient, having been traced to some five thousand years ago in Sumer. Sausage is mentioned in Homer's *Odyssey*, and one of the characters in *The Knights* by Aristophanes is a sausage seller named Agoracritus, who even carries a portable kitchen (history's first hot dog street cart?). Historians tell us that sausage vendors sold their wares in the aisles of Greek theaters—an uncanny forerunner to ballpark hot dog vendors. In the Middle

Ages, various cities and regions had their own varieties of sausage, such as bologna, Bavarian weisswurst, Irish blood sausage, and Thuringer from the German region of Thuringia. In Frankfurt, the story goes that in the seventeenth century, a butcher from Coburg named Johann Georghehner settled in the city, bringing his sausage recipe with him. Some sources, therefore, consider Georghehner the "inventor of the hot dog," although the Viennese point to the "wiener" to show that the hot dog originated in their metropolis. Some German sources state that a Frankfurt butcher named Johann Georg Lahner moved to Vienna in the early nineteenth century, which means that at least some "wieners" actually originated in Frankfurt.

And the Chicago hot dog? There's no doubt: it's a wiener.

German sausages have been eaten in America since German settlers arrived in the colonial era, but the American frankfurter or wiener as it is known and eaten today dates from a later period. One myth of long standing is that the hot dog in a bun was invented at the St. Louis World's Fair of 1904. As the legend tells it, a sausage vendor named Anton Feuchtwanger would lend his customers gloves so they would be able to handle his scalding sausages. Too many people walked off with the gloves, so Feuchtwanger asked his brother-in-law, a baker, to devise a roll to contain the sausages, thus creating the hot dog. A second version of the story says that Feuchtwanger began wrapping sausages in rolls in the late 1880s, and when Chris von der Ahe, owner of the St. Louis Browns, heard about it, he began selling hot dogs at his ballpark. Unfortunately, there is no evidence to support either of these tales, and the *Oxford Companion to Food* settles for, "All that can be said with any certainty is that in the closing decades of the 19th century frankfurters and wienies were being sold in buns in various cities in the USA."

However, Barry A. Popik, an investigator of expressions and slang, has discovered several nineteenth-century references to people eating sausage sandwiches, the earliest of which is from Charles Dickens in "The Key of the Street" (1851), where he speaks of crowds of people "clamorous for sandwiches. Ham sandwiches, beef sandwiches, German sausage sandwiches."

Dickens also says that "the cry is 'mustard,'" a serendipitous addition that lets us know that the practice of slathering mustard onto hot dogs is a venerable one. An article in the *Chicago News* from 1890, entitled "Chicago's Night Cooks," quotes a street sausage vendor (apparently German) who says, "Vill de shentlemens haf some red-hots und brod?" which is especially interesting not only because it's another indication of the pairing of hot dogs and bread but also because one might easily think that the term "hot dog" for a frankfurter or wiener preceded "red hot," and it evidently didn't.

The most informative clue is to be found in the New York City newspaper obituaries for a baker named Ignatz Frischman,

A hot dog vendor at Luna Park in Coney Island, New York, in 1904. It was at Coney Island that hot dogs became a national craze associated with beaches and summertime. (Library of Congress)

who was described as the "Frankfurter roll man." According to these articles, Frischman, who was born in Austria in 1850, in the early 1880s established a bakery in Coney Island, New York, where he began turning out Vienna rolls "of a special size" to serve as a superior replacement for the two slices of bread then being used for frankfurter sandwiches. The rolls were a triumph, and soon he was producing a hundred thousand of them on an average summer Sunday.[2] These sources reveal that the hot dog bun was well known a good two decades before the St. Louis World's Fair. They also show that almost certainly nobody ever needed gloves to eat one—some sort of bread covering or wrapping was standard practice.

The first person to make hot dogs a national craze associated with beaches and summertime was Nathan Handwerker, whose name is on the famous hot dog stand still located in Coney Island. Before Nathan, however, there was Charles Feltman, a German immigrant who owned a Coney Island entertainment empire that included nine restaurants. Feltman sold millions of ten-cent hot dogs, but his restaurants were better known for their shore dinners. In 1914, young Handwerker began working at Feltman's as a counterman dispensing hot dogs. According to Handwerker family lore, two of his friends, entertainers Eddie Cantor and Jimmy Durante, told him that ten cents was too much for a hot dog, giving Handwerker the idea of opening his own place. He opened his stand in 1916, and not only were the hot dogs just five cents, but also he threw in a root beer and a pickle. Today, Nathan's is a hot dog giant, with some eight thousand retail locations. Nathan's profile in Chicago, however, is very low. The Nathan's hot dog is a New York hot dog, not a Chicago hot dog.

Another early myth about the hot dog has to do with the origin of the term. For a long time, "hot dog" was attributed to a New York cartoonist named T. A. Dorgan. The story is that that Harry M. Stevens, who owned the food franchise at New York's Polo Grounds, was at the ballpark on a cold day in April 1901. The soda pop and ice cream were not moving, so he had the idea of sending some vendors to nearby butchers to buy some "long dachshund sausages" and to bakers for some soft rolls. The new food item was a hit. Dorgan, who was in the press box, thought—if these are called "dachshund sausages" and the vendors are touting them as something hot to eat, why not call them "hot dogs"? He thereupon drew a cartoon illustrating the new food item. The trouble with this story is that this legendary cartoon has never been found. There is a Dorgan cartoon of a six-day bicycle race in 1906 that does use the term "hot dog," but by 1906, the term "hot dog" was old news.

According to hot dog historian Bruce Kraig, the earliest recorded use of the term comes from, coincidentally, 1893, when an article in the September 28 edition of the *Knoxville Journal* said, "Even the wienerwurst men began preparing the 'hot dogs' ready for sale Saturday night."[3] Popik, however, has located a reference to "hot dog" peddlers in the New Brunswick (New Jersey) *Daily Times* that predates the Knoxville mention by five months. However that may be, the widespread popularity of "hot dog" appears to have arisen from college humor magazines of the 1890s. For example, Popik discovered in *The New Harvard Song Book* (copyright 1892) a verse that ran,

> Those little old hot dogs!
> Those little old hot dogs that Rammy sold!
> We would put fourteen away
> Just before we hit the hay—
> Those little old hot dogs that Rammy sold!

The first use of the term "hot dog" in the *Chicago Tribune* comes from 1904 in an article describing the visit of Democratic presidential candidate Alton B. Parker to a county fair in upstate New York.[4]

That the frankfurter or wiener would be viewed in terms of a dog is not surprising. Throughout the nineteenth and early twentieth centuries, humorists loved cracking jokes about the supposedly dubious contents of sausages. One well-known early example is the comic song of 1864 "Der Deitcher's Dog," the melody of which is still familiar ("Oh where, oh where has my little dog gone?"). Part of the ditty goes,

Un sasage ish goot, bolonie of course,
Oh where can he be.
Dey makes um mit dog und dey makes em mit horse,
I guess dey makes em mit he.

Newspapers also delighted in supposedly funny grisly cartoons depicting dogs being shoved into meat grinders and emerging as linked sausages.

The Hot Dog Comes to Chicago

The first mention of a "Vienna sausage" in the *Chicago Tribune* came on October 21, 1894, in a cartoon entitled "The Escaped Lion and the Vienna Sausage." The first panel shows a lion sauntering into a restaurant where a seated patron hands the

Many Americans got their first taste of an authentic "wiener" from vendors like these at *Old Vienna* at the Columbian Exposition. The price—ten cents—was not exactly cheap. (ICHi-02453, Chicago History Museum)

animal a sausage. The second panel shows the lion throwing up—presumably, the contents of that sausage were so toxic that even the king of beasts could not stomach it. That this cartoon dates from 1894 is telling: the editors at the *Tribune* had probably become familiar with "Vienna sausages" at the Columbian Exposition and couldn't resist the tried-and-true tainted-sausage joke. Because of the Columbian Exposition, Vienna sausages (wieners) were catching on in Chicago.[5]

Chicago was a very German city in the late nineteenth century. Germans constituted the largest ethnic group, and in 1900, the German population numbered some 470,000—one out of every four Chicagoans had either been born in Germany or had a parent who had been born there. Of course, some of the German that was spoken in Chicago was spoken by people who came from Austria. Immigration from the Austro-Hungarian Empire to Chicago occurred at a later date than the immigration from Germany, but beginning around 1890, Chicago became the city of choice for people emigrating from the Burgenland region of eastern Austria. According to 1890 census figures, there were about 14,738 Austrians in Chicago, and another source gives the number in 1905 as 29,760.[6] Together with the Germans, this meant a lot of butchers and a lot of sausage.

One German butcher who went on to fame was Oscar F. Mayer (1859–1955), who in 1893 had already been selling sausages in Chicago for a decade. He had emigrated to the United States in 1863 and had originally settled in Detroit. He then moved to Chicago, where in 1877 he went to work for the Armour meatpacking company as a buyer. His brother Gottfried, who had been a sausage maker in Nuremberg, joined him in Chicago in 1883, and the two purchased an existing German meat market. The pair made a success of the enterprise and by 1893 were displaying their wares at the Columbian Exposition and delivering their sausages throughout the city. Although the Oscar Mayer wiener went on to national renown, thanks in great measure to the company's marketing techniques, such as the Wienermobile, it did not become the Chicago hot dog. In 1919, Oscar F.'s son, Oscar G. Mayer, traveled to Wisconsin and discovered a large defunct packing plant for sale. The Mayers purchased the property and moved their business. Today, Oscar Meyer has its headquarters in Madison, Wisconsin. Anyone entering one of Chicago's estimated two thousand hot dog stands (more than all of its McDonalds, Burger Kings, and Wendys combined) is almost guaranteed to find either of two brands: Vienna Beef and Red Hot Chicago. Both of these dogs trace their origins to 1893 (and, before that, to Vienna).

The Germans and the Austrians had a strong presence at Chicago's Columbian Exposition of 1893. The seventeen-thousand-square-foot German Village had a castle and peasant homes, as well as a much-loved beer garden. The German Building, which looked like a flamboyant medieval *Rathaus*, was built as a permanent structure and served as a popular restaurant in Jackson Park until it burned down in 1925.[7] The Austrians were not to be outdone, and one of the most popular attractions on the Midway Plaisance was Old Vienna, a reproduction of a part of the Austrian capital as it was supposed to have looked in the early eighteenth century. There were no fewer than seventy buildings arranged along a curved street, some thirty-four of them stores filled with such items as Bohemian garnets and other jewelry, glass engravings, leather goods, Viennese candy, handkerchiefs, fans, and bentwood furniture. There were plenty of places at which to dine on Austrian delicacies; the official beer was Salvator, but many wines were available as well. The *Chicago Tribune* ran a humorous column describing the adventures of two friends who drank more than their share of Austrian "Gerspritzen," and after the fourth glass got into a dispute that had them "rolling upon the grass with the table as a third participant."[8] Old Vienna was visited by both former U.S. president Rutherford B. Hayes and the twenty-nine-year-old Archduke Franz Ferdinand (actually, the duke didn't exactly "visit" because the crowd was so huge that he was apparently intimidated and declined to enter). More than five hundred Austrians ran Old Vienna, and of course, they brought their sausages with them. A picture of two sausage vendors at Old Vienna shows them selling "Fine Vienna Sausages" for ten cents.

Old Vienna was one of the most popular attractions on the Midway Plaisance at the Columbian Exposition. (Author's collection)

Among the entrepreneurs at the Columbian Exposition were two young adventurers from Austria-Hungary—Samuel Ladany and his brother-in-law Emil Reichel. Ladany (the name is Hungarian and the original form was "Ladanyi") and Reichel were born in Budapest and went to Vienna to become apprentices in the sausage-making trade. They came to Chicago in 1890, and when the great fair arrived, they saw their chance. They bought a quantity of sausages from a small butcher shop and went to look for a promising spot. It is not known exactly where they set up their cart, although it was not inside Old Vienna. Most likely it was near one of the entrances to the Midway. The partners did so well that after the fair closed they were able to purchase their own store at 417 South Halsted Street, where they made their own sausages in the style they had learned in Vienna. Being Jewish, the founders did not, like many other companies, use pork in their product; the company became known as Vienna

Beef and it seems that many non-Jews came to prefer its recipe. As a result, although butchers were selling frankfurters and wieners in Chicago before the Columbian Exposition, we can say that the "Chicago hot dog" began in 1893 because Vienna Beef eventually came to dominate the market. Both Vienna Beef and Red Hot Chicago trace their origins to Samuel Ladany.

Samuel Ladany, the father of the "Chicago Hot Dog" and the founder of the Vienna Beef Company, began selling his sausages outside the gates of the Columbian Exposition in 1893. (Photo courtesy of Scott Ladany)

Ladany and Reichel were not content to simply peddle sausages from their own store. Soon they began selling their products to other stores and to restaurants, thus becoming a supplier. In 1908, Vienna Beef invested in a fleet of horse-drawn carriages to deliver its products throughout Chicago; in 1928, motorized vehicles replaced the wagons. The operation grew, rebuilding and remodeling were carried out, adjacent properties were acquired, new machinery was added, and efficiency was increased. Ladany's son Jules joined his father in the business in 1922, and the younger son, William, came aboard ten years later after graduating from the University of Chicago. In the 1950s, Vienna Beef began selling throughout the Midwest, and in 1962, its products began appearing in supermarkets. In 1957, *Tribune* reporter James Gavin interviewed Jules and William Ladany and wrote that they were of the opinion "that merchandise must be promoted with style and glamor. They contend that packaging is more and more assuming a prime position in merchandising"—which is likely a key to the company's continued growth and success.[9] In 1972, Vienna Beef moved into a large modern factory on North Damen Avenue, where it continues its operations. Jules and William Ladany died thirty-one days apart in 1978, and four years later, two of the company's top executives, James Eisenberg (who had married

The Vienna Beef Company originally delivered its wares by horse-drawn wagons but switched to a motorized fleet in 1928. (Photo courtesy of Vienna Beef, Ltd.)

Jules's daughter) and James W. Bodman, arranged a leveraged buyout and purchased the stock of the privately owned company from the estates of the founding families. Eighty percent of the proceeds went to the Ladany family, 10 percent went to the Reichels, and 10 percent went to others (the figures indicate how Reichel's interests and participation had declined over the years and how Vienna Beef had become a Ladany family business).[10]

But the sale did not mean that the Ladany family was finished in the Chicago hot dog trade. Scott Ladany, grandson of Samuel, went out on his own and in 1986 founded Red Hot Chicago, which made Ladany-family hot dogs at a factory on West Armitage Avenue. His slogan became "A Family Tradition Since 1893," and his products are found throughout Chicago; the presence of his son Billy in the company guarantees the Ladany presence in the Chicago hot dog business for at least another generation.

In June 2011, the Vienna Beef Company filed suit against Scott Ladany for allegedly claiming that his hot dogs were made with Vienna's original recipe, which he had agreed not to use when he left the company in 1983. This placed Ladany in the odd situation of being charged with having "stolen" his own family's recipe. The row ended amicably in February 2012, when Scott Ladany leased his Armitage Avenue plant to another company and returned to Vienna Beef as president of Red Hot Chicago, which became a separate division of the parent company.

Inventing the Chicago Hot Dog

Vendors who served Vienna Beef hot dogs in the early days were giving their customers hot dogs made in Chicago, but they were not giving them "Chicago hot dogs" as they are known today. The dogs were probably served simply—on a roll or on bread with a dash of mustard or maybe horseradish. The classic Chicago hot dog consists of a hot dog on a poppy seed bun (preferably from S. Rosen's) topped with seven ingredients—mustard, chopped onion, bright green relish, tomato wedges, a pickle spear, sport peppers, and a dash of celery salt (ketchup is prohibited[11]). At least, that's the formula according to the people at Vienna Beef, and it's the one given in all the Chicago guidebooks. The process by which the simple hot dog of Samuel Ladany became the "Chicago hot dog" unfolded in three stages. First, there was the creation of the hot dog itself, which, as has been seen, dates to 1893. The second step was the addition of all the toppings, which made the Chicago hot dog different from those in other parts of the United States. The final step was the recognition by Chicagoans and outsiders that the city had a unique food product that was worth cherishing, searching out, and writing about.

The idea of piling an abundance of ingredients onto a Chicago hot dog appears to have caught on during the Great Depression of the 1930s and is widely attributed to Abe Drexler, who ran a hot dog stand named Fluky's at the corner of Halsted and Maxwell Streets in a predominantly Jewish neighborhood. The Chicago hot dog, it should be pointed out, is by and large a Jewish

A Vienna Beef smokehouse in 1913. (Photo courtesy of Vienna Beef, Ltd.)

product (as is the New York hot dog). As mentioned, Ladany and Reichel were Jewish, which explains why their product was an all-beef hot dog and the company is called Vienna *Beef*, and several other Jewish hot dog manufacturers thrived in Chicago in the mid-twentieth century.[12] The original frankfurter/wiener pioneered by Johann Georg Lahner contained both pork and beef, which means that Ladany put a Jewish spin on the original wiener that he knew back home. In the early days of hot dogs, the idea that they were "kosher" (although many, including Vienna Beef, were not, strictly speaking) caused many purchasers to assume that they were uncontaminated.

In 1976, the *Chicago Tribune* interviewed Drexler. As he explained it, his father originally had a fruit stand, but "the fruit stand was converted into a hot dog stand. I was 19 when I started working there, a student at Medill High School. We sold hot dogs for a nickel apiece, seven items for a nickel: the hot dog,

onions, pickle, piccalilli, French fries, lettuce, hot peppers. . . .
Did we make money? We did marvelous. There was no income
tax, no sales tax."[13] (Piccalilli was a synonym for relish. In the
1970s, according to Fluky's lore, it was replaced—no one is sure
why—by the neon green relish that is now such a striking addition to the Chicago hot dog.) There has been some confusion
about the date of the first Fluky's. Most sources give the year
as 1929, which would mean it would not be correct to describe
their item as a "Depression dog" because the stock market crash
occurred in October 1929, and the Depression didn't really pick
up steam until the following year. However, Drexler told the
Tribune that Fluky's started in November 1932, which leads to
the conclusion that the 1929 date refers to his father's converted
fruit stand and that the famous Fluky's, which was actually a
second Drexler hot dog establishment, began three years later.
Abe Drexler died in 1986 at age seventy-six; his obituary said
that half of the original Fluky's was on the sidewalk and the
other half on the street; a fire hydrant, which was located inside, served as the water source. The Fluky's hot dog as Drexler
described it was not exactly the Chicago hot dog of today, but
it was very close, and Fluky's became famous.

As popular as Fluky's was, it's likely that other hot dog vendors were doing something similar in Chicago at the same time.
Hot dog historian Bruce Kraig interviewed several people who
recalled the early Chicago hot dog and came away with the
impression that Greek and Italian vendors began adding various toppings during the Depression in order to get an edge
on the competition:

> If Jews made hot dogs, Greeks, Macedonians, Bulgarians,
> Italians and Mexicans dressed them. In Chicago of 1900
> to the 1920s, Greeks and Italians competed in the fruit
> and vegetable market and a good number of each were
> street vendors. . . . Both developed many of the toppings
> on the classic Chicago hot dog, the classic "garden on
> a bun." Green relish (piccalilli), sport peppers (pickled
> mildly hot small chillies) and tomato are Mediterranean
> in origin, like a *giardiniere*. Mustard is German-Jewish, as

are the pickle spears and optional celery salt (this replaces a once ubiquitous vegetable on the American table). The ensemble gives a sweet-sour-spicy flavour profile that was dear to East European and Mediterranean taste buds. The Chicago hot dog is a palimpsest of early twentieth-century Chicago ethnicity.[14]

(Vienna Beef's Bob Schwartz, by the way, avers that the sport peppers were brought from Louisiana by African Americans who settled in Chicago during the Great Migration, which began during World War I.)

The seven ingredients on the traditional Chicago hot dog appear to have become canonical sometime in the 1960s or 1970s. One of the first, if not the first, guidebook to Chicago hot dogs, Rich Bowen and Dick Fay's *Hot Dog Chicago: A Native's Dining Guide* (1983), lists the seven condiments as standard.

At some point, the term "dragged through the garden" became attached to the preparation of this overloaded food treat. This imaginative phrase has become much beloved by writers of guidebooks to Chicago. Although it's possible the term has been in use since the Depression, the earliest citations date from the 1960s, and it has been used in places far from Chicago (at the famous Varsity drive-in in Atlanta, for example) and for hamburgers as well as hot dogs.[15] Another description that became attached to the Chicago hot dog was "banquet on a bun," although this term, too, has been used in other contexts. A few burger joints with that name were to be found in Chicago in the 1950s and up to at least the early 1980s. The phrase, which is still used to describe different kinds of sandwiches, seems to have been common in post–World War II America; in 1961, Chicago columnist Herb Lyon reported that a couple of local restaurateurs were set to open six Banquet on a Bun restaurants in Hollywood.[16]

In any case, few Chicagoans these days speak of their hot dogs as being "dragged through the garden" or being a "banquet on a bun." But they do take them seriously. Articles on where to find the best hot dog recur regularly in Chicago's magazines and newspapers, and plenty of Web sites and blogs argue the finer points. In 1995, the celebrated Chicago newspaper columnist Mike Royko wrote a famous column in which he upbraided the then U.S. senator from Illinois, Chicagoan Carol Moseley Braun, for incorrectly stating the ingredients for a Chicago hot dog. A coalition of organizations representing the meat business had put together a cookbook and had asked for contributions from politicians. Moseley Braun offered a hot dog topped with jalapenos, relish, mustard, and *ketchup*! "If the election were held today," Royko fumed, "I'd have to vote for just about anyone running against Senator Moseley-Braun."[17] After Barack Obama of Chicago entered the White House, he made sure to serve up correct Chicago-style dogs at the annual congressional picnic (the dogs were prepared by the owner of Byron's Hot Dogs).

The Chicago hot dog is ambitiously spiced, made for adult tastes, and not deadly bland . . .

By the time the Obamas were doling out the sport peppers in the nation's capital, the "Chicago hot dog" was firmly fixed in America's consciousness, and the third stage of the development was complete. The food item was no longer a hot dog consumed in Chicago but a "Chicago hot dog," and the entire nation recognized it as a bona fide regional food to rank with the New York bagel, the Philly cheese steak, and the New Orleans po' boy. This development is fairly recent; in fact, Chicagoans themselves don't seem to have appreciated that they had developed a distinctive American fast food until around 1970. One of the earliest recorded instances of that recognition came in an article by Norbert Blei in the June 6, 1971, edition of the *Chicago Tribune* entitled "The Great Chicago Hot Dog Quest." Blei began by saying, "I never gave any serious consideration to hot dog lore before," and then went on to surmise that hot dog eaters are an undiscriminating bunch: "As long as it looks like a hot dog, is stuck in a bun, the trimmings will take care of the rest." However, he discovered that some hot dogs were better than others. Peep's Hot Dogs, for example, had a good dog but not a great one. Lum's Famous Hot Dog (steamed in beer) was a little better and was covered in pickles, raw onion, and sliced tomatoes. Even better was the dog at Bob Elfman's on State Street; it came with half a pickle, half a green pepper, raw onion, and "the greenest piccalilli I have ever seen." He continued through a Mexican place on Twenty-Sixth Street and on to Jumbo Steaks Red Hots, with its "Garden Hot Dog." He then stopped by Maxwell Street, went on to G & D Red Hots on Milwaukee Avenue, and finally found contentment by discovering an actual pushcart vendor on the corner of Milwaukee and Mautene Court. Five years later, Charles Leroux, also writing in the *Tribune*, had a different take. To him, consumers of hot dogs were not indifferent; they "care passionately," he wrote.[18] During the 1970s, the hot dog passed from a being a simple fast food to being an object of debate among discriminating consumers, and the rules on making one were becoming fixed. Bowen and Fay's pioneering *Hot Dog Chicago* was an early sign that Chicagoans were now viewing the Chicago hot dog with pride and beginning to see that it was worth one's time to find a superior hot dog stand: "The hot dogs served in Chicago are finest quality, usually all-beef and pork without the fillers and additives found in supermarket vacuum-packed 'kiddie' hot dogs. . . . The Chicago hot dog is ambitiously spiced, made for adult tastes, and not deadly bland and cloying like the kiddie kind."[19]

Another reason that Chicago hot dogs came to acquire national recognition is that people in other parts of the United States began selling hot dogs in the Chicago style. This is also a trend that seems to date from the 1970s. In *Never Put Ketchup on a Hot Dog*, Bob Schwartz mentions many of these ambassadors of Chicago hot dog wisdom, including Fast Eddie Ermoian of Boulder, Colorado; Dick Malone, owner of Dickie's Dogs in Arizona; Skip Shababy of Skip's in Atlanta; and Mel Lohn, proprietor of Mel's Hot Dogs in Tampa, which was founded in 1972. The success of Taste Chicago, founded by actor Joe Mantegna and his wife, Arlene, in Burbank, California in 2003, indicates that Chicago dogs have become standard fare in Southern California.

It is probably not a coincidence that Charles Leroux's *Tribune* article on Chicago hot dogs appeared in the year of the American bicentennial. That event stirred serious investigations into the history of American customs and manners, with many local organizations and historical societies publishing regional histories and cookbooks. By the 1970s, Americans were coming around to a more democratic, egalitarian view of cooking; national pride, mixed with nostalgia, now made it viable to look for fine dining not, as in decades past, in classy French restaurants, but in local diners and hamburger palaces. It was kind of a reverse snobbism, a disinclination to appear elitist, an eagerness to achieve some sort of solidarity with regular folk, and an indication of a new casualness in manners. A much-admired early instance was the book *American Fried*, published by journalist-humorist Calvin Trillin in 1974. His tongue-in-cheek declaration that Arthur Bryant's, a barbecue joint in Kansas City, was "the single best restaurant in the world" was a major advance in kick-starting the regional food movement. Three years after *American Fried*, Jane and Michael Stern published *Roadfood*, a travelers' guide to dining in the American hinterlands that, like Trillin's book, found fine dining in unexpected places. The logic became inescapable: if a barbecue place can be sublime, if a roadside diner is worth driving miles to visit, why can't a hot dog stand be a destination restaurant? Today, *Roadfood*'s Web site lists several Chicago hot dog places, including the Vienna Beef Factory Store and Café, and many visitors to the Windy City feel their tourist agenda is not complete without sampling a "Chicago hot dog."

11

Wrigley's Gum

Although William Wrigley, who began selling Spearmint and Juicy Fruit in 1893, became the most famous name associated with chewing gum, he didn't invent it. Humans have been chomping on naturally derived sticky substances since the Neolithic period (archaeologists once found nine lumps of well-chewed birch bark tar at a Neolithic site in southern Germany). In 1993, researchers in western Sweden discovered a nine-thousand-year-old gob of honey-sweetened resin that contained tooth marks that, amusingly, appeared to be those of a teenager. The ancient Greeks chewed on a substance called mastic or mastiche, a sap derived from conifers, while Mayans favored the hardened latex of the sapodilla tree (*Manilkara zapota*), a substance known as chicle, which is the ancestor of modern chewing gum.[1]

The pioneer of chewing gum in the United States was John Bacon Curtis of Bangor, Maine. In 1848, the twenty-one-year-old "swamper," who worked clearing trees for roads, decided to look for a less arduous job. At the time, local Indians—as well as the settlers—were in the habit of chewing on the resin from spruce trees, and many lumberjacks collected and sold the stuff. Curtis got the idea that the spruce resin could be retailed in stores across the country, so he boiled up a batch, rolled it into a slab, cut it into strips, and bathed them in cornstarch so they wouldn't stick together. The first storekeeper who stocked the gum sticks quickly sold out, and Curtis's State of Maine Pure Spruce Gum was soon a success. By 1852, the young entrepreneur had built in Portland the world's first chewing gum factory and was selling his product nationwide. Spruce gum, of course, was soon replaced (although it can still be purchased). One of the problems was that the supply of spruce trees dwindled with increased demand for wood pulp. Another problem was that it was unsweetened and tasted "piney." Finally, it was tough to chew.

The next great breakthrough in gum history came in 1869. One of the participants was none other than Antonio López de Santa Anna—the very same Santa Anna whose troops had overrun the Alamo thirty-three years before. The Mexican dictator had been ousted from office in 1855, and one of the places he lived was Staten Island, New York, where in 1857, at age sixty-three, he still harbored dreams of regaining power. One of his schemes involved chicle. He had brought a quantity of the substance with him, and his secretary showed it to a local inventor and glass merchant named Thomas Adams. Santa Anna had the idea of devising a method of using chicle to replace the rubber in carriage tires and asked for Adams's help. Adams bought a ton of chicle, but despite his best efforts, he could not turn it into anything resembling rubber. But when Adams saw a young girl in a drugstore request a piece of paraffin wax gum, he came up with another plan. He whipped up some gumballs and sent them to the drugstore's owner. Adams turned his next batch of chicle into sticks and named them Adams' New York No. 1. In 1871, he created a gum-making machine and soon began adding flavors to his products, one of which became the licorice-based Black Jack. By the 1880s, Adams had more than 250 employees on his payroll. (Santa Anna had died in poverty in Mexico City in 1876.)

Many others tried to get into the chewing gum business in the late nineteenth century. John Colgan of Louisville flavored his Taffy-Tolu Chewing Gum with the sap of the balsam tolu tree, J. M. Clark played the sex-appeal angle with a gum called Kis-Me, and Edward E. Beeman, a Cleveland druggist, came up with a gum that incorporated a pepsin compound. William J. White was the first to put mint into gum, and he used increased amounts of corn syrup to help the gum's latex base absorb flavor. By 1893, White was the largest manufacturer of chewing gum in the country, while William Wrigley was an unknown just getting started in Chicago, where he had been living for about two years. But in that year, he came up with two flavors: Juicy Fruit and Spearmint. They would do pretty well for him.

Wrigley Makes His Fortune

William Wrigley Jr. was born in Philadelphia on September 30, 1861.[2] When he was nine, his father established the Wrigley Manufacturing Company, producers of "Wrigley's Scouring Soap." The business didn't enrich the family, but they were comfortable, although William early started showing his characteristic restlessness. He was bored in school, and at the age of eleven, he persuaded his pal Horace Yonker to take off with him for New York. There Wrigley worked as a newsboy and in a ship's galley, but the onset of cold weather convinced him to return home. The chastened lad agreed to work in the soap plant, but factory labor was not for him, and at age thirteen, he talked his father into letting him try his hand at being a salesman (he was big for his age). He got a horse and wagon, headed out across Pennsylvania and New York, and did remarkably well— he was always polite, he never argued, and people just liked him.

But the Golden West beckoned and, along with a friend named George Whitby, Wrigley headed for the wide open spaces. As the train pulled in to Kansas City, however, Wrigley's hat blew out the window, carrying the train tickets in the hat band. Wrigley was soon working for his father again, although his disappointment was diminished by his acquiring a bride—Ada Foote, who was barely eighteen when she married William on September 17, 1885. Wrigley had lots of grand ideas on how to expand the family soap business,

William Wrigley Jr., one of the towering figures of Chicago commerce, began selling Wrigley's Spearmint and Juicy Fruit gum in 1893. (Library of Congress).

but his father was either indifferent or opposed. As a result, the young Wrigley was drawn to America's most vigorous, most charismatic city—Chicago.

In later life, Wrigley liked to relate how he arrived in Chicago in March 1891 with just $32, and the story is still repeated. But it is misleading because he also had a check for $5,000 from his uncle William Scatchard, who had offered to stake Wrigley if he would take on his son, William Jr., on as a partner. The younger Scatchard was late in arriving in Chicago, so Wrigley, on his own, rented space in a building on Kinzie Street and prepared to start selling his father's soap. Wrigley and his partner took turns hitting the road, but Wrigley also got into the practice of relying on jobbers—people who bought small lots of merchandise from manufacturers and then resold the goods to retailers or users. This turned out to be the key strategy for Wrigley because he got the idea of including premiums with his product. Wrigley began this practice by procuring a quantity of umbrellas. He then sold his soap to jobbers for $3.34 a case and threw in a free umbrella with each case. This little bonus worked wonders, and the soap began selling, although not well enough to suit Wrigley.

"Anyone can make gum," he once said. "Selling it is the problem."

About this time, Wrigley became friends with a baking powder salesman who gave Wrigley the idea of branching out into that product. The competition in Chicago was not nearly as great as it was with soap, and his Spa Baking Powder was a winner. Once again, Wrigley offered premiums: a set of six silver-plated teaspoons proved quite popular. Another super idea was the "Wrigley Cook Book." The back cover said "Price $1.00," but a customer could buy a one-pound can of Spa Baking Powder *and* the cookbook for just fifty cents. Soon Wrigley was shipping nearly fifty thousand cookbooks every month, the baking powder business was flourishing, and Wrigley's Scouring Soap was almost an afterthought. A central element of the success was Wrigley's untiring sales efforts (in his first year of business, he once said, he spent 137 nights on sleeping cars). But he also trained an ace sales force; he befriended his salesmen, taught how to sell, and infected them with his own enthusiasm.

It's not exactly known how Wrigley got the idea of using chewing gum as one of his premiums, but the likeliest story recounts that he was approached by a salesman who wished to sell him sets of colored glass jars. Wrigley didn't believe the jars would find many buyers but thought that they might if they were filled with chewing gum. The meeting seems to have planted an idea in Wrigley's mind because in late 1892, he began looking for someone to manufacture chewing gum for him. He found the Zeno Manufacturing Company, his first gum was called "Lotta," he offered two packs of it with each half-pound can of baking powder, and gradually the baking powder–chewing gum combination sold out. It was then that Wrigley began hearing from his jobbers that it was easier to sell gum than baking powder, so now, he decided, he would be in the chewing gum business. Also, about this time, Wrigley opened an office in Philadelphia, and Scatchard moved to that city to take charge, leaving Wrigley the sole head of Chicago operations.

A setback occurred in 1895 when on the morning of January 27, a natural gas pipe underneath his building exploded, destroying both the structure and Wrigley's stock of gum. Wrigley estimated his losses at $11,000, but he had $6,000 worth of insurance. Ironically, Wrigley's building did not use natural gas; the pipe just happened to run under it. As a reporter put it, "Mr. Wrigley came over to the scene, viewed the wreck, found that some of his stock in the rear of the store and a load of potatoes in the basement were uninjured, and philosophically established his office next door at No. 89 Kinzie."[3]

There were at least a dozen successful chewing gum manufacturers in the United States, and in 1899, the six largest, including White's firm, formed a powerful "chewing gum trust," officially known as the American Chicle Company.[4] Wrigley refused to join. He had one thing his competitors lacked—he was an advertising genius. "Anyone can make gum," he once said. "Selling it is the problem." At first, Wrigley continued his practice of offering premiums along with his product. He tried different varieties of gum (Manna, Smyrna, and Youcanchu were three early varieties) and many premiums (lamps were popular). In the early days, Wrigley's most popular gum was Vassar. He created Juicy Fruit to compete with Adams, who sold a gum called California Fruit, and with Jonathan Primley, who marketed a gum of the same name.

Spearmint was initially a tough sell, but that would change when Wrigley got serious about advertising. Around 1907, Wrigley decided to push Spearmint hard. He spent $1.5 million on advertising, most of it for Spearmint, and sales soared. In the last eight months of 1907, Spearmint sales were $170,000. In 1908, they were $1,345,000; in 1909, $2,444,185; and in 1910, Spearmint sales totaled over $3.3 million, and it was the most popular gum in the United States. Zeno was still manufacturing Wrigley's gum, but Wrigley was friendly with Zeno's owner, and in 1910, the two concluded an affable merger, which put Wrigley in the manufacturing business. By 1913, Spearmint sales were just under $7 million, and Wrigley was spending nearly $2 million on advertising. His placards appeared all over streetcars and subways, and his electric sign in Manhattan's Times Square ran up an annual electric bill of more than $100,000. Wrigley's most impressive selling venture was the "mile-long" sign consisting of 117 linked billboards lining the railroad tracks between Atlantic City and Trenton, New Jersey. In 1924, the omnipresence of Spearmint in the United States was demonstrated by newspaper reports that two thieves had robbed a Chicago bank by affixing wads of the gum to the end of a long stick, inserting the stick into a teller's cage, and lifting out $50,000 worth of government certificates.[5] Wrigley eventually became the largest purchaser of advertising in the United States. In 1922, an advertising trade journal noted with satisfaction that since 1907 Wrigley had spent more than $20 million on advertising.[6] There's a story that Philip K. Wrigley, William's son and heir, was on a plane when someone asked him why he kept advertising so heavily even though Wrigley's products were so well-known. He answered that it was for the same reason that pilot keep their engines running even though their planes are twenty-nine thousand feet in the air.[7]

The Cubs and Catalina

In 1910, Wrigley built in Canada the first of his factories outside the United States. Five years later, he had a facility in Sydney,

Australia, which was followed by factories in Great Britain (1927) and New Zealand (1939). (Today, the Wrigley Company has nineteen factories around the world.) Large fields in Indiana and southern Michigan were being dedicated to the production of mint just for Wrigley. In 1930, the *Chicago Tribune* reported a "bumper crop" in the mint fields and noted that more than some three thousand farmers had planted thirty thousand acres, yielding a quantity of mint oil worth over $2 million. At that time, Michigan and Indiana were producing 90 percent of the mint in the United States.[8] Meanwhile, areas in Mexico and Central America were in great demand for chicle, which was harvested by workers who cut gashes into the sides of sapodilla trees to let the latex run out. Much of the production was centered in the Yucatan peninsula, where Mayan dissidents sometimes interfered with the harvest. The Mexican Revolution also interrupted production. Nevertheless, chicle production boomed; in 1917, the Mexican state of Quintana Roo in the Yucatan produced 45,291 kilos of chicle; four years later, it produced nearly a million. By the mid-1920s, U.S. chewing gum companies were importing nearly eighty-five million pounds of chicle annually, enough to provide the average American with 105 sticks of gum a year.[9] Wrigley, like the other gum manufacturers, negotiated concessions and land grants with foreign governments; he also built production centers, grand houses for the managers, and narrow-gauge railroads. Eventually, Wrigley and the other the gum makers were able to devise synthetic gum bases and end their reliance on chicle.

Wrigley put his rapidly growing fortune on display with a variety of unusual investments. The first was his takeover of the Chicago Cubs (see chapter 9, "The West Side Grounds"). In 1930, Wrigley explained that when he was a child he loved baseball but his father had no interest in the game. A frustrated Wrigley would walk past the stadium in Philadelphia and hear the crowds roaring within. "One day," he recalled, "when the cheering was particularly wild inside the park, I resolved that same day I would own a ball team and a ball park. . . . This incident also explains why I get a greater satisfaction out of this enterprise than any other in which I am interested."[10]

The gum mogul never entertained thoughts of making a lot of money on the Cubs. As he once put it, "No man is qualified to make a genuine success of owning a big-league team unless he is in the game for the love of it. On the other hand, it is no undertaking for a man who has not practically unlimited capital at his command, regardless of how much he loves the game. If he

Owning the Chicago Cubs was one of William Wrigley's greatest pleasures, and he rarely missed a home game. (DN-0085638, Chicago History Museum; photographer, *Chicago Daily News*)

regards it as merely a means of making money, he would do much better to invest his time and money in some business of a strictly commercial character."[11] The stadium was known as Cubs Park from 1920 until 1926 and was officially renamed Wrigley Field in 1926, although the name seems to have been used informally at least as early as 1922, when the *Chicago Tribune* mentioned a spring training game "at Wrigley field tomorrow."[12] Wrigley had great success with "Ladies' Day," when women were admitted free; he spent $2 million on improvements; and he added an upper deck in 1927. On certain days, school children got in free (they were actually excused from school), a gesture that helped expand the fan base. He spiffed up the ushering crew, hiring a young man named Andy Frain to train them and outfit them with handsome outfits, and he took meticulous care of the park. Ed Froelich, who served the team as batboy, equipment manager, and trainer, put it this way: "The Cubs were Mr. Wrigley's pride and joy. It didn't make any difference what he had scheduled; if the Cubs were home, he would be at the ballpark. . . . Before every home stand a ground crew of twenty-two men would start at the very top row with big fire hoses, and they'd wash down every aisle and every seat. The park was always spotless. . . . Every spring the park would be painted stem to stern. Not every other year or third year like some ball parks. No sir."[13]

No wonder that attendance was large. In those days, the seats were closer together, making it possible to squeeze in over fifty thousand people on some days. Wrigley also took care of the players. When a hit musical came to town, he made sure that each player was given two free tickets. In the spring, he gave each one $10 for a new straw hat; in the fall it was felt hats. Passing out cigars to home run hitters was another endearing gesture.

Wrigley was an athlete himself. In 1896, the *Chicago Tribune* listed the results of a swimming tournament and reported that "William Wrigley won the final in the handicap from G. A. Thorne by a handbreadth."[14] He also fought boxing matches, rode horses, played tennis, and enjoyed boating and golf—these were all reasons he began spending the winters in Pasadena, California. At some point, he took a trip to Catalina, a seventy-six-square mile island off the coast of California twenty-two miles south-southwest of Los Angeles. At that time, the island was owned by the Banning family, who had fallen into financial difficulty. A local real estate firm with which Wrigley did business wanted to buy the island but didn't have the funds, but in 1919, he agreed to form with them a syndicate to purchase it. Before the year was over, he bought out his partners and became the sole owner of Catalina Island. As he described his first visit: "The sun was just coming up. I had never seen a more beautiful spot. Right then and there I determined that the island should never pass out of my hands."[15]

But Wrigley also saw the island as an investment and set about making it comfortable for visitors. He established public utilities, schools, dams and reservoirs, steamships, glass-bottom boats, a hotel, and the twelve-story Casino building. He also constructed a furniture factory and a tile and pottery plant that utilized the island's native clay. One of Wrigley's finest legacies was the thirty-eight-acre Wrigley Memorial Botanical Garden, which specializes in plants native to California's Channel Islands. In 1972, Philip Wrigley established the Catalina Island Conservancy and donated most of the property on the island to that organization.

"The House That Gum Built"

Today, a 130-foot tower in Catalina's botanical garden stands a monument to Wrigley's memory, but few Chicagoans are likely to visit it. Chicago has a much taller structure that serves as a Wrigley memorial—the Wrigley Building. As the *AIA Guide to Chicago* expresses it, "London has Big Ben, Paris has the Eiffel Tower, and Chicago has the Wrigley Building."[16]

After World War I, Wrigley started looking for a location for a new office building. The property he finally bought on the north bank of the Chicago River was in a rough area of docks and flimsy structures, and many thought he was foolish to invest in such a neighborhood. In 1919, Wrigley hired the architectural firm of Graham, Anderson, Probst, and White to design "the house that gum built." The cornerstone was laid on November

11, 1920, and Wrigley spent freely to get the best. He spent extra money to dig deep enough to set the foundation on bedrock and to acquire the best grade of marble, and he directed that the tower be as high as city ordinances would permit (at 398 feet, it was just two feet under the limit). The head designer of the building, Charles Beersman, used "six different shades of a special enamel finish . . . on the terra cotta, varying from gray to pale cream and getting progressively lighter toward the top." One viewer said this technique made it seem "as if the sun were always shining on its upper reaches."[17] Although not a breakthrough in modern design, the Wrigley Building was an ingenious combination of tradition and height. The clock tower was modeled on the Giralda Tower in Seville, Spain, and the lower part is festooned with spires and pinnacles, but the finished structure was the tallest building in Chicago. The first tenants moved in in April 1921, and local wits had fun describing the building as a "tribute to the power of human jaws" and "built by nickels."[18] Wrigley then acquired the land to the north to build an annex connected by a sky bridge at the fourteenth floor, and although the two buildings were not originally designed together, they blend harmoniously into one grand edifice.

However, one of the most admired aspects of the Wrigley Building is not the structure itself but its illumination. From the very beginning, the building was bathed in floodlights, and the effect has only gotten more dramatic over time. (It was the first large building to use floodlight illumination, and it inspired many imitators.) In 1922, the building's rental brochure explained that "the building is lighted from hundreds of flood lights on adjacent buildings, as well as its own roof, so that at night, too, it stand forth in an ethereal beauty."[19] In 1970, the warehouse supporting the front floodlights was torn down; a battery of new lights twice as powerful as the old ones was then erected on the East Wacker Drive side. Today, the effect of the building might give viewers some feeling for the impression made by the original White City of 1893.

The Wrigley Building also had a powerful effect on the cityscape around it. For people boating on the Chicago River, the

One of William Wrigley's greatest gifts to Chicago was the beloved Wrigley Building of 1921, which was called a "tribute to the power of human jaws." (ICHi-35861, Chicago History Museum; photographer, Hedrich-Blessing)

tower acts as a dominant entry point to the city, and for people heading north over the Chicago River by foot or vehicle, it's the gateway to upper Michigan Avenue, the "Magnificent Mile." With the opening of the Michigan Avenue Bridge in 1920, Michigan Avenue was able to continue northward across the river, and two imposing structures quickly went up—the Wrigley Building at the south end and the Drake Hotel (1920) at the north. They were followed by the Allerton Hotel (1924), the Tribune Tower (1925), the Medinah Athletic Club (1929), and 919 North Michigan Avenue (1929). In early 1921, the *Chicago Tribune* ran a piece entitled "Boulevard Link See as Fifth Avenue's Rival," which began, "Michigan Avenue, north from the river, will be lined with smart shops, stores, banks, clubs, and hotels within the next five years." In the spring, the newspaper reported that many architectural firms were "deserting the Loop with its dirt and din for the calm and cleanliness of the upper Michigan Avenue district" and ran an article entitled "Upper Michigan Fast Becoming Grownup Street."[20]

In July 2011, the Wrigley Company announced that all employees working in the Wrigley Building would be moved to the firm's campus on Goose Island in the Chicago River. Like the Sears Tower, the company that built and named it would no longer operate, or even utilize it.

After Wrigley

By all accounts, Wrigley was a generous employer. The women who worked in his factories were given free manicures and shampoos once a month on company time, and their work clothes were cleaned without charge. The cafeteria served food at less than cost, and the company paid the medical expenses of all employees who became ill or who were injured on the job. After three months of work, every employee got a $300 life insurance policy, and after a year, one share of stock. The company began a five-day work week in 1924.

William Wrigley died in Phoenix on January 26, 1932. For years, his son, Philip K., who was born in 1894, had been working alongside him, learning the business, and he smoothly took over the company. Under Philip Wrigley's direction, the company's annual sales increased tenfold between 1932 ($23,369,000) and 1973 ($231,868,000).[21] During World War II, P. K. Wrigley became the owner of the All-American Girls Professional Baseball League; it lasted only two years but later gained fame as the subject of the film *A League of Their Own* (1992). In 1961, P.K. turned over the reins of the company to his son William Wrigley (P.K. died in 1977). The firm expanded globally, and several new brands of gum were developed (Freedent, Big Red, Extra, Orbit, and Winterfresh). William Wrigley died in 1999 and was succeeded by his son William (b. 1963), who became known as Bill Wrigley Jr. He represented the fourth Wrigley generation to administer the empire.

But he would be the last. The dynasty ended in 2008, when the Wrigley company, still the world's biggest gum maker, was sold to candy giant Mars Incorporated for $23 billion. The Wrigley family collected $80 a share, or nearly $3 billion, and Bill Wrigley was reported to have received close to $100 million—a pretty fair legacy from a man who had come to Chicago 117 years before as a soap salesman.

Chicago, the Candy Capital

Despite Wrigley's dominance, it was by no means the only company turning out sweet treats in the Windy City. For most of the twentieth century, Chicago was known as the "candy capital of the world." A little over a decade after Wrigley brought out Juicy Fruit and Spearmint, Emil J. Brach opened what he called his "palace of sweets" on North Avenue, selling caramels for twenty cents a pound. By 1918, Brach's was turning out a thousand tons of candy a week, and four years later, it built the nation's largest candy factory on the West Side. Another major Chicago candy company was Curtiss, founded in 1916 by Otto Schnering. The firm hit the jackpot in 1921 with its Baby Ruth candy bar and followed up that success with the Butterfinger. By the 1930s, Curtiss was employing over two thousand people in Chicago, the great majority of them women. Salvatore Ferrara, an Italian immigrant, founded Ferrara Pan Candy Company in Chicago in 1908. An accomplished pastry chef, he specialized in sugar-coated candy almonds. In addition to chocolates made in the European tradition, Ferrara went on to develop Lemonheads, Red Hots, Boston Baked Beans, and Jaw Busters. H. Teller Archibald opened the first Fannie May candy store in 1920 on North LaSalle Street, and within fifteen years, the company was operating some four dozen retail outlets in the Midwest. The company developed its best-selling Pixies in 1946. Tootsie Rolls were not invented in Chicago but in New York City in 1896 by an immigrant from Austria named Leo Hirshfield. However, in 1966, the company moved into a large facility in southwest Chicago and gradually consolidated all its operations in the city, where it turned out such delights as Tootsie Pops, Charleston Chew, Sugar Daddy, and Junior Mints. Like Tootsie Rolls, the Mars company had been launched outside of Chicago, being created in Tacoma, Washington, in 1911 by Frank C. Mars. Within a few years, however, Mars moved his operations to Minneapolis, and in 1929, he relocated to Chicago because of the better access to rail transportation. There the company gained worldwide renown as the maker of Milky Way, Snickers, and M&Ms—so even though the firm acquired Wrigley's in 2008, the chewing gum giant is still in business in Chicago (Wrigley's Global Innovation Center, a laboratory and innovation center on Chicago's Goose Island, now serves as the company's global headquarters). Blommer Chocolate was founded in Chicago in 1939 by three brothers—Henry, Al, and Bernard Blommer. Today, the company has factories in Chicago, California, and Pennsylvania. By the early 1950s, one out of every four candy bars in the United States was being made in Chicago, and the candy industry employed twenty-two thousand workers with an annual payroll of $86 million.[22]

Finally, one of America's most beloved confectionaries can, like the Chicago hot dog, trace its origin to Chicago's Columbian Exposition of 1893—Cracker Jack. Frederick W. Rueckheim, a German immigrant, along with his brother Louis, opened a candy and popcorn shop in Chicago in 1871. About a decade later, they expanded to a three-story building. When the world's fair came to Chicago, they began peddling a mixture of popcorn, peanuts, and molasses at the exposition. They continued their operations after the fair closed, with considerable success. At the time, Frederick Rueckheim said, "No matter how we try to plan for it, orders always exceed production."[23] As the story is told, some complained that the mixture was too sticky, leading Louis to tinker with the recipe and devise a superior product. A salesman is said to have tried it and remarked, "That's a cracker-jack!"—hence the name.

As the twenty-first century dawned, however, Chicago's position as the candy capital grew shaky. Firms began merging or being acquired or looking for cheaper places to manufacture their products. Brach's closed its Chicago plant in 2004 and moved its operations to Mexico. In the following year, Wrigley shuttered its ninety-four-year-old South Side plant. Nestle now owns most of the Curtiss brands, and Fannie May shut down its seventy-year-old Chicago candy factory in 2004. Between 1995 and 2005, nearly half of the 13,600 candy manufacturing jobs in the city disappeared. Industry analysts said that the main factor in this development was not the cost of labor or of factory maintenance, but the cost of sugar. The federal government's policy of subsidizing U.S. sugar production by placing quotas on sugar imports and purchasing excess sugar production caused U.S. candy makers to pay much more for sugar than their overseas counterparts. In 2005, Ferrara, for example, paid twenty-seven cents a pound while world sugar was going for about ten cents a pound.[24] Nevertheless, a lot of firms soldiered on, and the sweet smell of Blommer's continued to waft over the West Side. Boutique, high-end chocolate makers continued to do well, and some suburban plants stayed open. As the first decade of the twenty-first century ended, Chicagoans were not quite ready to cede the title of candy capital.

Finally, it's noteworthy that the thirty-third annual session of the American Dental Association kicked off in Chicago on Saturday, August 12, 1893. The attendees probably didn't know much about Wrigley's chewing gum and the Rueckheims' new popcorn treat. But they would learn.

12

The Chicago School of Architecture

On the very first day of 1893, the *Chicago Tribune* published an article titled "Chicago's Great Buildings," in which it proudly noted, "The remarkable down-town building activity of 1890 and 1891 was equaled if not outclassed by that of the year just closed. There has not been a month during the year in which a half-dozen prominent corners in the business district were not blocked by building operations. The demand for structural iron in the tall office buildings has been greater than the supply." The story noted that the buildings erected in the downtown area alone were valued at more than $10 million. Among the buildings it listed as being either completed or in the course of construction were the Art Institute, the Marshall Field Annex, the Auditorium Addition, the Old Colony Building, the Illinois Central Depot, and the Monadnock Addition.

The 1880s had witnessed a staggering upsurge in office building construction in Chicago. Architect Louis Sullivan wrote that "the progress of the building art from 1880 onward was phenomenal."[1] At the time of the Great Fire of 1871, there were an estimated three hundred thousand square feet of prime office space in the Loop; by 1893, there were almost two million.[2] In just the three-year period from 1889 to 1892, no fewer than twenty-one high-rise buildings were built.[3] Chicago's developers had found ways to raise large amounts of capital by forming investment groups, and money poured in not just from Chicago but also from outside the city. However, the author of that *Tribune* article could not have known that the first great age of Chicago architecture was reaching its apex. It was in 1893 that the city put a limit on building heights of 130 feet, or about ten stories. Considering that Chicago's tallest building, the Masonic Temple (1892), stood a bit over three hundred feet and had twenty-two floors, that was quite a comedown. A few tall buildings did open after 1893; building permits issued before the height restriction remained valid after it. But even without the height limit, the depression that began in 1893 would have curbed the real estate market anyway. Nevertheless, 1893 was still a year of great events in Chicago architecture. The Monadnock Building, at the time the largest office building in the world, was finished; Charles Atwood completed the Marshall Field Annex and began designing the Reliance Building; Adler and Sullivan's Chicago Stock Exchange was constructed; and Frank Lloyd Wright opened up his own business.

Chicago: City of Great Buildings

When people come to Chicago, the city's celebrated architecture is a must-see. In 2008, an independent study conducted by the architectural firm RMJM Hillier concluded that Chicago was the best city for architecture and design in the United States, and the first edition of the *AIA Guide to Chicago* begins, "Chicago's eminent position in the history of architecture has been so firmly established that it borders on cliché."[4] William Le Baron Jenney, Dankmar Adler, Louis Sullivan, John Wellborn Root, Daniel Burnham, and Frank Lloyd Wright, all of whom either launched or carried out their careers in Chicago in the nineteenth century, are still famous, and many equally celebrated architects came after them, from Mies van der Rohe to Bertrand Goldberg to Helmut Jahn to the firm of Skidmore, Owings, and Merrill (SOM). The innovative Aqua, a residential tower by Chicagoan Jeanne Gang, was named the 2009 Skyscraper of the Year by Emporis, a company that gathers data on tall buildings. SOM has gone far beyond Chicago, being the designer of the eighty-eight-story Jin Mao Tower in Shanghai (1999) and the

Cartoonist John T. McCutcheon's view of Chicago's architectural boom in the 1890s.
(*The French Emissary Studies Our Industrial Methods*; originally printed in the *Chicago Record-Herald*)

Burj Khalifa in Dubai (2010), which is as tall as the John Hancock Center and the Willis Tower stacked atop each other. And in August 2011, it was announced that the Chicago firm of Adrian Smith + Gordon Gill Architecture (AS+GG) were designing for Saudi Arabia a building named the Kingdom Tower that would be more than five hundred feet taller than the Burj Khalifa. The world's tallest buildings might no longer be in Chicago, but Chicagoans are still putting up the world's tallest buildings.

After the Fire

Historians of Chicago architecture usually begin their story with the Great Fire of 1871—once a city has burnt to the ground and its people are determined to rebuild, there is a lot of work for architects. Even better, the architects have a blank slate—they can try new things. As early as 1873, the *Chicago Tribune* said, "It is a common remark that Chicago was set forward ten years by the fire."[5] And in 1891, the authors of a book entitled *Industrial Chicago* commented that the Great Fire (along with some smaller ones) had been "fortunate events" because "the flames swept away forever the greater number of monstrous libels on artistic house-building" and opened the way for a vast amount of new construction.[6] They might have added that the Great Fire spurred the adoption of some stringent building codes about fireproofing.

. . . architects of the Chicago School invented metal-frame, or curtain-wall, construction . . .

Chicago is a sprawling metropolis, but its downtown is concentrated. In the late nineteenth century, the central business area was enclosed by Lake Michigan on the east, the Chicago River on the north and west, and a concentration of railroad tracks and stations on the south. As the *Chicago Tribune* explained in 1888, "Chicago has thus far had but three directions, north, south, and west, but there are indications now that a fourth is to be added . . . zenithward. Since water hems in the business centre on three sides and a nexus of railroads on the remaining, the south, Chicago must grow upward."[7] The architectural historian Joanna Merwood-Salisbury has commented that in the 1880s, "Chicago suffered under almost unbearable pressure . . . pressure that the economy would not hold; pressure that the city would destroy itself by growing too fast; pressure of imminent political revolution. With their designs for tall office buildings, architects and real estate developers provided not only an economic mechanism for unrestricted urban growth but also aesthetic and programmatic solutions to these social and political problems."[8]

In the mid-twentieth century, historians of art and architecture tended to evaluate the so-called Chicago School of the 1880s and 1890s from a teleological viewpoint. That is, twentieth-century modernism was thought to have achieved a near-perfect purity of expression; artworks that came before were rated according to how far they moved that process forward. In architecture, the International Style, represented especially by Mies van der Rohe, was seen as the zenith to which earlier buildings were striving, and the Chicago School was great because it produced so many of those buildings. The major critic of this school was the Swiss architectural historian Sigfried Giedion. In his *Space, Time, and Architecture* (1941), he praised the Chicago School as the forerunner of the European avant-garde. Ten years before Giedion's book, the critic and historian Lewis Mumford had made a similar claim that Chicago's architects were the godfathers of modernism, and an exhibition at the Museum of Modern Art in early 1933 entitled *Early Modern Architecture, Chicago 1870–1910: The Beginnings of the Skyscraper and the Growth of a National American Architecture* helped fix Mumford's opinion as canonical.

Nowadays, historians of architecture are less likely to see things this way. For one thing, historians have recently begun to question whether there ever was a true "Chicago School," in the sense of a group of like-minded architects working together to create a progressive style (the term itself was created by European modernists in the 1920s).[9] In addition, tall buildings of the nineteenth century are now hailed for their intrinsic aesthetic merit, which can include ornamentation as well as large windows and clean lines. Often cited is the well-known quotation from

Louis Sullivan, who insisted that the skyscraper was meant to be a "unitary utterance, Dionysian in beauty."[10] And factors beyond aesthetics have also been recognized. Chicago architects were concerned with more than just aesthetics but saw moral issues in the construction of tall buildings. As Root put it: "I do not believe it is possible to exaggerate the importance of the influence which may be exerted for good or evil by these distinctively modern buildings. . . . They are either gross and self-asserting shams, untrue both in the material realization of their aims, and in their art function as expressions of the deeper spirit of the age; or they are sincere, noble and enduring monuments to the broad and beneficent commerce of the age."[11]

There has also been a recent tendency to think about tall buildings with regard to their economic function—as works of commerce. Adler said, "In a utilitarian age like ours it is safe to assume that the real-estate owner and the investor in buildings will continue to erect the class of buildings from which the greatest possible revenue can be obtained with the least possible outlay. . . . The purpose of erecting buildings other than those required for the shelter of their owners is specifically that of making investments for profit."[12] The title of Carol Willis's *Form Follows Finance* neatly expresses this perception of skyscrapers. This examination of the business side of skyscrapers has rescued from oblivion some important figures. It takes more than an architect to erect a tall building; it also takes a developer, and developers are beginning to get their due. The most valuable volume in this regard is *They Built Chicago: Entrepreneurs Who Shaped a Great City's Architecture* by Miles L. Berger, which validates the importance of such entrepreneurs as Peter C. Brooks, Owen F. Aldis, Ferdinand W. Peck, and Edward C. Walker.[13] Louis Sullivan knew how things worked. He said that the Chicagoans most "responsible for the modern office building" were William E. Hale and Owen Aldis—real estate developers, not architects.[14] Even so, it's still difficult to regard a building like the Reliance and not be impressed by how far in advance of its time it was and what a milestone it is in the history of architecture.

The Birth of the Skyscraper

Although skyscrapers have been around a long time, historians are still debating which the first one was. The term "skyscraper" (often "sky-scraper") was used in the eighteenth century for a tall sail, and in the mid-nineteenth century, it was a jocular description of a very tall person, a high hat, or a high fly ball in baseball. The earliest citation in the *Oxford English Dictionary* for the use of the term to describe a building comes from an article in *American Architect and Building News* in June 1883, and reference books now commonly refer to that citation as the earliest known, but the *Chicago Tribune* used the word in an article of February 25 of that year, and in the context it doesn't appear as if the writer expected readers to find the word unfamiliar. Ironically, the article described conditions not in Chicago but in New York City and remarked that "there are more very high buildings in New York than in all the rest of the country put together."[15]

Some historians make a distinction between a mere tall building and a genuine skyscraper, with the difference depending on the method of construction. For most of history, buildings were made tall by piling brick upon brick (or concrete, marble, stones, and so on) in what is known as masonry construction. The problem with masonry construction is that the higher the building, the thicker the base has to be. Thus the walls of the sixteen-story masonry northern section of the Monadnock Building are six feet thick at the base. To get around that limitation, the architects of the Chicago School invented metal-frame, or curtain-wall, construction, which is essentially the construction of a metal cage on which the wall is hung like a curtain (another metaphor is a metal skeleton supporting the body or the skin). The wall can be thin and light and contain multiple large windows. Because metal-frame construction pointed the way to the skyscrapers of the twentieth century, some historians, when seeking the first skyscraper, look for the first tall metal-frame building.

Many books and Web sites state that the first skyscraper was Chicago's Home Insurance Building, which was the work of William Le Baron Jenney. This was the view of the architectural historian Carl Condit, whose *The Chicago School of Architecture* of

1952 was the pioneering work on Chicago's buildings. He wrote that the Home Insurance Building "represented the decisive step in the evolution of iron and steel framing" and was "the major progenitor of the true skyscraper."[16] However, as architects looked further into the matter, they realized that the building (which was demolished in 1931)[17] had in fact used some masonry walls, and in 1986, Condit himself concluded that "we can no longer argue that the Home Insurance Building was the first skyscraper." He altogether gave up defining a skyscraper by its use of a metal frame and speculated that the first one might have been the seven-and-a-half-story Equitable Life Assurance Building in New York, which had been built in 1870.[18]

However, if we do want to look for the true progenitor of the twentieth-century "glass box," it would have to be a metal-frame building, and Chicago has many candidates. An excellent one is the Tacoma Building (1889) of Holabird and Roche. In 1928, the *Architectural Record* published a brief article entitled "First Skyscraper Demolished." Discussing the Tacoma Building, it stated that it was a "true skyscraper," in which the "terra cotta casing served as curtains suspended from the framework." The article went on to say, however, that "no single person is recorded as the inventor of the steel frame. The developments of a generation were required to perfect the engineering principles involved in skyscraper construction. "[19]

The transition from masonry construction to the metal cage was not simply a matter of aesthetics or of finding a way to create larger windows. The 1880s were filled with labor strife and strikes. One of the more unusual commissions of Holabird and Roche was the design of Fort Sheridan on the city's North Side, which was established in 1887 expressly for the purpose of garrisoning troops to be used to put down labor demonstrations and strikes. A strike in that year by the bricklayers and carpenters unions over the eight-hour day put contractors and architects on notice that they were not immune from problems with organized labor, and few had more trouble than Adler and Sullivan, who were plagued by labor disputes during construction of the Auditorium Building of 1889. One advantage of metal

Which building is the first true skyscraper is much disputed, but a leading candidate is Chicago's Tacoma Building (1889) by Holabird and Roche. It was demolished in 1929. (ICHi-64433, Chicago History Museum)

cage construction was that it required fewer contributions from skilled craftsmen, especially those insubordinate bricklayers.

For most people, the most famous names in Chicago architecture are Louis Sullivan (1856–1924) and Frank Lloyd Wright (1867–1959). Not so well known is William Le Baron Jenney (1832–1907), who was the leading pioneer of metal-frame construction and might be described as the father (perhaps grandfather) of the skyscraper. The aesthetic merits of his facades have sometimes been faulted, but, as the chief engineer for Grant and Sherman during the Civil War, he was a master builder. Louis

Sullivan, William Holabird, and Martin Roche all worked in his firm, as did Daniel Burnham. Burnham (1846–1912) has become better known recently, but more for his directorship of the Columbian Exposition and his Plan of Chicago than for his buildings, which is unfortunate, for he put up several great ones. In recent times, Burnham's partner, John Wellborn Root (1850–91), has gradually become recognized as one of Chicago's supreme architects. In his design for the Montauk Building (1882), Root developed a unique method of erecting large structures on Chicago's soft, sandy soil. Called the "floating-raft" foundation, it consisted of a flat concrete slab reinforced with iron beams upon which the building rested; as Miles Berger has expressed it, the floating raft distributed "the weight of ten stories of brick and stone as evenly as a set of snowshoes."[20] Undeservedly lesser known is Charles Atwood (1849–96), who became Burnham's chief partner after Root's premature death in January 1891. As we shall see, in the Reliance Building, Atwood proved to be an architect of ingenuity and vision. Another major figure is Dankmar Adler (1844–1900), who, by the time he joined forces with Louis Sullivan in 1881, had already made his mark with the Central Music Hall of 1879, which marked him as the foremost acoustical engineer of his day. Sullivan himself, though perhaps the most famous of all the Chicago architects, was not as active as some others in the development of the skyscraper, despite his claims to have invented the form with the Wainwright Building (1892) in St. Louis.[21] Finally, there is the team of William Holabird (1854–1923) and Martin Roche (1855–1927). Among their eminent buildings were the Tacoma (1889), the Pontiac (1891), the Old Colony (1894), the Marquette (1895), and the 1893 South Addition of Burnham and Root's Monadnock Building, to which we now turn.

The Monadnock Building

One Chicago building offers a textbook example of the transition from masonry to metal-frame construction. One wonders how many people pass this bulky edifice on busy West Jackson Street without realizing that it is one of the most important buildings in the world. No other structure so clearly exhibits the end of the nineteenth-century architectural tradition and the beginning of the modern one. That's because the Monadnock Building, like the city itself, is divided into a North Side and a South Side. The 1891 northern half, designed by Burnham and Root, is a masonry, wall-bearing structure; Condit described it as "the last great building in the ancient tradition of masonry architecture."[22] The southern half, designed by Holabird and Roche, uses the steel-frame method of construction, which looks forward to the steel and glass giants of today. This dual nature makes the Monadnock Building *the* great transitional structure in modern architecture. The world's largest office building when the southern section opened in 1893, it was designated a Chicago landmark eighty years later.

The powers behind the northern section of the Monadnock were Peter Chardon Brooks III, a Massachusetts investor, and his agent in Chicago, Owen F. Aldis. Peter Brooks, along with his brother, Shepherd, was a major player in Chicago real estate, although he rarely, if ever, visited the city. He saw tall buildings as profitable investments, not as aesthetic statements. As he said of the Montauk Building (1882), his first commission for Burnham

The dual nature of Chicago's Monadnock Building makes it the great transitional structure in modern architecture. (Library of Congress)

and Root, "The building throughout is to be for use and not for ornament. Its beauty will be in its all-adaptation to its use."[23] Brooks also hired Burnham and Root to design the Rookery (1888), one of Chicago's most revered landmarks. In this building he permitted more ornate decoration, but when it came to the Monadnock, plainness was everything.[24] Not that Root would necessarily have had a problem with that. He went on record many times that for him simplicity was key. "Simple business principles . . . should dictate the utmost simplicity and straight-forwardness of plan, so arranged as to obtain the very best ven-tilation and light," he said.[25] It is clear from Root's writings that he (and other architects) hoped that plain facades and simple massing would create a sense of tranquility in an otherwise hectic urban setting.[26]

Edward A. Renwick, a member (and eventual partner) of Holabird and Roche, recalled that "When Owen Aldis put up the Monadnock on Jackson boulevard there was nothing on the south side of the street between State street and the river but cheap one-story shacks, mere hovels. Everyone thought Mr. Aldis was insane to build out there on the ragged edge of the city."[27] As it turned out, the Monadnock became the Brooks brothers' most profitable investment (and it remains a prime location).

Root's sixteen-story northern section of the Monadnock Building is a simple massive slab of dark, purplish-colored brick. Bay windows break up the surface, but the windows themselves have no trim or decoration, appearing as unadorned square cav-ities. The walls curve in at the second story and the cornice is flared. Critics have seen an Egyptian quality in the building, comparing its shape to an Egyptian pylon or a papyrus plant. Although we might think of the Gilded Age as one that adored profuse ornament, Root's structure earned considerable praise, with critics admiring its "naturalness." Louis Sullivan loved it, calling it "an amazing cliff of brickwork . . . that gave one the thrill of romance." But he recognized that it was the "last word of its kind . . . marking the high tide of masonry construc-tion as applied to commercial structures."[28] His praise was not unanimous. A contributor to a volume entitled *Industrial Chicago* wrote that "the commercial style if structurally ornamental becomes architectural. . . . Thus there is a distinction between the Woman's Temple and the Monadnock building. The first is an architectural house, the second an engineer's."[29] A French architect wrote that it was "no longer the work of an artist. . . . It is the work of a laborer who, without the slightest study, superimposes 15 strictly identical stories to make a block then stops when he finds the block high enough."[30]

Peter Brooks financed the Monadnock Building, but his brother, Shepherd, was the developer of the addition—perhaps that's why it is built in such a different style. Shepherd Brooks chose to drop Burnham and Root and give his business to Holabird and Roche, who designed a building that was both more and less progressive than the first Monadnock. It was less progressive in that it adhered to what might be called "classical ideals"—the building was, like a classical column, separated into three parts: a distinct three-story base, a central section (with classical ornament), and, at the top, arched windows and a dramatic cornice. Unlike the original Monadnock with its disproportionately small entranceways, the addition had large doors with archways that have been described as having "a kind of Roman scale and grandeur."[31] It was more progressive because it employed steel-frame technology.[32] Condit argued that because the windows are relatively small and the envelope of the frame is solid brick, the architects failed to "exploit the steel frame to full utilitarian and formal advantage."[33] Holabird and Roche did not repeat this mistake in their Marquette Building of 1895, which has been called "an exemplar of the Chicago style."[34] However, Aldis himself recognized the great step forward that Holabird and Roche had made with steel framing in the Monadnock addition. Renwick once recalled that "Mr. Aldis stated, in our office, that the new building cost 15% less than the north, contained 15 to 16% more available renting space and that space 15% lighter than the space of the north half. 'This makes me decide,' he said, 'that I can no longer afford to employ another architect.'"[35]

The Reliance Building

Meanwhile, Daniel Burnham had more to worry about than the loss of the Brooks brothers' business. His gifted, articulate partner, colleague, and friend John Wellborn Root had succumbed to pneumonia on January 15, 1891, just five days after his forty-first birthday. At the time, Burnham was supervising the team of architects that would design the buildings for the Columbian Exposition. Fortunately, he found a replacement for Root back East. Charles Bowler Atwood was born in Charlestown, Massachusetts, in 1849, went to the Lawrence Scientific School at Harvard University (today the Harvard School of Engineering and Applied Science), and got his training with the firm of Ware and Van Brundt in Boston. He worked on several important buildings in the East, including the twin William H. Vanderbilt mansions on Fifth Avenue in New York City, but after his five-year-old son died from typhoid fever in 1886, he went into a decline. However, after hearing of Root's death, Atwood, at the urging of a friend, asked William R. Ware (his former boss, who had become the head of the architecture school at Columbia University) to recommend him to Burnham. He joined Burnham in April 1891, and his career was reborn in Chicago.

The handsome and gifted architect Charles Bowler Atwood had everything going for him, but personal demons cut short his splendid career. (Chicago Public Library)

Atwood, who eventually became designer-in-chief of the Columbian Exposition, personally designed the fair's railroad station, the Court of

Honor Peristyle, and the Palace of Fine Arts, which is today the Museum of Science and Industry. Burnham also credited Atwood with the design of "the terraces, the bridges, the rostral columns, the Service building, the Forestry, and many minor decorative features," adding generously, "To his critical taste was largely due the final finish of the architecture of the Fair as a whole."[36] The Palace of Fine Arts, with its domes, caryatids, and Ionic colonnades, demonstrates Atwood's mastery of neoclassicism. Burnham recalled how Augustus Saint-Gaudens, America's preeminent sculptor, came to see him in late summer 1893 and "seizing me by the shoulders, said, 'Do you realize the rank of Atwood's Art Building among all the structures of the world?' and without waiting for a reply, he continued 'There has been nothing equal to it since the Parthenon.'"[37] Two other major events in Atwood's career also took place in 1893: he completed the Marshall Field Annex, his first building as a member of Burnham's firm, and he took over the design work on the Reliance Building.

The Chicago entrepreneur Marshall Field was in 1893 the sole proprietor of one of the grandest department stories in the country. Anticipating the crowds that would pour into Chicago for the fair, he determined that he would need even more selling space, and by March 1892, he had completed the purchase of six adjacent lots.[38] He then hired Burnham's firm to design the new annex. Demolition of the existing structures began on May 1, and Atwood's design was completed by May 29.[39] To maximize revenues, Field requested a nine-story structure with the first four floors for retail and the rest for rentable office space. The building opened with showy spectacle on August 7, 1893. Atwood's mastery of historical styles is as evident in the annex as in the Palace of Fine Arts, although the annex is not modeled after Hellenic designs. Instead, it drew on the Italian Renaissance, especially the Florentine *palazzo*. It is a light-colored building with a three-story granite base. Three tall arches run through the center of the façade of the next three floors, which are garbed in gray-white terra-cotta. The seventh and eighth floors are in gray-white brick and terra-cotta, as are the shorter top floor and the prominent overhanging cornice.

Charles B. Atwood designed the Marshall Field Annex, which opened in 1893, in the style of a Florentine *palazzo*. (Chicago Public Library)

The Palace of Fine Arts and the Marshall Field Annex might have left contemporaries with the impression that Atwood was a conservative, not to say hidebound, architect. If so, his next project must have come as an astonishment. As Thomas J. O'Gorman has expressed it, the Reliance Building at State and Washington (just down the block from the annex) "was the doorway to a new era of American architecture. So advanced was its design that no other building in America came close to it."[40] The Chicago Landmarks Commission has described Atwood's edifice as "internationally recognized as the direct ancestor of today's glass-and-steel skyscrapers."

Skyscrapers could never have been built had not the elevator been invented. The credit for creating the modern elevator is traditionally given to Elisha Graves Otis, who in 1852 unveiled a safety brake that convinced a dubious public that elevators could be made entirely secure. However, in Chicago it was not Otis who was the leader in elevator technology; it was William Ellery Hale, who perfected and marketed the hydraulic elevator. He patented the "Hale Water-Balance Elevator" in 1869 and bought out Otis in 1883. Hale was also a developer and as early as 1867 had built a six-story building at the southeast corner of State and Washington. In 1882, he bought a narrow, but ideally situated, property across the street on the southwest corner. The First National Bank of Chicago occupied the premises but moved out in 1890, whereupon Hale announced plans to put up a new building with the department store Carson, Pirie, Scott as its principal tenant. Hale, however, had one problem: the bank had moved out, but the tenants on the upper floors had not. Rather than wait for their leases to expire on May 1, 1894, Hale had the upper floors jacked up and a new foundation and first floor constructed beneath them. Then when the tenants finally did depart, he was free to construct the upper floors of his fifteen-story tower. As he had done with his previous buildings, he commissioned Burnham and Root to do the design. Root having died, in July 1893, Burnham turned to Atwood to complete the project.

Today's office workers, in their climate-controlled buildings, couldn't open their windows even if they wanted to. Things were different in the 1890s, when the catchphrase for architects was "light and air." Some buildings had mechanical ventilation systems, but air conditioning didn't exist, and the ability to open a large window on a hot day was prized. Similarly, although by the 1890s just about every tall building was wired for electricity, the power of the incandescent light bulb was slight. Until the development of the fluorescent light in the 1940s, the only real way to sufficiently light an office was with sunlight (even on cloudy days, daylight was adequate enough to light interiors).[41] The beauty of the steel cage was its ability to permit large windows.

Large windows, however, are heavy and difficult to raise. So what architects in the Windy City did—notably in the Reliance Building—was to create the "Chicago window," which consists of a large unmovable square central pane with narrow vertical sliding sash windows of the same height on each side. The center window lets in the light, the side windows let in the air, and the ensemble creates a pleasant rhythmical effect on the outside. The Chicago window can also be an element of a projecting bay, a device used by Atwood in the Reliance, which gives it its distinctive undulating façade (the bays project a full three feet over the sidewalk). The bay allows the window to admit light from three directions and breezes from two. The Reliance Building is also distinctive in that the glass fills two full structural bays instead of just one. The windows are set flush with the wall plane, which makes the building, as one observer put it, appear "to be sealed with a transparent membrane"—a forerunner of Mies van der Rohe, indeed.[42] As another writer remarked, "Not until the 1950s would Chicago again build an office tower with so much glass."[43]

Another innovation that makes Atwood's design so distinctive is his use of glazed white enameled terra-cotta, which, in its extent, was unique at the time (Root had used red Scotch granite for the first two floors). It was the terra-cotta, not the windows, that brought the most attention when the edifice was new. Atwood likely turned to this bright material because it carried over the look of the White City.[44] A contemporary reviewer called the façade "indestructible and as hard and smooth as any porcelain ware. It will be washed by every rainstorm and may if necessary

The Reliance Building by Charles B. Atwood has been called the "doorway to a new era of American architecture." (Library of Congress)

be scrubbed like a dinner plate."[45] The *Architectural Record*, in an article entitled "A White Enameled Building," commented that "there is one most important feature . . . which will make this building stand out in the history of architecture in America, namely, the use of enameled terra cotta for the exterior."[46] The terra-cotta contains Gothic detailing in the form of quatrefoils on the spandrels and clustered colonettes that frame the windows.

A hundred years after it opened, the Reliance Building was again in the news as an example of innovation. This time it demonstrated how an old building could acquire new life through imaginative restoration. By the 1970s, the Reliance was in a shabby state; the cracked and darkened terra-cotta was deteriorating. The building was on preservationists' "most threatened" lists, and demolition seemed likely. However, the City of Chicago acquired the property through eminent domain for $1.2 million, made a commitment to save it, and in 1994 began a $6.6-million exterior restoration. Some two thousand of the twelve thousand terra-cotta pieces were replaced. A private development team then bought the building from the city in 1999 and began the interior restoration. Some parts of the interior were rebuilt, and the mosaic floors, marble ceilings and walls, and ornamental metal elevator grills, stairways, and archways were refurbished. Today, the Reliance Building is the home of the Hotel Burnham. The first floor houses the aptly named Café Atwood, which, with its eighteen-foot-high ceilings and enormous windows, is an impressive space. The building has won several awards for its restoration, including ones from the National Trust for Historic Preservation and the American Institute of Architects. That it has become a hotel gives guests the chance to gaze out from the inside—an experience not easily realized in Chicago's other historic skyscrapers, which remain for the most part office buildings.

Atwood went on to design the Ellicott Square Building in Buffalo, which opened in May 1896, and Chicago's terra-cotta-clad, Gothic-inspired Fisher Building of the same year. Then his career abruptly ended. On December 10, 1895, he was fired for absenteeism, and just nine days later he was dead. In a sketch of Atwood written shortly after his death, Burnham recalled, "During the last two years his health was such as to prohibit any steady concentrated effort."[47] However, Burnham later told his biographer, Charles Moore, that Atwood had been a drug addict.[48] Atwood, Burnham said, "got himself into difficulty and started to use dope. I did not know it, none of us did."[49] About Atwood, Moore wrote, "Tall, slender, of elegant figure and bearing, with a head remarkable for its beauty, with gray, lustrous eyes, a voice with rare charm and a diction that completed the spell, Atwood gradually changed from one of the most companionable of men and became a recluse. At the age of forty-six, with the greatest possibilities before him, and after having given up a position in which he was free to work out his conceptions without financial worries, he succumbed to his only enemy—himself."[50] Atwood's obituary in the *Chicago Tribune* praised his "artistic skill and exquisite architectural conceptions" and said that "he will be principally remembered by his three creations in the White City—the Terminal Station, the Peristyle, and the Art Gallery."[51] It made no mention of the Reliance Building.

The Chicago Stock Exchange

For Louis Sullivan, 1893 was an exciting, fulfilling year. Both his striking red-brick skyscraper, the Wainwright Building in St. Louis, and his Schiller Building on Randolph Street in Chicago, a multiuse structure with a spectacular auditorium, had been completed the year before, and his Transportation Building at the 1893 fair, which is still hailed for bucking Burnham's neoclassical mandate with its great multihued Golden Doorway, was a splendid achievement.[52] But his greatest feat was the Chicago Stock Exchange.

Sometimes, the date of an important building can be arguable. Is it when it was designed? Or when construction began? Or when it opened its doors? Construction began on the Chicago Stock Exchange in May 1893, and the brokers moved in twelve months later.[53] A large medallion decorated each side of the ornamented archway that spanned the LaSalle Street entrance. One of them showed the Philip Peck residence (1837), which was the first building to stand on the site. The other said, "The First Brick Building Erected in Chicago Was Built Upon This Site." Later, it was learned that this inscription wasn't true, so it was replaced with the large numbers "1893," which indicates that, as far as the builders were concerned, that was the date of the structure.

In this thirteen-story building, Sullivan and Adler fully embraced steel-cage construction, although Sullivan clad the exterior in beautifully ornamented terra-cotta as if to demonstrate that a steel skeleton did not preclude a glamorous surface. The two-story base contained tall semicircular arches, and the floors above had projecting bays and Chicago windows. The heart of the building, the Trading Room, measured sixty-four by eighty-one feet and had a thirty-foot ceiling. One contemporary described this space, tastefully decorated with art glass, multicolored stencils, and gilded capitals, as "unexcelled in the magnificence of its appointments and decoration by any room used for like purposes in the country."[54] The razing in 1972 of the Stock Exchange despite worldwide opposition was one of Chicago's greatest artistic tragedies. An equal tragedy was the death of the Chicago historian, preservationist, and photographer Richard Nickel, who died in 1972 when a steel beam collapsed within the weakened building as he was attempting to document it. But the building's demise

The Chicago Stock Exchange of 1893, one of Louis Sullivan's finest achievements. Its demolition in 1972 was one of Chicago's greatest architectural tragedies. (Library of Congress)

(along with the demolition of Sullivan's Schiller Building a decade before) electrified the city's preservationists, and the preservation movement was greatly strengthened (few Adler and Sullivan buildings were demolished after Nickel's death). The Landmarks Preservation Council of Illinois was created for the express purpose of attempting to save the Stock Exchange, and today the organization uses its entry arch as its logo. Sections of the Trading Room were preserved, and in the late 1970s, the Art Institute of Chicago reconstructed it in a new wing. Many other fragments of the Stock Exchange were preserved in Chicago and in collections around the world, and the LaSalle Street entrance was moved to the East Garden of the Art Institute, where it can still be seen, still bearing the medallion that reads "1893." The

Medallion on the Chicago Stock Exchange's entry arch, now on the grounds of the Art Institute. The arch has been called the "Wailing Wall" of Chicago's preservationists. (Photograph by the author)

historian Donald Miller has called it the "Wailing Wall" of Chicago's preservationists.[55]

Yet, unlike Daniel Burnham, who would go on after his success in organizing the Columbia Exposition to become a celebrated city planner, Louis Sullivan reached his peak in 1893 and then began a sad decline. While the economic depression was raging in 1894, Sullivan broke with Adler, who was the partner with the greater business sense. He had one great building left in him—the Schlesinger and Meyer store of 1899 (it became the Carson, Pirie, Scott store in 1904 and the Sullivan Center in 2008)—but for the most part, the rest of Sullivan's life was plagued by financial hardship, a lack of commissions, and alcoholism.

Frank Lloyd Wright Sets Out on His Own

But if 1893 can be viewed as the year in which Sullivan's deterioration began, just the opposite might be said for the twenty-six-year-old architect who had been working in Sullivan's office for some five years. For it was in 1893 that Frank Lloyd Wright left the employ of Adler and Sullivan and opened his own office, which just happened to be in the very Schiller Building that Wright had helped design. Wright later admitted that being in that building made him feel a little closer to his former employers (he also liked the view).

Nearly alone among Chicago's famous architects, Frank Lloyd Wright was a native midwesterner. Wright was born in Richland Center, Wisconsin, and the characteristic long horizontal lines of his "Prairie School" architecture have often been attributed to his affection for the midwestern landscape. In 1939, he advised a group of Londoners that if they wanted to see the United States, they should forget about the East. "America," he said, "begins west of Buffalo."[56] His activity as an architect proves his affinity for the Midwest. Of the three hundred Wright buildings extant at the time of his death, over half were in just three states—Michigan (thirty-seven), Wisconsin (forty-three), and Illinois (eighty-eight)—and there were many houses in Minnesota, Iowa, and Ohio as well.[57]

Wright attended high school in Madison, Wisconsin, and entered the University of Wisconsin in January 1886. In that era, it was still possible, even common, for professionals in the arts and sciences to learn their craft without attending a university or other school, and this was the case with Wright. Even before going to college he worked for an architect, and he spent just one year at the university before joining the firm of Joseph Lyman Silsbee, a Chicago architect. It is not clear exactly when Wright went to work for Adler and Sullivan (probably 1888 or early 1889, more likely the earlier year), but he was quickly recognized for his ability, becoming head draughtsman with his own office. His talent was put strikingly on display in the Charnley House of 1892. There has been debate over which architect—Sullivan or Wright—was responsible for the look of the building, but it is absolutely original and forward-looking (Wright was not shy about calling it the "first modern house in America") and clearly foreshadows Wright's Prairie Style.

The story of how Wright left Sullivan's employ commonly runs something like this. Without Sullivan's knowledge, Wright began receiving and executing commissions on his own—that is, moonlighting; the ten or so houses he designed are known

Frank Lloyd Wright's studio and home in Oak Park. Wright's employer, Louis Sullivan, lent him the money he needed to purchase the house. (Wikimedia Commons)

as his "bootleg" houses. When Sullivan found out, he was furious and fired his young assistant, who thereupon went out on his own. This was sometime in 1893. That the split occurred in that year is certain, but that an angry Sullivan fired Wright for moonlighting, seems, on closer inspection, questionable. In his autobiography, Wright explained that Sullivan had lent him the money he needed to purchase his home in Oak Park; in addition to that debt, Wright had others (as he would throughout his life). He related that he had worked off-hours at home on projects for Adler and Sullivan so he believed there was nothing improper about working off-hours on his own. When Sullivan confronted him about the bootleg projects, Wright admitted he was in the wrong, but he resented Sullivan's "haughty" tone. "I therefore threw my pencil down," he wrote, "and walked out of the Adler and Sullivan office never to return."[58] Autobiographies are seldom the most reliable place to turn for accurate information about a person's career, and that's especially true with Wright, but experts on Wright acknowledge that the story that he was fired is difficult to corroborate. Thomas A. Heinz even disputes the idea that Sullivan had a problem with Wright's moonlighting. As he puts it, "Contrary to popular opinion, there were no provisions for prohibiting additional work being undertaken outside Frank's terms of employment with Adler & Sullivan. Indeed, it would have been to Sullivan's advantage if Wright was making extra money as he would have been able to pay the loan back more rapidly."[59] Heinz also points out that Wright's stay in Sullivan's office was likely to have ended in 1893, bootleg houses or not, because the depression had caused a severe slowdown in business, and the firm of Sullivan and Adler was down to fewer than five employees.

Wright's busy career lasted until the 1950s, and, unlike the other architects discussed in this chapter, he was primarily a designer of houses, so we will break away from his story as he ventures out on his own. However, he will be remembered for such structures such as the Unity Temple in Oak Park, the Imperial Hotel in Tokyo, and the Solomon R. Guggenheim Museum in New York, and he did keep Sullivan's flame burning

One of Frank Lloyd Wright's so-called bootleg houses, the Robert Parker house in Oak Park. (Photograph by the author)

by maintaining an interest in the skyscraper. His Larkin Building in Buffalo (1906) was an early triumph, and soon after he designed for a San Francisco newspaper a dramatic reinforced concrete skyscraper that was never built. Throughout the 1920s, he sketched various plans for tall buildings, but he was then at the low point of his career and couldn't find a client. At the end of that decade the rector of a church in Manhattan commissioned Wright to design a tower to be built on church property for the purpose of generating income. The architect came up with a bold proposal for several towers, but the ambitious plan was not realized. In the late 1930s, he began designing a building complex for S. C. Johnson and Son (the maker of Johnson's Wax) in Racine, Wisconsin. The Administration Building (1939) was a low windowless brick structure lit by skylights and by Pyrex tubing beneath the cornice. The Johnson Company found that it generated welcome publicity and asked Wright to add a fourteen-story Research Tower, which opened in 1950. As tall buildings go, it's not that tall, but it does stand out, rising above the landscape as it does. When Wright finally was able to actually build a skyscraper in the sense that he envisioned one, it was in the unlikely location of Bartlesville, Oklahoma, where Harold C. Price, the owner of a pipeline company, commissioned him to erect the multiuse nineteen-story Price Tower. That building, however, was not finished until 1956. In that same year, Wright had a bit of fun by unveiling a twenty-two-foot-high drawing of a proposed Chicago building called "Mile High Illinois" that would indeed be one mile high (528 stories). Given the near zero chance that this mother of all skyscrapers would be built, the project says more about Wright's gift for self-promotion than it does about his practicality.

Wright died just two months shy of his ninety-second birthday, on April 9, 1959. This was four years after the completion of Naess and Murphy's Prudential Building, the structure that ended a two-decade drought in the construction of new skyscrapers in Chicago. This building was the tallest in Chicago, but not for long because many skyscrapers followed it, such as the Inland Steel Building (1958), Marina City (1964), the Chicago Civic Center (1965, now the Richard J. Daley Center), the Lake Point Tower (1968), the First National Bank of Chicago (1969, now Bank One Plaza), the John Hancock Center (1969), Mies van der Rohe's IBM Building (1973), the Standard Oil Building (1973, now the Aon Center), and, the biggest of them all, the 108-story Sears Tower (1974, now the Willis Tower).

Thus came into being the second great age of skyscraper building in Chicago, and, as the construction of the Trump Tower (2009), now Chicago's second tallest building, has shown, it is still going on. Frank Lloyd Wright had lived to see the decline of one era and the dawn of another.

13

Reforming Chicago

Anyone curious to see how much a city can change in a century can walk down South Federal Street just south of the Loop in Chicago. It's in the heart of what's now known as Printers Row, where condo conversion has been transforming this once commercial district into one of Chicago's hotter neighborhoods. The street between Harrison and Polk is monotonous, with few storefronts, although it is distinguished by the Printers Square Apartments, a condo conversion of a handsome commercial building built in 1913.

In 1893, however, the street was named Custom House Place, and it was probably the most scandalous red-light district in the United States. A map published in 1894 shows no fewer than twenty-nine brothels and ten saloons lining both sides of the street in the single block between Harrison and Polk.[1] Nearby was "Hell's Half Acre," an area so rough that policemen would enter only in pairs, and "Whiskey Row," where in 1896 a tavern owner named Mickey Finn would concoct his eponymous knockout drink. Another celebrated nearby vice neighborhood was "Little Cheyenne," home to the black madam Hattie Briggs, who stood six feet tall and weighed 320 pounds. Historian Karen Abbott describes the city in the decades after the fire in this way: "The vice districts, slung like a tawdry necklace across the city's South Side, were more brazen than ever. Junkies shot one another up with 'guns'—hypodermic needles—in the middle of drugstore aisles. Women lounged stark naked against door-ways, calling out obscene suggestions to passersby. And the competition grew fiercer as hundreds of newcomers settled in the red-light district every week."[2]

The famous "map of sin" was the work of William T. Stead, a celebrated British journalist. He came to Chicago in 1893 to study the city's newspapers, but once he got a good look around, he changed his plans. Chicago, he concluded, was a city that needed cleaning up. The best-known vice district was the "Levee," a loosely defined term that many used to describe the vice-ridden South Side in general, although after Mayor Carter Harrison II began cleaning up portions of the South Loop, the Levee district settled in the area between Eighteenth and Twenty-Second Streets. The Levee will forever be associated with "Bathhouse" John Coughlin and Michael "Hinky Dink" Kenna, the aldermen of the First Ward, which included the Loop, the Levee, and the Prairie Avenue district (in that era, Chicago's wards were represented by two aldermen). This notorious pair ruled the First Ward for nearly half a century—actually, they formed their political alliance in 1893—profiting mightily from payoffs, bribes, and "boodle" (the selling of votes by aldermen to entrepreneurs seeking city contracts).

But such powerful evil provoked an equally powerful reaction. As *Scribner's Magazine* put it in the 1880s, Chicago was a city of both "wickedness and piety."[3] And those on the side of piety, against considerable opposition, meant to purge the iniquity. These efforts did not achieve success until the 1910s, but much of the impetus can be traced to 1893. This chapter will look at two champions of moral improvement who set their sights on Chicago in that year. The success of one, who relied on traditional religious reform aimed at individual sinners, was initially electrifying but ultimately ephemeral. The other, whose Victorian reformist zeal meshed in the United States with the Progressive movement, did a great deal to motivate the reformers who would eventually succeed in eliminating the city's unconcealed excesses.

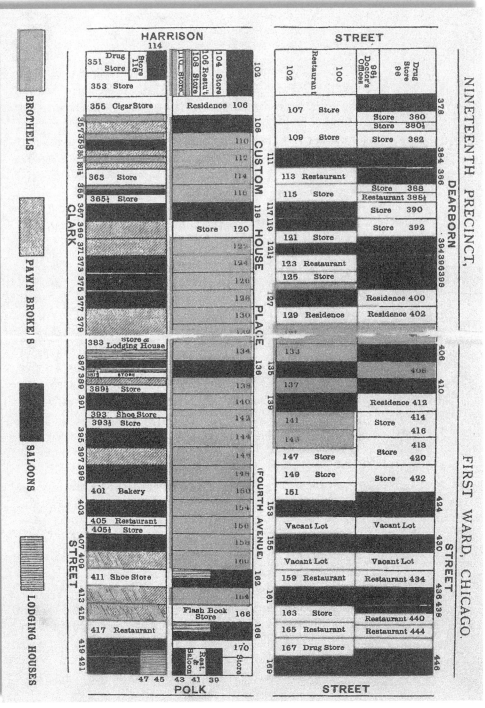

William T. Stead's famous "Map of Sin" showed no fewer than twenty-nine brothels and ten saloons lining both sides of the street in a single block in Chicago. (Author's collection)

Moody's Crusade

Before Billy Graham, Oral Roberts, and Pat Robertson, there was Dwight Lyman Moody, who is considered the precursor, if not the inventor, of modern large-scale evangelism. It was Moody who pioneered the mass merchandising of religion, the reach-out techniques, the welcoming ecumenicalism, the employment of slangy language, and the use of popular music.[4] Moody became a tycoon of religion who followed a business model. Previous revival preachers tended to operate in rural areas or in smaller cities; Moody headed for the metropolises. An observer of his work in New York in 1876 called it "a vast business enterprise, organized and conducted by business men, who put their money into it on business principles, for the purpose of saving souls."[5] Operations on the scale of Moody's required planning and organization. They also required money, which Moody was able to raise on a grand scale, and Chicago magnates like Marshall Field, Philip Armour, and Cyrus McCormick contributed generously. Another innovation pioneered by Moody was the use of publicity and advertising (Moody was not shy about twisting the arms of newspaper reporters). He was criticized by some clergymen for taking out newspaper advertisements, but he responded, "It seems to me a good deal better to advertise and have a full house, than to preach to empty pews. . . . This is the age of advertisement and you have to take your chance"[6]

Moody, like his predecessor Charles Grandison Finney (1792–1875), the progenitor of modern revivalism, practiced what was known as "heart religion" as opposed to "head religion." Fine points of theology did not much interest Moody, who was not an ordained minister. He would wring tears from his listeners (and

The Chicago-based evangelist Dwight Lyman Moody considered the Columbian Exposition to be "the opportunity of a century" and in 1893 staged his great World's Fair Evangelistic Campaign. (Library of Congress)

sob himself) when telling stories of deceased children awaiting their erring parents in heaven. His vocabulary was colloquial, and he would transition quickly from pathos to humor. He was a round, burly man (five-foot-six and 280 pounds) and threw himself into his preaching with physicality, acting out Bible stories.

Born in Northfield, Massachusetts, in 1837, he came to Chicago in 1856, not long after he had found religion while working in his uncle's shoe store in Boston. He became a shoe clerk in Chicago, too, but his energy propelled him into other enterprises, and he thrived both as a businessman and as an active member of Plymouth Congregational Church. In 1861, Moody made the momentous decision to devote all his time to evangelical activity; ten years later, he formed a partnership with Ira D. Sankey, a musically gifted evangelist with a fine singing voice.

Moody and Sankey carried their message to Britain in 1873 and were a sensation. In Edinburgh, they spoke to audiences of two thousand people every night, and when the pair reached Birmingham in January 1874, they drew over 156,000 people in just eight days. They then spent four months in London, during which time some three million people came to hear them. When Moody he returned to the United States, he was an international celebrity. He drew great crowds to New York's Hippodrome, made a tour of the South and West, and then returned to Chicago in 1876.

As 1893 approached, many Chicago clergymen were apprehensive about the upcoming Columbian Exposition. They feared, first, that the fair would draw many of the country's worst elements to the city and, second, that the excitement would distract both visitors and Chicagoans from their religious duties. Some proposed a boycott of the exposition; others considered somehow using the law to close it. Moody, however, realized that the exposition actually offered a glorious prospect. He didn't have to go out to reach people; they were coming to him. "Here is the opportunity of a century!" he exulted.[7]

Moody launched what he called his World's Fair Evangelistic Campaign at the Chicago Avenue Church, better known as "Moody's Church," on the first Sunday in May. His target was not the comfortable citizens who were already attending his services. He was going to go right into Hades—West Madison Street, an area of "saloons, brothels, gambling-hells, murderers' dens, and all kinds of vile resorts."[8] He found a four-story building, used the ground floor for a mission hall, and housed on the other floors some thirty students to help him. While revival meetings were being held in the hall, the students would fan out into the neighborhood.

But Moody wanted a larger venue and found the Haymarket Theater, with a capacity of three thousand. His student helpers mostly succeeded in rounding up enough patrons, although not all were of the destitute sort that Moody would have liked to convert. As one observer put it, "Side by side stood rough men and fashionably dressed ladies, negroes and working-women and gentlemen."[9] Clergymen from all across the country poured in to work at Moody's side, along with allies from England, Scotland, Ireland, France, Germany, Austria, and, from Russia, one Rabbi Joseph Rabinowitz, a Jewish convert to Christianity. Female associates were also present in considerable numbers. The churches, theaters, schools, and recreational centers in which Moody and his assistants preached numbered in the dozens, and he was not above holding services in Forepaugh's Circus Tent, which held ten thousand people. He took out an advertisement in the newspapers that ran:

Ha! Ha! Ha!
Three Big Shows!
Moody in the Morning!
Forepaugh in the Afternoon and Evening![10]

As one observer of his revival in the circus tent put it, "The surroundings were the usual circus furniture—ropes, trapezes, gaudy decorations, etc., while in an adjoining building was a large menagerie, including eleven elephants. Clowns, grooms, circus riders, men, women, and children, drinking and betting men, pickpockets, all gathered we were informed, into this unique assembly. What a crowd it was! Men, women, and children, 18,000 of them, and on a Sunday morning, too!"[11]

Moody's ministry also employed five other "large canvas tabernacles," as well as a "gospel wagon" used to hold open-air meetings in warm weather. Moody even sent ministers to hold meetings in police stations just before roll call. Nor were the spiritual needs of children overlooked. Meetings held for them featured pictures projected onto a canvas by a stereopticon, or "magic lantern."

The evangelists who had come from Europe were vital in reaching out to Chicago's ethnic neighborhoods, with sermons being given in Dutch, Swedish, German, Polish, French, and Czech. The extent of Moody's activity—and the number of preachers he employed—can be assessed from the report that on the second Sunday of October 1893 some seven-

Moody himself came to understand that his revivals were not enough to turn the United States into an evangelical nation.

ty-two thousand people gathered in 109 separate Moody-sponsored meetings. And it seemed that the Columbian Exposition had a synergy with Moody's campaign. Moody claimed that at one meeting in the Haymarket Theater, fully twenty-eight hundred of the three thousand attendees were World's Fair visitors.

The final meeting of the World's Fair Evangelistic Campaign was held on October 31, 1893. One of Moody's colleagues was convinced that for years afterward many people would reflect, "It was at the World's Fair in '93 that I learned for the first time that Jesus Christ died to save men."[12] After the campaign ended, Moody reported that the enterprise had cost $60,000 for the activities themselves and $40,000 to "enlarge the buildings before the time of the campaign." This great sum, he said, was "provided for by the gifts of generous Christian individuals and societies all over the United States, England, and Canada. Some of this money was given in answer to personal appeals, and some without any suggestion from me."[13]

Although it is reasonable to believe that Moody's campaign inspired some reprobates to give up strong drink and some prodigals to return home, it would be impossible to assess the long-term effectiveness of the World's Fair Evangelistic Campaign or to say how many souls were "saved." The evidence indicates, however, that this campaign, like Moody's other revivals, did not boost church attendance very much in the long run. In some cities, such as Philadelphia and Boston, it was found that a Moody revival would raise church attendance for a year or so, but then the numbers would slip back to what they were before—or even decline.[14] Even more telling was Moody's inability to reach workers or criminals or what was then called "the unchurched." Despite Moody's claims that he would preach to anyone, anywhere, observers of Moody's rallies reported that the audiences were generally middle class and composed of already committed Christians.

Moody himself came to understand that his revivals were not enough to turn the United States into an evangelical nation. This realization helped spur his establishment of the Moody Bible Institute in 1886. He hoped that he could educate an entire generation of ministers who would spread the word more effectively and extensively in the years to come. The success of this establishment has meant that Moody still has a large presence in Chicago. The school, which offers both undergraduate and graduate courses, still stands on the corner of Chicago and La-Salle Streets, where Moody founded it. The Moody Church on North Clark Street opened in 1925, a generation after Moody's death in 1899, and holds more than four thousand people.

Moody expressed sympathy for the poor and for the working class, but his strategy for helping them was to convert them, not to give them handouts. Judicious charity was fine (too much might make them dependent and idle), but the acquisition of Christian virtues was key to their escape from poverty. At the time of Moody's campaign, reformist forces were inaugurating the era of Progressivism, which sought to better the lives of workers and the poor through legislation and government action, while some churchmen were preaching a "social gospel"— among their goals were a shorter workweek, the abolition of child labor, and the regulation of factories. These issues did not especially interest Moody. He did not see social progress on the horizon, he saw the Second Coming, and he advised his listeners to think about heaven: "if we don't find everything down here just as we want it, we shall be satisfied there."[15] "Don't let Sunday be given up to talking on topics you don't understand such as capital and labor," he advised.[16] Moody viewed organized labor with suspicion and thought that unionism, atheism, and anarchy formed a three-headed monster.

Even the suffering brought by the depression of 1893 did not substantially change the minds of Moody and other ministers who shared his theology, although some came to believe that some action had to be taken to ameliorate the misery.[17] As historian William G. McLoughlin Jr. has pointed out, this unresponsiveness to social reform movements has been characteristic of American revivalism in general: "the logic of their theology disparaged collective efforts at reform. Since all sin was personal, all reform must be personal. Regeneration, not legislation, changed the human heart, and until that was changed all else was useless."[18]

Moody's individualistic theology was the main reason that, despite all his hard work during the World's Fair Evangelistic Campaign, he would not be the one to clean out Custom House Place. That street of sin did indeed vanish in time, but it would be other reformers who would make it happen.

William Stead and Civic Reform

Although Moody backed moral reform, other Chicago leaders were more interested in social, political, and civic reform—the kind of changes that would expunge vice, confront political corruption and fraud, improve urban services, and help raise living standards. William Stead, who came to Chicago in 1893, was instrumental in sparking that type of reform.

William Thomas Stead was born in the village of Embleton in England on July 5, 1849. His father, a Congregational minister, practiced home schooling and had his son reading Latin by age five. At age twelve, Stead underwent a religious awakening, but he did not follow his father into the ministry. Instead he went into journalism, and at age twenty-two he took charge of the *Northern Echo* and became the youngest newspaper editor in Britain. Newspaper work did not dilute his religious zeal; it increased it. Stead saw his job as "a glorious opportunity of attacking the devil" and vowed to use his power "on behalf of the poor, the outcast and the oppressed." His motto was "Everything wrong in the world is a divine call to use your life in righting it."[19] In 1880, he went to London to become assistant editor of the *Pall Mall Gazette.* Three years later, he became the newspaper's editor.

In the 1970s, American literary life was enlivened by a movement called "the New Journalism," but there was a "New Journalism" in Britain a century earlier that was associated with Stead. In addition to its crusading spirit, this movement invigorated newspapers with a greater use of illustrations, interviews with prominent people, and a deliberate outreach to the common reader with the goal of swaying public opinion. This New Journalism also called upon reporters to mix in an intimate way with daily life. Two of Stead's earliest journalistic campaigns involved an exposé of slum conditions and an article called "The Truth about the Navy," criticizing the status of Britain's fleet; both efforts resulted in parliamentary legislation. But Stead's most sensational effort was "Maiden Tribute of Modern Babylon," published in July 1885. It was a shocking exposé of child prostitution—a subject simply not discussed in Victorian high society, much less published in a newspaper. Stead sent a reformed prostitute into the Marylebone district to purchase a thirteen-year-old girl, who, Stead avowed, was sold by her own mother for £5. This action resulted in the passage of the Criminal Law Amendment Bill, which, among other things, raised the female age of consent from thirteen to sixteen. However, Stead was charged with abduction and indecent assault and spent three months in prison. In 1890, he

The British journalist and reformer William T. Stead. When he was in Chicago it was said that he "consorted wholly with the lost souls of the underworld." (Victoria and Albert Museum)

left the *Pall Mall Gazette* and launched a magazine entitled the *Review of Reviews*, which became a global success.

Many visitors to London had told Stead of the wonders of Chicago and the promise of the great fair. He had also gotten a tantalizing glimpse of the city's low life by reading a volume entitled *Chicago's Dark Places* (1891), which brought to light Chicago's seamy underworld. Stead, along with his son, departed from Southampton on October 21, 1893, and he barely arrived in time to view the Columbian Exposition. The story goes that one of the first places Stead went to see was Custom House Place, where he walked into a saloon run by one Hank North, a former performer in minstrel shows. A group of ruffians thought to have a bit of fun with this unexpected gentleman, but North sprayed them with a seltzer bottle, calling out, "Back away, boys! This is Mr. Stead from England." Stead, one of the greatest interviewers of his time, buttonholed one of the toughs, the infamous Frank Brown (known as "Brownie, King of the Bums") and soon had him engaged in long talks about the real Chicago.

As a journalist who knew Stead wrote, "He took up his residence in a little room over a disreputable saloon and consorted wholly with the lost souls of the underworld. All this, he assured, for a high and holy purpose. He was in the mire, but not of it."[20] After the depression arrived, Stead wrote about how the unemployed "wandered through the streets, seeking work and finding none." He told how the "foot-sore, leg-swollen tramp" would seek shelter "wherever he could find a roof to shelter him and warmth to keep the frost out of his bones. Some kenneled in empty trucks on the railway sidings, rejoicing even in a fireless retreat; others crept into the basement of saloons, or coiled themselves up in outhouses, but the bulk of them were accommodated in the police stations, in the Pacific Garden Mission and in the City Hall. Such improvised shelters were all the appliances of civilization which Chicago in the year of the World's Fair had to offer to the homeless out-of-works."[21]

What made Stead especially angry was that whatever help the destitute were able to get came not from the better sort but from the saloonkeepers. North, for example, was doing what he could by providing free lunches: "How he keeps it up is a marvel, but the free lunch goes on, hot soup with bread, apparently dispensed with equal freedom to those who take a drink and those who do not." Stead calculated that North was giving away thirty-six gallons of soup and seventy-two loaves of bread every day. Many saloon-keepers allowed the unemployed to take shelter in their basements, and when Stead visited "Hinky Dink" Kenna's saloon, he learned that the proprietor had set up a Workingmen's Exchange that fed thousands. Whatever their morals, these people, unlike the "predatory rich," were practicing the "fundamental principles of human brotherhood which Christ came to preach."[22]

Stead arranged, at his own expense, a great meeting of Chicagoans high and low. The assembly, held at the Central Music Hall, turned out to be one of the pivotal moments in Chicago history. On November 11, the eve of Stead's meeting, invitations went out to "two thousand residents of the toughest parts of the levee" as well as to "every minister of the gospel who could be reached and to a large number of wealthy and prominent men."[23] The gathering took place in two sessions, both headed by Stead, the first at 2:30 and the second at 7:30. The rhetoric at times was fiery. At the afternoon assembly a leading socialist named Thomas J. Morgan created a sensation when he said:

> If this crime of silence, this infernal desire of the well-to-do to crush out of sight this awful suffering is persisted in, do not think that you will rest in security. If you well-to-do people do not listen—will not wake up—you do not know but that . . . a desperate man, feeling in himself all the injustice that is inflicted on his fellows, will kill, will destroy. This is no fancy picture. The reality exists from day to day everywhere. And if the pleadings of Editor Stead in the name of Christ and for justice cannot shake you out of your false security may somebody use dynamite to blow you out.[24]

Hundreds called out in protest and some left the building before Stead calmed things down. Stead himself spoke for over an hour.

He said that he was dismayed to discover that Chicago had not only imported all the evils of Europe, "but had improved upon them, and more than that had originated new scandals which not even a third-rate town in Europe would endure." The evening session also had its stormy moments, especially when the clergy was censured, but it was calmer than the afternoon meeting. Stead concluded by expressing his hope that a newly proposed organization, the Civic Federation of Chicago, would help "drive the devil out of Chicago." In Stead's view, the city faced three evils: first, the depression; second, the manner in which the police permitted the red-light district to flourish; third, the failure of city government to deal with either of the first two ills, or very many others for that matter.

The next day, Stead left for Toronto, telling reporters that he had "started a ball rolling" and that he hoped the newspapers would keep it going. When asked if he shouldn't remain longer, he said, "There are plenty of men to continue—plenty of them, and they can do it better than I could."[25] But he was back in Chicago in early December, and in a lecture at a meeting of the women's clubs, he so berated the ladies for their "self-indulgent lives" that many of the attendees stormed out. He also made headlines by briefly taking a job shoveling snow with destitute unemployed workers. On December 10, he returned to the Central Music Hall, where he reiterated his criticisms. He then traveled to other parts of the Midwest and, upon returning to Chicago, expressed optimism that reform efforts seemed to be taking place. He left New York for home on March 7. But although Stead would no longer be physically present in Chicago, his influence would grow. In 1894, he published his book.

If Christ Came to Chicago!

If Christ Came to Chicago! seems at first glance like a reformist tract. It is that, but it is also one of the finest feats of reportage in Chicago's history, a thick volume filled with descriptions, anecdotes, statistics, and interviews—a huge resource for historians.

Stead begins by declaring that faith is not enough; action is what's wanted. And that means action from government: "the

The frontispiece of William Stead's *If Christ Came to Chicago!* depicts Jesus dispersing Chicago's moneychangers. The structure in the background is the Administration Building of the Columbian Exposition.

assistance of the municipal authority is indispensable . . . before we can make men divine, we must cast out the devils who are brutalizing them out of even human semblance. But this cannot be accomplished excepting by the use of means, which can only be wielded by the City Council . . . all roads lead to City Hall."[26]

If Christ came to Chicago, Stead argues, the first and most dispiriting thing he would find would be the army of unemployed. Stead's tour begins at the Harrison Street police station. Although it housed some of "the most dissolute ruffians of both sexes," desperate men, out of work, applied each night to be admitted for shelter from the frost. The cells resembled "cages of wild beasts," and an "open gutter at the back provide[d] the only sanitary accommodation." Stead relates that when he described such horrors to Chicago's leaders, he was met with a universal response: these people are "bums" and deserve no better. To counter this attitude, Stead explains that a university professor canvassed a group of a hundred unemployed persons and discovered that 90 percent of them were not working class but were bakers, waiters, sailors, shoemakers, painters, carpenters, and so on—even university graduates.

Stead goes on to describe the situation of the city's prostitutes, with an angry aside about churches that refuse to relieve penitent "harlots." Stead's anecdotes are plentiful, from the practices carried on in the houses, to the policemen who "get their women cheap," to the routine arrests and bailing-outs. The chapter "Whisky and Politics" describes how a good-natured, honest saloonkeeper educated Stead on the workings of Chicago politics, on how the saloon played a pivotal role in the political process, on the price of votes, and on the "secret ballot" being not so secret. Stead found a paradox in the system. On the one hand, Chicago's politics were rife with "bribery, intimidation, bull-dozing of every kind, knifing, shooting, and the whole swimming in whisky." On the other hand, however, these saloon-keeper/politicians took care of people: "Rough and rude though it might be, the Democratic party organization, and, of course, the Republican party organization to a less extent in the same way, are nevertheless doing the work which the churches ought to do. . . . In its own imperfect manner this rough, vulgar, faulty substitute for religion is at least compelling the heeler and the bartender and the tough, whom none of the churches can reach, to recognize that fundamental principle of human brotherhood which Christ came to teach."[27]

Stead's favorable opinion of saloon-keepers is followed by a jaundiced view of Chicago's millionaires, especially those he calls the "Chicagoan Trinity" of Marshall Field, Philip Armour, and George Pullman. Despite their charitable efforts (Stead was pleased with the Armour Institute), Stead takes a dim view of their determination to avoid paying their fair share of taxes. In a scathing chapter entitled "Who Are the Disreputables?" Stead slams Chicago's "respectable" wealthy, charging, "Rich men and women are often, owing to the temptations which beset them, the most disreputable members of the community." Those rich who weren't corrupt and rapacious were simply idle and unproductive—these tended to be the heirs. In Europe, Stead argues, such people would enter Parliament, but that a rich man in Chicago would consider running for alderman was unthinkable. Stead's disparagement of the upper classes likely represents his failure to appreciate how the "saloon Democrats" so thoroughly controlled real power in the city by means of the political machine devised by gambling boss and political kingmaker Michael McDonald in the 1870s and 1880s. It was an impediment that obstructed even the sincerest reformers.[28]

In the section of the book entitled "Satan's Invisible World Displayed," Stead castigates the "boodler" system through which Chicago's politicians took payoffs to grant favors to entrepreneurs, a process known, Stead explains, as "squaring" the alderman. Stead reports the remark of a lawyer who said, "There are sixty-eight Aldermen in the City Council and sixty-six of them can be bought. This I know because I have bought them myself." (Stead himself believed there might be as many as ten honest aldermen).[29] Also coming in for censure were the "Gas Trust," an illegal combination of private gas suppliers who gouged their customers; the telephone company (another boodled franchise); and the tax assessors, who "never assess any item of property at its fair cash value," thus depriving the city of revenue and thrusting most of the tax burden onto the poor. (The Auditorium, he asserted, was "assessed at just about the sum which it cost to fit it with radiators.") In a chapter entitled "Gambling and Party Finance," Stead marvels at how Chicago's politicians contrived a system by which they allowed illegal gambling to flourish as long as they took a percentage of the profits.

In part 4, "Christ's Church in Chicago," Stead casts his withering gaze upon the churches. He has a few kind words for the Catholic Church but regrets its unwillingness to push for civic reform—he points out the presence of so many Catholics in city politics and lamented that most seemed in it for the boodle. He praises the work of the Salvation Army, but, as for the rest of the Protestant churches, they are, in his view, pretty much nothing more than social clubs. Stead then goes on to a grim assessment of the police force, most of whose members he saw as corrupt beneficiaries of the political spoils system who "flourish upon black mail," and the courts, which he thought would almost never convict someone of a political crime.

Was there hope? Stead thought so. "Chicago," he wrote, "is in the throes of what for the want of a better name may be called a Civic Revival. The good men and women of all parties have begun to realize how disgraceful to the city is the condition of its municipal administration."[30] What was needed was the establishment of a "Civic Church," in which religious and secular forces would unite: "what preaching cannot do, what the personal religion of the individual would be powerless to effect, civic religion practically applied by the election of honest men would assuredly accomplish."[31]

Organizing for Reform

Efforts to organize a municipal association to effect civic reform took place long before Stead came to Chicago. In July 1874, the city witnessed the birth of the first of what might be called "good government" movements. This group, the Citizens' Association, was founded by businessmen and attorneys after a ruinous blaze showed the need for a reform of the fire department, but its scope came to include taxation, corruption, the police, and civic administration. The president, Franklin MacVeagh, organized committees to investigate a range of issues, and by November, the organization had five hundred members, representing "the very best citizens of Chicago."[32] In their view, the lower classes had captured the political system and the "better portion of the community" was "disenfranchised," making it necessary, as MacVeagh put it, to organize an "organization supplemental to our city institutions."[33] The group, however, tended to be elitist and to stay neutral in politics. As one historian has put it, "the structural weaknesses such as class antagonism remained untouched because the mugwumpish reform attitudes of the Citizens' Association did little to alleviate the problem and often exacerbated the situation. Indeed not very many people could or would cope with the problems urbanization and industrialism created because of the class and physical barriers these processes erected."[34] Another problem was the difficulty in following up transient successes. Scandals would erupt and felons would be convicted, but Mike McDonald's machine would sputter a bit and then resume chugging away. As one contemporary put it, "The trouble with reform is that the reformers won't stay mad more than six months."[35]

William Stead had a better idea, and it was he who kick-started the Civic Federation of Chicago. It happened at the November 12 afternoon meeting. After Morgan made his rabble-rousing remarks about dynamite, Graham Taylor, a social worker and minister, tried to calm the tumult, and during his speech, a woman cried out, "Give us a plan for action." The president of the waiters' union, W. C. Pomeroy, offered a motion "that it is the sense of this meeting that the formation of a civic confederation is feasible and practical and that a committee of twenty-one be selected as an organizing committee."[36] After the evening assembly, a panel of five, one of whom was Jane Addams, convened to select a committee of not twenty-one, but forty. The membership, comprised of business and professional people, clergy, women, and labor leaders, was much more broad-based than that of the earlier Citizens' Association. The president was the banker Lyman Gage and the two vice presidents were Bertha Honoré Palmer, wife of the hotel magnate Potter Palmer, and the labor leader J. J. McGrath.

At first, it appeared that the thrust of the new organization would be towards political reform, but as the depression got worse, its efforts turned toward relief of the poor, and during the winter of 1893–94, it disbursed $133,000 in aid, along with large quantities of food and other essentials. One of its earliest and most visible successes was its eradication of open gambling. In May 1894, a committee of the Civic Federation reported that between fifteen hundred and two thousand professional gamblers were operating in Chicago and that they were paying from $9,000 to $30,000 a month for protection, and on September 20, Mayor John Patrick Hopkins ordered the closing of all gambling houses.[37] The next day, a small law enforcement army descended on Clark Street, and within that one day, seventy-eight gambling joints were put out of business.[38] No one would pretend that illegal gambling thereby disappeared from Chicago, not with the growth of the policy racket, bookie joints, illegal slot machines, and so on in the 1920s and 1930s. But wide-open illegal casino gambling would henceforth be gone.

The same is true of prostitution, which has hardly disappeared from Chicago or any other big city. But the contrast between Custom House Place and today's South Federal Street speaks volumes. Those forces dedicated to the closing down of the bordellos had to contend with those who favored segregated vice districts, arguing that vice was part of human nature and that it was better to confine it to a single location. But here again reform efforts prevailed. Nevertheless, although a series of raids in 1894 shuttered a few of the houses, it took nearly two decades for the brothels to fade away. In 1910, Mayor Fred Busse appointed a commission to look into matter, and their report, *The Social Evil in Chicago*, called for the "absolute annihilation" of the Levee. On October 24, 1911, the subsequent mayor, Carter Harrison II, ordered the closing of the city's most famous and expensive brothel, the Everleigh Club, and a little over a year later, he shuttered the rest of the houses. Other factors that contributed to the eventual disappearance of the Levee were rising property values in the neighborhood, the desire of the railroads to reclaim the area for passenger terminals, and the onset of automobiles and highways, which made it possible for thrill seekers to easily travel to outlying protected vice havens, such as Cicero and Calumet City, Indiana. Economic considerations had also been instrumental in the removal of the Clark Street gambling houses—the property was of too great commercial value to escape development. Sometimes real estate developers prove to be more powerful agents of improvement than reformers.[39]

The Civic Federation itself was not much involved with the antiprostitution effort, having by then transformed itself into a watchdog group concerned mostly with public finance and taxation (which it remains today), but by this point, other reform groups, such as the Municipal Voters League, the Chicago Bureau of Charities, the City Club, and the Bureau of Public Efficiency, had sprung up. By 1912, the Progressive Era had been in full swing for years, reformers across the country were agitating for urban reform, and other cities were also pushing vice underground. It was inevitable, therefore, that Chicago would have been part of this movement, and when Stead first arrived he had assessed that Chicago already was, as was the rest of the country, "in the incipient stages of a civic revival." But it was Stead who, as he put it, "started a ball rolling" in Chicago.

Upon returning home, Stead became involved with other issues, such as European unity, Russian affairs, and international peace. His opposition to the Boer War earned him great hostility. He did travel to the United States again and even returned briefly to Chicago as part of an extended speaking tour. In 1912, he was invited to come to New York to address a meeting entitled "World's Peace." The ship on which he sailed was the *Titanic*, and he was among the 1,523 passengers who perished.

Moody died on December 22, 1899, at his home in Northfield, Massachusetts. He had prepared for the occasion earlier by stating, "Some day you will read in the papers that D. L. Moody of East Northfield is dead. Don't you believe a word of it! At that moment I shall be more alive than I am now."[40] However, several years earlier—in 1893 to be exact—a rising evangelist named John Wilbur Chapman, who was assisting Moody's crusade, had hired as his assistant at a salary of $40 a week a former professional ballplayer for the Chicago White Stockings.[41] His name was Billy Sunday, and he would be the one who would bring evangelism into the twentieth century.

14

Epidemics and Clean Water

Chicago suffered its first epidemic before it even was Chicago. In 1832, a year before the state legislature incorporated the tiny settlement, a ship arriving at Fort Dearborn brought troops to fight in the Black Hawk War; these troops brought cholera with them. About one-fifth of the passengers died, and most of the village's three hundred inhabitants got out of town as fast as they could.

Not surprisingly, therefore, one of the first things the citizens of newly incorporated Chicago did was to create, in 1835, the Chicago Board of Health. This body did heroic (although intermittent) work in devising health policies and advising the city government to pass and enforce public health regulations, but its labors took some time to bear fruit. By 1893, Chicago had known sixty years of sporadic epidemics, and the population was much too large to be fleeing into the countryside.

For some three years after canal boats began arriving in 1849 from New Orleans and other southern localities after the opening of the Illinois and Michigan Canal, nearly thirteen hundred people died from cholera. That same disease struck just six years later when more than fifteen hundred Chicagoans died. By this time, according to the historian Harold L. Platt, Chicago was "the unhealthiest place in the United States."[1] Between that outbreak and 1893, Chicago suffered repeated epidemics of cholera, dysentery, scarlet fever, typhoid, and smallpox.[2]

In 1893, yet another smallpox epidemic struck Chicago. But this episode was, in an odd way, actually something to applaud. That's because in its limited scope and in the city's vigorous response it was demonstrated that Chicago was nearing victory in its battle against epidemic disease and in its quest for a clean water supply. The 1893 smallpox epidemic was the *last* significant outbreak of that disease in the city's history. As the historian Thomas Bonner has explained, "An examination of Chicago mortality tables reveals the effectiveness of empirical sanitary measures undertaken before 1895. During the period between 1855 and 1895, roughly the years of greatest growth for Chicago, the mortality rate was actually reduced, and no epidemic took a toll comparable to the great cholera and typhoid fever outbreaks of the earlier years."[3] A chart of the death rate in Chicago from 1844 to 1920 shows a spike in 1891 due to a typhoid fever outbreak and then a steady decline thereafter, with an especially steep drop from 1893 to 1894.[4]

The Epidemic of 1893

In the 1890s, about a quarter of Chicago's population lived in unimaginably crowded slums—and things seemed to be getting worse as tenement-style buildings began to sprout, with greedy landlords successfully evading the city's health regulations and sanitary codes. In some of these buildings, 150 people were squeezed into six apartments.[5] In the summer of 1893, health inspectors made an investigation of "the lodging houses habited by Italians." To cite just two examples, in a State Street house the inspector found "sixty-one cots and bunks in the cellar six feet six inches in height. . . . The whole room is impregnated with bad odors which arise from defective plumbing." At a Canal Street habitation, the inspector reported, "I found fifteen beds in a cellar. The walls and ceiling were unplastered. The floor is rotted and unsafe. The sink is used for all purposes. . . . It is one of the most filthy places I have visited."[6] In 1901, a survey found at least twelve people living in a three-room apartment that had not a single window.[7] The year before, a physician determined that in Chicago's worst slums, the population density was nine hundred people per acre, which meant that if the entire city had an equal density it could contain the population of the Western Hemisphere.[8]

Many of these new tenements were what were known as "double deckers." The old wooden house on the property was pushed to the back, and a new brick three-story or four-story dwelling was built flush against it in the front. Often the worst conditions were to be found in the rear house; as a contemporary reported, "The front houses cut off the source of light, and the rooms were dark. . . . The demoralization and degradation to which people living in the filthy surroundings of these alley houses eventually descend is obvious. . . . Rear tenements make the worse possible dwellings for human beings."[9] Few of these slum residents had any place to bathe outside of the overcrowded public baths, mounds of garbage and filth were everywhere, and sewerage was often inadequate, if not nonexistent. One of the city's densest areas was the West Side, where Jane Addams's Hull-House was located, and this neighborhood became the epicenter of the 1893 smallpox epidemic.

According to the reformer and Hull-House resident Florence Kelley, who was appointed Illinois' chief factory inspector in 1893, the epidemic "followed a neglected case on the Midway of the Exposition." "At the close of the Fair," she wrote, "the hideous fact could no longer be concealed that smallpox had been gradually spreading from the Midway to the homes of some garment workers on the West Side."[10] Smallpox, however, had been occurring in Chicago before the fair opened. There were a small number of cases in 1892, and in 1893, there were three in January, three in February, and five in April. The city health commissioner, Dr. Arthur R. Reynolds, believed that workers, both foreign and domestic, laboring on the fair in 1892 had brought the disease to Chicago.[11] In 1894, he noted, "Up to April 1892, Chicago had been free from smallpox for the longest period in its history, from December, 1889, a period of twenty-nine months. In 1892 began the heaviest immigration

Kelley's job . . . was to confiscate and destroy newly made clothing that had become contaminated by infected garment workers.

since 1882, and for a year or two previous large numbers of artisans, workingmen, and laborers have been flocking to the city." Some of these workers, he noted, came from abroad: "Emigrant carrying steamers infected of smallpox arrived repeatedly at the Atlantic seaports and a bulk of their steerage passengers came to Chicago either for residence or for distribution."[12] However, others speculated that the smallpox might have spread from Indiana, where several towns had recently experienced epidemics.

Kelley's job (and the job of other inspectors) was to confiscate and destroy newly made clothing that had become contaminated by infected garment workers. Understandably, workers refused to give up the garments and suffer the loss of income. An example of the inspectors' difficulties can be seen in what happened to one Inspector Bisno. He visited the home of a garment worker named John Cerenak, who made coats in a tenement room. There Bisno found a coat that Cerenak was making for A. A. Devore and Sons; he also found the body of a boy who had recently died from smallpox. Cerenak claimed that the coat was actually his own, but Bisno checked with the Devore Company and was told that it was theirs and they preferred to see it destroyed. When Bisno went back to Cerenak, this time in the company of Dr. Reynolds, he was told that Cerenak would not relinquish the coat unless he was paid $16. Reynolds told Bisno that he would return the next day with the police to seize it. For some reason, Reynolds was unable to return, and when inspectors later asked about the coat's whereabouts, they were told it had disappeared.[13] Factory owners were as uncooperative as the workers, and it wasn't until Illinois governor John Peter Altgeld threatened to organize a five-state embargo on "all shipments of products of the needle trades from Chicago" that they agreed to allow inspection and promote vaccination in their shops.

The health department initiated a citywide vaccination campaign, although it was hindered by fear of the procedure, especially in poor neighborhoods with many immigrants. Dr. Reynolds called it "a heart-breaking struggle with ignorance and prejudice, where every weapon of resistance to the efforts of the department, even to acts of personal violence, was employed."[14]

Kelley recounted seeing babies and small children wrapped up and hidden on closet shelves so the doctors wouldn't find them. She also told of a young physician who was "disabled for life" after being shot in the elbow by a panicky tailor. As a rule, when health inspectors found contagious diseases, they put warning cards on the doors of houses. Investigators found that residents often placed the cards on the inside of the front door, or on the back door, or on the basement door—when they simply didn't destroy the cards altogether. Such antivaccination sentiments occurred in other U.S. cities—for many immigrants, heavy-handed coercion reminded them of the tyrannical regimes they had come to America to escape.[15]

Another source of friction was parents' fears that their children would be sent to the smallpox hospital (also known as the "pest house") which, even Kelley had to agree, was a fearsome place. Dr. Reynolds reported, "No department rules or statutory law could overcome the horror of a pest house. Fear of the pest house led to the secretion of cases. Sick children were wrapped up and carried through the alley to a neighboring house when the family saw the health department conveyance arrive. Open violence was early threatened and occasionally attempted."[16]

The smallpox hospital soon became overcrowded; tents were set up on the grounds, but these too were soon overflowing. Several instances were reported of persons with the disease walking into police stations for help. In one case, it was proposed to convert a school into a temporary hospital. At a heated meeting, one objector complained that the building was too good to be used in such a manner, to which the chairman replied, "No building was too good for the care of the sick."[17] The plan fell through, however, when it was realized that the conversion would be too expensive. Finally, a temporary hospital was erected, more tents were found, and overcrowding ceased. The immigrants' fear of vaccination was not characteristic of most other parts of the city. As Dr. Reynolds explained, "It is not the better sanitary environment alone through our best residence districts that secure practical immunity from smallpox to their inhabitants; it is the active appreciation of the virtue of vaccination."[18]

Almost a hundred thousand vaccinations were performed in the last six months of 1893, but that was just the beginning. Letters went out to the heads of private and parochial schools as well as to railroads, factories, and businesses urging the vaccination of students and employees. Health officials spread the word by giving interviews to both English- and foreign-language newspapers. Even though the depression of 1893 had left the city strapped for cash, Mayor John Patrick Hopkins eventually found the funds—some $100,000—for the vaccination campaign. Hundreds of doctors and medical students were pressed into service. The city was divided into districts and subdistricts, five hundred vaccinators went door to door, and within the first three to four months of 1894, half a million vaccinations were administered. By May 1894, as Dr. Reynolds expressed it, "the backbone of the epidemic was broken."[19]

Improving Sanitation

A key element in the fight against epidemic disease in Chicago was the establishment of housing ordinances.[20] In the late nineteenth century, many reformers and reporters were raising the alarm about the "tenement threat": diseases bred in overcrowded slums. Much of the blame was placed upon the unsanitary habits of immigrants, who were considered genetically inferior to the "better sort" and culturally habituated to squalor—for this reason tenants, and not landlords, were held responsible for the unsanitary state of their dwellings. Progressives and labor leaders, on the other hand, found that the fault lay with landlords. As one contemporary writer expressed it, there were "thousands of families living in this city renting houses who do not know where or how to seek relief from the imposition of landlords, who build pest houses by contract to the lowest bidder."[21] City government also came in for censure for failing to fund sanitary improvements.

It might have been convenient to blame the immigrants, but Chicago's elite began to realize that they were not protected from the impact of the slums. Not only could disease spill into the better neighborhoods, but also a host of social ills were being bred in the tenements—"squalor, discomfort, intemperance, herding like cattle, filth, chronic disease, sweeping epidemics and decimation by death, the little children being the chief victims, family disruption, growth in immorality and vicious habits, and the creation of and fostering of crime," as one source expressed it.[22] It was in everyone's interest to ameliorate slum conditions: a cleaner city would be a safer city. For example, after a 1902 typhoid epidemic, Jane Addams wrote a report on how city officials were being bribed not to enforce sanitation laws. Her report pointed out that "the river wards cannot be isolated from the other residential portions of the town." Many produce vendors and delivery wagons originate in the West Side, she said, and "with these go the houseflies, bearing, as we may believe, the typhoid germ."[23]

Although Chicago had established a board of health in 1835, its effectiveness varied over the years, and sometimes it didn't even exist. In 1876, however, Mayor Monroe Heath established a permanent Department of Health headed by a single commissioner, a physician named Oscar Coleman De Wolf, who served until 1889, by which time a local newspaper reported, "The department has since developed into the most active and efficient health service in the United States."[24] At De Wolf's urging, the city passed its first health ordinance in 1880, giving the board of health the power to inspect and regulate health conditions in both factories and dwellings. Property owners were now provided with garbage cans and faced fines for not using them. Retired police officers, now hired as "sanitary policemen," were charged with inspecting "the ventilation of rooms, light and air shafts, windows, ventilation of water closets, drainage and plumbing."[25] New construction also had to be reviewed for sanitary purposes—De Wolf wrote articles for the *Inland Architect* magazine in which he explained the role of architects in providing ventilation, sanitation, fire prevention, and other salubrious measures.[26]

One aspect of Jane Addams's philosophy maintained that as long as women were being relegated to the traditional role of housekeeper, they could become housekeepers for the city as a whole. Consequently, she and many other women became involved in such issues as poisonous sewage, impure milk, and smoke-laden air.[27] Proper garbage disposal became one of their chief interests, and Addams herself actually tried to get hired as a garbage collector. That attempt failed, but in 1895, she was appointed garbage inspector of the Nineteenth Ward and with the help of her cohorts was instrumental in reporting hundreds of sanitary violations. At six in the morning, Addams and a female colleague would climb into their inspection buggy, follow the garbage trucks, and report landlords who were not providing sufficient trash receptacles.

Efficient trash collection was one of the many interests of the social worker and reformer Jane Addams, who had herself appointed garbage inspector of Chicago's nineteenth ward. (Library of Congress)

In 1893, Chicago newspapers were filled with articles recording complaints about inadequate garbage collection; as expected, such grievances multiplied in the summer. They intensified after the *Chicago Tribune* published an interview with Superintendent George S. Welles of the Bureau of Street and Alley Cleaning, in which he claimed that every garbage box in the city was emptied at least three times a week. The newspaper sent out reporters to verify his claim, and they had no trouble finding scandalous conditions. The garbage box behind a residence on Congress Street, for example, "was filled yesterday with refuse to such an extent that both of its lids were open six inches. The garbage was thick with maggots, and the stench was offensive at a distance of fifty feet." The homeowner, J. H. Howenstein, said, "It is more than two weeks since this box has been cleaned." Henry Hannigan of Loomis Street reported, "I moved into this house six weeks ago and the garbage man has cleaned our box only once since we have lived here."[28] Chicagoans were well aware of the connection between poor garbage control and disease. In July, the residents of the Grand Crossing neighborhood railed against the health department for keeping a garbage dump in their area and not maintaining it, referring to it as the "cholera bed."[29]

Chicago would eventually control its garbage problem, mostly through a system of landfills (incinerators, which Superintendent Welles promoted in 1893, were tried for a time, but concerns over air pollution forced their closing). Landfill garbage was something of a valuable resource in early Chicago because the low-lying city used refuse for filling in swamps and marshes. Grant Park, for example, sits on mounds of nineteenth-century rubbish (along with debris from the Great Fire), and many populated areas in the region of Lake Calumet owe their existence to landfills. Today, with landfill space becoming harder to find, the city has begun employing a recycling program in the hopes of reducing the amount of waste.

But garbage was not the knottiest problem with regard to urban sanitation. That problem involved the most basic of things: water.

Water In, Water Out

Any city, to survive as a functioning entity, has to deal with two water issues: bringing clean water in and carrying dirty water out. Cities on rivers, like St. Louis or Cincinnati, have a simple answer—the river brings in clean water from upstream and carries dirty water downstream. Municipalities downstream might not appreciate it, but the system works for the city in question. Cities on seacoasts can dump their waste water into the ocean; clean water is usually derived from a river or from aqueducts.[30] But cities on lakes have a special challenge—if they dump their waste water into the lake, they pollute the water supply, which was Chicago's problem.

In the 1840s, Chicago had no sewers. Ditches lined the sides of roads and streets, and waste was discarded into them to await the rains that would wash the refuse into the Chicago River. It was widely recognized that this system was unsatisfactory. As one observer put it in 1850, "Many of the populous localities are noisome quagmires, the gutters running with filth at which the very swine turn up their noses in supreme disgust. . . . The gutters at the crossings are clogged up, leaving standing pools of an undescribable liquid, there to salute the noses of passers by."[31] According to then prevalent theories of disease, wet ground was the source of illness. A Chicago physician said, "One thing is certain. This disease [cholera] develops itself most in the crowded and poorly ventilated parts of cities and large towns, in low damp places, and especially when stagnant pools and water-courses abound."[32] The solution, then, was to somehow to drain the city or to raise it out of the mud.

In 1850, Ellis Sylvester Chesbrough came to Chicago from Boston, where he had been city engineer, and took charge of the city's waterworks. Five years later, he was given the job of designing a comprehensive sewer system for Chicago. He weighed several alternatives for disposing of sewage, and the board of sewerage commissioners chose the least costly—the construction of a network of sewers that would empty waste into the Chicago River and then into Lake Michigan. Chesbrough recognized that Chicago was so flat that waste water would not easily flow down into the river. His solution was to build his sewers above ground down the middle of the streets. The system was graded so that the more distant sewers were higher, thus allowing the waste water to stream down to the river. The sewers were connected to the buildings and covered up; the streets were designed to be rounded, higher in the center so that water would run into side gutters connected to the sewer. There was one major problem, however—the streets were now higher than the entrances to the buildings.

The solution: raise the buildings up to road level. In a massive enterprise that required some twenty years, Chicago's buildings were literally jacked up—as much as ten feet in some cases. The owners of the properties were expected to bear the costs, and, predictably, not all of them did, which left some Chicago structures in a hole. To this day some older Chicago neighborhoods contain homes with their second-story windows at the level of the sidewalk. One of the most spectacular edifice raisings was that of the Briggs House. As a traveler described it, "The Briggs House, a gigantic hotel, five storeys high, solid masonry, weighing 22,000 tons, was raised four and a half feet, and new foundations built below. The people were in it all the time, coming and going, eating and sleeping—the whole business of the hotel proceeding without interruption."[33] One of the most prominent building raisers was George Pullman, later famous as the developer of the railroad sleeping car, who had previously been involved in moving buildings during the widening of the Erie Canal. He would have holes dug beneath the foundation of a building and heavy boards inserted below. Hundreds of jack-screws were then placed underneath. A small army of workers would, at Pullman's signal, turn the jacks, and the building would rise—so slightly that those inside couldn't even tell.

Chesbrough's sewers functioned as intended, but the waste, being channeled into the Chicago River, ended up in Lake Michigan. This was not a problem as long as drinking water was being drawn from a point far enough out in the lake that the pollution didn't reach it, but Chesbrough's very success saw to it that it soon did. And the muck that the sewers carried into the Chicago River also made that waterway even dirtier. After an epidemic of erysipelas in 1863, a prominent Chicago lawyer labeled the waterway a "River of Death," describing it as "a gigantic sewer . . . here red with blood, there slimy with grease, and black with filth and putrid matter."[34] The South Branch of the Chicago River became notorious because that was where the refuse from the slaughterhouses and stockyards was dumped. Methane and hydrogen sulfide gases rose to the surface, giving the waterway the nickname "Bubbly Creek."

Chesbrough then realized the city would have to build a new tunnel extending two miles out into Lake Michigan and running sixty-nine feet below the lakebed. At the far end of the tunnel would be an intake pipe—the "Two-Mile Crib." Work went on around the clock, and the huge project—it was at the time the longest tunnel ever built—was finished in 1866

The foul crust on Chicago's notorious "Bubbly Creek" was so thick that a rooster could walk on it. (DN-0056899, Chicago History Museum; photographer, *Chicago Daily News*)

at an estimated cost of $600,000 (a larger parallel tunnel was dug in 1872). Essential to the operation of the new system was the Water Tower and its adjacent pumping station, now one of Chicago's most distinctive landmarks. The city's citizens were euphoric, rejoicing in the belief that pure water would end epidemics forever, and the opening-day ceremony was glorious and self-congratulatory. A British visitor noted that "from the time I left New York till I reached Chicago, I had nowhere seen in the towns clear drinking water." But, he went on, "At Chicago . . . the whole city is supplied with the purest water."[35]

Problem solved. Or was it? When heavy spring rains sped the flow of the Chicago River, the waste began creeping out to the intake crib once again, and it was determined that even a four-mile tunnel would not likely keep the water supply free from contamination.[36] An even more radical plan would have to be adopted, and Chesbrough proposed something truly audacious—reversing the course of the Chicago River. Instead of flowing into Lake Michigan, the river would have to flow backward into the Illinois and Michigan Canal, then into the Des Plaines River, then to the Illinois River, and finally to the Mississippi, by which point the waste would be "deodorized." As a result, the canal was deepened for 26 miles from Bridgeport in the city to downstate Lockport, and large pumping facilities at Bridgeport were employed to aid the flow of the water. This project, which took five years and cost some $3 million, was completed in 1871.

Once again, the "solution" to Chicago's wastewater problem was short-lived. The enlarged canal proved too small and sluggish. It usually worked, but when heavy rains came, waste backed up into the lake. As the *Chicago Tribune* explained, "In spring time and times of heavy rain, so much water runs into the new canal by underground channels from the land on both

How Chicago got its water in the 1850s. (Chicago Public Library)

sides . . . that its force overcomes the fall of 3 feet in 30 miles and the water turns the current back into the Chicago River."[37] In the summer of 1879, for example, sewage poured into Lake Michigan for thirty days in a row.[38] In 1885, the city was hit by five and a half inches of rain in ten hours. At first, many considered the deluge a blessing that would "purge" the sewers, but when river water spilled into the Two-Mile Crib and cholera and typhoid broke out, officials realized the seriousness of what had happened. Even Chesbrough had to admit that "the purifying power of the canal is limited."[39]

Three million dollars might have seemed a great deal to spend on widening the Illinois and Michigan Canal, but ten times that sum would be paid out before Chicago's wastewater dilemma would be resolved once and for all. That solution would be a new dig—the twenty-eight-mile Sanitary and Ship Canal. As the name indicates, it was to have two purposes, waste management and transportation, but as far as most Chicagoans were concerned, the sanitation aspect was by far the more important. Because the area of the project would expand beyond Chicago's borders and suburban areas had their sanitation problems, too, a regional sanitary district was established in 1889.

Construction began just four months before the start of 1893. The Sanitary and Ship Canal was then, and still is, one of the greatest engineering triumphs in U.S. history (the American Society of Civil Engineers listed it as one of the seven wonders of American engineering). More land was excavated in its building than in the construction of the Panama Canal. In addition, the Chicago River itself was enlarged in order to allow water to flow freely from Lake Michigan to the new waterway.

The new canal was opened on January 2, 1900. Two later canals completed the massive enterprise: the North Shore Channel (1910) and the CalSag Channel (1922). Together, they flushed Chicago's wastewater down to the Mississippi River and the Gulf of Mexico. In 2001, the American Society of Civil Engineers named the Chicago Wastewater System a "Civil Engineering Monument of the Millennium." In addition to the canal system, the award cites seven water reclamation plants, including

Construction of the Sanitary and Ship Canal began just four months before the start of 1893. The massive enterprise finally solved Chicago's sewage problem. (Wikimedia Commons)

the Stickney Water Reclamation Plant, one of the largest in the world. When Chicago added chlorination and began filtering its drinking water, the city finally possessed one of the finest water supplies anywhere in the world—it had come a long way from the days in which residents occasionally found minnows in their bathtubs.

One might expect that the municipalities downstream from Chicago were not thrilled that the sewage of a huge city would now be flowing past them. Actually, as the historian Louis P. Cain has said, "The only two Illinois cities to object were Joliet and Peoria. . . . The Illinois River was a commercial waterway and was little used for drinking water or recreation. Most river towns were constructed with their backs to the river. Chicago's diversion was welcomed in that the increased water volume would ensure against low-water navigational problems."[40]

St. Louis was another matter, however, and officials there tried to get a federal injunction against the opening of the canal. They moved too slowly, however, and it was opened before action could be taken. Nevertheless, in January 1900, the state of Missouri brought the matter to the U.S. Supreme Court, asking that Chicago be barred from using the canal for waste disposal. Two years later, however, a chemistry professor named Arthur W. Palmer determined that the Illinois River was effectively oxidizing the sewage and that the water was clean by the time it reached Peoria. When it got to the Mississippi, he reported, "little more than a harmless salt remained to tell of the enormous pollution 320 miles above."[41] It must have been a major embarrassment when the citizens of St. Louis learned that the water in the Illinois River was cleaner than the Mississippi River water that they were drinking. The Supreme Court dismissed the case.

Today, Chicago has two treatment plants to process the water it takes from Lake Michigan—one for the northern part of the city and adjacent suburbs and another for the southern areas. The water goes through a complex treatment process in which it is passed through a purification plant, filtered through screens, given chemical treatment, passed through mixing basins in what is called a flocculation, sent to settling basins, filtered through sand and gravel, and then given a final chemical application. Raw sewage no longer flows down the canal to the Mississippi. The Sanitary District began building sewage treatment plants in the 1910s, and by 1970, Chicago had the world's largest sewage treatment facilities.

The Chicago River is now home to ducks, blue herons, nearly seventy species of fish, and so many beavers that some shoreline trees have to be protected from their teeth. But those conditions apply only in parts of the river; much of it is hardly pristine. In May 2011, the Environmental Protection Agency (EPA) placed the waterway on its list of "America's Most Endangered Rivers." Most of the river water, it said, contains sewage only partially treated, and after rainstorms a mix of untreated waste and runoff sometimes flows into it. Pointing out that Chicago is the only major U.S. city that leaves out a step in the disinfecting process and discharges undisinfected wastewater into its river, and citing the presence of bacterial sewage in the water, the EPA urged that sewage treatment plants be fitted with disinfection equipment and that the river be made safe for "primary contact," a term that includes such things as kayaking, boating, and swimming. Some Chicagoans liked the idea of splashing around in sight of the Willis Tower. Others asked whether, given the river's unpredictable currents and its barge traffic, taking a dip in it would be advisable even if it were as clean as it was when Father Marquette first laid eyes on it.

Epilogue

Chicago's Next Great Year

In its issue of April 19, 2010, *Newsweek* magazine published an article entitled "100 Places to Remember before They Disappear." To the surprise of a lot of midwesterners, Chicago was one of those places. According to the piece, which pictured what might happen to the planet if climatologists' predictions of climate change turned out to be accurate, Chicago "could experience a gradual yet dramatic increase in heat waves and flooding."

Chicago's city government recognizes the perils of climate change and has developed what it calls the "Chicago Climate Action Plan," but not too many people consider *Newsweek*'s gloomy scenario when they ponder Chicago's future. Rather, they look at the city's strengths and challenges from other points of view: economic, cultural, social, political, and so on.

Will Chicago ever have another year like 1893? It's not likely because the thesis of this book has been that such a concentration of events was possible only because Chicago was growing so fast. Chicago is no longer an "adolescent" city, and its growth is more measured. But, barring such a catastrophic spike in world temperatures that Lake Michigan inundates the Loop, Chicago's future contains many favorable prospects, not least because, as it did at the beginning of the twentieth century, it has civic organizations dedicated to its betterment. Nor is its immense geographical advantage at the center of the midland empire going to go away. The political scientist Larry Bennett has written that Chicago has gone through two historical stages and is now entering a third. The first stage was Chicago's emergence as a great industrial center in the period from the Civil War to the mid-twentieth century. The second consists of the "Rust Belt" years from around 1950 to 1990. The present stage is that of Chicago's reinventing itself as a postindustrial world metropolis. This city has a revitalized urban core but a belt of impoverished neighborhoods at its edges. It has a large group of middle-class professionals who value its "urban amenities" and a changing ethnic mix involving large numbers of immigrants from Mexico and a growing population of Asian heritage. This city, he says, is a "work in progress."[1]

A major thing that Chicago has going for it is the diversity of its economy. In 2003, a report by Moody's Investors Service ranked Chicago as the city with the most diverse economy in the United States. Even when the recession of 2008 arrived, the city was seen as less vulnerable than others to large economic swings. The city's economic diversity can be seen in the impressive number of major corporations that are based in either Chicago or its environs. Among them are Kraft Foods, Abbot Laboratories, Boeing, McDonald's, Sara Lee, Aon, Archer Daniels Midland, Allstate, Sears, Caterpillar, OfficeMax, Motorola, UAL, Navistar, Walgreen, and R. R. Donnelley. The administration of Mayor Richard M. Daley was assiduous in courting corporations and scored some significant successes, and Mayor Rahm Emanuel has strenuously continued these efforts. The city has never been, like Detroit, a one-industry town, and this diversity not only has saved it from the declines suffered by other "Rust Belt" cities but also has positioned it well for the challenges of the twenty-first century.

A second important factor in the city's future is demographics. As journalist Alan Ehrenhalt has explained it, for the past few decades Chicago has been undergoing what is known as a "demographic inversion." This phenomenon is sometimes described as "gentrification," but it involves deeper changes than that term suggests. Chicago, according to this analysis, is becoming more like a European city. The poor and the recent arrivals are being pushed to the periphery, and the city center is becoming a place where the prosperous both work and live—a "24/7" downtown. It's not that swarms of people are abandoning the suburbs and flocking back into the city, but, as Ehrenhalt puts it, "We are living at a moment in which the massive outward migration of the affluent that characterized the second half of the twentieth century is coming to an end."[2] The reasons for this trend are varied. They include highway congestion and the rising price of gasoline, which make suburban commuting increasingly difficult; different lifestyle choices by young people, who increasingly prefer congregating in urban neighborhoods; the removal of industrial grime and manufacturing from the downtown area; the availability of large loft spaces and homes suited for renovation; declining crime rates; and the desire of retirees to live in a place that offers walkability, convenience, and first-rate medical services and cultural institutions. The journalist Richard Florida has described what he calls the rise in U.S. cities of the "creative class"—people "who add economic value through their creativity." These people's work habits are highly flexible, and they value the round-the-clock options and amenities that cities provide, the diversity of different neighborhoods, and the ability to easily circulate among other "knowledge workers."[3] All these factors have produced a set of circumstances that has transformed Chicago since the gloomy 1970s, when cities throughout the United States seemed to be entering into crisis mode, and has brought excitement and reinvigoration not only to the downtown but also to many reviving neighborhoods. Some urban analysts, however, question how successful Chicago will be in continuing to generate the well-paying jobs that make further neighborhood revitalization possible.[4]

The centennial of Daniel Burnham's 1909 *Plan of Chicago* was intensively commemorated in Chicago, and the city's urban planners used the moment to publicize their efforts to follow in his path. In 2010, the Chicago Metropolitan Agency for Planning issued a 404-page draft of what it called "Go to 2040," a long-range series of strategies to prepare the city for the challenges of the global economy of the twenty-first century.

Interestingly, "Go to 2040" was created at the request of the Commercial Club of Chicago, the same group that initiated Burnham's plan. According to the plan's developers, the future will no longer see a struggle between the city and the suburbs for business and power; Chicago will be part of a super-region that will compete against India, China, and Brazil. A key element of the plan is greater emphasis on mass transportation, with the creation of a new West Loop Transportation Center to serve as a hub for commuter trains, buses, and the El and a high-speed rail network reaching out to other cities. Other considerations stress conservation, economic innovation, tax reform, sustainable local food, a more efficient freight network, green technology, and job growth, as well as education, health care, safety, the expansion of parks and open spaces, and what might in general be called "livability." The creation of "Go to 2040" underscores what many observers have cited as one of Chicago's strengths— the dedicated involvement of the public sector in decisions affecting the city's development.

. . . Chicagoans still refer to 1893 when thinking about their city's achievements.

Writing in 1905, the authors of a book on Chicago said, "It will require more wisdom to prepare the present city to become the wonderful city Chicago should be in 2070 than was required of its founders and builders to produce the city of to-day."[5] This might well be true, given the challenges the city faces. The decision by Mayor Richard M. Daley to step down after presiding over the city for twenty-two years and his replacement by Rahm Emanuel in 2011 prompted assessment of Chicago in many quarters. It was noted that at the beginning of Daley's tenure, Chicago was so divided that it was known as "Beirut on the Lake" and its government was fractured by "Council Wars." Although those problems were largely solved, Daley did leave his successor with others. Corruption scandals continued to trouble Chicago, and the school system, though improved, had an outsized deficit and a poor graduation rate. The city itself was in an even bigger hole, facing a structural deficit that could top $1 billion when unfunded pension plans were factored in and a dropping bond rating. Daley's attempts to privatize certain city services had mixed results, with the privatization of parking meters being the most unpopular of these efforts.

Contrasting with those ongoing problems were the many achievements. Under Daley, Chicago saw the building of Cellular Field (White Sox), and the United Center (Bulls and Blackhawks) and the openings of the Peggy Notebaert Nature Museum and the Museum of Contemporary Art. The Field Museum acquired Sue, the finest *Tyrannosaurus rex* ever discovered; the Museum of Science and Industry added several new exhibits and underground parking; the Adler Planetarium underwent extensive renovation and added four new galleries and a "Sky Pavilion"; and the Art Institute added an enormous wing devoted to modern art. Navy Pier was turned into a major tourist destination; Lake Shore Drive was rerouted to create a museum campus; Soldier Field was rebuilt; a "Riverwalk" was begun along Wacker Drive; and Orchestra Hall was rebuilt and expanded. The mayor oversaw a program that beautified the city with plantings of trees and flowers, he moved to make it bicycle friendly, and he helped make Chicago a world leader in biotechnology, nanotechnology, and other innovations. A downtown theater district was established, and Chicago's medical facilities kept expanding, making the city a medical center of international importance. The South Loop came to house a massive number of college and university students, and construction of a New McCormick Place, along with the resolution of labor issues, helped Chicago retain its prominent position as a convention center. The program remains controversial, but the decision to tear down public housing high-rises removed some of the sorest blights in the city. Just in the years between 2006 and 2010, Chicago's skyline was strikingly changed with the addition of several new skyscrapers—One Museum Park, Legacy Tower, Blue Cross Blue Shield Tower, Aqua, 340 on the Park, and Trump International Hotel and Tower, which at 1,362 feet, was, when it opened in 2009, the twelfth tallest building in the world. Any of these events would be enough to serve as the basis of a chapter in a book on modern Chicago.

Finally, although it was considerably over budget, the 24.5-acre Millennium Park, which opened in 2004, has become a major tourist attraction and source of civic pride. Chris Jones of the *Chicago Tribune* went so far as to call it "arguably the most expansive cultural project in Chicago since the 1893 Columbian Exposition." It was an interesting remark. It shows that Chicagoans still refer to 1893 when thinking about their city's achievements. But it also shows that the events of that year can be equaled—or even surpassed.

Notes · Index

Notes

Introduction

1. Stephen Longstreet, *Chicago, 1860–1919* (New York: David McKay, 1973), 190.

2. Quoted in Donald L. Miller, *City of the Century: The Epic of Chicago and the Making of America* (New York: Simon and Schuster, 1996), 516.

3. Henry B. Fuller, "The Upward Movement in Chicago," *Atlantic Monthly*, October 1897 (vol. 80, no. 480), 534.

4. Anselm Strauss, *Images of the American City* (New York: Free Press of Glencoe, 1961), 20.

5. Julian Ralph, quoted in Bessie Louise Pierce, ed., *As Others See Chicago* (Chicago: University of Chicago Press, 1933), 295.

6. Jane Addams, *Twenty Years at Hull-House* (New York: Signet Classics, 1961), 192.

7. Rufus Blanchard, *Columbian Memorial Songs, Historical Geography and Maps* (Chicago: Blanchard, 1892).

8. R. L. Duffus, writing in the *New York Times Magazine*, quoted in Pierce, 370.

9. Strauss, 26.

10. Quoted in Pierce, 338–39.

11. There are various rankings of global cities, and Chicago is usually high on the list. For example, in 2008, the journal *Foreign Policy* listed Chicago as number six in the world (behind New York, London, Tokyo, Paris, and Hong Kong). A lot of these analyses are based on the work of sociologist Saskia Sassen, who places New York, London, and Tokyo as the top three and ranks Chicago in the "second tier" of twenty or so global cities.

12. Quoted in Carl Smith, *Urban Disorder and the Shape of Belief* (Chicago: University of Chicago Press, 1995), 267.

13. Perry R. Duis, *Challenging Chicago* (Champaign: University of Illinois Press, 1998), 49.

14. Lewis Mumford, *The City in History* (New York: Harcourt, Brace and World, 1961), 531.

15. "Last Words about the World's Fair," in *Skyscraper: The Search for an American Style, 1891–1941*, ed. Roger Shepherd (New York: McGraw-Hill, 2003), 35.

16. Strauss, 162.

17. Smith, 212.

18. Smith, 216.

19. Quoted in Robert G. Spinney, *City of Big Shoulders* (DeKalb: Northern Illinois University Press, 2000), 120.

20. See Spiro Kostof, *The City Shaped: Urban Patterns and Meanings through History* (New York: Bullfinch Press, 1993), 75–77.

21. Quoted in Strauss, 12.

22. Harold M. Mayer and Richard C. Wade, *Chicago: Growth of a Metropolis* (Chicago: University of Chicago Press, 1969), 196.

23. Quoted in Pierce, 288.

24. Quoted in Pierce, 338.

25. "A City of Vast Enterprise," *New York Times*, December 24, 1893.

1. The White City and the Gray City

1. James Fullarton Muirhead, *America the Land of Contrasts: A Briton's View of his American Kin* (New York: John Lane, 1911), 205. See also: James Fullarton Muirhead and Karl Baedeker, *The United States, with an Excursion into Mexico: Handbook for Travellers* (New York: Charles Scribner's Sons, 1899). The section of the guidebook on Chicago has many details on the city of interest to historians—a list of recommended restaurants, for example.

2. Some writers, such as the Chicago novelist Henry Blake Fuller (see chapter 8, "The Birth of Urban Literature") preferred the term "Black City" as a contrast to the "White City" of the fair, but the idea was the same. See the chapter "The White City and the Black" in Clarence A. Andrews, *Chicago in Story: A Literary History* (Iowa City: Midwest Heritage, 1982).

3. The article from the *Sun*, entitled "Bets on the Fair," was reprinted in the *Chicago Tribune*, March 1, 1890, 13.

4. "The Would-Be Army of Utah," *Chicago Tribune*, April 7, 1858, 2.

5. "We Will Have the Fair," *Chicago Tribune*, February 25, 1890, 1.

6. Stanley Appelbaum, *The Chicago World's Fair of 1893: A Photographic Record* (New York: Dover, 1980), 5.

7. Bessie Louise Pierce, ed., *As Others See Chicago* (Chicago: University of Chicago Press, 1933), 356–57. For more on William T. Stead, see chapter 13, "Reforming Chicago."

8. A good way to get a sense of how visitors viewed the fair is to look at some contemporary works of fiction that related the adventures of rural Americans who came to Chicago in 1893. Two such are Marietta Holley, *Samantha at the World's Fair* (New York: Funk and Wagnall's, 1893) and C. M. Stevens, *The Adventures of Uncle Jeremiah and Family at the Great Fair* (Chicago: Laird and Lee, 1893). The common reactions were of awe and pride, with a good dose of rural-urban culture clash.

9. Quoted in Donald L. Miller, *City of the Century* (New York: Simon and Schuster, 1996), 495.

10. Pierce, 251.

11. Pierce, 232, 382.

12. "Dark As a Dungeon," *Chicago Tribune*, December 1, 1892, 3.

13. Arnold Lewis, *An Early Encounter with Tomorrow: Europeans, Chicago's Loop, and the World's Columbian Exposition* (Champaign: University of Illinois Press, 1997), 32.

14. "A City's Smoke and Soot," *Chicago Tribune*, August 18, 1888, 3.

15. "Their Losses Are Great," *Chicago Tribune*, August 25, 1888, 9.

16. Paul F. Bird, "Chicago's Smoke Problem," *Journal of the Western Society of Engineers* 15.3 (June 1910): 279–345.

17. "Year's Smoke War," *Chicago Tribune*, December 17, 1892, 1.

18. "To Fight the Anti-smoke Society," *Chicago Tribune*, February 26, 1893, 3. The society quickly issued a rejoinder in which it stated, "The principal aim of the society . . . has been to convince people that bituminous coal can be burned without making smoke, and, if necessary, to show people how to do this."

19. "Means Business Now," *Chicago Tribune*, August 9, 1892, 9.

20. Joe Sherman, *Gasp! The Swift and Terrible Beauty of Air* (Berkeley, CA: Counterpoint Press, 2004), 204.

21. On Annie Sergel and the antismoke campaign, see Harold L. Platt, *Shock Cities: The Environmental Transformation and Reform of Manchester and Chicago* (Chicago: University Of Chicago Press, 2005).

22. Officials of the University of Chicago sometimes liked to refer to their campus as a "Gray City" (because of the building stone) that compared favorably with the "White City." Whereas the latter was ephemeral and meant to last but a season, the university's "Gray City" would be a permanent utopia.

23. Carl Smith, *The Plan of Chicago: Daniel Burnham and the Remaking of the American City* (Chicago: University of Chicago Press, 2006), 19.

2. Three Museums and a Library

1. Steven Conn, *Museums and American Intellectual Life, 1876–1926* (Chicago: University of Chicago Press, 1998), 21.

2. Kathleen D. McCarthy, *Noblesse Oblige: Charity and Cultural Philanthropy in Chicago, 1849–1929* (Chicago: University of Chicago Press, 1982), 61.

3. "Matthew Arnold," *Chicago Tribune*, January 23, 1884, 6.

4. On how the development of the political machine discouraged the elite from entering politics, see Richard C. Lindberg, *The Gambler King of Clark Street: Michael C. McDonald and the Rise of Chicago's Democratic Machine* (Carbondale: Southern Illinois University Press, 2009).

5. On the early history of the Art Institute, see Anna Felicia Cierpik, "History of the Art Institute of Chicago from Its Incorporation on May 24, 1879, to the Death of Charles L. Hutchinson" (master's thesis, De Paul University, 1957); and Linda S. Phipps, "The Art Institute of Chicago 1890–97: Patrons and Architects" (master's thesis, University of Wisconsin, 1986).

6. "Art Institute Congresses," *New York Times*, June 23, 1893.

7. "In Chicago but Not of It," in George Ade, *Stories of Chicago* (Champaign: University of Illinois Press, 2003), 18–19, 21.

8. W. M. R. French, *The Art Institute of Chicago: Historical and Descriptive* (Chicago: R. Blanchard, 1901), 3–11. Cierpik, "History of the Art Institute of Chicago," 26.

9. Thomas Wakefield Goodspeed, quoted in Helen Lefkowitz Horowitz, *Culture and the City: Cultural Philanthropy in Chicago from the 1880s to 1917* (Chicago: University of Chicago Press, 1976), 51.

10. McCarthy, *Noblesse Oblige*, 87.

11. Donald Hoffman, *The Architecture of John Wellborn Root* (Chicago: University of Chicago Press, 1973), 54.

12. Phipps, 118.

13. "Removing Art Institute Halls," *Chicago Tribune*, October 31, 1893, 13.

14. "Art Institute Open," *Chicago Tribune*, December 9, 1893, 6.

15. Inter Ocean, *Centennial History of the City of Chicago: Its Men and Institutions, Biographical Sketches of Leading Citizens* (Chicago: Inter Ocean, 1905), 65.

16. On Bertha Palmer's collection, see the chapter entitled "Art Collector" in Ishbel Ross, *Silhouette in Diamonds: The Life of Mrs. Potter Palmer* (New York: Harper, 1960).

17. Conn, 194.

18. Conn, 42.

19. A detailed description of the exhibits and the efforts to collect them, written by Putnam himself, can be found in Trumbull White and William Igleheart, *The World's Columbian Exposition, Chicago, 1893* (Boston: John K. Hastings, 1893), 415–35.

20. "Token of the Fair," *Chicago Tribune*, November 29, 1891, 2.

21. "Planning a Museum," *Chicago Tribune*, December 5, 1891, 9.

22. "Columbian Museum Is Incorporated," *Chicago Tribune*, September 17, 1893, 12.

23. "The Museum's First Million," *Bulletin of the Field Museum of Natural History* 41.8 (August 1970), 13.

24. *The Field Museum 2006 Annual Report to the Board of Trustees: Collections and Research* (Chicago: Office of Collections and Research, Field Museum, 2006), 3.

25. Patricia M. Williams, "The Burnham Plan and Field Museum; A Chicago Original," *Bulletin of the Field Museum of Natural History* 39.5 (May 1968): 10.

26. "Field Museum Gets Site," *Chicago Tribune*, January 22, 1901, 9.

27. Lois Wille, *Forever Open, Clear and Free: The Struggle for Chicago's Lakefront*, 2nd ed. (Chicago: University of Chicago Press, 1991), 78.

28. "Begin Today New $5,000,000 Field Museum," *Chicago Tribune*, July 15, 1915, 1.

29. Williams, 11.

30. The novelist Arthur Meeker, quoted in Jay Pridmore, *Inventive Genius: The History of the Museum of Science and Industry Chicago* (Chicago: Museum of Science and Industry, 1996), 37.

31. "Restore the Fine Arts Building," *Chicago Tribune*, April 1, 1923, 8.

32. Herman Kogan, *A Continuing Marvel: The Story of the Museum of Science and Industry* (Garden City, NY: Doubleday, 1973), 8.

33. "Saarinen Sees Artistic Glory in Old Museum," *Chicago Tribune*, March 24, 1923, 17.

34. "Move to Save Old Fine Arts Building Grows," *Chicago Tribune*, May 22, 1921, 24.

35. "6,000 Women in Move to Save Old Arts Bldg.," *Chicago Tribune*, February 19, 1922, 7.

36. Kogan, 9.

37. "Notable Chicagoans Revive World's Fair Memories," *Chicago Tribune*, February 1, 1923, 3.

38. "6,000 Women," 7.

39. Peter M. Ascoli, *Julius Rosenwald: The Man Who Built Sears, Roebuck and Advanced the Cause of Black Education in the American South* (Bloomington: Indiana University Press, 2006), 265.

40. Pridmore, 20–22.

41. Daniel Bluestone, *Constructing Chicago* (New Haven: Yale University Press, 1991), 164.

42. Bluestone, 169.

3. Sears, Roebuck and Company

1. For the history of Sears, see Louis E. Asher and Edith Heal, *Send No Money* (Chicago: Argus, 1942); Boris Emmet and John E. Jeuck, *Catalogs and Counters: A History of Sears, Roebuck & Company* (Chicago: University of Chicago Press, 1950); and Gordon Weil, *Sears, Roebuck, U.S.A.* (New York: Stein and Day, 1977). Also useful is the chapter "Sears, Roebuck and Co." in Tom Mahoney and Leonard Sloane, *The Great Merchants: American's Foremost Retail Institutions and the People Who Made Them Great* (New York: Harper and Row, 1974), which also has a chapter on Marshall Field.

2. There has been some uncertainly about the exact date of Sears's birth, but both the *Dictionary of American Biography* and Alvah Roebuck, Sears's partner, agreed on the December 7, 1863, date.

3. Hollis W. Field, "The Multimillionaires of Chicago. III. Richard W. Sears," *Chicago Tribune*, June 16, 1907. A slightly different account of the first version of the story is given in David L. Cohn's *The Good Old Days*, which was published in 1940, two years before *Send No Money*. Cohn relates that the local merchant refused the watches not because they were unsatisfactory but because they had never been ordered. This was, according to Cohn, a common ruse by wholesalers, who claimed that the shipment had been a mistake but went on to offer the merchandise at a discount.

4. Emmet and Jeuck, 10.

5. See William Cronon, *Nature's Metropolis: Chicago and the Great West* (New York: W. W. Norton, 1991), 334–40.

6. This circular is reproduced in Frank Brown Latham, *1872–1972: A Century of Serving Consumers; the Story of Montgomery Ward* (Chicago: Montgomery Ward, 1972), 9.

7. Latham, 12.

8. Day Allen Willey, "The Rural Free Delivery Service," *American Monthly Review of Reviews* 27. 1 (January 1903): 56.

9. "To Be a Fine Park," *Chicago Tribune*, January 24, 1893, 6.

10. "Ward Explains War on Museum," *Chicago Tribune*, November 26, 1908, 4.

11. "Moving to Block Victory of Ward," *Chicago Tribune*, October 27, 1909, 1. On the ongoing battle to preserve Chicago's lakefront, see Lois Wille, *Forever Open, Clear, and Free* (Chicago: University of Chicago Press, 1972).

12. Latham, 45.

13. Robert Marion La Follette, ed., *The Making of America*, vol. 1 (Chicago: The Making of America Co., 1906), 396.

14. Weil, 61.

15. Emmet and Jeuck, 46.

16. John M. Oharenko, *Historic Sears, Roebuck and Co. Catalog Plant (Images of America)* (Charleston, SC: Acadia, 2005), 8.

17. Emmet and Jeuck, 183–84.

18. Emmet and Jeuck, 324.

19. Many of the original Rosenwald school buildings have disappeared, a development that has led the National Trust for Historic Preservation to form the Rosenwald Schools Initiative to develop a plan for saving them.

20. Weil, 94–96.

21. William Grimes, "Bruce J. Graham, Chicago Architect Who Designed Sears Tower, Dies at 84," *New York Times*, March 10, 2010.

22. Bruce Graham, *Bruce Graham of SOM* (New York: Rizzoli, 1989), 56.

23. Alice Sinkevitch, ed., *AIA Guide to Chicago*, 2nd ed. (New York: Harcourt, 2004), 93.

24. From an interview with Bruce Graham compiled under the auspices of the Chicago Architects Oral History Project of the Department of Architecture at the Art Institute of Chicago (1988), accessed March 12, 2010, http://digital-libraries.saic.edu/cdm4/index_caohp.php?CISOROOT=/caohp.

25. Ada Louise Huxtable, "Chicago: A City of Architectural Excellence," *New York Times*, June 8, 1975.

26. Paul Gapp, "A Symbol of Today Towers above the Cracker Boxes," *Chicago Tribune*, February 3, 1974, E3.

4. Frances Willard's Bicycle

1. Ruth Bordin, *Frances Willard: A Biography* (Chapel Hill: University of North Carolina Press, 1986), 206–7.

2. Actually, if Willard had had her way, she would also have taken swimming and trapeze lessons! See Carolyn De Swarte Gifford, ed., *Writing Out My Heart: Selections from the Journal of Frances E. Willard, 1855–1896* (Champaign: University of Illinois Press, 1995), 382. "We always reach for the impossible!" Willard wrote at the time.

3. Mary Earhart, *Frances Willard: From Prayers to Politics* (Chicago: University of Chicago Press, 1944), 321–22.

4. Frances E. Willard, *A Wheel within a Wheel: How I Learned to Ride the Bicycle with Some Reflections by the Way* (Bedford, MA: Applewood, n.d.), 19.

5. Willard, *Wheel*, 25.

6. Willard, *Wheel*, 25

7. Willard, *Wheel*, 47.

8. Willard, *Wheel*,. 59.

9. Willard, *Wheel*, 74–75.

10. "The Greatest American Woman: Miss Frances E. Willard's Last Autobiographical Interview," *Our Day* 18 (March 1898): 107–16.

11. "Miss Willard Hopeful," *New York Times*, April 19, 1896.

12. Frances E. Willard, *The Autobiography of an American Woman: Glimpses of Fifty Years* (Chicago: Woman's Temperance Publishing Association, 1892), 25.

13. Willard, *Wheel*, 72.

14. Willard, *Autobiography*, 69.

15. Earhart, 40.

16. Earhart, 44.

17. Bordin, 63.

18. In a journal entry written on her twentieth birthday, Willard described herself as "plain" and said, "I settled it long ago with my heart, that God saw it to be right that I should have 'no beauty that I should be desired.'"

See Gifford, 45–47. At the time, Willard was, she said, slightly more than five-foot-two and weighed ninety-five pounds, with "freckles not a few."

19. Ruth Bordin, *Woman and Temperance: The Quest for Power and Liberty, 1873–1900* (Philadelphia: Temple University Press, 1981), 157.

20. Alice L. Williams, *Brilliants, Selected from the Writings of Frances E. Willard* (Boston: Samuel E. Cassino, 1893), 15, 39.

21. Bordin, *Woman and Temperance*, 3–4.

22. Carol Mattingly, *Well-Tempered Women: Nineteenth-Century Temperance Rhetoric* (Carbondale: Southern Illinois University Press, 1998), 124.

23. Mattingly, 14.

24. Bordin, *Woman and Temperance*, 95.

25. Bordin, *Woman and Temperance*, 98.

26. According to Perry R. Duis, "by 1908 the City Club found that many had gone dry or had been vandalized by removing the hand-held drinking cup." See *The Saloon: Public Drinking in Chicago and Boston, 1880–1920* (Champaign: University of Illinois Press, 1983), 190. The WCTU is currently compiling a list of surviving WCTU water fountains and has identified fountains in over sixty locations, some still giving water, with one as distant as Melbourne, Australia. See the organization's Web site at *www.wctu.org*.

27. "Drop a Penny and Get a Drink," *Chicago Daily Tribune*, July 21, 1895, 31.

28. See Kristen Schaffer, *Daniel H. Burnham: Visionary Architect and Planner* (New York: Rizzoli, 2003), 54; Robert Bruegmann, *The Architects and the City: Holabird & Roche of Chicago, 1880–1918* (Chicago: University of Chicago Press, 1997), 117–18; Rachel E. Bohlmann, "Our 'House Beautiful': The Woman's Temple and the WCTU Effort to Establish Place and Identity in Downtown Chicago, 1887–1898," *Journal of Women's History* 11.2 (Summer 1999): 110–34; and Donald Hoffman, *The Architecture of John Wellborn Root* (Chicago: University of Chicago Press, 1973), 193–95.

29. Carl W. Condit, *The Chicago School of Architecture* (Chicago: University of Chicago Press, 1964), 104. Burnham found Root's first design for the building to be too simple for an organization like the WCTU with its high-minded goals and persuaded him to add the roof and extra ornamentation. For this and more on the Temple, see Joanna Merwood-Salisbury, *Chicago 1890: The Skyscraper and the Modern City* (Chicago: University of Chicago Press, 2009), 78.

30. See Earhart, 373–77.

31. Merwood-Salisbury, 79.

32. "Champion of Her Sex," *New York Sunday World*, February 2, 1896.

33. See the chapter entitled "Women Move Out-of-Doors" in Patricia Campbell Warner, *When the Girls Came Out to Play: The Birth of American Sportswear* (Amherst: University of Massachusetts Press, 2006).

34. Warner, 105–7. Bloomer did not exactly invent the outfit, but because she wore it, wrote about it so extensively, and published pictures of it, it became associated with her.

35. Quoted in Richard Lindberg, *Chicago Ragtime: Another Look at Chicago, 1880–1920* (South Bend, IN: Icarus, 1985), 77–78.

36. Perry R. Duis, *Challenging Chicago: Coping with Everyday Life* (Urbana: University of Illinois Press), 191. Private carriages, of course, were beyond the means of any women who needed to go to work; even the cost of keeping a horse was prohibitive for many.

37. "The Wheel as a Reformer," *New York Times*, December 1, 1895.

38. See the chapter entitled "Bicycling and the Bloomer" in Warner.

39. Warner, 113.

40. "Rainy Day Skirts Longer," *New York Times*, March 2, 1899.

41. "Short Skirts and Ridicule," *New York Times*, February 28, 1897.

42. "May Wear Bloomers," *Chicago Daily Tribune*, July 21, 1895, 14.

43. Quoted in Warner, 124.

44. "Bikes Defy Old Sol," *Chicago Daily Tribune*, June 3, 1895, 1.

45. Warner, *Wheel*, 76.

46. Duis, *Challenging Chicago*, 190.

47. "Bicycling," in *The Encyclopedia of Chicago,* edited by James R. Grossman, Ann Durkin Keating, and Janice L. Reiff (Chicago: University of Chicago Press, 2004). See also George D. Bushnell, "When Chicago Was Wheel Crazy," *Chicago History* 4.3 (Fall 1975): 169.

48. Lindberg, 76.

49. Robert Muccigrosso, *Celebrating the New World: Chicago's Columbian Exposition of 1893* (Chicago: Ivan R. Dee, 1993), 158.

50. Duis, *Challenging Chicago*, 190.

51. Lindberg, *Chicago Ragtime*, 76. The *Encyclopedia of Chicago* has it this way: "By the late 1890s, 54 clubs boasted more than 10,000 members."

52. "When Chicago Was Wheel Crazy," 172.

53. "Bikes Defy Old Sol," *Chicago Daily Tribune*, June 3, 1895.

54. Peter Levine, *A. G. Spalding and the Rise of Baseball* (New York: Oxford University Press, 1985), 91.

55. "Arnold, Schwinn & Co.," in *The Encyclopedia of Chicago.*

56. Duis, *Challenging Chicago*, 190.

57. "Like a River of Fire," *Chicago Daily Tribune*, August 11, 1893, 3.

58. Steven A. Riess, *City Games: The Evolution of American Urban Society and the Rise of Sports* (Champaign: University of Illinois Press, 1989), 64. Reformers also championed asphalt as a sanitary measure—it was easier to keep clean than cobblestones.

59. Willard, *Wheel*, 12.

60. Duis, *Challenging Chicago*, 191.

61. "Bicycling's Relation to the Cause of Temperance," *Chicago Tribune*, September 22, 1895, 26.

62. Stephen Longstreet, *Chicago, 1860–1919* (New York: David McKay, 1973), 223.

63. "Bicycling," *The Encyclopedia of Chicago.*

5. Open-Heart Surgery

1. "Takes Its Vacation," *Chicago Tribune*, July 9, 1893, 11.

2. Quoted in Scotti Cohn, *It Happened in Chicago* (Guilford, CT: Globe Pequot Press, 2009), 51. William's paper on the surgery was published as "Stab Wound of the Heart and Pericardium," *New York Medical Record*, March 27, 1897, 1:437–39.

3. "Chicago Colored People," *Chicago Tribune*, May 4, 1890, 33. Among the others were the exclusive tailor Lloyd G. Wheeler, the lawyer Edward H. Morris, and the builder Richard M. Hancock. Admiring their success, the article's author took a most optimistic view that "the old prejudice against the dark skin is dying out—at all events in Chicago."

4. Helen Buckler, *Daniel Hale Williams: Negro Surgeon* (New York: Putnam, 1954), 100.

5. Allan H. Spear, *Black Chicago: The Making of a Negro Ghetto, 1890–1920* (Chicago: University of Chicago Press, 1967), 15, 19.

6. Spear, 26.

7. Spear, 22–23.

8. Edward Glaeser, *Triumph of the City* (New York: Penguin, 2011), 82.

9. Irving Cutler, *Chicago: Metropolis of the Mid-Continent* (Carbondale: Southern Illinois University Press, 2006), 157.

10. Spear, 6.

11. The law was made more specific in 1896 and spelled out "hotels, soda fountains, saloons, bathrooms, skating rinks, concerts, cafes, bicycle rinks, elevators, ice cream parlors, railroads, omnibuses, stages, streetcars, and boats."

12. Spear, 46.

13. On the history of Provident Hospital, see Richard M. Krieg, *Provident Hospital: A Living Legacy* (Chicago: Provident Foundation, 1998).

14. "Chicago's New Hospital," *Chicago Tribune*, July 5, 1891, 25.

15. "Hospital for Colored People," *Chicago Tribune*, May 5, 1891, 3.

16. Buckler, 78.

17. A poster for the event is reproduced in Krieg, 4.

18. "Echoes from Dixie Days," *Chicago Tribune*, May 13, 1896, 2.

19. "Inspect New Provident Hospital," *Chicago Tribune*, November 18, 1896, 5.

20. Harris B. Shumacker Jr., *The Evolution of Cardiac Surgery* (Bloomington: Indiana University Press, 1992), 12. To go even further back, historians point to the case of the Spanish physician Francisco Romero, who drained a pericardial effusion (an accumulation of excess fluid around the heart) in 1801.

21. Cutler, 396.

22. For an impressively complete catalog of nineteenth-century physicians in Chicago, see *History of Medicine and Surgery and Physicians and Surgeons of Chicago* (Chicago: Biographical Publishing, 1922).

23. Thomas Neville Bonner, *Medicine in Chicago, 1850–1950* (Champaign: University of Illinois Press, 1991), 36.

24. Dr. H. Gradle, *Bacteria and the Germ Theory of Disease* (Chicago: W. T. Keener, 1883), 1–2.

25. Bonner, 84.

26. "For Graduate Work," *Chicago Tribune*, July 21, 1893, 10.

6. A Church for Father Tolton

1. It's been estimated that 55 percent of the immigrants from Germany were Catholic. See the article "Germans" in the *Encyclopedia of Chicago* (Chicago: University of Chicago Press, 2004).

2. Charles Shanabruch, *Chicago's Catholics* (Notre Dame, IN: University of Notre Dame Press, 1981), 77.

3. Bessie Louise Pierce, *A History of Chicago*, vol. 3, *The Rise of a Modern City 1871–1893* (Chicago: University of Chicago Press, 1957), 424.

4. Father Tolton's first name is often given as "Augustine," but many sources indicate it was "Augustus." The most prominent is the biographical essay on Tolton in William J. Simmons, *Men of Mark: Eminent, Progressive, and Rising* (Cleveland: Geo. M. Rewell, 1887). This volume, by a black author, contains dozens of sketches of prominent black persons, and Simmons's information surely came from Tolton himself. Cyprian Davis, in his *The History of Black Catholics in the United States* (New York: Crossroad, 1990), points to several records showing that Tolton was known as "Augustus." His book reproduces the front page of the *American Catholic Tribune* of March 11, 1887, which carries a photograph of "Rev. Augustus Tolton." Other contemporary sources also use "Augustus," as, for example, the *Chicago Tribune* did in reporting on Tolton's activities and his death.

5. The only full-length biography of Father Tolton is *From Slave to Priest* by Caroline Hemesath (San Francisco: Ignatius Press, 2006, originally published in 1973). Although the author's research was thorough and she spoke with people who knew Father Tolton (including St. Katharine Drexel), she invents dialogue and scenes, which sometimes makes it difficult to assess the reliability of certain passages. Cyprian Davis's research, however, presented in *The History of Black Catholics in the United States*, rounds out the picture considerably, as does Simmons's *Men of Mark*.

6. Francis J. Butler, *American Catholic Identity: Essays in an Age of Change* (Lanham, MD: Rowman and Littlefield, 1994), 207.

7. Quoted in Davis, 43–44.

8. Freedmen and Southern Society Project, Ira Berlin, *Freedom, a Documentary History of Emancipation, 1861–1867* (New York: Cambridge University Press, 1993), 586.

9. Father John J. Plantevigne, quoted in Albert J. Raboteau, *A Fire in the Bones: Reflections on African-American Religious History* (Boston: Beacon, 1996), 128.

10. Davis, 155.

11. Quoted in Davis, 155. The cardinal's name was actually Giovanni *Simeoni*.

12. Quoted in Simmons, 445–46.

13. Quoted in Hemesath, 166.

14. Davis, 156–57.

15. Shanabruch, 34.

16. Allan H. Spear, *Black Chicago: The Making of a Negro Ghetto, 1890–1920* (Chicago: University of Chicago Press, 1967), 94.

17. "Church for Colored Catholics," *Chicago Tribune*, January 15, 1894, 2.

18. Hemesath, 203.

19. Davis, 159.

20. See Suellen Hoy, *Good Hearts: Catholic Sisters in Chicago's Past* (Champaign: University of Illinois Press, 2006), 88.

21. "Two New Churches," *Chicago Tribune*, January 20, 1893, 5.

22. "Sta. Monica Church," *Chicago Tribune*, December 3, 1893, 29.

23. "Church for Colored Catholics."

24. Robert L. Ruffin, speaking to the third meeting of the Colored Catholic Congress. Quoted in Raboteau, 129.

25. Hemesath, 213.

26. Hemesath, 209

27. Hemesath, 215.

28. Hemesath, p. 167.

29. Hemesath, 161.

30. Hemesath, 210–11.

31. From the Web site of St. Elizabeth's Chicago, accessed May 1, 2009, www.stelizabethchicago.com.

32. "Die in Scorching Air," *Chicago Tribune*, July 10, 1897, 1.

33. "Two Priests Die from the Heat," *Chicago Tribune*, July 10, 1897, 5.

34. Stephen J. Ochs, *Desegregating the Altar: The Josephites and the Struggle for Black Priests, 1871–1960* (Baton Rouge: Louisiana State University Press, 1990), 90.

35. Ochs, 172.

36. Ochs, 102.

37. Quoted in Raboteau, 124.

38. Martin A. Marty, "Priests and Prejudice" (a review of Stephen J. Ochs, *Desegregating the Altar*), *New York Times*, September 23, 1990.

39. Raboteau, 128.

7. The Illinois Institute of Technology

1. A. N. Waterman, *Historical Review of Chicago and Cook County* (Chicago: Lewis, 1908), 194. No text of the sermon survives, and probably there never was one because Gunsaulus usually spoke from notes. Even the date is unknown, and the best estimate is that it was in early 1890.

2. S. Parkes Cadman, "Introductory Tribute," in *In Memoriam: Frank Wakely Gunsaulus, 1856–1921* (Mrs. F. W. Gunsaulus, 1921), 5.

3. The Art Institute's Gunsaulus Hall, an addition built in 1911, was restored in 2009. The Field Museum's Gunsaulus Hall contains the Japanese collections to which Gunsaulus donated his collection of Japanese sword mounts in 1916. His daughter, Helen Gunsaulus, became the museum's assistant curator of Japanese ethnology three years later. Her book, *Japanese Sword Mounts*, is still in print.

4. Cadman, p. 8.

5. Harper Leech and John Charles Carroll, *Armour and His Times* (New York: D. Appleton-Century, 1938), 212.

6. Quoted in Stephen Longstreet, *Chicago, 1860–1919* (New York: David McKay, 1973), 71.

7. Kathleen D. McCarthy, *Noblesse Oblige: Charity & Cultural Philanthropy in Chicago, 1849–1929* (Chicago: University of Chicago Press, 1982), 93.

8. *Rand, McNally & Co.'s Handy Guide to Chicago* (New York: Rand, McNally, 1893), 150.

9. James Peebles, *A History of the Armour Institute of Technology* (Chicago, 1955?), 8.

10. Leech and Carroll, 213.

11. Peebles, 8.

12. In 1898, Patton and Fisher took on a third partner, Grant Miller. Thus Machinery Hall is the work of Patton, Miller, and Fisher.

13. Chicago Department of Planning and Development, *Main Building and Machinery Hall, Illinois Institute of Technology (originally Armour Institute of Technology): Preliminary Summary of Information Submitted to the Commission on Chicago Landmarks in January 2004* (Chicago Department of Planning and Development, 2004), 2, 12.

14. Leech and Carroll, 214.

15. Peebles, 12.

16. Quoted in Peebles, 11.

17. Arthur Warren, "Philip D. Armour," *McClure's Magazine* 2 (December 1893–May 1894).

18. Charles R. Morris, *The Tycoons: How Andrew Carnegie, John D. Rockefeller, Jay Gould, and J. P. Morgan Invented the American Supereconomy* (New York: Times Books, 2005), 115.

19. Quoted in William Cronon, *Nature's Metropolis: Chicago and the Great West* (New York: Norton, 1991), 208.

20. Robert G. Spinney, *City of Big Shoulders: A History of Chicago* (DeKalb: Northern Illinois University Press, 2000), 62.

21. There actually was a "big four," but George Hammond's operations were across the state line in Indiana.

22. Bessie Louise Pierce, *A History of Chicago*, vol. 3, *The Rise of a Modern City 1871–1893* (Chicago: University of Chicago Press, 1957), 109.

23. See Louise Carroll Wade, *Chicago's Pride: The Stockyards, Packingtown, and Environs in the Nineteenth Century* (Champaign: University of Illinois Press, 1987).

24. Emmett Dedmon, *Fabulous Chicago* (New York: Random House, 1953), 186.

25. Leech and Carroll, 45–46.

26. From *Outre-mer Impressions of America* (1895), in *As Others See Chicago*, ed. Bessie Louise Pierce (Chicago: University of Chicago Press, 2004), 389.

27. Andrew F. Smith, *Eating History: 30 Turning Points in the Making of American Cuisine* (New York: Columbia University Press, 2009), 89.

28. See chapter 5, "Annihilating Space: Meat," in Cronon.

29. See Marco d'Eramo, *The Pig and the Skyscraper*, trans. from the Italian by Graeme Thomson (New York: Verso, 2002).

30. *Rand, McNally & Co.'s Handy Guide to Chicago*, 119.

31. "Higher Education in the Loop and South Loop: An Impact Study," January 2005, accessed September 2, 2009, http://hwashington.ccc.edu /pdfs/hes_finalreport12505.pdf.

32. "2009 Higher Education in the Loop and South Loop Study," accessed September 2, 2009, http://www.chicagoloopalliance.com/db_ images/includes/233InterimReport6-10-09.pdf.

33. Recycling historic buildings is a deliberate strategy. As the executive director of the Chicago Loop Alliance has put it, "Much of the vibrancy in the Loop today is the result of a determined effort to foster higher education here, which has been part of the City of Chicago's vision for re-using South Loop office buildings that are economically obsolete." See "College Enrollment in Loop Up 25 Percent, Boosting Downtown Real Estate Investment and Employment," accessed September 2, 2009, http://www.chicagoloopalliance.com/business.php?id=233.

34. Richard Galehouse, "The American University: City Planner of the Twenty-First Century," in *The Plan of Chicago @ 100: 15 Views of Burnham's Legacy for a New Century*, ed. Ely Chapter, Lambda Alpha International (St. Paul: Lambda Alpha International, 2009), 121–22.

35. Peebles, 13–14.

36. Peebles, 25.

37. Marjorie Warvelle Bear, *A Mile Square of Chicago* (Oak Brook, IL: TIPRAC, 2007), 427.

38. See Agness Joslyn Kaufman, "Lewis Institute," IIT Archives of the Paul Galvin Library, accessed September 2, 2009, http://archives.iit.edu /history/lewis/index.html.

39. Werner Blaser, *Mies van der Rohe: IIT Campus* (Boston: Birkhäuser, 2002), 13.

40. A good concise biography and analysis of Mies van der Rohe's work is Peter Blake, *Mies van der Rohe: Architecture and Structure* (New York: Penguin, 1964).

41. Blake, 8.

8. The Birth of Urban Literature

1. Howells's essay, "Certain of the Chicago School of Fiction," appeared in the May 1903 issue of the *North American Review*.

2. Mencken's article, entitled "Civilized Chicago," first appeared in the *New York Evening Mail* and was reprinted in the *Chicago Tribune* on October 28, 1917.

3. In 1907, Hamlin Garland spearheaded the establishment of a cultural association called the Cliff Dwellers (it still exists). Despite the name, Fuller was not associated with the group and was never a member. Although Hamlin and others claimed that the name was taken not from Fuller's novel, but from the Anasazi dwellings in the Southwest, it's difficult to imagine that they did not have Fuller's book somewhere in the back of their minds.

4. Henry Regnery, *Creative Chicago* (Evanston, IL: Chicago Historical Bookworks, 1993), 93.

5. Two comprehensive surveys of early Chicago literature are Kenny J. Williams, *Prairie Fire: A Literary History of Chicago from the Frontier to 1893* (Nashville: Townsend, 1980) and Clarence A. Andrews, *Chicago in Story: A Literary History* (Iowa City: Midwest Heritage Publishing, 1982).

6. A lengthy description of *Wau-Nan-Gee* can be found in Williams, 50–53.

7. Williams's *Prairie Fire* contains lengthy appendices that list nineteenth-century Chicago newspapers, magazines, novels, and publishers.

8. Williams, 180.

9. Hugh Dalziel Duncan, *The Rise of Chicago as a Literary Center from 1885 to 1920* (Totowa, NJ: Bedminster, 1964), 9.

10. Williams, 442.

11. Andrews, 65.

12. Andrews, 11.

13. Kenneth Scambray, *A Varied Harvest: The Life and Works of Henry Blake Fuller* (Pittsburgh: University of Pittsburgh Press, 1987), 93.

14. Hamlin Garland came to Chicago in May 1893; he is still well known as a pioneer of realism, but he wrote only two books set in Chicago.

15. Carl S. Smith, *Chicago and the American Literary Imagination, 1880–1920* (Chicago: University of Chicago Press, 1894), 130–31.

16. Henry B. Fuller, *The Chevalier of Pensieri-Vani* (New York: Century, 1899), 105.

17. "Discovering Authors," *Chicago Tribune*, July 26, 1891, 26.

18. Constance M. Griffin, *Henry Blake Fuller: A Critical Biography* (Philadelphia: University of Pennsylvania Press, 1939), 33.

19. Scambray, 84.

20. Scambray, 87.

21. Scambray, 84–85.

22. John Pilkington Jr., *Henry Blake Fuller* (New York: Twayne, 1970), 96.

23. Pilkington, 110.

24. Samuel Putnam, "Personal Portraits: The Cliff Dweller," *Chicagoan*, April 9, 1927, reprinted in Neil Harris, *The Chicagoan: A Lost Magazine of the Jazz Age* (Chicago: University of Chicago Press, 2008), 227.

25. Pilkington, 132.

26. Joel Connaroe, "Seven Types of Ambiguity," *New York Times*, August 9, 1998.

27. Jacques Barzun, *From Dawn to Decadence: 500 Years of Western Cultural Life* (New York: Perennial, 2001), 596–97.

28. In the foreword to Finley Peter Dunne, *Mr. Dooley*, ed. Barbara Schaff (Springfield, IL: Lincoln Herndon Press, 1988), iii.

29. Stephen Longstreet, *Chicago, 1860–1919* (New York: David McKay, 1973), 379.

30. The influential McGarry, whose saloon was an important meeting place for Chicago's politicos, had little in common with the genial Mr. Dooley. On one occasion, the Chicago political boss and gambling czar Michael McDonald entered his establishment with a loaded pistol and pointed it at McGarry's head (it was snatched from his hand before he could fire.) See Richard C. Lindberg, *The Gambler King of Clark Street: Michael C. McDonald and the Rise of Chicago's Democratic Machine* (Carbondale: Southern Illinois University Press, 2009), 59–61.

31. Here is an example: "One nite time I comed home on mine house, und dook mine leetle daughter, Gretchen, Jr., on mine kneees. I told her some shtory riddles, und vas make her some lafe. Pooty gwick she vas creeb on my bosom, und vas so shleepy, I dook her on her leedle ped." Quoted in Will M. Clemens, *Famous Funny Fellows: Brief Biographical Sketches of American Humorists* (Cleveland: William W. Williams, 1882), 163.

32. John M. Harrison, "Finley Peter Dunne and the Progressive Movement," *Journalism Quarterly* 44 (Autumn 1967): 475–81. Quoted in James DeMuth, *Small Town Chicago: The Comic Perspective of Finley Peter Dunne, George Ade, and Ring Lardner* (Port Washington, NY: Kennikat, 1980), 41.

33. Walter Blair and Raven I. McDavid Jr., eds., *The Mirth of a Nation: America's Great Dialect Humor* (Minneapolis: University of Minnesota Press, 1983), xii. This book is an excellent source on the humorists who preceded Dunne and Ade.

34. Hugh Henry Brackenridge, *Modern Chivalry* (Philadelphia: Carey and Hart, 1846), 43.

35. Finley Peter Dunne, *Mr. Dooley and the Chicago Irish: The Autobiography of a Nineteenth-Century Ethnic Group*, ed. Charles Fanning (Washington, DC: Catholic University of America Press, 1976), xvii–xix.

36. DeMuth, 30.

37. Elmer Ellis, *Mr. Dooley's America: A Life of Finley Peter Dunne* (Hamden, CT: Archon, 1969), 103. Dunne did attempt, more than once, to write standard fiction, but without success.

38. Fred C. Kelly, *George Ade: Warmhearted Satirist* (Indianapolis: Bobbs-Merrill, 1947), 109.

39. From the introduction to George Ade, *Stories of Chicago*, ed. Franklin J. Mein (Champaign: University of Illinois Press, 2003), xvii.

40. Introduction to George Ade, xiii.

41. Kelly, 136.

42. Kelly, 174.

43. Lee Coyle, *George Ade* (New York: Twayne, 1964), 70–71.

44. Emmett Dedmon, *Fabulous Chicago* (New York: Random House, 1953), 282–83.

45. Regnery, 130–11.

46. Regnery, xvii.

47. See the article "Literary Cultures" in James R. Grossman et al., *The Encyclopedia of Chicago* (Chicago: University of Chicago Press, 2004).

9. The West Side Grounds

1. Peter Golenbock, *Wrigleyville: A Magical History Tour of the Chicago Cubs* (New York: St. Martin's, 1999), 17.

2. Glenn Stout, *The Cubs* (Boston: Houghton Mifflin, 2007), 37.

3. Peter Levine, *A. G. Spalding and the Rise of Baseball* (New York: Oxford University Press, 1985), 8.

4. John Thorn, et al., eds., *Total Baseball* (New York: Viking, 1997), 1862.

5. John Thorn, "The True Father of Baseball," in Thorn, 106–8.

6. Adrian C. Anson, *A Ball Player's Career* (Chicago: Era Publishing, 1900), 21.

7. "Baseball," in *The Encyclopedia of Chicago* (Chicago: University of Chicago Press, 2004). Federal Writers' Project, *Baseball in Old Chicago* (Chicago: A. C. McClurg, 1939), 1.

8. Federal Writers' Project, 1.

9. Federal Writers' Project, 4.

10. Warren Jay Goldstein, *Playing for Keeps: A History of Early Baseball* (Ithaca, NY: Cornell University Press, 1991), 84.

11. Andrew J. Schiff, *"The Father of Baseball": A Biography of Henry Chadwick* (Jefferson, NC: McFarland, 2008), 112.

12. Federal Writers' Project, 10.

13. Benjamin G. Rader, *Baseball: A History of America's Game* (Champaign: University of Illinois Press, 2008), 32.

14. Steven A. Riess, *Touching Base: Professional Baseball and American Culture in the Progressive Era* (Champaign: University of Illinois Press, 1999), 20.

15. Rader, 32.

16. Elliott J. Gorn, *A Brief History of American Sports* (Champaign: University of Illinois Press, 2004), 140.

17. "The Value of an Athletic Training," quoted in Gorn, 147.

18. Riess, 24. Ironically, current research indicates that viewing aggressive sports tends to make viewers more belligerent, not less.

19. Riess, p. 18.

20. Riess, p. 29.

21. Riess, 159, 181–82. In his book *City Games*, Riess argues that "the evolution of the city, more than any other single factor, influenced the development of organized sport . . . in America." After all, he points out, "the city was the place where sport became rationalized, specialized, organized, commercialized, and professionalized." See Steven A. Riess, *City Games: The Evolution of American Urban Society and the Rise of Sports* (Champaign: University of Illinois Press, 1989), 1.

22. Riess, *City Games*, 88.

23. Roger I. Abrams, *The First World Series and the Baseball Fanatics of 1903* (Boston: Northeastern, 2005), 5, 10.

24. Robert G. Spinney, *City of Big Shoulders* (DeKalb: Northern Illinois University Press, 2000), 142.

25. See Rob Edelman, "Baseball, Vaudeville, and Mike Donlin," *Base Ball: A Journal of the Early Game*, Spring 2008, 44–57. Also see Richard Pioreck, "Baseball and Vaudeville and the Development of Popular Culture in the United States, 1880–1930," in Alvin L. Hall, ed., *The Cooperstown Symposium on Baseball and American Culture, 1999* (Jefferson, NC: McFarland, 2002). One might argue that boxing was also a form of mass entertainment, but it drew a mostly male crowd of lower status. Minstrel shows were also a national phenomenon but began as a lower-class form of entertainment aimed almost exclusively at young working-class men.

26. Spinney, p. 85.

27. Levine, 99.

28. Levine, xiii.

29. Levine, p. 42.

30. "'Pop' Anson, Famed in Baseball, Dead," *New York Times*, April 15, 1922.

31. Levine, 47.

32. Federal Writers' Project, 12–13, 22–23.

33. Stout, 7, 9. See the description of the park in Philip J. Lowry, *Green Cathedrals: The Ultimate Celebration of Major League and Negro League Ballparks* (New York: Walker, 2006), 47–48.

34. Levine, 46.

35. John Snyder, *Cubs Journal: Year-by-Year and Day-by-Day with the Chicago Cubs Since 1876* (Cincinnati: Emmis, 2005), 36; Lowry, 48.

36. Snyder, 44.

37. Anson, 292.

38. Anson, 293.

39. Paul Dickson, *The New Dickson Baseball Dictionary* (Orlando, FL: Harvest, 1999), 361.

40. Riess, *Touching Base*, 13–14.

41. "Has Confidence Yet," *Chicago Tribune*, May 12, 1893.

42. "Chicago Sad Sunday Defeat," *Chicago Tribune*, May 15, 1893.

43. "Their Memory Dear," *Chicago Tribune*, August 21, 1893.

44. "Flames Stop a Ball Game," *New York Times*, August 6, 1894.

45. "Panic at a Fire," *Chicago Tribune*, August 6, 1894.

46. Figures and dates are from Lowry.

10. The Chicago Hot Dog

1. On the history of the hot dog, see David Graulich, *Hot Dog Companion* (New York: Lebhar-Friedman, 1999); Robert W. Bly, *All-American Frank* (Baltimore: PublishAmerica, 2007); and Bruce Kraig, *Hot Dog* (London: Reaktion, 2009), the most scholarly and informative account.

2. "Frankfurter Roll Man Dead," *New York Times*, March 7, 1904, 12. Popik's research can be found on his Web site, The Big Apple: www.barrypopik.com.

3. Kraig, 23.

4. "Parker at County Fair," *Chicago Tribune*, September 1, 1904, 4. In 2004, etymologist Gerald Cohen, along with Barry A. Popik and David Shulman, self-published *Origin of the Term "Hot Dog,"* which, at nearly three hundred pages, is a uniquely comprehensive analysis of the subject.

5. Chicagoans were also familiar with the term "frankfurter." When a group of *Tribune* editors visited the Turkish Village at the Columbian Exposition and encountered a "kabob," the best thing they could come up to compare it to was to say that it looked like a "Frankfurter sausage."

6. The *Inter Ocean, Centennial History of the City of Chicago: Its Men and Institutions, Biographical Sketches of Leading Citizens* (Chicago: Inter Ocean, 1905), 26.

7. On the German exhibits at the fair, see Joseph C. Heinen and Susan Barton Heinen, *Lost German Chicago* (Mount Pleasant, SC: Arcadia, 2009), 22–25.

8. "They Tried Gerspritzen Once," *Chicago Tribune*, August 6, 1893, 25.

9. James Gavin, "Chicagoland Fair Is Good Omen for Sausage Maker," *Chicago Tribune*, June 23, 1957, A7.

10. Interview with Scott Ladany, July 29, 2010.

11. Bob Schwartz of Vienna Beef has underscored this ban with his book *Never Put Ketchup on a Hot Dog* (Chicago: Chicago Books Press, 2008), which is a history/guidebook about Chicago hot dogs.

12. Although recipes are well guarded secrets, the proprietors of Vienna Beef are willing to acknowledge that the Chicago hot dog differs from the New York version in that it has less garlic and more paprika.

13. "Meet the Seasoned Pros of Hotdogdom," *Chicago Tribune*, July 29, 1976, B1.

14. Kraig, 78. See also Heather Shouse, "Dynamite Dogs," *Time Out Chicago*, July 3–9, 2008, 13–24.

15. See Popik's Web site for citations of "dragged through the garden."

16. Herb Lyon, "Tower Ticker," *Chicago Tribune*, November 16, 1961, 22.

17. Mike Royko, *For the Love of Mike: More of the Best of Mike Royko* (Chicago: University of Chicago Press, 2002), 154–56.

18. Charles Leroux, "Hey, Getcher Red Hot Facts Right Here: Truth and Fiction on Franks," *Chicago Tribune*, July 29, 1976, B1.

19. Rich Bowen and Dick Fay, *Hot Dog Chicago: A Native's Dining Guide* (Chicago: Chicago Review Press, 1983), 1.

11. Wrigley's Gum

1. Jennifer P. Mathews, *Chicle: The Chewing Gum of the Americas, from the Ancient Maya to William Wrigley* (Tucson: University of Arizona Press, 2009).

2. On Wrigley, see William Zimmerman Jr., *William Wrigley, Jr.: The Man and His Business, 1861–1932* (private edition, 1935).

3. "Gum Store Blows Up," *Chicago Tribune*, January 28, 1895, 2.

4. In addition to White, the members of the trust were Beeman, Adams, Jonathan Primley, S. T. Britten, and the Kis-Me Gum Company.

5. "Pull $50,000 from Bank by Quid of Gum," *Chicago Tribune*, February 20, 1924, 1.

6. "Why 'The Flavor Lasts,'" *Printers' Ink* 119 (April 6, 1922), 124.

7. Sarah Murray, *Moveable Feasts: From Ancient Rome to the 21st Century, the Incredible Journeys of the Food We Eat* (New York: Picador, 2008), 64.

8. "Bumper Crop Predicted in Mint Fields," *Chicago Tribune*, July 2, 1930, 24.

9. Mathews, 54.

10. Peter Golenbock, *Wrigleyville: A Magical History Tour of the Chicago Cubs* (New York: St. Martin's Griffin, 1999), 199.

11. Quoted in Paul M. Angle, *Philip K. Wrigley: A Memoir of a Modest Man* (Chicago: Rand McNally, 1975), 58.

12. "Choose Up Sides," *Chicago Tribune*, March 4, 1922, 10.

13. Golenbock, 202.

14. "Swim in Fast Time at C.A.A.," *Chicago Tribune*, February 16, 1896, 7.

15. Angle, 52.

16. Alice Sinkevitch, ed., *AIA Guide to Chicago*, 2nd ed. (New York: Harcourt, 2004), 102.

17. Sally Anderson Chappell, *Architecture and Planning of Graham, Anderson, Probst and White, 1912–1936* (Chicago: University Of Chicago Press, 1992), 123.

18. Zimmerman, 153.

19. Chappell, 126.

20. "Boulevard Link See as Fifth Avenue's Rival," *Chicago Tribune*, February 6, 1921, A5; "Architects Keep On Flocking to Upper Michigan Ave. Zone," *Chicago Tribune*, May 1, 1921, 25; Al Chase, "Upper Michigan Fast Becoming Grownup Street," *Chicago Tribune*, May 5, 1921, 20.

21. Angle, 9.

22. Dominic A. Pacyga, *Chicago: A Biography* (Chicago: University of Chicago Press, 2009), 320.

23. Andrew F. Smith, *Popped Culture: A Social History of Popcorn in America* (Columbia: University of South Carolina Press, 1999), 85.

24. "Sugar Prices May Cost Chicago Candy Crown," *Chicago Tribune,* June 15, 2005, 1.

12. The Chicago School of Architecture

1. Louis H. Sullivan, *The Autobiography of an Idea* (New York: Dover, 1956), 306, 308.

2. Robert Bruegmann, *The Architects and the City: Holabird & Roche of Chicago, 1880–1918* (Chicago: University of Chicago Press, 1997), 101.

3. Carol Willis, *Form Follows Finance: Skyscrapers and Skylines in New York and Chicago* (New York: Princeton Architectural Press, 1995), 169.

4. Alice Sinkevitch, ed., *AIA Guide to Chicago* (New York: Harcourt, 2004), xiii.

5. Bessie Louise Pierce, *A History of Chicago*, vol. 3, *The Rise of a Modern City 1871–1893* (Chicago: University of Chicago Press, 1957), 63.

6. Quoted in Harold M. Mayer and Richard C. Wade, *Chicago: Growth of a Metropolis* (Chicago: University of Chicago Press, 1969), 120.

7. Quoted in Daniel Bluestone, *Constructing Chicago* (New Haven, CT: Yale University Press, 1991), 109.

8. Joanna Merwood-Salisbury, *Chicago 1890: The Skyscraper and the Modern City* (University of Chicago Press, 2009), 1.

9. On this, see especially Robert Bruegmann, "The Myth of the Chicago School," in *Chicago Architecture: Histories, Revisions, Alternatives*, ed. Charles Waldheim and Katerina Rüedi Ray (Chicago: University of Chicago Press, 2005), 15–29. One of the problems with positing a "Chicago School" is that it devalues the works of excellent Chicago architects that are not assigned to it.

10. Louis Sullivan, "The Tall Building Artistically Considered" (1896), in *Kindergarten Chats and Other Writings* (New York: Dover, 1979), 206.

11. Quoted in Carl Condit, *The Chicago School of Architecture* (Chicago: University of Chicago Press, 1964), 50.

12. Quoted in Donald Hoffman, *Frank Lloyd Wright, Louis Sullivan, and the Skyscraper* (New York: Dover Publications, 1998), 5.

13. Miles L. Berger, *They Built Chicago: Entrepreneurs Who Shaped a Great City's Architecture* (Chicago: Bonus Books, 1992).

14. Quoted in Hoffman, 5.

15. "New York Gossip," *Chicago Daily Tribune*, February 25, 1883, 9.

16. Condit, 81–83.

17. The Home Insurance Building was torn down in order to erect the building now known as 135 South LaSalle Street (1934), which was the last skyscraper built in Chicago until the 1950s. In their book *Chicago's Famous Buildings* (Chicago: University of Chicago Press, 2003), authors Fred Schulze and Kevin Harrington write that this building is a "Chicago rarity" in that it is "excellent enough to justify the demolition of a comparably important structure to make room for it" (100).

18. Ivars Peterson, "The First Skyscraper—New Theory That Home Insurance Building Was Not the First," *Science News*, April 5, 1986.

19. Quoted in Roger Shepherd, ed., *Skyscraper: The Search for an American Style, 1891–1941* (New York: McGraw-Hill, 2003), 29. Shepherd himself says that "the year 1891 saw [the steel skeleton] accepted as more than a mere experiment, and we may say that from that year dates its definitive adoption in American architecture."

20. Berger, 30.

21. Sullivan's disinclination to compromise with developers, his rebuke of the classicism of the Columbian Exposition, the poetic and visionary language of his writings, and his financial struggles have combined to give him a Romantic aura. When the American Institute of Architects posthumously awarded Sullivan its Gold Medal in 1946, it said that he "fought almost alone in his generation, lived unhappily, and died in poverty." Few things raise an artist's reputation more than dying in poverty. He also originated the phrase "form follows function" (originally "form ever follows function"), which became so popular with modernists.

22. Condit, 66. The Monadnock, however, is not the world's tallest masonry building. That distinction belongs to the Mole Antonelliana in Turin (1863–89).

23. Kristen Schaffer, *Daniel H. Burnham: Visionary Architect and Planner* (New York: Rizzoli, 2003), 24.

24. The Massachusetts Brooks brothers are not to be confused with the Brooks Brothers men's clothing firm, which is New York based and began in 1818. It's a nice touch that, at this writing, a Brooks Brothers clothing store is in the Rookery Building, which was commissioned by the other Brooks brothers.

25. Donald Hoffman, *The Architecture of John Wellborn Root* (Chicago: University of Chicago Press, 1973), 87.

26. See Merwood-Salisbury, 66–67.

27. Quoted in Condit, 66. Miles Berger, however, has pointed out that when the northern section of the Monadnock opened, developer Charles C. Heisen had already put three buildings in the area—the Como Block (1887), the Monon Building (1890), and the Manhattan Building (1891) (106.)

28. Sullivan, 309.

29. Quoted in Bruegmann, *The Architects and the City*, 119–20.

30. Jacques Hernant, quoted in Merwood-Salisbury, 46.

31. Bruegmann, *The Architects and the City*, 120.

32. Although most architectural guides describe the building as a steel cage, it is not purely one, in that it employs some load-bearing wall, but in general it fits the description.

33. Condit, 119.

34. Sinkevitch, 65.

35. From Renwick's "Recollections," quoted in Bruegmann, *The Architects and the City*, 490.

36. Daniel H. Burnham, "Charles Bowler Atwood," *The Inland Architect and News Record* 36.6 (January 1896): 56.

37. Burnham, 56.

38. After arriving in Chicago from Massachusetts in 1856, Marshall Field entered into a partnership with Potter Palmer and Levi Leiter. Palmer sold his share of the business, and the first Field and Leiter store opened on State Street in 1868. This store burned in the Great Fire, and its replacement burned in a fire in 1877. Field and Leiter's third store opened the following year; it was this one for which Atwood's annex was built. Field bought Leiter out in 1879. The third Field and Leiter store was replaced in 1907 by the present building, which was at the time, with 73 acres of space and 13 floors, the largest department store in the world. The annex also still stands.

39. On the building and Atwood's career, see Ann Lorenz Van Zanten, "The Marshall Field Annex and the New Urban Order of Daniel Burnham's Chicago," *Chicago History* 11.3 (Fall and Winter 1982): 130–41.

40. Thomas J. O'Gorman, *Architecture in Detail: Chicago* (Canton, OH: PRC Publishing, 2003), 32.

41. This is one reason that older buildings have high ceilings—to allow daylight to reach into the interior as far as possible.

42. Commission on Chicago Historical and Architectural Landmarks, *Reliance Building* (Chicago: City of Chicago, Commission on Chicago Historical and Architectural Landmarks, 1979), 5.

43. David Dunlap, "Restoring a Century-Old Glass Tower in Chicago," *New York Times*, July 25, 1999, section 11, 7.

44. According to the *Chicago Tribune*, the building was to "compare in strength and certain other features to the Fair, and the interior to be after the style of the Rookery." The lease of the corner property to the Reliance Company was for 198 years beginning July 1, 1893. See "New Building Company Formed," *Chicago Daily Tribune*, July 23, 1893, 14.

45. "New Building Company," 11. See also Jay Pridmore, *The Reliance Building* (Rohnert Park, CA: Pomegranate Communications, 2003), 38.

46. Commission on Chicago Historical and Architectural Landmarks, *Summary of Information on the Reliance Building* (Chicago: City of Chicago, Commission on Chicago Historical and Architectural Landmarks, 1971), 3. Holabird and Roche had used white terra cotta on the Champlain Building (1894), but the material was not glazed.

47. Burnham, 57.

48. Van Zanten, 133. Apparently, Atwood's drug of choice was opium.

49. Hoffman, *The Architecture of John Wellborn Root*, 220. According to Hoffman, Moore never published this statement of Burnham's; it was found in the original typescript of Moore's interview.

50. Charles Moore, *Daniel Burnham, Architect, Planner of Cities* (Boston: Houghton Mifflin, 1921), 85–86.

51. "A White City Architect Passed Away," *Chicago Daily Tribune*, December 21, 1895, 12. The article attributed his death (and Root's) to "overwork." Interestingly, it commented that the art gallery "is at best but a temporary structure, though it was built more securely than the other buildings. . . . It would be a fitting tribute to Mr. Atwood's genius if this noble temple could be reproduced in permanent shape and stand as a monument to his memory."

52. Sullivan's original plan was to have two smaller doorways, and it was Burnham who advised him instead "to have one grand entrance . . . much richer than either of the others you had proposed." See Mario Manieri Elia, *Louis Henry Sullivan* (New York: Princeton Architectural Press, 1996), 97.

53. "Brokers' Fine Home," *Chicago Daily Tribune*, April 22, 1894, 25.

54. Richard Nickel and Aaron Siskind, *The Complete Architecture of Adler & Sullivan* (Chicago: Richard Nickel Committee, 2010), 403.

55. Donald L. Miller, *City of the Century: The Epic of Chicago and the Making of America* (New York: Simon and Schuster, 1996), 374.

56. Robert C. Twombly, *Frank Lloyd Wright: His Life and His Architecture* (New York: John Wiley and Sons, 1979), 416.

57. Twombly, 416.

58. Frank Lloyd Wright, *An Autobiography* (New York: Duell, Sloan and Pearce, 1943), 111.

59. Thomas A. Heinz, *The Vision of Frank Lloyd Wright* (New York: Barnes and Noble, 2005), 21.

13. Reforming Chicago

1. The map is excellently reproduced in Robert A. Holland, *Chicago in Maps: 1612–2002* (New York: Rizzoli, 2005), 159.

2. Karen Abbott, *Sin in the Second City* (New York: Random House, 2007), 10.

3. Emmett Dedmon, *Fabulous Chicago* (New York: Random House, 1953), 135.

4. Bernard A. Weisberger, "Evangelists to the Machine Age," *American Heritage* 6.5 (August 1955): 20–23, 100–101.

5. William G. McLoughlin Jr., *Modern Revivalism: Charles Grandison Finney to Billy Graham* (New York: Ronald, 1959), 166.

6. Bruce J. Evensen, *God's Man for the Gilded Age: D. L. Moody and the Rise of Modern Mass Evangelism* (New York: Oxford University Press, 2003), 25.

7. Richard K. Curtis, *They Called Him Mister Moody* (Garden City, NY: Doubleday, 1962), 271.

8. H. B. Hartzler, *Moody in Chicago, or the World's Fair Gospel Campaign* (New York: Fleming H. Revell, n.d.), 28.

9. Hartzler, 33–34.

10. Curtis, 276.

11. Hartzler, 49.

12. Hartzler, 74.

13. Hartzler, 232.

14. McLoughlin, 265–66.

15. McLoughlin, 259.

16. Curtis, 267.

17. On the reluctance of the Protestant churches to move away from a philosophy of individualism and competition during the depression of 1893, see Donald D. Marks, "Polishing the Gem of the Prairie: The Evolution of Civic Reform Consciousness in Chicago," (Ph.D. diss., University of Wisconsin, 1974).

18. McLoughlin, 526.

19. Grace Eckely, *Maiden Tribute: A Life of W. T. Stead* (Philadelphia: Xlibris, 2007), i.

20. Melville E. Stone, *Fifty Years a Journalist* (Garden City, NY: Doubleday, 1921), 202.

21. William T. Stead, *If Christ Came to Chicago!* (Chicago: Laird and Lee, 1894), 18.

22. Donald L. Miller, *City of the Century: The Epic of Chicago and the Making of America* (New York: Simon and Schuster, 1996), 537.

23. "Stead in the Slums," *Chicago Tribune*, November 12, 1893, 1.

24. "Strong Words Used," *Chicago Tribune*, November 13, 1893, p. 1.

25. "He Starts the Ball," *Chicago Tribune*, November 14, 1893, 5.

26. Stead, 16.

27. Stead, 68.

28. See Richard C. Lindberg, *The Gambler King of Clark Street: Michael C. McDonald and the Rise of Chicago's Democratic Machine* (Carbondale: Southern Illinois University Press, 2009). In 1893, McDonald was proudly presiding over the opening of the Lake Street elevated line, one of the undoubted benefits he brought to Chicago.

29. Stead, 182.

30. Stead, 324.

31. Stead, 359.

32. Marks, 64.

33. "Address by President Franklin MacVeagh, September 11, 1874," in *Address and Reports of the Citizens' Association of Chicago* (Chicago: Hazlitt and Reed, 1876), 7.

34. Marks, 89.

35. Lindberg, 137.

36. Douglas Sutherland, *Fifty Years on the Civic Front* (Chicago: Civic Federation, 1943), 6.

37. Sutherland, 10.

38. Perry R. Duis, *The Saloon: Public Drinking in Chicago and Boston, 1880–1920* (Champaign: University of Illinois Press, 1983), 246.

39. Lindberg, 167.

40. Evensen, 3.

41. McLoughlin, 405.

14. Epidemics and Clean Water

1. Harold L. Platt, *Shock Cities: The Environmental Transformation and Reform of Manchester and Chicago* (Chicago: University of Chicago Press, 2005), 80.

2. One of Chicago's most persistent urban legends, one repeated in the *Chicago Tribune Magazine* as recently as March 21, 2004, is that some ninety thousand people perished from cholera and typhoid in 1885. This fable has been thoroughly debunked.

3. Thomas Neville Bonner, *Medicine in Chicago, 1850–1950* (Champaign: University of Illinois Press, 1991), 25.

4. See the article "Demography" in *The Encyclopedia of Chicago*, ed. James R. Grossman et al. (Chicago: University of Chicago Press, 2004), 235. One analysis estimates that 30 to 50 percent of Chicago's mortality decline from 1850 to 1925 was due to the cleansing of the water supply. See Edward Glaeser, *Triumph of the City* (New York: Penguin, 2011), 101.

5. Donald L. Miller, *City of the Century: The Epic of Chicago and the Making of America* (New York: Simon and Schuster, 1996), 457.

6. "Inspectors Examine Lodging-Houses," *Chicago Tribune*, August 16, 1893, 6.

7. Harold M. Mayer and Richard C. Wade, *Chicago: Growth of a Metropolis* (Chicago: University of Chicago Press, 1969), 256.

8. Mayer and Wade, 256.

9. Robert Hunter, quoted in Mayer and Wade, 256.

10. Florence Kelley, *Notes of Sixty Years: the Autobiography of Florence Kelley* (Chicago: Charles H. Kerr, 1986), 87.

11. Arthur R. Reynolds, "History of the Chicago Smallpox Epidemic of 1893, 1894 and 1895. With Side Lights and Recollections," in *The Rise and Fall of Disease in Illinois*, ed. Isaac D. Rawlings (Springfield, IL: Schnepp and Barnes, 1927), 313–20.

12. "Record of the Pest," *Chicago Tribune*, May 28, 1894, 12.

13. Bayard Holmes, "The Sweatshops and Smallpox in Chicago," *Journal of the American Medical Association* 23 (September 15, 1894), 420.

14. "Record of the Pest," 12.

15. See Michael Willrich, *Pox: An American History* (New York: Penguin, 2011). An increase in childhood diseases in the United States in the early twenty-first century has demonstrated that antivaccination sentiments have by no means disappeared.

16. Reynolds, 318.

17. Reynolds, 316.

18. "Record of the Pest," 12.

19. Reynolds, 314.

20. See Margaret Garb, "Regulating Urban Living," *Chicago History* 25.3 (Spring 2008): 4–29.

21. Garb, 10.

22. Quoted in Perry R. Duis, *Challenging Chicago: Coping with Everyday Life, 1837–1920* (Champaign: University of Illinois Press, 1998), 98.

23. Platt, 350.

24. The *Chicago Inter Ocean*, quoted in Garb, 17.

25. Garb, 18.

26. Joanna Merwood-Salisbury, *Chicago 1890: The Skyscraper and the Modern City* (Chicago: University of Chicago Press, 2009), 109.

27. See Eileen Maura McGurty, "Trashy Women: Gender and the Politics of Garbage in Chicago, 1890–1917." *Historical Geography* 26 (1998): 27–43.

28. "Garbage Boxes Are Seldom Emptied," *Chicago Tribune*, June 24, 1893, 14.

29. "A Bed of Reeking Refuse," *Chicago Tribune*, July 20, 1983, 1.

30. For a survey of American urban sanitation strategies, see Martin V. Melosi, *The Sanitary City: Environmental Services in Urban America from Colonial Times to the Present* (Pittsburgh: University of Pittsburgh Press, 2008).

31. Louis P. Cain, *Sanitation Strategy for a Lakefront Metropolis: The Case of Chicago* (DeKalb: Northern Illinois University Press, 1978), 23.

32. Platt, 119.

33. Quoted in Mayer and Wade, 96.

34. Edwin C. Larned, quoted in Platt, 144.

35. F. Barnham Zincke, quoted in Bessie Louise Pierce, ed., *As Others See Chicago* (Chicago: University of Chicago Press, 2004), 219.

36. M. N. Baker, "The Chicago Drainage Canal," *Outlook* 64 (February 10, 1900): 356.

37. Platt, 187.

38. Cain, 63.

39. Miller, 131.

40. Cain, 80.

41. Cain, 81.

Epilogue: Chicago's Next Great Year

1. Larry Bennett, *The Third City: Chicago and American Urbanism* (Chicago: University of Chicago Press, 2010).

2. Alan Ehrenhalt, "Trading Places: The Demographic Inversion of the American City," *New Republic*, August 13, 2008.

3. Richard Florida, *The Rise of the Creative Class* (New York: Basic, 2004).

4. Bennett, 150.

5. The *Inter Ocean, Centennial History of the City of Chicago: Its Men and Institutions, Biographical Sketches of Leading Citizens* (Chicago: Inter Ocean, 1905), 14.

Index

Abbott, Karen, 265–66
Abbott, Margaret (later Dunne), 169
Abrams, Roger I., 188
Academy of Design, Chicago, 36
Academy of Fine Arts, Chicago, 36
Adams, Daniel "Doc," 184
Adams, Frederick Upham, 165
Adams, Thomas, 222, 226
Addams, Jane, 7, 282, 291–92
Ade, Bill, 178
Ade, George, 35–36, 165, 170–79
Ade, John, 175, 178
Adler, Dankmar, 1, 238, 242, 244, 246, 258, 260–61
Administration Building, Columbian Exposition, 18, 21
Administration Building, Johnson Company, 264
advertising, 63, 67–68, 225–26, 268, 270
AEW Capital Management, 74
Agassiz, Louis, 43
air pollution, 24–28, 311n18
Aldis, Owen F., 242, 247–48, 249
Allerton Hotel, 233
Altgeld, John Peter, 288
American Chicle Company, 225
American College of Surgeons, 107
American Dental Association, 236
American Institute of Architects, 50, 256, 330n21
American League, 183
American Medical Association (AMA), 111, 112
American Museum of Natural History, 31
American Society of Civil Engineers, 298–99
Anderson, Harry, 98
Anson, Adrian "Cap," 183, 184, 189, 193–94, 195, 196–97, 198
Anthony, Susan B., 87
Anthropological Building, 44–45
anti-smoke movement, 25–29, 311n18
Aon Center, 264
Aqua building, 238
Archer, William, 11
Archibald, H. Teller, 235

architectural styles: Armour Mission, 135–36; Art Gallery, 332n51; Chicago's reputation, 238–40, 241–42; churches, 114–15, 124; Columbian Exposition, 14f, 17–18, 20–21, 47, 250–51, 332n52; education buildings, 133, 137, 146, 149–50; geographical constraints, 240–41; high ceiling purposes, 331n41; library, 54, 55–56; Montauk Building, 246; museums, 36, 37f, 40, 50, 53f; social services facilities, 135–36; Woman's Temple, 85–86, 316n29
architectural styles, business/office buildings: Chicago Stock Exchange, 257–59; Field Annex, 238, 251–53; Monadnock Building, 246–49, 331n32; Reliance Building, 253–56, 331n44; Rookery Building, 248; Sears complex and tower, 69–71, 72–74; skyscraper beginnings, 243–46, 330n19; Wrigley Building, 230–33
Aristophanes, 203
Armour, Andrew, 141
Armour, Charles, 141
Armour, George, 36
Armour, Herman, 140, 141
Armour, J. Ogden, 148
Armour, Joseph Francis, 135, 141
Armour, Malvina Belle (earlier Ogden), 105, 140
Armour, Philip Danforth, 103, 138, 139, 140–45, 148, 268, 280
Armour, Simeon, 141
Armour Flats, 136
Armour Institute of Technology, 56, 133–39, 147–49
Armour Mission, 135–36
Armour Scientific Academy, 136
Arnold, Matthew, 33
Art Gallery, 257, 332n51
Arthur Bryant's, Kansas City, 220
Artie (Ade), 172–73
Art Institute of Chicago, 34–42, 134, 259, 320n3
Asher, Louis E., 58
attendance statistics: baseball, 195, 197–98, 199, 229; Columbian

Exposition, 1, 18–19; museums, 47
Atwood, Charles B.: architectural designs, 40, 47, 53f, 238, 246, 250–56, 332n51; career decline/death, 256–57, 332n49; with Chicago Exposition Company colleagues, 16f
Auditorium Building, 244
Austrian population, 209, 210
Ayer, Edward E., 45–47

Baker, Newton D., 61
baking powder business, Wrigley's, 224–25
ballparks, 194–98
The Banditti of the Prairies, 153
Bank One Plaza, 264
"banquet on a bun," 217–18
Baptist community, 111, 146
Barat University, 146
Barnett, F. L., 102
Barriers Burned Away (Roe), 154
Bartlett Memorial Collection, 42
Barzun, Jacques, 162
Base Ball Association, Chicago, 185–86
baseball history, 183–89, 196, 200–201, 234, 326n21. See also Cubs; White Stockings
"A Basket of Potatoes" (Ade), 175
Beeman, Edward E., 222
Beersman, Charles, 231
Belfield, William T., 110
Bellow, Saul, 179
Bennett, Larry, 301–2
Berger, Miles L., 242, 246, 330n27
Bernardoni, Brian, 202
Bernhardt, Sarah, 141
Bertram Cope's Year (Fuller), 161–62
bicycling, 76–79, 86–93
Bigot, Mary Healy, 154
Bisno, Inspector, 288
black characters, literary, 167–68, 173
black community, 99–105, 117–18, 119, 128–30, 132, 193–94, 318n11. See also Tolton, Augustus
Black Jack gum, 222
Blei, Norbert, 218–19
Blenk, James H., 129

Blommer, Al, 235
Blommer, Bernard, 235
Blommer, Henry, 235
Bloom, Sol, 21
Bloomer, Amelia, 87, 316n34
Bluestone, Daniel, 55
Bob Elfman's, 219
Bodman, James W., 213
Bonner, Thomas, 110, 111, 286
Bonney, Edward, 153
boodler system, 280
Booth, Emma Scarr, 155
bootleg houses, Wright's, 261–62, 263f
Borden Block, 53
Bordin, Ruth, 82, 84
Boston baseball, 190, 200
Bourget, Paul, 24, 143
Bowen, Rich, 217, 219
boxing, 326n25
Brach, Emil J. (and company), 234, 236
Brackenridge, H. H., 168
Brainard, Daniel, 110–11
Braun, Adolphe, 40
Braun, Carol Moseley, 218
Braves' Field, Boston, 200
Breckenridge, Sophonisba, 101
Breton, Jules, 41
Bridgeport, 165, 297
Briggs, Hattie, 265
Briggs House, 295
Bronzeville, 100, 101f
Brooks, Peter Chardon, III, 247–49
Brooks, Shepherd, 247, 249
Brooks Brothers clothing, 330n24
Bross, William, 153
brothels, 265–66, 267f, 283
Brotherhood Park, 196
Brown, Frank, 275
Brown, G. W., 124
Browne, Charles Farrar, 167
Bruce, H. Addington, 186
Bruwaert, François Edmond, 8, 12
Bubbly Creek, 295, 296f
building activity, statistics, 237. See also architectural styles entries
Burgess, A. H., 55
Burj Khalifa, Dubai, 240
Burnham, Daniel: on Atwood, 257, 332n49; Columbian Exposition leadership, 21, 22, 246; on Field Museum location, 48; planning career, 11, 29, 303

Burnham, Daniel (architectural designs): Armour Mission, 135; Art Institute, 36, 37f; Columbian Exposition buildings, 1, 16–17, 250–51, 332n52; Monadnock Building, 247–48; Reliance Building, 253; Rookery Building, 248; Woman's Temple, 85, 316n29
Burns, Tom, 197
Burritt Durand (McGovern), 153
Bushnell, George D., 90
Bushnell, William H., 153
Busse, Frank, 29
Busse, Fred, 283
Butterick and Company, 88
Byron's Hot Dogs, 218

Café Atwood, 256
Cain, Louis P., 299
CalSag Channel, 298
canals, 39, 66, 297–99
candy production, 234–36
Cantor, Eddie, 206
car bungee-jumping, Columbian Exposition, 22
Carl Pretzel's Magazine Pook, 166, 324n31
Carson, Pirie, Scott store, 57–58, 253
Cartwright, Alexander, 184
Catalina Island, 229–30
catalogs. See mail order companies
Catholic community, 111, 113–15, 122, 146, 281. See also Tolton, Augustus
Cazenovia Academy, 140
Central Music Hall, 33, 246, 276–77
Century of Progress International Exposition, 54
Cerenak, John, 288
Chadwick, Henry, 189
Chamberlain, J. E., 153
Chamber of Commerce Building, 53
Champlain Building, 331n46
Chance, Frank, 181
Chap-Book, 153
Chapman, John Wilbur, 284
Charnley House, 261
The Chatelaine of La Trinité (Fuller), 158
Chatfield-Taylor, Hobart C., 154, 165
Chesbrough, Ellis Sylvester, 294–98

The Chevalier of Pensieri-Vani (Fuller), 157–58
chewing gum business, 221–23, 225–28, 233
Chicagoan, 160–61
Chicago Avenue Church, 269–70
Chicago Baptist Hospital, 111
"Chicago Colored People," 97, 318n3
Chicago Daily News, 165, 183
Chicago Evening Post, 147–48, 162, 165–69
Chicago Exposition Company, 16
Chicago Herald, 28, 165
Chicago Hospital for Women and Children, 112
Chicago Inter Ocean, 97, 139
Chicago Medical College, 110, 111
Chicago News, 205
Chicago Public Library, 54–56
Chicago Record, 35–36, 170
Chicago River, water quality, 294, 295–98
Chicago's greatest year, overview, 1–12. See also specific topics, e.g., architectural styles entries; Columbian Exposition; museums; reform activity
"Chicago's Night Cooks," 205
"Chicago's Soliloquy on Here Childhood," 7
Chicago State University, 146
Chicago Sun, 14–15
Chicago Times-Herald, 168
Chicago Tribune (article/editorial topics): air pollution, 25, 28; Atwood obituary, 257, 332n51; black professionals, 97, 318n3; buildings/architecture, 50, 51, 74, 233, 237, 240–41, 243, 331n44; Catholic community, 123, 124; Columbian Exposition, 11–12, 15, 22, 91, 210; disease problems and control, 292, 297–98, 334n2; farming, 227; hot dogs, 207, 208–9, 212, 215–16, 218–19; literary figures, 157–58; medical profession, 97, 103, 112; military expedition, 15; Millennium Park, 306; museums, 45, 49, 52; Sears, Roebuck, 58–59; sports, 91, 92, 189, 199, 200, 201, 229; temperance-related activity, 85; weather, 95, 127; women's dress, 88–89
chicle production, 222, 227

Chisley, Martha Jane (later Tolton), 116, 117, 125
cholera, 285, 294, 298, 334*n*2
churches. *See* religious communities
Church of St. Benedict the Moor, 119
Cincinnati baseball teams, 185, 198–99, 202
cities, developmental stages, 6–10
Citizens' Association, 281–82
Citizens Protective Association, 28
Civic Center, Chicago, 264
Civic Federation of Chicago, 277, 282–84
civic leaders, role changes, 32–33
civic reform. *See* reform activity
Civil War, 117, 140–41, 184
Clark, Henry A., 153
Clark, J. M., 222
Cleveland, Grover, 17, 18*f*
The Cliff Dwellers (Fuller), 152, 155, 158–59
Cliff Dwellers organization, 323*n*3
climate change, 301
clothing changes, women's, 87–89, 316*n*34
coal soot, 25–28, 311*n*18
Cobb, Henry Ives, 1, 17, 56, 146
Cohen, Gerald, 327*n*4
Cohn, David L., 61, 313*n*3
Cole, Thomas, 6–7
Colgan, John, 222
colleges. *See* schools/colleges
The College Widow (Ade), 174, 177–78
Collier, Price, 11
Collins, Morris Allen, 165
The Colossus (Read), 154
Colts, Chicago, 183, 196–200
Columbia College, 146
Columbian Exposition: architects for, 1, 17, 250–51, 257, 332*n*52; Armour Institute relationship, 138*f*, 139; attendance statistics, 1, 18–19; bicycling activity, 91; Chicago's goal, 8, 15; as city operation lesson, 30; commercial activities, 65, 69; competition for, 14–15; "Darkies' Day" portrayal, 99*f*; disease, 287; dress reform symposium, 88; education approach, 20; entertainment activities, 21–23; evangelism activity, 269–72; expanse of, 18–19; food wares, 208*f*, 209,

210, 211, 235–36, 327*n*5; location, 16–17; opening of, 17–18, 19*f*; parade, 24*f*; project managers, 16; visitor impressions, 11–12
Columbian Exposition, museum relationships: art, 34–35, 38, 39, 41; natural history, 43–45, 46; science and industry, 49–51
Comiskey, Charles, 199
Commercial Club, 44–45, 304
Como Block, 330*n*27
Condit, Carl W., 85, 243–44, 247, 249
Coney Island, 205*f*, 206
Congress, U.S., 15
Congress Parkway, West, 56
Connaroe, Joel, 161–62
Conservator, 102
cookbook, Wrigley's, 224
Cook County Board of Commissioners, 106
Cook County Hospital, 107, 109, 110
Cooke, Horatio, 152–53
cooking school, Armour Institute, 139
Cooper, Johnson Jones, 167
Cornish, James, 95–97
corruption, 280, 283, 292
Cotton Stealing (Chamberlain), 153
Coughlin, John, 266
The County Chairman (Ade), 177
Course of Empire paintings (Cole), 6–7
Court of Honor, 17, 18, 20
Cracker Jack, 235–36
Crane, Stephen, 155
creative class, urban settings, 303
Crerar Library, 48
Crockett, Davy, 167
Crown Hall, Illinois Institute of Technology, 149–50
Cubs, Chicago, 181–83, 198, 201, 202, 227–30. *See also* White Stockings
Cultural Center, Chicago, 54–55
curtain-wall construction, advantages, 243, 244–45
Curtis, John Bacon, 221–22
Curtiss candy, 234
Custom House Place, 265, 275
cycling, 76–79, 86–93

Daggett, Sarah E., 39
Daley, Richard J., 93
Daley, Richard M., 93, 302, 304–5

Dalton, H. C., 108
Dana, Charles, 14–15
"Darkies' Day," 99*f*
Davis, Cyprian, 115, 319*n*4
Davis, Nathan S., 111
Debs, Eugene V., 10–11
Decker, George, 199
Dedication Day, Columbian Exposition, 24*f*
Dedmon, Emmett, 179
Demidoff Collection, 41
demographic inversion, 302–3. *See also* population statistics
Dennis, Charles H., 176
DePaul University, 146
"Der Deitcher's Dog," 207–8
Des Plaines River, 297
Deventer, Emma Murdock, 154
Devore Company, 288
De Wolf, Oscar Coleman, 291
Dexter Park, 194–95
Dial, 9, 153
dialect humor, 163, 166, 167–68, 324*n*31
Dickens, Charles, 204–5
Dickie's Dogs, 219
disease problems and control: housing conditions, 286–87, 290–91; sanitation improvements, 290–93; types of, 285–86, 287–90, 294, 298, 334*n*2; water quality, 293–300
Doc Horne (Ade), 172, 173–74
Doering, Otto, 70
Donelson, Kathryn, 154–55
Dooley character, Dunne's, 162–63, 165–69
Dorgan, T. A., 206–7
Dorsey, John Henry, 129
Doubleday, Abner, 187
Douglas, Frederick, 102–3
Douglas, Joseph H., 105
Douglass, Adam, 168
"dragged through the garden," 217–18
Drake Hotel, 233
Drexel, Katharine, 123, 124*f*, 126, 130
Drexler, Abe, 213–16
Dreiser, Theodore, 177
Drucker, Mrs. Joseph, 120–21
Duis, Perry R., 90
Duncan, Hugh Dalziel, 154
Dunne, Ellen (earlier Finley), 164
Dunne, Finley Peter, 162–70
Dunne, Margaret (earlier Abbott), 169

Index

Dunne, Peter, 164
Dunne, Philip, 163, 169
Durante, Jimmy, 206

economic conditions, 2–3, 28, 102, 275–76, 279, 302
Edison Company, Chicago, 26
education. *See* schools/colleges
Edwards Law, 113
Ehrenhalt, Alan, 302–3
Eisenberg, James, 212–13
Elder, William Henry, 116–17
Electricity Building, 17, 138*f*, 139
elevators, 253
Eliott, Stephen, 116, 117
Eliott, Susan (earlier Manning), 116
Ellicott Square Building, 256
Elliot, Daniel Giraud, 47
Ellis, Elmer, 169
Emanuel, Rahm, 93, 302, 304
employment patterns, 2–3, 102, 275–76, 279
Emporis, 238
entertainment, 21–23, 189, 326*n*25. *See also* baseball history; museums
Environmental Protection Agency (EPA), 300
epidemics. *See* disease problems and control
Epiphany College, 129
Episcopal community, 111
Epstein, Joseph, 180
Equitable Life Assurance Building, 244
Ermoian, Fast Eddie, 219
erysipelas epidemic, 295
evangelism, 268–73, 284
Everleigh Club, 283
Excelsiors, Chicago, 185

Fables in Slang (Ade), 174
Fair department store, 57–58
Fannie May candy, 235, 236
Fanning, Charles, 168
farmers, 62–63
Farwell, Charles, 185–86
Fay, Dick, 217, 219
Federal League, 200–201
Federation of Women's Clubs, Chicago, 50–51
Feehan, Patrick Augustine, 121–22, 123
Feltman, Charles, 206
Fenger, Christian, 110

Ferdinand, Archduke Franz, 210
Ferguson Building, 42
Ferrara, Salvatore (and company), 234–35, 236
Ferris, George Washington, Jr., 22
Ferris wheel, 22–23, 91
Feuchtwanger, Anton, 204
Field, Eugene, 151, 165, 169
Field, Hollis W., 58–59
Field, Marshall, 46–47, 48, 57, 251, 268, 280, 331*n*38
Field Annex, 238, 251–53
Field Collection, 41
Field Museum, 42–49, 134, 320*n*3
Fields, W. C., 173–74
Fine Arts Building, 51, 53*f*
Finley, Ellen (later Dunne), 164
Finn, Mickey, 265
Finney, Charles Grandison, 268
fires, 130, 140, 199–200, 210, 281. *See also* Great Fire
First National Bank, 253, 264
Fisher, Reynolds, 133, 136, 321*n*12
Fisher Building, 256
Fisheries Building, 17
Flagg, Newton, 117
"floating-raft" foundations, 246
Florida, Richard, 303
Fluky's, 214–16
football, 54
Foote, Ada (later Wrigley), 223
For Her Daily Bread (Sommers), 154
Fort Sheridan, 243
Fowler, Charles Henry, 81
Frain, Andy, 229
frankfurters. *See* hot dogs
Franklin, Benjamin, 167
Freedman's Hospital, 107
Frémont, John, 117
Frischman, Ignatz, 205–6
Froelich, Ed, 229
Fuller, George Wood, 156–57
Fuller, Henry Blake, 6, 151, 152, 155–62, 180
Fullerton, Hugh, 187
Fullerton Auditorium, 42
future prospects, Chicago's, 301–6

Gage, Lyman, 282
Galehouse, Richard, 147
gambling, 183, 193, 280, 283–84
Gang, Jeanne, 238
Gapp, Paul, 74
garbage collection, 291, 292–93
Gardens of this World (Fuller), 161

Garland, Hamlin, 158, 180, 323*n*3, *n*14
garment workers, smallpox control, 287–88
Gavin, James, 212
Gay and Lesbian Hall of Fame, Chicago, 161
Gem of the Prairie, 153
George, Cardinal Francis, 128
George, Henry, 10
Georghehner, Johann, 204
German population, 113, 114, 117–18, 122, 209
German Village, Columbian Exposition, 210
Germany, 51–52, 136
Gill, Gordon, 240
Girls Professional Baseball League, All-American, 234
Gladys, Willard's bicycle, 77–79, 93
Glaeser, Edward, 101
Gleanings of Thought (Cooke), 152–53
global city designation, 8–9, 309*n*11
Golden Doorway, 17, 257, 332*n*52
Goldman, Henry, 69
Goode, George Brown, 31–32
Goodman Theater, 42
Goose Island campus, Wrigley's, 233
"Go to 2040" document, 303–4
Gradle, Henry, 110
Graham, Anderson, Probst, and White, 230
Graham, Bruce, 73–74
Graham, Burnham and Company, 49
Graham, Ernest, R., 16*f*
Grand Crossing neighborhood, 293
Grange, 62–63
Grant Park, 65–67, 293. *See also* museums
Gray City, 24–31, 311*n*18, *n*22
Great Fire, 36, 55, 63, 111, 195, 240, 331*n*38. *See also* fires
Gresham, Walter Q., 107
Groenbaum, Otto, 127
Guggenheim Museum, 262
gum business, 221–23, 225–28, 233
Gunsaulus, Frank W., 134–35, 136, 138
Gunsaulus, Helen, 320*n*3
Gunsaulus Halls, 320*n*3

Hahnemann Hospital, 111
Hale, William E., 242, 253
Haliburton, Thomas Chandler, 167
Hall, George Cleveland, 107–8
Hall, William C., 167
Hall Collection of Sculpture, 40
Hallowell, Sara Tyson, 41
Hammond, George, 321n21
Hancock, Richard M., 318n3
Hancock Center, 73–74, 264
Handwerker, Nathan, 206
Hannigan, Henry, 292–93
Hardscrabble (Richardson), 153
Harold Washington College, 146
Harold Washington Library
  Center, 56
Harper, William Rainey, 146
Harrington, Kevin, 330n17
Harris, Charles H., 166, 324n31
Harris, George Washington, 167
Harris, Joel Chandler, 168
Harrison, Carter, 28
Harrison, Carter, II, 92, 266, 283
Hart, Jim, 194
Hayes, Rutherford B., 210
Haymarket affair, 34
Haymarket Theater, 270, 271
Heal, Edith, 58
Heald, Henry, 150
Health Culture Club, 88
health departments, 99, 285, 291
Healy, Alexander Sherwood, 115
Healy, James Augustine, 115
Healy, Michael Morris, 115
Healy, Patrick Francis, 115
heart surgery, 95–97, 108, 318n20
Heath, Monroe, 291
Hecht, Ben, 5
height restrictions, buildings, 231,
  238. See also skyscrapers
Heinz, Thomas A., 262
Heisen, Charles C., 330n27
Hell's Half Acre, 265
Hemesath, Caroline, 319
Hibbard bicycles, 92
Higinbotham, Harlow N., 16, 21,
  41, 48
Hirshfield, Leo, 235
History Museum, Chicago, 56
Hodnett, Father, 124–25
Holabird, John, 149–50
Holabird, William, 244, 246, 247,
  249, 331n46
Holt, Charlotte, 87
Home Insurance Building,
  243–44, 330n17

Hopkins, John Patrick, 283, 290
Horowitz, Helen Lefkowitz, 6
Horticulture Building, 17
hospitals. See medical facilities
hot dogs: classic Chicago version,
  214–20; Columbia Exposition,
  208f, 209, 210–11, 327n5; historic
  stories/myths, 203–9; Mayer
  brothers activity, 209–10; Red
  Hot Chicago business, 213–14;
  Vienna Beef business, 211–13,
  327n12
Hotel Burnham, 256
House of Representatives, U.S., 15
housing, 61, 136, 142, 286–87,
  290–91, 305
Howard, Ebenezer, 11
Howard, Lillian, 175
Howells, William Dean, 151–52,
  155, 156f, 159, 160
Howenstein, J. H., 292
Hughes, Thomas, 55, 186
Hulbert, William, 183
Hull, Mrs. Perry A., 88
Hull House, 287
Huneker, James, 160
Hunt, Richard M., 1, 17, 21
Hutchinson, Benjamin F., 3, 36, 38
Hutchinson, Charles L., 36, 38, 41
Huxtable, Ada Louise, 74
Hyde Park, 8, 101, 106

IBM Building, 264
If Christ Came to Chicago (Stead),
  277–79
Illinois and Michigan Canal,
  297–98
Illinois Central Railroad, 28–29,
  196
Illinois Institute of Technology,
  56, 133–39, 147–49
Illinois Library Act, 55
Illinois Medical District, 201
Illinois River, 297, 299–300
illumination, Wrigley Building,
  231
Imperial Hotel, 262
Inland Steel Building, 264
Inner-City Association of Chi-
  cago, 186
Insurance Exchange, 52–53
international designs, Chicago
  architects, 238, 240
Interstate Industrial Exposition
  Building, 38–39
Ireland, John, 126

Jackson, Kate, 81
Jackson Park, 16–17, 210
James, William, 186
Jarrold, Ernest, 168
Jefferson, annexation, 8
Jenney, William Le Baron, 243,
  245–46
Jewish population, 111, 213–15
John Hancock Center, 73–74, 264
Johnson, Alice (later Williams),
  107
Johnson Company, 264
Jones, Chris, 306
Juicy Fruit gum, 225–26

Kahn, Fazlur R., 73
Kelley, Florence, 287–89
Kelly, Edward, 52
Kelly, Mike, 193
Kenna, Michael, 266, 276
Kennicott, Mark, 91
Kenyon, William Asbury, 153
ketchup prohibition, hot dogs,
  214, 218, 327n11
"The Key of the Street" (Dick-
  ens), 204–5
Keyser, Harriete, 168
Kinzie, Juliette Augusta Magill, 153
Kipling, Rudyard, 24
Kirkland, Joseph, 153
Kis-Me Chewing Gum, 222
Kraig, Bruce, 207, 216–17

Ladany, Billy, 213
Ladany, Jules, 212
Ladany, Samuel, 211–12, 215
Ladany, Scott, 213–14
Ladany, William, 212
Ladies College, Northwestern
  University, 81
Lahner, Johann Georg, 204, 215
Lake Forest College, 146
Lakefront Park, 195–96
Lake/Lakeview, annexations, 8
Lake Michigan, water quality,
  294, 295–96, 298
Lake Park/Lake Shore Park, 195
Lake Point Tower, 264
Lakeville (Bigot), 154
Lamb Bicycle Company, 90
landfills, garbage, 293
Landmarks organizations, 137,
  253, 259
Lardner, Ring, 201
Larkin Building, 263
The Last Refuge (Fuller), 160

Index

League of American Wheelmen, 91

legislation, anti-discrimination, 102, 318*n*11

Leiter, L. Z., 36

Leiter, Levi, 57, 331*n*38

Leland, Warren F., 39

Leroux, Charles, 219

Levee district, 6, 266, 283–84

Levine, Peter, 183–84, 190, 193

Lewis, Alfred Henry, 165

Lewis, Sinclair, 61

Lewis Institute, 148–49

libraries, 42, 54–56

The Lily, 87

Lindberg, Richard, 90

Lind University Medical School, 111

Lister, Joseph, 96

"Literary Chicago" *(Payne)*, 151

Little Cheyenne, 265

Lloyd, William Demarest, 10

Locke, David Ross, 167

Lockport, canal project, 297

Lohn, Mel, 219

Longstreet, Stephen, 5

Loraine, William, 177

Lotta chewing gun, 225

Louisiana Purchase Exposition, 23

Lowell, James Russell, 157, 167

Loyola University., 146

Luetgert, Adolph, 200

Lum's Famous Hot Dog, 218

Luna Park, 205*f*

Lurie Children's Hospital, 110

Lutheran community, 111, 113

Lyon, Herb, 217

Machinery Hall, 137, 321*n*12

MacVeagh, Franklin, 281–82

Madden, James, 103

Maggie: A Girl of the Streets (Crane), 155

mail order companies: Montgomery Ward, 62–67; Sears, Roebuck, 49–50, 58–61, 65, 67–72, 313*n*3

Main Building, Armour Institute, 133, 137

Malone, Dick, 219

Mandel Brothers department store, 58

mandolins, Sears catalog, 60

Manhattan Building, 330*n*27

Manning, Susan (later Eliott), 116

Mantegna, Arlene, 219

Mantegna, Joe, 219

Manufacturers and Liberal Arts Building, 20–21

Map of Sin, 265–66, 267*f*

Marina City building, 264

Marquette Building, 246, 249

Mars, Frank C. (and company), 234, 235

Masonic Temple, 238

masonry construction, limitations, 243

Matz, Rudolph, 28

Mayan buildings display, 44*f*

Mayer, Gottfried, 209

Mayer, Oscar F., 209

Mayer, Oscar G., 209–10

Mayor's Bicycle Advisory Council, 93

McAuliff, Cornelius, 168

McCormick, Cyrus, 268

McCutcheon, John T., 144*f*, 165, 171, 176, 239*f*

McDonald, Michael, 280, 282, 324*n*30, 333*n*28

McGarry, James, 165, 324*n*30

McGirr, Peter, 118

McGovern, John, 153

McGrath, J. J., 282

McKim, Charles, 1, 17

McKinlock Court, 42

McLoughlin, Maurice E., 168

McLoughlin, William G., Jr., 273

McNeery character, Dunne's, 165

Mead, William, 1, 17

meatpacking industry, 13, 57, 140–45, 321*n*21

medical facilities: for baseball stadium fire, 200; early history, 110–11, 127; education institutions, 98, 107, 110–11, 112; modern concentration of, 109–10, 111–12, 201; Provident Hospital, 95–97, 103–6

medical innovations, 95–97, 108–9, 318*n*20

Medill, Joseph, 185–86

Medinah Athletic Club, 233

Meharry Medical College, 107

Mel's Hot Dogs, 219

Mencken, H. L., 152, 179

Merchandise Building, Sears, 70–71

Mercy Hospital, 127

Merwood-Salisbury, Joanna, 241

metal cage construction, advantages, 243, 244–45

Metcalf, Gordon M., 74

Methodist community, 111

Metropolitan Agency for Planning, Chicago, 303–4

Mexico, chicle production, 222, 227

Michael Reese Hospital, 111

Michigan, 227, 260

Michigan Avenue, 63, 66, 90, 98, 132, 195, 233. *See also* Grant Park

Midway Plaisance, 1, 18, 21

Mies van der Rohe, Ludwig, 149–50, 241, 264

"Mile High Illinois," 264

Millennium Park, 66, 306

Miller, Donald L., 3, 259

Miller, Grant, 321*n*12

Million Dollar Sermon, Gunsaulus,' 134–35

Milwaukee Female College, 80

minstrel shows, 326*n*25

mint production, 227

Miscellaneous Poems (Kenyon), 153

Mississippi River, 297, 298, 299–300

Modern Chivalry (Brackenridge), 168

Modern Wing, Art Institute, 42

Monadnock Building, 238, 243, 246–49, 331*n*32

Monon Building, 330*n*27

Monroe, Harriet, 151

Montauk Building, 53, 246, 247–48

Montgomery Ward, 62–67

Moody, Dwight Lyman, 268–73, 284

Moody Bible Institute, 272

Moore, Charles, 257, 332*n*49

Morgan, Thomas J., 276, 282

Morning News, 176

Morning World, 178

Morris, Edward H., 318*n*3

Morris, John S., 130

Morris, Nelson, 141

Morton Wing, 42

Mr. Dooley in Peace and in War (Dunne), 169

Muirhead, James Fullarton, 13

Mumford, Lewis, 9, 241

Munger Collection, 41

Museum of Modern Art, 241

Museum of Science and Industry, 49–54

museums: art, 34–42, 134, 259, 320*n*3; civic importance, 31–32; leadership characterized, 32–34; natural history, 42–49, 134,

320*n3*; science and industry,
49–54
mustard on hot dogs, 205

Naess and Murphy, 264
National American Woman Suf-
frage Association, 82
National Association of Base Ball
Players, 185
National Association of Colored
People (NAACP), 102
National Association of Profes-
sional Base Ball Players, 182–83
National Board of Trade of Cy-
cling Manufacturers, 91
National Historic Landmark
designations, 108
National League of Professional
Baseball Players, 183, 190
National Medical Association,
107–8
National Trust for Historic Preservation, 53, 256, 314*n19*
natural history museum, 42–49,
134, 320*n3*
Nestle, 236
Neuropsychiatric Institute, 197,
202
Newberry Library, 56
New England Magazine, 151
The New Flag (Fuller), 160
newspapers: as literary incubators,
164–65, 176–77; New Journalism
movement, 274; Stead's background with, 273–74. *See also*
specific publications, e.g., *Chi-
cago Tribune; New York Times*
New York City: baseball, 184, 200,
206–7; Coney Island, 205*f*;
global city designation, 309*n11*;
museums, 31; skyscraper abundance, 243; Tolton's church
service, 119; World's Fair competition, 14
New York Knickerbockers, 184
New York Sun, 14–15
New York Times, 12, 74, 87–88, 119,
161–62, 193
Nickel, Richard, 258
Nickerson, Samuel M., 41
The Night of the Fourth (Ade), 177
North, Hank, 275–76
North American Review, 151–52
North Central College, 146
Northeastern Illinois University,
146

Northern Echo, 273–74
North Shore Channel, 298
North Western Female College,
80, 81
Northwestern University, 81,
109–10, 146
Norton, Charles Eliot, 157
Not on the Screen (Fuller), 161
Nusbaum, Aaron, 69

Oak Park home, Wright's, 261*f*,
262
Obama, Barack, 218
Ogden, Malvina Belle (later Ar-
mour), 105, 140
O'Gorman, Thomas J., 253
Old Colony Building, 246
The Old Time Saloon (Ade), 178
The Old Town (Ade), 178
Old Vienna, Columbian Exposi-
tion, 210, 211*f*
Olmsted, Frederick Law, 16
O'Neil, Mrs. Patrick, 124
On the Stairs (Fuller), 160
Opening Day, Columbian Expo-
sition, 17–18, 19*f*
Opera House, Chicago, 53
Otis, Elisha Graves, 253

Palace of Fine Arts, 21, 47, 49–51,
251
Pall Mall Gazette, 274–75
Palmer, Arthur W., 299–300
Palmer, Bertha Honoré, 41, 282
Palmer, Henry, 98
Palmer, Potter, 41, 57, 185–86,
331*n38*
Paris Exhibition, 18
Parker, Alton B., 207
Parker, Robert, 263, 263*f*
Passavant, William, 111
Pasteur, Louis, 96
Patrons of Husbandry, 62–63
Patton, Normand, 133, 136, 321*m12*
Paulding, James Kirke, 167
Payne, William Morton, 151
Peabody and Stearns, 17
Pearsons, Mrs. D. K., 40
Peck, Philip, 257–58
Peep's Hot Dogs, 218
Peggy from Paris (Ade), 177
Pelouze, William Nelson, 50
Philadelphia, Shibe Park, 200
Piano, Renzo, 42
The Pickwick Papers (Dickens), 173
Pilkington, John, 161

Pink Marsh (Ade), 172, 173
Pirates, Chicago, 196
Plainfield College, 146
Plankinton, John, 140
Plan of Chicago (Burnham), 11,
29, 303
Plantevigne, John Joseph, 129
Platt, Harold L., 285
Players' National League, 196–97
Plymouth Congregational
Church, 133–34, 135, 269
political machine, 33–34, 266,
279–82, 333*n28*
Polo Grounds, New York, 200,
206–7
Pomeroy, W. C., 282
Pontiac Building, 246
Poole, William Frederick, 55
Poor Richard, Franklin's, 167
Popik, Barry A., 204–5, 207, 327*n4*
population statistics, 1, 8, 99, 209,
286–87
Post, George B., 17
Post Graduate Medical School,
112
Prairie Fire (Bushnell), 153
premiums practice, Wrigley's, 224
preservation activity, 50–51, 52–53,
256, 259
Press Club, 165
Pretzel character, 166
Price, Sarah (later Williams),
97–98
prices: baseball tickets, 188; bi-
cycles, 89; hot dogs, 206, 208*f*,
215–16; meat, 140; in Sears
catalog, 60, 61, 67; sugar, 236;
Wrigley's cookbook, 224
Price Tower, 264
Printers Row, 265
Progressive movement, 82, 84–86,
272, 284, 290
prohibition movement, 79, 82–86,
92
prostitution, 265–66, 267*f*, 274,
279, 283
Protestant Orphan Asylum, 98
Provident Hospital, 95–97, 103–8,
110
Prudential Building, 264
Pullman, George, 166–67, 280, 295
The Puppet-Booth (Fuller), 160, 161
Purdue University, 176, 178
Putnam, Frederick Ward, 21,
43–45
Putnam, Samuel, 160–61

Quigley, James, 129
Quincy, Illinois, 117–18, 120–21, 128

Rabinowitz, Joseph, 270
racial discrimination, 99–103, 193–94, 318*n*11. *See also* Tolton, Augustus
railroads: air pollution problems, 26, 28–29; in Dooley piece, 166–67; Lakefront Park property, 196; meatpacking industry, 141–42, 144–45, 148; rural economies, 63
Ralph, Julian, 12
Rand McNally Building, 52–53
Read, Opie, 154, 165
realism school, literature, 155, 323*n*14. *See also* urban literature, Chicago's role
reclamation plants, water, 298–99
Red Hot Chicago, 212, 213–14
reform activity: with Civic Federation, 281–84; evangelism's perspective, 272–73; incentives for, 5–6, 265–67; Stead's role, 275–81, 284
refrigerator cars, railway, 144
Regnery, Henry, 152
Rehn, Ludwig, 108
Reichel, Emil, 211–12, 213
Reidsdelle, Marie, 88
Reischl, Mike, 201–2
Reliance Building, 238, 246, 251, 253–56, 331*n*44
religion, in Dooley pieces, 166
religious communities: education facilities, 129, 130, 132, 146, 272; evangelist activity, 268–73, 284; hospital operations, 111; World Parliament congress, 34–35. *See also* Stead, William T.; Tolton, Augustus
Rembrandt, 41
Renoir, 41
Renwick, Edward A., 248, 249
Repasi, Ildiko, 132
Research Tower, Johnson Company, 264
reserve clause, baseball's, 190, 196
revivalism, 268–73, 284
Reynolds, Arthur R., 287–90
Reynolds, Emma, 103
Reynolds, Louis, 103
Rice Building, 42
Richardson, John, 153
Richardt, Michael, 118

Riess, Steven A., 185, 186–87, 326*n*21
Riordan, Father, 126–27
RMJM Hillier, 238
Roadfood (Stern and Stern), 220
Robert Morris University, 146
Roche, Martin, 244, 246, 247, 249, 331*n*46
Rockefeller, John D., 146
Rockfort baseball, 185, 190
Rodger Latimer's Mistake (Donelson), 154–55
Roe, E. P., 154
Roebuck, Alvah Curtis, 59–60, 68
Romero, Francisco, 318*n*20
Rookery Building, 248, 330*n*24
Roosevelt, Theodore, 186
Roosevelt University, 146
Root, John Wellborn: comment on tall buildings, 242; death, 250
Root, John Wellborn (architectural designs): Armour Mission, 135; Art Institute buildings, 36, 37*f*, 40; Colombian Exposition, 16–17; Monadnock Building, 247–48; Montauk Building, 246; Reliance Building, 254; Rookery, 248; Woman's Temple, 85, 316*n*29
Rosa, Joseph, 73
Rosenwald, Julius, 51–52, 69, 70–72
Rosenwald, William, 52
Rosenwald schools, 72, 314*n*19
Ross, David, 178
Rover Safety Bicycle, 93
Royko, Mike, 218
Rueckheim, Frederick W., 235–36
Rueckheim, Louis, 235–36
rural free delivery, 65
Rush Medical College, 110–11
Rush University Medical Center, 107
Ryerson, Martin, 38, 41, 42

Saarinen, Eliel, 50
safety bicycles, 76–77
Sainte-Gaudens, Augustus, 47, 251
Saint Xavier University, 146
saloons, 265, 267*f*, 275–76, 279–80, 324*n*30. *See also* Dooley character, Dunne's
Salvation Army, 281
Sandburg, Carl, 165
Sanitary and Ship Canal, 298, 299*f*

sanitation improvements, 290–93
Sankey, Ira D., 269
Santa Anna, Antonio López de, 222
Sassen, Saskia, 309*n*11
sausage making. *See* hot dogs
Savage, Henry W., 177
Scambray, Kenneth, 158
Scatchard, William, 224
Scatchard, William, Jr., 224, 225
Schaeffermeyer, Herman, 117–18
Schiller Building, 257, 259, 260
Schlesinger and Mayer, 57–58
Schnering, Otto, 234
schools/colleges: abundance of, 4, 145–47, 322*n*33; English requirement, 113; medical institutions, 98, 107, 109–11, 112; racial discrimination, 117–18; religious institutions, 129, 130, 132, 146, 272; Rosenwald's philanthropy, 72; women's institutions, 80, 81. *See also* Illinois Institute of Technology; University of Chicago
Schulze, Fred, 330*n*17
Schuyler, Montgomery, 9
Schwartz, Bob, 217, 219, 327*n*11
Schwinn, Ignaz, 91
Science and Industry, Museum of, 49–54
Sears, Richard Warren, 58–60, 67–69, 71
Sears, Roebuck and Company, 49–50, 58–61, 65, 67–72, 313*n*3
Sears Tower (Willis Tower), 69–70, 71, 72–75
Seattle Mariners, 181
Selee, Frank, 183
Sergel, Annie, 28–29
sewage systems, 293–300
Shababy, Skip, 219
Shadowed by Three (Deventer), 154
Shanabruch, Charles, 113–14
Sharps and Flats column, Field's, 165
Shepherd, Roger, 330*n*19
Shepley, Rutan and Coolidge, 40, 54–55, 56
Sheridan, Philip, 185–86
Shibe Park, Philadelphia, 200
The Sho-Gun (Ade), 178
Shulman, David, 327*n*4
Siedon, Sigfried, 241
Silsbee, Joseph Lyman, 260
Simmons, William J., 319*n*4

Simoni, Cardinal, 119
Sinclair, Upton, 141
Sisters of Mercy, 111
Sisters of the Blessed Sacrament, 130
Skidmore, Owings, and Merrill (SOM), 238
Skiff, Frederick, 47, 49
Skip's, 219
skyscrapers, 243–49, 263–64. *See also* architectural styles *entries; Cliff Dwellers* (Fuller)
Slattery, John R., 128–30
slavery, 116–17
smallpox, 285–86, 287–90, 334n2
Smith, Adrian, 240
Smith, Carl S., 30, 155
Smith, Seba, 167
Smith, William, 110
soap business, Wrigley's, 223–24
social reform. *See* reform activity
social services, 32, 135–36
Society for the Prevention of Smoke in Chicago, 25–28, 311n18
Somerset, Isabel, 77
Sommers, Lillian, 154
Spa Baking Powder, 224–25
Spalding, Albert G., 90–91, 183, 187, 189–93, 195, 197
Spalding, Byron, 190
Spanish-American War, 160, 169
Spear, Allan H., 100
Spearmint gum, 226
Spinney, Robert G., 188
sports, 54, 76–79, 86–93, 184–89, 326n21, n25. *See also* Cubs; White Stockings
Sportsman's Park, St. Louis, 200
spruce gum, 221–22
St. Augustine's Church, 122
St. Boniface Church, 117, 120, 121
St. Elizabeth's parish, 130–32
St. Joseph Advocate, 119–20
St. Joseph's parish, Quincy, 120–21
St. Joseph's Society of the Sacred Heart, 128, 130
St. Louis, Missouri, 14, 23, 200, 299–300
St. Louis Browns, 204
St. Louis Post-Dispatch, 168, 187–88
St. Louis World's Fair, 204
St. Luke's Hospital, 108, 111
St. Mary of the Angels, 114–15, 122–23

St. Monica's parish, 115, 122–27, 129, 130
Standard Oil Building, 264
Starley and Sutton, 93
Stead, William T., 18, 266, 267f, 273–81, 282, 284
Stern, Jane, 220
Stern, Michael, 220
Stevens, Harry M., 206–7
Stevenson, Sarah Hackett, 112
Stickney Water Reclamation Plant, 299
St Ignatius University., 146
Stine, W. M., 138–39
Stock Exchange, Chicago, 238, 257–60
Stock Yard, Union, 142
Stoney, William S., 108
Stories of the Streets and of the Towns column, Ade's, 170–74
Stout, Glenn, 195
Street of All Nations, 21
strikes, labor, 9, 244–45
Strong, Josiah, 10
sugar prices, 236
Sullivan, Louis: architectural designs, 1, 17, 238, 244, 256–60, 332n52; on building activity, 237; career decline, 259–60; characterized, 330n21; Jenny relationship, 245–46; on Monadnock Building, 248; on skyscrapers, 242; Wright's employment, 260–62
The Sultan of Sulu (Ade), 177
Sunday, Billy, 284
Supreme Court, Illinois, 49, 67
Supreme Court, U.S., 299–300
Swift, Gustavus, 141, 144
Symphony Orchestra, Chicago, 6, 9, 39

Tacoma Building, 53, 244, 245f
Taffy-Tolu Chewing Gum, 222
Taft, Lorado, 51
Taste Chicago, 219
Taylor, Benjamin Franklin, 153
Taylor, Graham, 282
temperance movement, 79, 82–86, 92
terra-cotta designs, 231, 244, 251, 254–56, 258, 331n46
Theophilus Trent (Taylor), 153
Thirty-Fifth Street Grounds, 196–97, 198
"Thirty Years of Freedom"

fundraiser, 105
Thompson, Mary Harris, 112
Thompson, William Tappan, 167
Thorns in Your Sides (Keyser), 168
Titanic, 284
Toledo Blue Stockings, 193–94
Tolton, Augustus: background, 116–19; death, 127–28; mural memorial, 131f, 132; in New York City, 119–20; Quincy parish, 119–21; St. Monica's parish, 122–26
Tolton, Martha Jane (earlier Chisley), 116, 117, 125
Tolton, Peter Paul, 116, 117
Tom Brown's Schooldays (Hughes), 186
Tom Quick (Bross), 153
Tootsie Rolls, 235
Transportation Building, 1, 17, 257
Transportation Center, West Loop, 304
trash collection, 291, 292–93
Tribune Tower, 233
Trillin, Calvin, 220
Truman, Harry, 53
Trump Tower, 264
tugboat war, 24, 26–28
Turkish Village, Columbian Exposition, 327n5
Turner, Frederick Jackson, 34
Twain, Mark, 167, 170, 173
Twenty-Third Street Grounds, 103
Two-Mile Crib, 294–97
typhoid fever, 285, 286, 291, 298

Uncles, Charles Randolph, 128–29
unemployment patterns, 2–3, 275–76, 279
Union Baseball Club, 185
Union Base-Ball Grounds, 195
Union League, 50, 51
Union Stock Yards, 142, 194
Unity Temple, 262
University of Chicago, 56, 106, 110, 134, 145–46, 311n22
University of Illinois, 107, 146, 147
urban literature, Chicago's role: overview, 151–52, 179–80; Ade's work, 170–79; Dunne's work, 162–70; fiction foundation, 152–55; Fuller's work, 152, 155–62

vaccinations, smallpox, 288–90
Valle, Lincoln C., 123

Vanderbilt, William H., 250
Vatican, 118–19
vaudeville shows, 189
vice district, 6, 265–66, 267f, 283–84
Vienna Beef Company, 211–13, 214, 215, 327n12
Vienna sausages, 208–9
Viking Bicycle Club, 92
Virginia Hotel, 53
Vivekananda, 34–35
von der Ahe, Chris, 204

Wacker Drive, 72, 231
Wainwright Building, 246, 257
Walker, Moses Fleetwood, 193–94
Ward, Aaron Montgomery, 39, 48–49, 62–67
Ware, William R., 250
Warner, Charles Dudley, 11
Warren, Arthur, 139
Warren Company, 59
The War Scout of Eighteen Hundred Twelve (Clark), 153
Washington, D.C., World's Fair competition, 14
watches story, Sears,' 58–59, 313n3
water fountains, WCTU's, 84–85, 316n26
water quality, 293–300
Water Tower, 296
Wathall, Alfred, 177
Wau-bun, the "Early Day" in the North-West (Kinzie), 153
Wau-Nan-Gee (Richardson), 153
Way Out in Left Field Society, 201–2
weather, 95, 127, 176
Weeghman, Charles, 201
Weeghman Field, 201
Wegman, Julius, 124
Wegmann, Theodore, 118
Weiss, Michael, 121
Welles, George S., 292, 293
Wells, Ida B., 102

Wertenbaker, Lael, 108
Wesley Memorial Hospital, 111
West Side Grounds, 182, 194, 197–202
West Side Park, 196
Whales, Chicago, 200–201
Wheaton College, 146
Wheeler, Lloyd G., 318n3
A Wheel within a Wheel (Willard), 77, 79
Whiskey Row, 265
Whitby, George, 223
White, Stanford, 1, 17
White, William J., 222–23
Whitechapel Club, 165
White City. *See* Columbian Exposition
White Stockings, Chicago, 164, 182–83, 189–90, 191f, 193–97. *See also* Colts
Whitney, Payne, 169
wieners. *See* hot dogs
A Wilful Heiress (Booth), 155
Willard, Frances E.: background, 79–81; bicycle use, 76–79, 89; home of, 85, 93–94; physical appearance, 82, 315n18; temperance leadership, 79, 82–86, 92
Willard, Oliver, 80
Willard Hall, Woman's Temple, 85
Williams, Alice (earlier Johnson), 107
Williams, Daniel Hale, 3, 95–99, 103–4, 105, 107–9
Williams, Kenny J., 154
Williams, Price, 98
Williams, Sarah (earlier Price), 97–98
Williamson, Ned, 195
Willis, Carol, 242
Willis Group Holdings, 75
Willis Tower, 69–70, 71, 72–75
windows, Chicago-style, 254, 258

"Windy City" nickname, 14–15
With Edge Tools (Chatfield-Taylor), 154
With the Procession (Fuller), 155, 159–60
Wolcott, Alexander, 110
Woman's Christian Temperance Union (WCTU), 79, 82–86, 93–94, 316n26
Woman's Hospital Medical College of Chicago, 112
Woman's Temple, 53, 85–86, 249, 316n29
Woman Suffrage Association, National American, 82
Workingman's Exchange, 276
World Parliament of Religions, 34–35
World's Congress Auxiliary, 34–35, 40
World's Fair Evangelistic Campaign, 269–72
Wright, Frank Lloyd, 238, 260–64
Wrigley, Ada (earlier Foote), 223
Wrigley, Philip K., 226, 230, 233–34
Wrigley, William, Jr., 201, 223–30, 233
Wrigley, William (grandson), 234
Wrigley, William (great grandson), 234
Wrigley Building, 230–33
Wrigley Field, 182, 201, 229
Wrigley Memorial Botanical Garden, 230

yoga, introduction of, 35
"A Young Man in Upper Life" (Ade), 170

Zeno Manufacturing Company, 225, 226
Zury, the Meanest Man in Spring County (Kirkland), 153

Joseph Gustaitis is a freelance writer and editor living in Chicago. He received his A.B. from Dartmouth College and his M.A. and Ph.D. in history from Columbia University. He is the author of many articles in the popular history field. After working as an editor at *Collier's Year Book*, he became the humanities editor for *Collier's Encyclopedia*. He has also worked in television and won an Emmy Award for writing for ABC-TV's *FYI* program.